RxSwift

Reactive Programming with Swift

By Florent Pillet, Junior Bontognali, Marin Todorov & Scott Gardner

RxSwift: Reactive Programming with Swift

Florent Pillet, Junior Bontognali, Marin Todorov & Scott Gardner

Copyright ©2017 Razeware LLC.

Notice of Rights

All rights reserved. No part of this book or corresponding materials (such as text, images, or source code) may be reproduced or distributed by any means without prior written permission of the copyright owner.

Notice of Liability

This book and all corresponding materials (such as source code) are provided on an "as is" basis, without warranty of any kind, express of implied, including but not limited to the warranties of merchantability, fitness for a particular purpose, and noninfringement. In no event shall the authors or copyright holders be liable for any claim, damages or other liability, whether in action of contract, tort or otherwise, arising from, out of or in connection with the software or the use of other dealing in the software.

Trademarks

All trademarks and registered trademarks appearing in this book are the property of their own respective owners.

ISBN: 978-1-942878-46-9

Dedications

"For my father."
— *Marin Todorov*

"For Fabienne and Alexandra"
— *Florent Pillet*

"For my grandfather."
— *Junior Bontognali*

"For Betty 😺"
— *Scott Gardner*

About the authors

Florent Pillet is an author of this book. Florent has been developing for mobile platforms since the last century and moved to iOS on day 1. He adopted reactive programming before Swift was announced and has been using RxSwift in production since 2015. A freelance developer, Florent also uses Rx on Android and likes working on tools for developers like the popular NSLogger when he's not contracting for clients worldwide. Say hello to Florent on Twitter at @fpillet.

Junior Bontognali is an author of this book. Junior has been developing on iOS since the first iPhone and joined the RxSwift team in the early development stage. Based in Switzerland, when he's not eating cheese or chocolate, he's doing some cool stuff in the mobile space, without denying to work on other technologies. Other than that he organizes tech events, speaks and blogs. Say hello to Junior on Twitter at @bontoJR.

Marin Todorov is an author of this book. Marin is one of the founding members of the raywenderlich.com team and has worked on seven of the team's books. Besides crafting code, Marin also enjoys blogging, teaching, and speaking at conferences. He happily open-sources code. You can find out more about Marin at www.underplot.com.

Scott Gardner is an author of this book. Scott has been developing iOS apps since 2010, Swift since the day it was announced, and RxSwift since before version 1. He's authored several video courses, tutorials, and articles on iOS app development, presented at numerous conferences, meetups, and online events, and this is his second book. Say hello to Scott on Twitter at @scotteg.

About the editors

Ash Furrow is the technical editor of this book. Ash is a Canadian iOS developer and author, currently working at Artsy. He has published a number of books, built many apps, and is a contributor to the open source community. On his blog ashfurrow.com, he writes about a range of topics, from interesting programming to explorations of analogue film photography.

Chris Belanger is the editor of this book. Chris Belanger is the Book Team Lead and Lead Editor for raywenderlich.com. If there are words to wrangle or a paragraph to ponder, he's on the case. When he kicks back, you can usually find Chris with guitar in hand, looking for the nearest beach, or exploring the lakes and rivers in his part of the world in a canoe.

Marin Todorov is the final pass editor of this book. Marin is one of the founding members of the raywenderlich.com team and has worked on seven of the team's books. Besides crafting code, Marin also enjoys blogging, teaching, and speaking at conferences. He happily open-sources code.

Table of Contents:

Introduction 15
- What you need 16
- Who this book is for 16
- How to use this book 17
- What's in store 17
- Book source code and forums 18
- Digital editions 19
- License 19
- About the cover 20

Section I: Getting Started with RxSwift 21

Chapter 1: Hello RxSwift! 23
- Introduction to asynchronous programming 24
- Foundation of RxSwift 31
- App architecture 38
- RxCocoa 39
- Installing RxSwift 40
- Community 42
- Where to go from here? 43

Chapter 2: Observables 45
- Getting started 46
- What is an observable? 47
- Lifecycle of an observable 48
- Creating observables 49
- Subscribing to observables 51
- Disposing and terminating 56
- Creating observable factories 61
- Using Traits 62
- Challenges 65

Chapter 3: Subjects 67
Getting started 68
What are subjects? 69
Working with publish subjects 69
Working with behavior subjects 72
Working with replay subjects 74
Working with variables 78
Challenges 80

Chapter 4: Observables and Subjects in Practice 83
Getting started 84
Using a variable in a view controller 85
Talking to other view controllers via subjects 89
Creating a custom observable 94
RxSwift traits in practice 97
Completable 98
Challenges 101

Section II: Operators and Best Practices ... 103

Chapter 5: Filtering Operators 105
Getting started 106
Ignoring operators 106
Skipping operators 110
Taking operators 114
Distinct operators 118
Challenges 121

Chapter 6: Filtering Operators in Practice 125
Improving the Combinestagram project 126
Sharing subscriptions 127
Improving the photo selector 135
Trying out time based filter operators 142
Challenges 145

Chapter 7: Transforming Operators 147
Getting started 148
Transforming elements 148
Transforming inner observables 151
Observing events 156
Challenges 160

Chapter 8: Transforming Operators in Practice 163
Getting started with GitFeed 164
Fetching data from the web... 165
Transforming the response 169
Intermission: Handling erroneous input............................. 174
Persisting objects to disk... 175
Add a Last-Modified header to the request....................... 177
Challenges 181

Chapter 9: Combining Operators 185
Getting started 186
Prefixing and concatenating 186
Merging 190
Combining elements 192
Triggers 197
Switches 199
Combining elements within a sequence 202
Challenges 204

Chapter 10: Combining Operators in Practice 207
Getting started 208
Preparing the web backend service 208
Categories view controller 212
Adding the event download service 214
Getting events for categories 216
Events view controller 220
Wiring the days selector 222

    Splitting event downloads 223
    Challenges 227

Chapter 11: Time Based Operators 229
    Getting started 230
    Buffering operators 232
    Time-shifting operators 242
    Timer operators 244
    Challenges 247

Section III: iOS Apps with RxCocoa 249

Chapter 12: Beginning RxCocoa 251
    Getting started 252
    Using RxCocoa with basic UIKit controls 253
    Binding observables 261
    Improving the code with Traits 264
    Disposing with RxCocoa 268
    Where to go from here? 269
    Challenges 270

Chapter 13: Intermediate RxCocoa 271
    Getting started 272
    Showing an activity while searching 272
    Extending CLLocationManager 275
    How to extend a UIKit view 283
    One more thing: a signal! 290
    Conclusions about RxCocoa 291
    Challenges 291

Section IV: Intermediate RxSwift/ RxCocoa 293

Chapter 14: Error Handling in Practice 295
    Getting started 296

Managing errors 296
Handle errors with catch 298
Catching errors 300
Retrying on error 301
Custom errors 306
Advanced error handling 309
Where to go from here? 313
Challenges 313

Chapter 15: Intro To Schedulers 315
What is a Scheduler? 316
Setting up the project 317
Switching schedulers 317
Pitfalls 321
Best practices and built-in schedulers 325
Where to go from here? 328

Chapter 16: Testing with RxTest 331
Getting started 332
Testing operators with RxTest 333
Testing RxSwift production code 341

Chapter 17: Creating Custom Reactive Extensions 347
Getting started 348
How to create extensions 348
Use custom wrappers 354
Testing custom wrappers 355
Common available wrappers 358
Where to go from here? 361
Challenges 362

Section V: RxSwift Community Cookbook . 363

Chapter 18: Table and Collection Views 365
Basic table view 365

    Multiple cell types 367
    Providing additional functionality 368
    RxDataSources 368

Chapter 19: Action 371
    Creating an Action 372
    Connecting buttons 373
    Composing behavior 373
    Passing work items to cells 374
    Manual execution 375
    Perfectly suited for MVVM 375

Chapter 20: RxGesture 377
    Attaching gestures 377
    Supported gestures 378
    Advanced usage 380

Chapter 21: RxRealm 383
    Auto-updating results 383
    Arrays 384
    Asynchronous first item 384
    Changesets 385
    Single objects 385
    Adding objects 386
    Deleting objects 387

Chapter 22: RxAlamofire 389
    Basic requests 389
    Request customization 391
    Response validation 391
    Downloading files 392
    Upload tasks 392
    Tracking progress 393

Section VI: Putting it All Together 395

Chapter 23: MVVM with RxSwift 397
Introducing MVVM 398
Getting started with Tweetie 401
Challenges 416

Chapter 24: Building a Complete RxSwift App 419
Introducing QuickTodo 420
Architecting the application 420
Bindable view controllers 422
Task model 423
Tasks service 424
Scenes 426
Coordinating scenes 427
Binding the tasks list with RxDataSources 431
Binding the Task cell 436
Editing tasks 437
Challenges 441

Conclusion 445

Introduction

> *"If you've ever used an asynchronous callback based API, you've probably dealt with handling the response data ad-hoc all across your codebase, and have most likely decided there was no way to unit test it all... But, let me tell you - there is a better way, and it's called Rx!"*
>
> — Krunoslav Zaher, creator of RxSwift

There's no denying it: Rx is one of the hottest topics in mobile app development these days!

If you visit international conferences, or even local meetups, it might feel like everyone is talking about observables, side effects, and (gulp) schedulers.

And no wonder — Rx is a multi-platform standard, so no matter if it's a web development conference, local Android meetup, or a Swift workshop, you might end up joining a multi-platform discussion on Rx.

The RxSwift library (part of the larger family of Rx ports across platforms and languages) allows you to use your favorite Swift programming language in a completely new way. The somewhat difficult-to-handle asynchronous code in Swift becomes much easier and a lot saner to write with RxSwift.

To create responsive and robust applications, you have to handle a multitude of concurrent tasks like playing audio, handling user interface input, making networking calls, and more. Sometimes, passing data from one process to another or even just observing that tasks happen in the correct sequence one after another asynchronously might cause the developer a lot of trouble.

In this book, you'll learn how RxSwift solves the issues related to asynchronous programming and master various reactive techniques, from observing simple data sequences, to combining and transforming asynchronous value streams, to designing the architecture and building production quality apps.

By the end of this book, you'll have worked through the chapter content and you'll have hands-on experience solving the challenges at the end of the chapters — and you'll be well on your way to coming up with your own Rx patterns and solutions!

What you need

To follow along with the tutorials in this book, you'll need the following:

- **A Mac running the latest point release of macOS Sierra or later**: You'll need this to be able to install the latest version of Xcode.

- **Xcode 9 or later**: Xcode is the main development tool for iOS. You can download the latest version of Xcode for free on the Mac app store here: http://apple.co/2aL9StL

- **An intermediate level** knowledge of Swift and iOS development. This book is about learning RxSwift specifically; to understand the rest of the project code and how the accompanying demo projects work you will need at least an intermediate understanding of Swift and UIKit.

If you want to try things out on a physical iOS device, you'll need a developer account with Apple, which you can obtain for free. However, all the sample projects in this book will work just fine in the iOS Simulator bundled with Xcode, so the paid developer account is completely optional.

Who this book is for

This book is for iOS developers who already feel comfortable with iOS and Swift, and want to dive deep into development with RxSwift.

If you're a complete beginner to iOS, we suggest you first read through the latest edition of The iOS Apprentice. That will give you a solid foundation of building iOS apps with Swift from the ground up but you might still need to learn more about intermediate level iOS development before you can work through all chapters in this book.

If you know the basics of iOS development but are new to Swift, we suggest you read through Swift Apprentice first, which goes through the features of Swift using playgrounds to teach the language.

You can find both of these books at our online store:

http://store.raywenderlich.com

How to use this book

Generally, each chapter in this book includes a starter project and covers a small number of programming techniques in detail. Some of the chapters deal mostly with theory so you get to try isolated pieces of code, while learning the process in a Swift playground.

Other chapters provide you with a starter project that includes some non-Rx logic inside and lead you through Rx-ifying the project by adding code in key places. In the process, you'll see what difference RxSwift makes in the project code and how to approach different common problems.

We do suggest that you work through the chapters in order, since the concepts build upon each other. Remember you'll get the most out of the book if you follow along with the tutorials and perform the hands-on challenges.

For advanced developers, there's still value in the early chapters since they cover the basics. However if you're comfortable with those concepts, feel free to jump ahead to the topics that interest you the most.

What's in store

This book is divided into six sections. You can find more details on each section in its introduction. Here's a brief overview.

Section I: Getting Started with RxSwift

The first section of the book covers RxSwift basics. Don't skip this section, as you will be required to have a good understanding of how and why things work in the following sections.

Section II: Operators and Best Practices

In this section, once you've mastered the basics, you will move on to building more complex Rx code by using operators. Operators allow you to chain and compose little pieces of functionality to build up complex logic.

Section III: iOS Apps with RxCocoa

Once you've mastered RxSwift's basics and know how to use operators, you will move on to iOS specific APIs, which will allow you to use and integrate your RxSwift code with the existing iOS classes and UI controls.

Section IV: Intermediate RxSwift/RxCocoa

In this section, you will look into more topics like building an error-handling strategy for your app, handling your networking needs the reactive way, writing Rx tests, and more.

Section V: RxSwift Community Cookbook

Many of the available RxSwift-based libraries are created and maintained by the community – people just like you. In this section, we'll look into a few of these projects and how you can use them in your own apps.

Section VI: Putting it All Together

This part of the book deals with app architecture and strategies for building production-quality, full-blown iOS applications. You will learn how to structure your project and explore a couple of different approaches to designing your data streams and the project navigation.

Book source code and forums

You can get the source code for the book here:

www.raywenderlich.com/store/rxswift/source-code

You'll find all the code from the chapters, as well as the solutions to the challenges for your reference.

We've also set up an official forum for the book at forums.raywenderlich.com. This is a great place to ask questions about the book, discuss debugging strategies or to submit any errors you may find.

Digital editions

We also have PDF and ePub digital editions of this book available, which can be handy if you want a soft copy to take with you, or you want to quickly search for a specific term within the book.

Buying the digital edition of the book also has a few extra benefits: free updates each time we update the book, access to older versions of the book, and you can download the digital editions from anywhere, at anytime.

Visit the book store page here:

- https://store.raywenderlich.com/products/rxswift

And since you purchased the print version of this book, you're eligible to upgrade to the digital edition at a significant discount!

Simply email support@razeware.com with your receipt for the physical copy and we'll get you set up with the discounted digital edition of the book.

License

By purchasing RxSwift: Reactive Programming in Swift, you have the following license:

- You are allowed to use and/or modify the source code in *RxSwift: Reactive Programming in Swift* in as many apps as you want, with no attribution required.

- You are allowed to use and/or modify all art, images and designs that are included in *RxSwift: Reactive Programming in Swift* in as many apps as you want, but must include this attribution line somewhere inside your app: "Artwork/images/designs: from RxSwift: Reactive Programming in Swift book, available at http://www.raywenderlich.com."

- This book is for your personal use only. You are NOT allowed to sell this book without prior authorization, or distribute it to friends, co-workers or students; they would need to purchase their own copy.

All materials provided with this book are provided on an "as is" basis, without warranty of any kind, express or implied, including but not limited to the warranties of merchantability, fitness for a particular purpose and non-infringement. In no event shall the authors or copyright holders be liable for any claim, damages or other liability, whether in an action of contract, tort or otherwise, arising from, out of or in connection with the software or the use or other dealings in the software. All trademarks and registered trademarks appearing in this book are the property of their respective owners.

About the cover

The electric eel is a unique kind of beast. In fact, it's been reclassified few times, since it's not *exactly* like any other animal. It can grow to two meters in length and twenty kilograms in weight.

Its size however, is not what should worry you, should you have the chance to meet one in person. That little devil sports a natural taser gun that can discharge up to 860 volts and 1 amp of current! Where was that electric eel when you were trying to jump-start your car that cold morning last February, right?

The electric eel was chosen for the Rx project logo since its pre-release code name was Volta. Now you know!

Section I: Getting Started with RxSwift

In this part of the book, you're going to learn about the basics of RxSwift. You are going to have a look at what kinds of asynchronous programming problems RxSwift addresses, and what kind of solutions it offers.

Further, you will learn about the few basic classes that allow you to create and observe event sequences, which are the foundation of the Rx framework.

You are going to start slow by learning about the basics and a little bit of theory. Please don't skip these chapters! This will allow you to make good progress in the following sections when things get more complex.

Chapter 1: Hello RxSwift!

Chapter 2: Observables

Chapter 3: Subjects

Chapter 4: Observables and Subjects in Practice

Chapter 1: Hello RxSwift!

By Marin Todorov

This book aims to introduce you, the reader, to the RxSwift library and to writing reactive iOS apps with Swift.

But what exactly *is* RxSwift? Here's a good definition:

> *RxSwift is a library for composing asynchronous and event-based code by using observable sequences and functional style operators, allowing for parameterized execution via schedulers.*

Sounds complicated? Don't worry if it does. Writing reactive programs, understanding the many concepts behind them, and navigating a lot of the relevant, commonly used lingo might be intimidating — especially if you try to take it all in at once, or when you haven't been introduced to it in a structured way.

That's the goal of this book: to gradually introduce you to the various RxSwift APIs and Rx concepts by explaining how to use each of the APIs, and then covering its practical usage in iOS apps.

You'll start with the basic features of RxSwift, and then gradually work through intermediate and advanced topics. Taking the time to exercise new concepts extensively as you progress will make it easier to master RxSwift by the end of the book. Rx is too broad of a topic to cover completely in a single book; instead, we aim to give you a solid understanding of the library so that you can continue developing Rx skills on your own.

We still haven't quite established what RxSwift *is* though, did we? Let's start with a simple, understandable definition and progress to a better, more expressive one as we waltz through the topic of reactive programming later in this chapter.

> *RxSwift, in its essence, simplifies developing asynchronous programs by allowing your code to react to new data and process it in a sequential, isolated manner.*

As an iOS app developer, this should be much more clear and tell you more about what RxSwift is, compared to the first definition you read earlier in this chapter.

Even if you're still fuzzy on the details, it should be clear that RxSwift helps you write asynchronous code. And you know that developing good, deterministic, asynchronous code is *hard*, so any help is quite welcome!

Introduction to asynchronous programming

If you tried to explain asynchronous programming in a simple, down to earth language, you might come up with something along the lines of the following.

An iOS app, at any moment, might be doing any of the following things and more:

- Reacting to button taps
- Animating the keyboard as a text field loses focus
- Downloading a large photo from the Internet
- Saving bits of data to disk
- Playing audio

All of these things seemingly happen at the same time. Whenever the keyboard animates out of the screen, the audio in your app doesn't pause until the animation has finished, right?

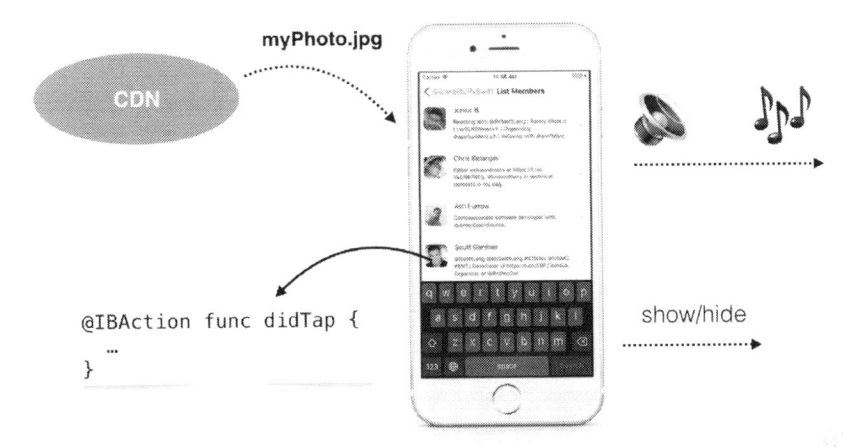

All the different bits of your program don't block each other's execution. iOS offers you all kind of APIs that allow you to perform different pieces of work on different threads and perform them across the different cores of the device's CPU.

Writing code that truly runs in parallel, however, is rather complex, especially when different bits of code need to work with the same pieces of data. It's hard to argue about which piece of code updates the data first, or which code read the latest value.

Cocoa and UIKit Asynchronous APIs

Apple has provided lots of APIs in the iOS SDK that help you write asynchronous code. You've used these in your projects, and probably haven't given them a second thought because they are so fundamental to writing mobile apps.

You've probably used most of the following:

- **NotificationCenter**: To execute a piece of code any time an event of interest happens, such as the user changing the orientation of the device, or the software keyboard showing or hiding on the screen.
- **The delegate pattern**: To define methods to be executed by another class or API at arbitrary times. For example, in your application delegate you define what should happen when a new remote notification arrives, but you have no idea when this piece of code will be executed, or how many times it will execute.

- **Grand Central Dispatch**: To help you abstract the execution of pieces of work. You can schedule code to be executed sequentially in a serial queue, or run a multitude of tasks concurrently on different queues with different priorities.
- **Closures**: To create detached pieces of code that you can pass between classes so each class can decide whether to execute it or not, how many times, and in what context.

Since most of your typical classes would do something asynchronously, and all UI components are inherently asynchronous, it's impossible to make assumptions in what order the **entirety** of your app code will get executed.

After all, your app's code runs differently depending on various external factors, such as user input, network activity, or other OS events. Each time the user fires up your app, the code may run in a completely different order depending on those external factors. (Well, except for the case when you have an army of robots testing your app, then you can expect all events to happen with precise, kill-bot synchronization.)

We're definitely not saying that writing good asynchronous code is impossible. After all, the great APIs from Apple listed above are very advanced, very specialized for the task, and to be fair, quite powerful compared to what other platforms offer.

The issue is that complex asynchronous code becomes very difficult to write in part because of the variety of APIs that Apple's SDK offers:

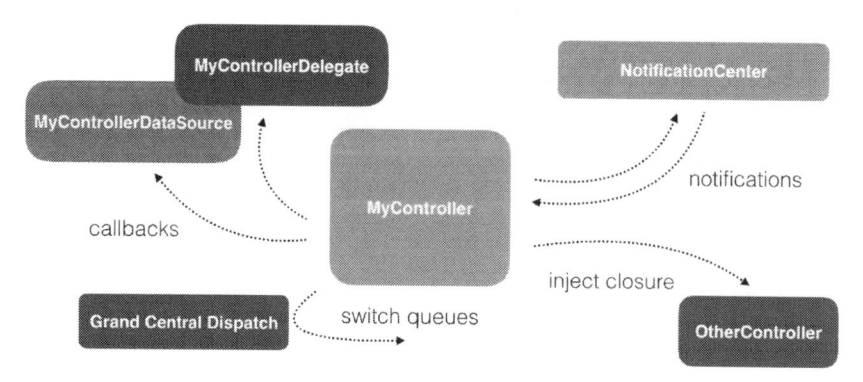

Using delegates requires you to adopt one particular pattern, another one for closures, yet another approach for subscribing to `NotificationCenter`, and so on. Since there is no universal language across all the asynchronous APIs, reading and understanding the code, and reasoning about its execution, becomes difficult.

To wrap up this section and put the discussion into a bit more context, you'll compare two pieces of code: one synchronous, and one asynchronous.

Synchronous code

Performing an operation for each element of an array is something you've done plenty of times. It's a very simple yet solid building block of app logic because it guarantees two things: it executes *synchronously*, and the collection is *immutable* while you iterate over it.

Take a moment to think about what this implies. When you iterate over a collection, you don't need to check that all elements are still there, and you don't need to rewind back in case another thread inserts an element at the start of the collection. You assume you always iterate over the collection in *its entirety* at the beginning of the loop.

If you want to play a bit more with these aspects of the `for` loop, try this in a playground:

```
var array = [1, 2, 3]
for number in array {
  print(number)
  array = [4, 5, 6]
}
print(array)
```

Is `array` mutable inside the `for` body? Does the collection that the loop iterates over ever change? What's the sequence of execution of all commands? Can you modify `number` if you need to?

Asynchronous code

Consider similar code, but assume each iteration happens as a reaction to a tap on a button. As the user repeatedly taps on the button, the app prints out the next element in an array:

```
var array = [1, 2, 3]
var currentIndex = 0

//this method is connected in IB to a button
@IBAction func printNext(_ sender: Any) {
  print(array[currentIndex])

  if currentIndex != array.count-1 {
    currentIndex += 1
  }
}
```

Think about this code in the same context as you did for the previous one. As the user taps the button, will that print all of the array's elements? You really can't say. Another piece of asynchronous code might remove the last element, *before* it's been printed.

Or another piece of code might insert a new element at the start of the collection *after* you've moved on.

Also, you assume only `printNext(_:)` will ever change `currentIndex`, but another piece of code might modify `currentIndex` as well — perhaps some clever code you added at some point after crafting the above function.

You've likely realized that some of the core issues with writing asynchronous code are: a) the order in which pieces of work are performed and b) shared mutable data.

Luckily, these are some of RxSwift's strong suits!

Next, you need a good primer on the language that will help you start understanding how RxSwift works, what problems it solves, and ultimately let you move past this gentle introduction and into writing your first Rx code in the next chapter.

Asynchronous programming glossary

Some of the language in RxSwift is so tightly bound to asynchronous, reactive, and/or functional programming that it will be easier if you first understand the following foundational terms.

In general, RxSwift tries to address the following issues:

1. State, and specifically, shared mutable state

State is somewhat difficult to define. To understand state, consider the following practical example.

When you start your laptop it runs just fine, but after you use it for a few days or even weeks, it might start behaving weirdly or abruptly hang and refuse to speak to you. The hardware and software remains the same, but what's changed is the state. As soon as you restart, the same combination of hardware and software will work just fine once more.

The data in memory, the one stored on disk, all the artifacts of reacting to user input, all traces that remain after fetching data from cloud services — the sum of these is the state of your laptop.

Managing the state of your app, especially when shared between multiple asynchronous components, is one of the issues you'll learn how to handle in this book.

2. Imperative programming

Imperative programming is a programming paradigm that uses statements to change the program's state. Much like you would use imperative language while playing with your dog — *"Fetch! Lay down! Play dead!"* — you use imperative code to tell the app exactly *when* and *how* to do things.

Imperative code is similar to the code that your computer understands. All the CPU does is follow lengthy sequences of simple instructions. The issue is that it gets challenging for humans to write imperative code for complex, asynchronous apps — especially when shared mutable state is involved.

For example take this code, found in `viewDidAppear(_:)` of an iOS view controller:

```
override func viewDidAppear(_ animated: Bool) {
  super.viewDidAppear(animated)

  setupUI()
  connectUIControls()
  createDataSource()
  listenForChanges()
}
```

There's no telling what these methods do. Do they update properties of the view controller itself? More disturbingly, are they called in the right order? Maybe somebody inadvertently swapped the order of these method calls and committed the change to source control. Now the app might behave differently due to the swapped calls.

3. Side effects

Now that you know more about mutable state and imperative programming, you can pin down most issues with those two things to **side effects**.

Side effects are any change to the state outside of the current scope. For example, consider the last piece of code in the example above. `connectUIControls()` probably attaches some kind of event handler to some UI components. This causes a side effect, as it changes the state of the view: the app behaves one way *before* executing `connectUIControls()`, and differently *after* that.

Any time you modify data stored on disk or update the text of a label on screen, you cause side effects.

Side effects are not bad in themselves. After all, causing side effects is the ultimate goal of *any* program! You need to change the state of the world somehow after your program has finished executing. Running for a while and doing nothing makes for a pretty useless app.

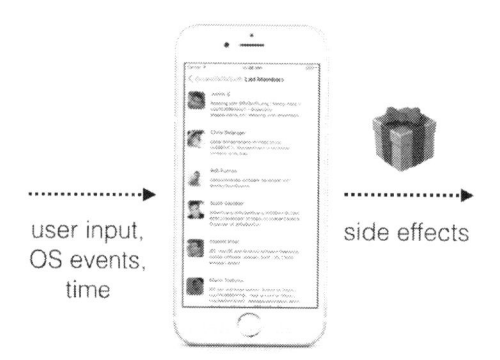

The issue with producing side effects is doing it in a controlled way. You need to be able to determine which pieces of code cause side effects, and which simply process and output data.

RxSwift tries to address the issues (or problems) listed above by tackling the following couple of concepts.

4. Declarative code

In imperative programming, you change state at will. In functional code, you don't cause any side effects. Since you don't live in a perfect world, the balance lies somewhere in the middle. RxSwift combines some of the best aspects of imperative code and functional code.

Declarative code lets you define pieces of behavior, and RxSwift will run these behaviors any time there's a relevant event and provide them an immutable, isolated data input to work with.

This way you can work with asynchronous code, but make the same assumptions as in a simple `for` loop: that you're working with immutable data and you can execute code in sequential, deterministic way.

5. Reactive systems

Reactive systems is a rather abstract term and covers web or iOS apps that exhibit most or all of the following qualities:

- **Responsive**: Always keep the UI up to date, representing the latest app state.
- **Resilient**: Each behavior is defined in isolation and provides for flexible error recovery.
- **Elastic**: The code handles varied workload, often implementing features such as lazy pull-driven data collections, event throttling, and resource sharing.

- **Message driven**: Components use message-based communication for improved reusability and isolation, decoupling the lifecycle and implementation of classes.

Now that you have a good understanding of the problems RxSwift helps solve and how it approaches these issues, it's time to talk about the building blocks of Rx and how they play together.

Foundation of RxSwift

Reactive programming isn't a new concept; it's been around for a fairly long time, but its core concepts have made a noticeable comeback over the last decade.

In that period, web applications have became more involved and are facing the issue of managing complex asynchronous UIs. On the server side, reactive systems (as described above) have become a necessity.

A team at Microsoft took on the challenge of solving the problems of asynchronous, scalable, real time application development that we've discussed in this chapter. They worked on a library, independently from the core teams in the company, and sometime around 2009, offered a new client and server side framework called Reactive Extensions for .NET (Rx).

It was an installable add-on for .NET 3.5, and later became a built-in core library in .NET 4.0. It's been an open source component since 2012. Open sourcing the code permitted other languages and platforms to reimplement the same functionality, which turned Rx into a cross-platform standard.

Today you have RxJS, RxKotlin, Rx.NET, RxScala, RxSwift, and more. All these libraries strive to implement the same behavior and same expressive APIs. Ultimately, a developer creating an iOS app with RxSwift can freely discuss app logic with another programmer using RxJS on the web.

Like the original Rx, RxSwift also works with all the concepts you've covered so far: it tackles mutable state, it allows you to compose event sequences and improves on architectural concepts such as code isolation, reusability, and decouplings.

Let's revisit that definition:

> *RxSwift finds the sweet spot between traditionally imperative Cocoa code and purist functional code. It allows you to react to events by using immutable code definitions to process asynchronously pieces of input in a deterministic, composable way.*

You can read more about the family of Rx implementations at http://reactivex.io. This is the central repository of documentation about Rx's operators and core classes. It's also probably the first place you'll notice the Rx logo, the electric eel (a slightly more realistic image of which you'll find on the cover of this book):

> **Note**: I personally thought for some time that it was a techno-shrimp, but research shows that it is, in fact, an electric eel. (The Rx project used to be called Volta.)

In this book, you are going to cover both the cornerstone concepts of developing with RxSwift as well as real-world examples of how to use them in your apps.

The three building blocks of Rx code are **observables**, **operators**, and **schedulers**. The sections below cover each of these in detail.

Observables

The `Observable<T>` class provides the foundation of Rx code: the ability to asynchronously produce a sequence of events that can "carry" an immutable snapshot of data T. In the simplest words, it allows classes to subscribe for values emitted by another class over time.

The `Observable<T>` class allows one or more observers to react to any events in real time and update the app UI, or otherwise process and utilize new and incoming data.

The `ObservableType` protocol (to which the `Observable<T>` conforms) is extremely simple. An `Observable` can emit (and observers can receive) only three types of events:

- **A `next` event**: An event which "carries" the latest (or "*next*") data value. This is the way observers "receive" values.

- **A `completed` event**: This event terminates the event sequence with success. It means the `Observable` completed its life-cycle successfully and won't emit any other events.

- **An `error` event**: The `Observable` terminates with an error and will not emit other events.

When talking about asynchronous events emitted over time, you can visualize an observable sequence of integers on a timeline, like so:

Observable<Int>

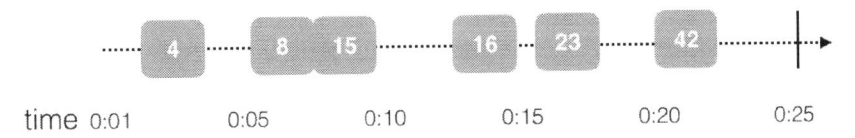

time 0:01   0:05   0:10   0:15   0:20   0:25

This simple contract of three possible events an `Observable` can emit is anything and everything in Rx. Because it is so universal, you can use it to create even the most complex application logic.

Because the observable contract does not make any assumptions about the nature of the `Observable` or the `Observer`, using event sequences is the ultimate decoupling practice. You don't ever need to use delegate protocols, or inject closures to allow your classes to talk to each other.

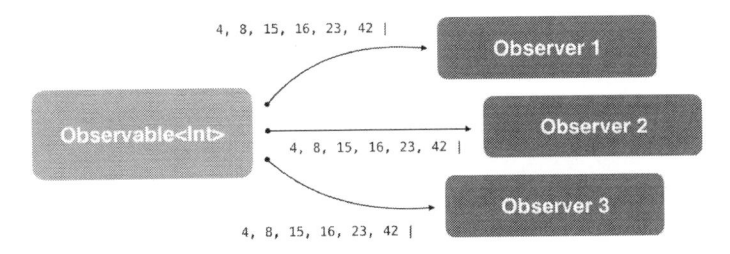

To get an idea about some real-life situations, you'll look at two different kinds of observable sequences: **finite** and **infinite**.

Finite observable sequences

Some observable sequences emit zero, one, or more values, and at a later point, either terminate successfully or terminate with an error.

In an iOS app, consider code that downloads a file from the Internet:

- First, you start the download and start observing for incoming data.
- Then you repeatedly receive chunks of data as parts of the file come in.
- In the event the network connection goes down, the download will stop and the connection will time out with an error.
- Alternatively, if the code downloads all the file's data, it will complete with success.

This workflow accurately describes the lifecycle of a typical observable. Take a look at the related code below:

```
API.download(file: "http://www...")
  .subscribe(onNext: { data in
    ... append data to temporary file
  },
  onError: { error in
    ... display error to user
  },
  onCompleted: {
    ... use downloaded file
  })
```

`API.download(file:)` returns an `Observable<Data>` instance, which emits `Data` values as chunks of data come over the network.

You subscribe for `next` events by providing the `onNext` closure. In the downloading example, you append the data to a temporary file stored on disk.

You subscribe for an `error` by providing the `onError` closure. In the closure, you can display the `error.localizedDescription` in an alert box or do something else.

Finally, to handle a `completed` event, you provide the `onCompleted` closure, where you can push a new view controller to display the downloaded file or anything else your app logic dictates.

Infinite observable sequences

Unlike file downloads or similar activities, which are supposed to terminate either naturally or forcefully, there are other sequences which are simply infinite. Often, UI events are such infinite observable sequences.

For example, consider the code you need to react to device orientation changes in your app:

- You add your class as an observer to `UIDeviceOrientationDidChange` notifications from `NotificationCenter`.

- You then need to provide a method callback to handle orientation changes. It needs to grab the current orientation from `UIDevice` and react accordingly to the latest value.

This sequence of orientation changes does not have a natural end. As long as there is device, there is a possible sequence of orientation changes. Further, since the sequence is virtually infinite, you always have an initial value at the time you start observing it.

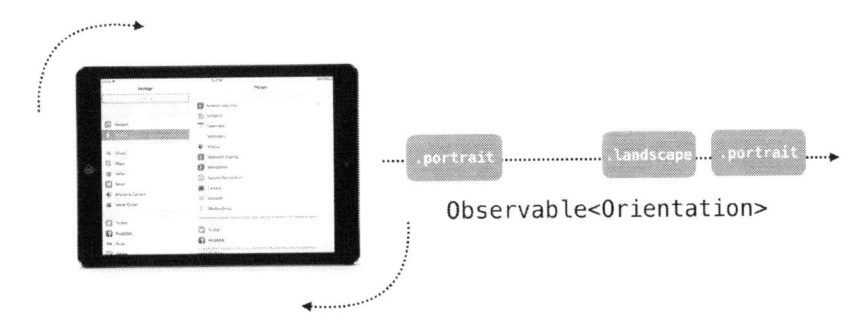

It may happen that the user never rotates their device, but that doesn't mean the sequence of events is terminated. It just means there were no events emitted.

In RxSwift, you could write code like this to handle device orientation:

```
UIDevice.rx.orientation
  .subscribe(onNext: { current in
    switch current {
      case .landscape:
        ... re-arrange UI for landscape
      case .portrait:
        ... re-arrange UI for portrait
    }
  })
```

`UIDevice.rx.orientation` is a fictional control property that produces an `Observable<Orientation>` (this is very easy to code yourself; you'll learn how in the next chapters). You subscribe to it and update the app UI according to the current orientation. You skip the `onError` and `onCompleted` parameters, since these events can never be emitted from that observable.

Operators

`ObservableType` and the implementation of `Observable` class include plenty of methods that abstract discrete pieces of asynchronous work, which can be composed together to implement more complex logic.

Because they are highly decoupled and composable, these methods are most often referred to as `operators`. Since these operators mostly take in asynchronous input and only produce output without causing side effects, they can easily fit together, much like puzzle pieces, and work to build a bigger picture.

For example, take the mathematical expression (5 + 6) * 10 - 2.

In a clear, deterministic way, you can apply the operators *, ( ), + and − in their predefined order to the pieces of data that are their input, take their output and keep processing the expression until it's resolved.

In a somewhat similar manner, you can apply Rx operators to the pieces of input emitted by an `Observable` to deterministically process inputs and outputs until the expression has been resolved to a final value, which you can then use to cause side effects.

Here's the previous example about observing orientation changes, adjusted to use some common Rx operators:

```
UIDevice.rx.orientation
  .filter { value in
    return value != .landscape
  }
  .map { _ in
    return "Portrait is the best!"
  }
  .subscribe(onNext: { string in
    showAlert(text: string)
  })
```

Each time `UIDevice.rx.orientation` produces either a `.landscape` or `.portrait` value, Rx will apply couple of operators to that emitted piece of data.

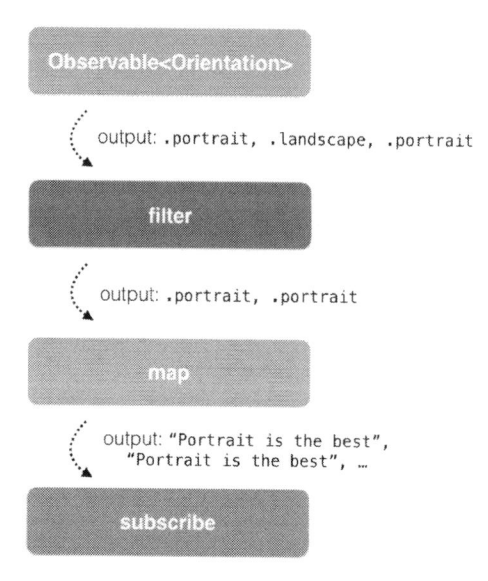

First, `filter` will only let through values that are not `.landscape`. If the device is in landscape mode, the subscription code will not get executed because `filter` will suppress these events.

In case of `.portrait` values, the `map` operator will take the `Orientation` type input and convert it to a `String` output — the text `"Portrait is the best!"`.

Finally, with `subscribe` you subscribe for the resulting `next` event, this time carrying a `String` value, and you call a method to display an alert with that text onscreen.

The operators are also highly *composable* — they always take in data as input and output their result, so you can easily chain them in many different ways achieving so much more than what a single operator can do on its own!

As you work through the book, you will learn about more complex operators that abstract more involved pieces of asynchronous work.

Schedulers

Schedulers are the Rx equivalent of dispatch queues — just on steroids and much easier to use.

RxSwift comes with a number of predefined schedulers, which cover 99% of use cases and hopefully means you will never have to go about creating your own scheduler.

In fact, most of the examples in the first half of this book are quite simple and generally deal with observing data and updating the UI, so you won't look into schedulers at all until you've covered the basics.

That being said, schedulers are very powerful.

For example, you can specify that you'd like to observe for `next` events on `SerialDispatchQueueScheduler`, which uses Grand Central Dispatch to serialize running your code on a given queue.

`ConcurrentDispatchQueueScheduler` will run your code concurrently. `OperationQueueScheduler` will allow you to schedule your subscriptions on a given `NSOperationQueue`.

Thanks to RxSwift, you can schedule the different pieces of work of the same subscription on different schedulers to achieve the best performance.

RxSwift will act as a dispatcher between your subscriptions (on the left hand side below) and the schedulers (on the right hand side), sending the pieces of work to the correct context and seamlessly allowing them to work with each other's output.

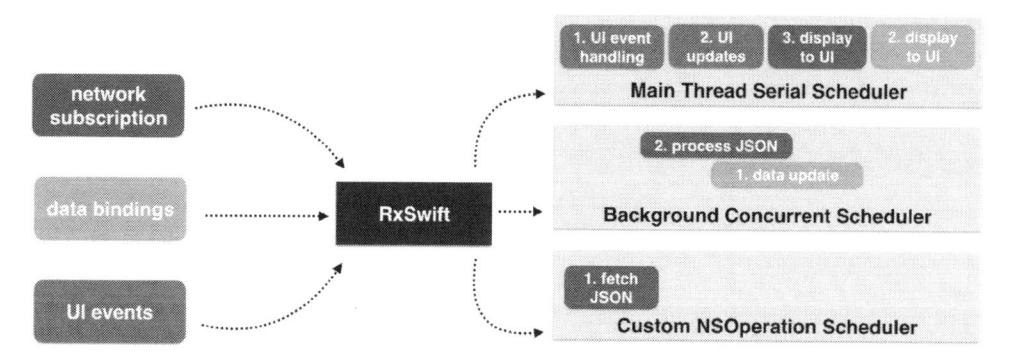

To read this diagram, follow the colored pieces of work in the sequence they were scheduled (1, 2, 3, ...) across the different schedulers. For example:

- The blue network subscription starts with a piece of code (1) that runs on a custom NSOperation based scheduler.

- The data output by this block serves as the input of the next block (2), which runs on a different scheduler, which is on a concurrent background GCD queue.

- Finally, the last piece of blue code (3) is scheduled on the Main thread scheduler in order to update the UI with the new data.

Even if it looks very interesting and quite handy, don't bother too much with schedulers right now. You'll return to them later in this book.

App architecture

It's worth mentioning that RxSwift doesn't alter your app's architecture in any way; it mostly deals with events, asynchronous data sequences, and a universal communication contract.

You can create applications with Rx by implementing MVC architecture as defined in the Apple developer documentation. You can also choose to implement MVP architecture or MVVM if that's what you prefer.

In case you'd like to go that way, RxSwift is also very useful for implementing your own unidirectional data flow architecture.

It's important to note that you definitely do *not* have to start a project from scratch to make it a reactive app; you can iteratively refactor pieces of an exiting project, or simply use RxSwift when appending new features to your app.

Microsoft's MVVM architecture was developed specifically for event-driven software created on platforms which offers data bindings. RxSwift and MVVM definitely do play nicely together, and towards the end of this book you'll look into that pattern and how to implement it with RxSwift.

The reason MVVM and RxSwift go great together is that a ViewModel allows you to expose `Observable<T>` properties, which you can bind directly to UIKit controls in your View Controller glue code. This makes binding model data to the UI very simple to represent, and to code:

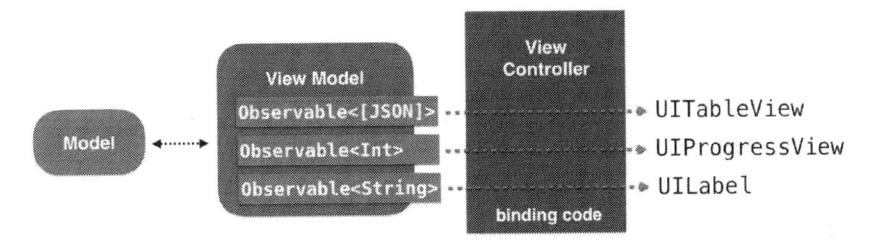

All other examples in the book use the MVC architecture in order to keep the sample code simple and easy to understand.

RxCocoa

RxSwift is the implementation of the common Rx API. Therefore it doesn't know anything about any Cocoa or UIKit-specific classes.

RxCocoa is RxSwift's companion library holding all classes that specifically aid development for UIKit and Cocoa. Besides featuring some advanced classes, RxCocoa adds reactive extensions to many UI components so that you can subscribe for various UI events out of the box.

For example, it's very easy to use RxCocoa to subscribe to the state changes of a `UISwitch`, like so:

```
toggleSwitch.rx.isOn
  .subscribe(onNext: { enabled in
    print( enabled ? "it's ON" : "it's OFF" )
  })
```

RxCocoa adds the `rx.isOn` property (among others) to the `UISwitch` class so you can subscribe to generally useful event sequences.

Observable<Bool>

Further, RxCocoa adds `rx` namespaces to `UITextField`, `URLSession`, `UIViewController`, and more.

Installing RxSwift

RxSwift is available for free at https://github.com/ReactiveX/RxSwift.

RxSwift is distributed under the MIT license, which in short allows you to include the library in free or commercial software, on an as-is basis. As with all other MIT-licensed software, the copyright notice should be included in all apps you distribute.

There is plenty to explore in the RxSwift repository. It includes the **RxSwift** and **RxCocoa** libraries, but you will also find **RxTest** and **RxBlocking** in there, which allow you to write Rx tests.

Besides all the great source code (definitely worth peeking into), you will find **Rx.playground**, which interactively demonstrates many of the operators. Also check out **RxExample**, which is a great showcase app that demonstrates many of the concepts in practice.

The easiest way to include RxSwift/RxCocoa in your projects is via CocoaPods or Carthage. You can also use the Swift Package Manager.

The projects in this book use CocoaPods. Even if you usually use a different dependency manager, **please make sure to use CocoaPods** while you work through the projects in this book.

Before starting on this book, the authors discussed several approaches, and they decided using CocoaPods is a bit more useful when learning RxSwift, since you can always **Cmd-click** on a method and jump straight to its source code. In your own project, you are free to use CocoaPods, Carthage, or another manager — go with the one that suits your own workflow best.

> **Note:** If you're a Carthage guru and want to go that route, feel free; be aware the book only includes instructions for CocoaPods.

RxSwift via CocoaPods

You can install RxSwift via CocoaPods like any other pod library. A typical Podfile would look something like this:

```
use_frameworks!

target 'MyTargetName' do
  pod 'RxSwift', '~> 4.0'
  pod 'RxCocoa', '~> 4.0'
end
```

Of course, you can include just RxSwift, both RxSwift and RxCocoa, or even all the libraries found in the GitHub repository.

Installing RxSwift in the book projects

As for the projects in this book, they all come with a completed Podfile, but without the dependency files included. We looked into this option, but it didn't make sense to include all the files for RxSwift in every single project for each chapter in the book download.

Before you start working on the book, make sure you have the latest version of CocoaPods installed. You need to do that just once before starting to work on the book's projects. Usually executing this in Terminal will suffice:

```
sudo gem install cocoapods
```

If you want to know more, visit the CocoaPods website: https://guides.cocoapods.org/using/getting-started.html.

As the start of **each chapter**, you will be asked to open the starter project for that chapter and install RxSwift in the starter project. This is an easy operation:

1. In the book folder, find the directory matching the name of the chapter you are working on.
2. Copy the **starter** folder in a convenient location on your computer. A location in your user folder is a good idea.
3. Open the built-in Terminal.app or another one you use on daily basis and navigate to the **starter** folder. Type `cd /users/yourname/path/to/starter`, replacing the example path with the actual path on your computer.
4. Type `pod install` to fetch RxSwift from GitHub and install it in the chapter project.

5. Finally, inside the starter folder, find the newly created `.xcworkspace` file and launch it. Build the workspace one time in Xcode, and you're ready to work through the chapter!

> **Note:** In case CocoaPods complains it can't find the latest version of RxSwift, run once `pod update` to refresh the pods index.

RxSwift via Carthage

Installing RxSwift via Carthage is almost equally streamlined. First make sure you've installed the latest version of Carthage from here: https://github.com/Carthage/Carthage#installing-carthage.

In your project, create a new file named Cartfile and add the following line to it:

```
github "ReactiveX/RxSwift" ~> 4.0
```

Next, within the folder of your project execute `carthage update`.

This will download the source code of **all libraries** included in the RxSwift repository and build them, which might take some time. Once the process finishes, find the resulting framework files in the Carthage subfolder created inside the current folder and include them in your project.

Build once more to make sure Xcode indexes the newly added frameworks, and you're ready to go.

Community

The RxSwift project is alive and buzzing with activity, not only because Rx is inspiring programmers to create cool software with it, but also due to the positive nature of the community that formed around this project.

The RxSwift community is very friendly, open minded, and enthusiastic about discussing patterns, common techniques, or just helping each other.

Besides the official RxSwift repository, you'll find plenty of projects created by Rx enthusiasts here: http://community.rxswift.org.

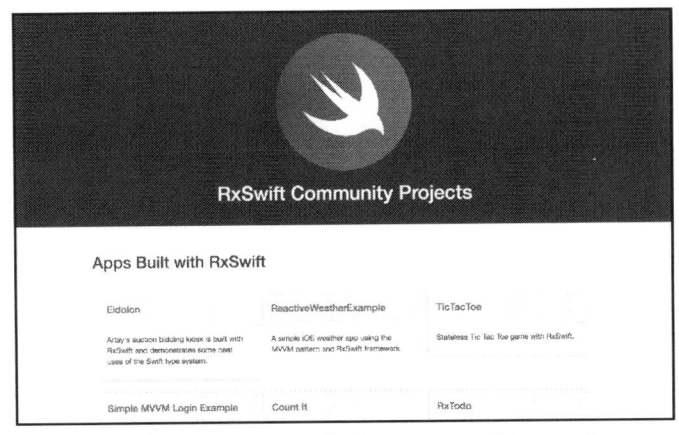

Even more Rx libraries and experiments, which spring up like mushrooms after the rain, can be found here: https://github.com/RxSwiftCommunity

Probably the best way to meet many of the people interested in RxSwift is the Slack channel dedicated to the library: http://rxswift-slack.herokuapp.com.

The Slack channel has over 3,900 members! Day-to-day topics are: helping each other, discussing potential new features of RxSwift or its companion libraries, and sharing RxSwift blog posts and conference talks.

Where to go from here?

This chapter introduced you to many of the problems that RxSwift addresses. You learned about the complexities of asynchronous programming, sharing mutable state, causing side effects, and more.

You haven't written any RxSwift yet, but you now understand why RxSwift is a good idea and you're aware of the types of problems it solves. This should give you a good start as you work through the rest of the book.

And there is plenty to work through. You'll start by creating very simple observables and work your way up to complete real-world apps using MVVM architecture.

Move right on to Chapter 2, "Observables"!

Chapter 2: Observables

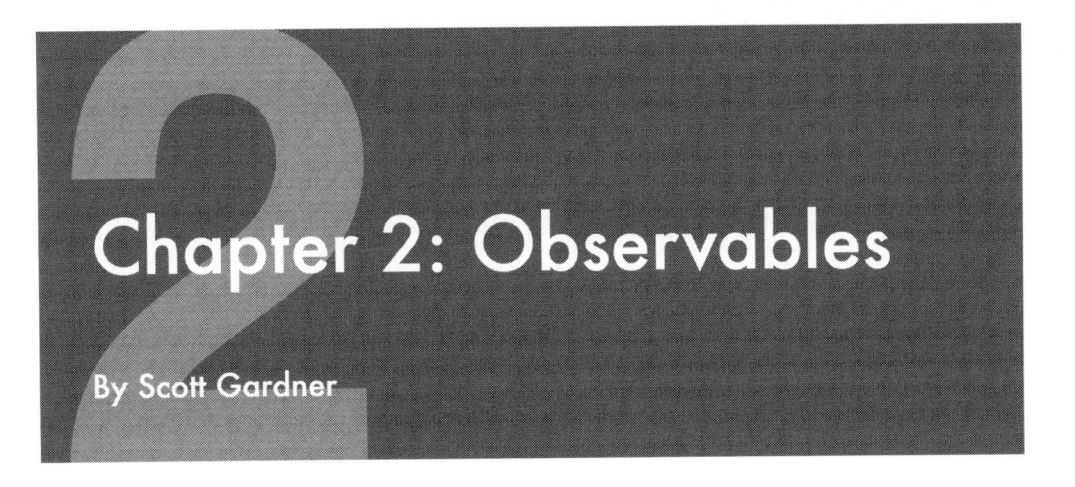

By Scott Gardner

Now that you're set up to use RxSwift and have learned some of the basic concepts, it's time to make the jump and play with some observables.

In this chapter, you're going to go over several examples of creating and subscribing to observables. The real-world use of some of the observables may seem a bit obscure, but rest assured you'll be acquiring important skills and learning a lot about the types of observables available to you in RxSwift. You'll use those skills throughout the rest of this book, and beyond!

Getting started

The starter project for this chapter is an Xcode project named **RxSwiftPlayground** that contains a playground. It's already been set up for you with the RxSwift library using CocoaPods. So after running `pod install` as explained in Chapter 1, open up the Xcode *workspace*, and then select **RxSwiftPlayground.playground** in the Project Navigator to open it in the Source Editor.

> **Note:** Be sure to open **RxSwiftPlayground.xcworkspace** from Finder and not the playground file directly.

As the comment at the top indicates, build the project first to make RxSwift available and clear any errors. (You can build by pressing the default keyboard shortcut Cmd + B.)

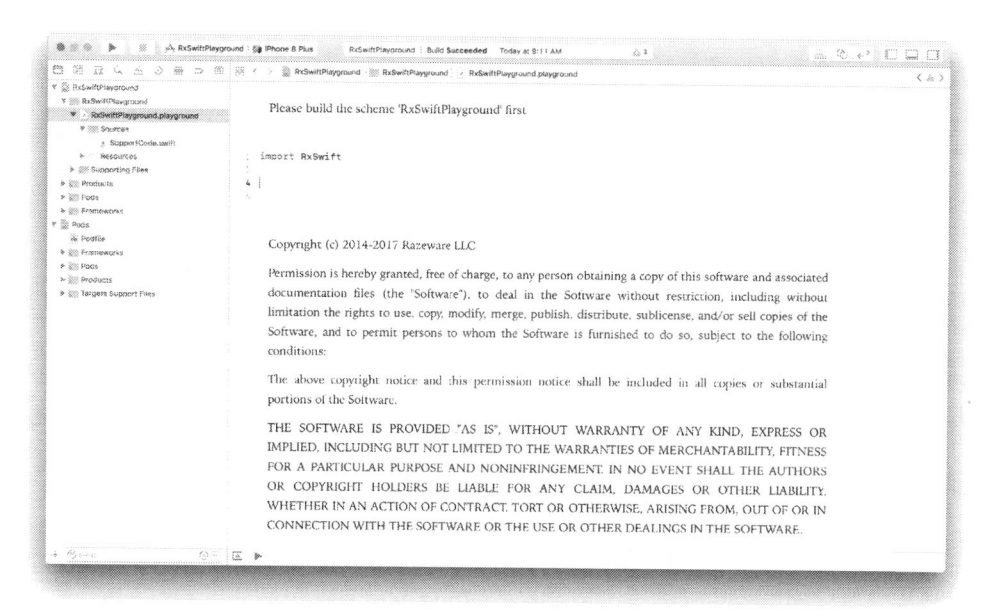

Twist down the playground page, through the **Sources** folder in the **Project navigator**, and select **SupportCode.swift**. It contains the following helper function `example(of:)`:

```
public func example(of description: String, action: () -> Void)
{
  print("\n--- Example of:", description, "---")
  action()
}
```

You're going to use this function to encapsulate different examples as you work your way through this chapter. You'll see how to use this function shortly.

But before you get too deep into that, now would probably be a good time to answer the question: what *is* an observable?

What is an observable?

Observables are the heart of Rx. You're going to spend some time discussing what observables are, how to create them, and how to use them.

You'll see "observable," "observable sequence," and "sequence" used interchangeably in Rx. And really, they're all the same thing. You may even see an occasional "stream" thrown around from time to time, especially from developers that come to RxSwift from a different reactive programming environment. "Stream" also refers to the same thing, but in RxSwift, all the cool kids call it a sequence, not a stream. In RxSwift...

...or something that *works* with a sequence. And an `Observable` is just a sequence, with some special powers. One of them, in fact the most important one, is that it is *asynchronous*. Observables produce events, the process of which is referred to as *emitting*, over a period of time. Events can contain values, such as numbers or instances of a custom type, or they can be recognized gestures, such as taps.

One of the best ways to conceptualize this is by using marble diagrams (which are just values plotted on a timeline).

The left-to-right arrow represents time, and the numbered circles represent elements of a sequence. Element 1 will be emitted, some time will pass, and then 2 and 3 will be emitted. How much time, you ask? It could be at *any* point throughout the life of the observable. Which brings you to the lifecycle of an observable.

Lifecycle of an observable

In the previous marble diagram, the observable emitted three elements. When an observable emits an element, it does so in what's known as a **next** event.

Here's another marble diagram, this time including a vertical bar that represents the end of the road for this observable.

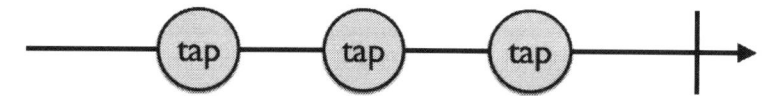

This observable emits three tap events, and then it ends. This is called a **completed** event, as it's been *terminated*. For example, perhaps the taps were on a view that had been dismissed. The important thing is that the observable has terminated, and can no longer emit anything. This is normal termination. However, sometimes things can go wrong.

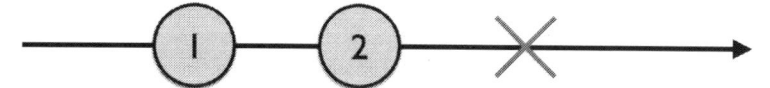

An error has occurred in this marble diagram; it's represented by the red X. The observable emitted an **error** event containing the error. This is no different than when an observable terminates normally with a **completed** event. If an observable emits an **error** event, it is also terminated and can no longer emit anything else.

Here's a quick recap:

- An observable emits **next** events that contain elements. It can continue to do this until it either:
- ...emits an error **event** and is terminated, or
- ...emits a **completed** event and is terminated.
- Once an observable is terminated, it can no longer emit events.

Taking an example straight from the RxSwift source code, these events are represented as enumeration cases:

```
/// Represents a sequence event.
///
/// Sequence grammar:
/// **next\* (error | completed)**
public enum Event<Element> {
    /// Next element is produced.
    case next(Element)

    /// Sequence terminated with an error.
    case error(Swift.Error)

    /// Sequence completed successfully.
    case completed
}
```

Here you can see that `.next` events contain an instance of some `Element`, `.error` events contain an instance of `Swift.Error` and `.completed` events are simply stop events that don't contain any data.

Now that you understand what an observable is and what it does, you'll create some observables to see them in action.

Creating observables

Switch back from the current file to **RxSwift.playground** and add the code below:

```
example(of: "just, of, from") {

    // 1
    let one = 1
    let two = 2
    let three = 3

    // 2
    let observable: Observable<Int> = Observable<Int>.just(one)
}
```

Here's what you do in the code above:

1. Define some integer constants you'll use in the following examples.

2. Create an observable sequence of type `Int` using the `just` method with the `one` integer.

`just` is aptly named, since all it does is create an observable sequence containing *just* a single element. `just` is a type method on `Observable`. However, in Rx, methods are referred to as "operators." And the eagle-eyed among you can probably guess which operator you're going to check out next.

Add this code to the trailing closure of `example(of:)`:

```
let observable2 = Observable.of(one, two, three)
```

This time you didn't explicitly specify the type. You *might* think that because you give it several integers, the type is `Observable` of `[Int]`. **Option-click** on `observable2` to show its inferred type and you'll see that it's an `Observable` of `Int`, not an array.

```
// 2
let observable: Observable<Int> = Observable<Int>.just(one)
let observable2 = Observable.of(one, two, three)
```

Declaration `let observable2: Observable<Int>`
Declared in RxSwiftPlayground.playground

That's because the `of` operator takes a *variadic* parameter of the type inferred by the elements passed to it.

```
// 2
let observable: Observable<Int> = Observable<Int>.just(one)
let observable2 = Observable.of(one, two, three)
}
```

Declaration `static func of(_ elements: Int..., scheduler: ImmediateSchedulerType = default) -> Observable<Int>`
Description This method creates a new Observable instance with a variable number of elements.
Parameters   elements   Elements to generate.
             scheduler   Scheduler to send elements on. If nil, elements are sent immediately on subscription.
Returns   The observable sequence whose elements are pulled from the given arguments.
Declared In RxSwift

If you *want* to create an observable array, you can simply pass an array to `of`.

Add this code to the bottom of the example:

```
let observable3 = Observable.of([one, two, three])
```

Option-click on `observable3` and you'll see that it is indeed an `Observable` of `[Int]`. The `just` operator can also take an array as its single element, which may seem a little weird at first. However, it's the *array* that is the single element, not its contents.

Another operator you can use to create observables is `from`. Add this code to the bottom of the example:

```
let observable4 = Observable.from([one, two, three])
```

The `from` operator creates an observable of individual type instances from a regular array of elements. Option-click on `observable4` and you'll see that it is an `Observable` of `Int`, not `[Int]`. The `from` operator *only* takes an array.

Your console is probably looking quite bare at the moment. That's because you haven't printed anything except the example header. Time to change that by *subscribing* to observables.

Subscribing to observables

As an iOS developer, you may be familiar with `NotificationCenter`; it broadcasts notifications to observers, which are different than RxSwift `Observables`. Here's an example of an observer of the `UIKeyboardDidChangeFrame` notification, with a handler as a trailing closure:

```
let observer = NotificationCenter.default.addObserver(
  forName: .UIKeyboardDidChangeFrame,
  object: nil,
  queue: nil
) { notification in
  // Handle receiving notification
}
```

Subscribing to an RxSwift observable is fairly similar; you call observing an observable *subscribing* to it. So instead of `addObserver()`, you use `subscribe()`. Unlike `NotificationCenter`, where developers typically use only its `.default` singleton instance, each observable in Rx is different.

More importantly, an observable won't send events until it has a subscriber. Remember that an observable is really a sequence definition; subscribing to an observable is really more like calling `next()` on an `Iterator` in the Swift standard library.

```
let sequence = 0..<3

var iterator = sequence.makeIterator()
```

```
while let n = iterator.next() {
  print(n)
}

/* Prints:
 0
 1
 2
*/
```

Subscribing to observables is more streamlined than this, though. You can also add handlers for each event type an observable can emit. Recall that an observable emits `.next`, `.error`, and `.completed` events. A `.next` event passes the element being emitted to the handler, and an `.error` event contains an error instance.

To see this in action, add this new example to the playground (insert the code somewhere *after* the closing curly bracket of the previous example):

```
example(of: "subscribe") {
    let one = 1
    let two = 2
    let three = 3

    let observable = Observable.of(one, two, three)
}
```

This is similar to the previous example, except this time you're simply using the `of` operator. Now add this code at the bottom of this example's closure, to subscribe to the observable:

```
observable.subscribe { event in
    print(event)
}
```

> **Note:** The Console should automatically appear whenever there is output, but you can manually show it by selecting **View ▸ Debug Area ▸ Activate Console** from the menu. This is where the `print` statements in the playground display their output.

Option-click on the `subscribe` operator, and you'll see that it takes an escaping closure that takes an `Event` of type `Int` and doesn't return anything, and `subscribe` returns a `Disposable`. You'll cover disposables shortly.

```
                    25
                          observable.subscribe { event in
                            nrint(event)
         Declaration  func subscribe(_ on: @escaping (Event<Int>) -> Void) ->
                      Disposable
         Description  Subscribes an event handler to an observable sequence.
         Parameters     on   Action to invoke for each event in the observable sequence.
             Returns  Subscription object used to unsubscribe from the observable sequence.
         Declared in  RxSwift
```

The result of this subscription is that each event emitted by the `observable` prints out.

```
--- Example of: subscribe ---
next(1)
next(2)
next(3)
completed
```

The observable emits a `.next` event for each element, then emits a `.completed` event and finally is terminated. When working with observables, you'll usually be more interested in the *elements* emitted by `.next` events, than you will be with the events themselves.

To see how you might access them; replace the subscribing code from above with the following code:

```
observable.subscribe { event in
   if let element = event.element {
      print(element)
   }
}
```

`Event` has an `element` property. It's an optional value, because only `.next` events have an element. So you use optional binding to unwrap the element if it's not `nil`. Now, only the elements are printed, not the events containing the elements, and not the `.completed` event.

```
1
2
3
```

That's a nice pattern, and it's so frequently used that there's a shortcut for it in RxSwift. There's a `subscribe` operator for each type of event an observable emits: **next, error,** and **completed**.

Replace the previous subscription code with this:

```
observable.subscribe(onNext: { element in
    print(element)
})
```

> **Note**: If you have code completion suggestions turned on in Xcode preferences, you may be asked for handlers for the other events. Ignore these for now.

Now you're only handling `.next` event elements and ignoring everything else. The `onNext` closure receives the `.next` event's element as an argument, so you don't have to manually retrieve it from the event like you did before.

You've seen how to create observable of one element and of many elements. But what about an observable of zero elements? The `empty` operator creates an empty observable sequence with zero elements; it will only emit a `.completed` event.

Add this new example to the playground:

```
example(of: "empty") {
    let observable = Observable<Void>.empty()
}
```

An observable must be defined as a specific type if it can't be inferred. So, since `empty` has nothing from which to infer the type, the type must be defined explicitly. In this case, `Void` is as good as anything else. Add this code to the example to subscribe to it:

```
observable
    .subscribe(
        // 1
        onNext: { element in
            print(element)
        },
        
        // 2
        onCompleted: {
            print("Completed")
        }
    )
```

Taking each numbered comment in turn:

1. Handle `.next` events, just like you did in the previous example.
2. A `.completed` event does not include an element, so simply print a message.

In the console, you'll see that `empty` simply emits a `.completed` event:

```
--- Example of: empty ---
Completed
```

But what use is an *empty* observable? Well, they're handy when you want to return an observable that immediately terminates, or intentionally has zero values.

As opposed to the `empty` operator, the `never` operator creates an observable that doesn't emit anything and *never* terminates. It can be use to represent an infinite duration. Add this example to the playground:

```
example(of: "never") {
    let observable = Observable<Any>.never()
    
    observable
      .subscribe(
        onNext: { element in
            print(element)
        },
          onCompleted: {
            print("Completed")
        }
      )
}
```

Nothing is printed, except for the example header. Not even `"Completed"`. How do you know if this is even working? Hang on to that inquisitive spirit until the **Challenges** section.

So far, you've been working mostly with observables of explicit variables, but it's also possible to generate an observable from a range of values. Add this example to the playground:

```
example(of: "range") {
    // 1
    let observable = Observable<Int>.range(start: 1, count: 10)
    
    observable
      .subscribe(onNext: { i in
        
        // 2
        let n = Double(i)
        let fibonacci = Int(((pow(1.61803, n) - pow(0.61803, n)) / 2.23606).rounded())
        print(fibonacci)
    })
}
```

Taking it section-by-section:

1. Create an observable using the `range` operator, which takes a `start` integer value and a `count` of sequential integers to generate.
2. Calculate and print the *nth* Fibonacci number for each emitted element.

There's actually a better place, than in the `onNext` handler, to put code that transforms the emitted element. You'll learn about that in Chapter 7, "Transforming Operators."

Except for the `never()` example, up to this point you've been working with observables that automatically emit a `.completed` event and naturally terminate. This permitted you to focus on the mechanics of creating and subscribing to observables, but that brushed an important aspect of subscribing to observables under the carpet. It's time to do some housekeeping and deal with that aspect before moving on.

Disposing and terminating

Remember that an observable doesn't do anything until it receives a subscription. It's the subscription that triggers an observable to begin emitting events, up until it emits an `.error` or `.completed` event and is terminated. You can manually cause an observable to terminate by canceling a subscription to it.

Add this new example to the playground:

```
example(of: "dispose") {

  // 1
  let observable = Observable.of("A", "B", "C")

  // 2
  let subscription = observable.subscribe { event in

    // 3
    print(event)
  }
}
```

Quite simply:

1. Create an observable of some strings.
2. Subscribe to the observable, this time saving the returned `Disposable` as a local constant called `subscription`.
3. Print each emitted `event` in the handler.

To explicitly cancel a subscription, call `dispose()` on it. After you cancel the subscription, or *dispose* of it, the observable in the current example will stop emitting events.

Add this code to the bottom of the example:

```
subscription.dispose()
```

Managing each subscription individually would be tedious, so RxSwift includes a `DisposeBag` type. A dispose bag holds disposables — typically added using the `.disposed(by:)` method — and will call `dispose()` on each one when the dispose bag is about to be deallocated. Add this new example to the playground:

```
example(of: "DisposeBag") {

  // 1
  let disposeBag = DisposeBag()

  // 2
  Observable.of("A", "B", "C")
    .subscribe { // 3
      print($0)
    }
    .disposed(by: disposeBag) // 4
}
```

Here's how this disposable code works:

1. Create a dispose bag.

2. Create an observable.

3. Subscribe to the observable and print out the emitted event using the default argument name $0 rather than explicitly defining an argument name.

4. Add the return value from `subscribe` to the `disposeBag`.

This is the pattern you'll use the most frequently; creating and subscribing to an observable and immediately adding the subscription to a dispose bag.

Why bother with disposables at all? If you forget to add a subscription to a dispose bag, or manually call `dispose` on it when you're done with the subscription, or in some other way cause the observable to terminate at some point, you will *probably* leak memory. Don't worry if you forget; the Swift compiler should warn you about unused disposables.

In the previous examples, you've created observables with specific `.next` event elements. Another way to specify all events that an observable will emit to subscribers is by using the `create` operator.

Add this new example to the playground:

```
example(of: "create") {

  let disposeBag = DisposeBag()

  Observable<String>.create { observer in

  }
}
```

The `create` operator takes a single parameter named `subscribe`. Its job is to provide the implementation of calling `subscribe` on the observable. In other words, it defines all the events that will be emitted to subscribers. Option-click on `create`.

> Observable<String>.create { observer in
>
> **Declaration**   static func create(_ subscribe: @escaping
>   (AnyObserver<String>) -> Disposable) ->
>   Observable<String>
>
> **Description**   Creates an observable sequence from a specified subscribe method implementation.
>
> **Parameters**   subscribe   Implementation of the resulting observable sequence's subscribe method.
>
> **Returns**   The observable sequence with the specified implementation for the subscribe method.
>
> **Declared In**   RxSwift

The `subscribe` parameter is an escaping closure that takes an `AnyObserver` and returns a `Disposable`. AnyObserver is a generic type that facilitates adding values *onto* an observable sequence, which will then be emitted to subscribers.

Change the implementation of `create` to the following:

```
Observable<String>.create { observer in
  // 1
  observer.onNext("1")

  // 2
  observer.onCompleted()

  // 3
  observer.onNext("?")

  // 4
  return Disposables.create()
}
```

Here's the play-by-play:

1. Add a `.next` event onto the observer. `onNext(_:)` is a convenience method for `on(.next(_:))`.
2. Add a `.completed` event onto the observer. Similarly, `onCompleted` is a convenience method for `on(.completed)`.
3. Add another `.next` event onto the observer.
4. Return a disposable.

> **Note** The last step, returning a `Disposable`, may seem strange but remember that the `subscribe` operators *return* a disposable representing the subscription. Here, `Disposables.create()` is an empty disposable, but some disposables have side-effects.

Do you think the second `onNext` element (?) could ever be emitted to subscribers? Why or why not? To see if you guessed correctly, subscribe to the observable by adding the following code on the next line after the `create` implementation:

```
.subscribe(
  onNext: { print($0) },
  onError: { print($0) },
  onCompleted: { print("Completed") },
  onDisposed: { print("Disposed") }
)
.disposed(by: disposeBag)
```

You've subscribed to the observable, and implemented all the handlers, using default argument names for element and error arguments passed to the `onNext` and `onError` handlers respectively. The result is that the first `.next` event element, `"Completed"` and `"Disposed"` print out. The second `.next` event doesn't print because the observable emitted a `.completed` event and terminated before it.

```
--- Example of: create ---
1
Completed
Disposed
```

What would happen if you added an error to the `observer`? Add this code at the top of the example:

```
enum MyError: Error {
    case anError
}
```

You've created an `Error` type with a single case `anError`. Now add the following line of code between the `observer.onNext` and `observer.onCompleted` calls:

```
observer.onError(MyError.anError)
```

The observable emits the error and then is terminated.

```
--- Example of: create ---
1
anError
Disposed
```

What would happen if you emitted neither a `.completed` nor a `.error` event, and didn't add the subscription to `disposeBag`? Comment out the `observer.onError`, `observer.onCompleted` and `disposed(by: disposeBag)` lines of code to find out.

Here's the complete implementation:

```
example(of: "create") {
  
  enum MyError: Error {
    case anError
  }
  
  let disposeBag = DisposeBag()
  
  Observable<String>.create { observer in
    // 1
    observer.onNext("1")
    
//    observer.onError(MyError.anError)
    
    // 2
//    observer.onCompleted()
    
    // 3
    observer.onNext("?")
    
    // 4
    return Disposables.create()
  }
  .subscribe(
    onNext: { print($0) },
    onError: { print($0) },
    onCompleted: { print("Completed") },
    onDisposed: { print("Disposed") }
  )
//  .disposed(by: disposeBag)
}
```

Congratulations — you've just leaked memory! The observable will never finish, and the disposable will never be disposed of.

```
--- Example of: create ---
1
?
```

Feel free to uncomment the line adding the `.completed` event or the ones adding the subscription to the `disposeBag` if you just can't stand to leave this example in a leaky state.

Creating observable factories

Rather than creating an observable that waits around for subscribers, it's possible to create observable factories that vend a new observable to each subscriber.

Add this new example to the playground:

```
example(of: "deferred") {
    let disposeBag = DisposeBag()

    // 1
    var flip = false

    // 2
    let factory: Observable<Int> = Observable.deferred {

        // 3
        flip = !flip

        // 4
        if flip {
            return Observable.of(1, 2, 3)
        } else {
            return Observable.of(4, 5, 6)
        }
    }
}
```

Here's the explanation:

1. Create a `Bool` flag to flip which observable to return.

2. Create an observable of `Int` factory using the `deferred` operator.

3. Invert `flip`, which will be used each time `factory` is subscribed to.

4. Return different observables based on whether `flip` is `true` or `false`.

Externally, an observable factory is indistinguishable from a regular observable. Add this code to the bottom of the example to subscribe to `factory` four times:

```
for _ in 0...3 {
  factory.subscribe(onNext: {
    print($0, terminator: "")
  })
  .disposed(by: disposeBag)

  print()
}
```

Each time you subscribe to `factory`, you get the opposite observable. You get 123, then 456, and the pattern repeats each time a new subscription is created.

```
--- Example of: deferred ---
123
456
123
456
```

Using Traits

Traits are observables with a narrower set of behaviors than regular observables. Their use is optional; you can use a regular observable anywhere you might use a trait instead. Their purpose is to provide a way to more clearly convey your intent to readers of your code or consumers of your API. The context implied by using a trait can help make your code more intuitive.

There are three kinds of traits in RxSwift: `Single`, `Maybe`, and `Completable`. Without knowing anything more about them yet, can you guess how each one is specialized?

`Single`s will emit either a `.success(value)` or `.error` event. `.success(value)` is actually a combination of the `.next` and `.completed` events. This is useful for one-time processes that will either succeed and yield a value or fail, such as downloading data or loading it from disk.

A `Completable` will only emit a `.completed` or `.error` event. It doesn't emit any value. You could use a completable when you only care that an operation completed successfully or failed, such as a file write.

And `Maybe` is a mashup of a `Single` and `Completable`. It can either emit a `.success(value)`, `.completed`, or `.error`. If you need to implement an operation that could either succeed or fail, and optionally return a value on success, then `Maybe` is your ticket.

You'll have an opportunity to work more with traits in Chapter 4 and beyond. For now, you'll run through a basic example of using a single to load some text from a text file named **Copyright.txt** in the **Resources** folder of the playground, because who doesn't love some legalese once in a while?

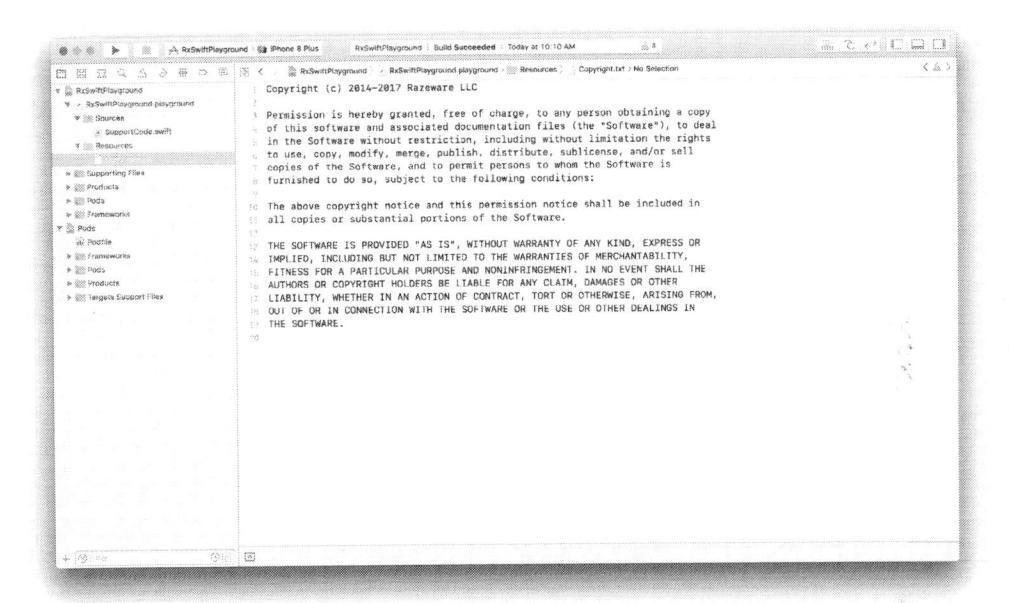

Add this example to the playground:

```
example(of: "Single") {

  // 1
  let disposeBag = DisposeBag()

  // 2
  enum FileReadError: Error {
    case fileNotFound, unreadable, encodingFailed
  }

  // 3
  func loadText(from name: String) -> Single<String> {
    // 4
    return Single.create { single in

    }
  }
}
```

Here's what you do in this code:

1. Create a dispose bag to use later.
2. Define an `Error` enum to model some possible errors that can occur in reading data from a file on disk.
3. Implement a function to load text from a file on disk that returns a `Single`.
4. Create and return a `Single`.

Add this code inside the `create` closure to complete the implementation:

```
// 1
let disposable = Disposables.create()

// 2
guard let path = Bundle.main.path(forResource: name, ofType:
"txt") else {
  single(.error(FileReadError.fileNotFound))
  return disposable
}

// 3
guard let data = FileManager.default.contents(atPath: path) else
{
  single(.error(FileReadError.unreadable))
  return disposable
}

// 4
guard let contents = String(data: data, encoding: .utf8) else {
  single(.error(FileReadError.encodingFailed))
  return disposable
}

// 5
single(.success(contents))
return disposable
```

From the top:

1. The `subscribe` closure of the `create` method must return a disposable (Option-click on `create` to see this for yourself), so you create one here that you'll return at various points.

2. Get the path for the filename, or else add a file not found error onto the `Single` and return the `disposable` you created.

3. Get the data from the file at that path, or add an unreadable error onto the `Single` and return the disposable.

1. Convert the data to a string; otherwise, add an encoding failed error onto the `Single` and return the `disposable`. Starting to see a pattern here?
2. Made it this far? Add the contents onto the `Single` as a success, and return the `disposable`.

Now you can put this function to work. Add this code to the example:

```
// 1
loadText(from: "Copyright")
// 2
  .subscribe {
    // 3
    switch $0 {
    case .success(let string):
      print(string)
    case .error(let error):
      print(error)
    }
  }
  .disposed(by: disposeBag)
```

Here, you:

1. Call `loadText(from:)`, passing the root name of the text file.
2. Subscribe to the `Single` it returns.
3. Switch on the event, printing the string if it was successful, or printing the error if not.

You should see the text from the file printed to the console, the same as the copyright comment at the bottom of the playground:

```
--- Example of: Single ---
Copyright (c) 2014-2017 Razeware LLC
...
```

Try changing the filename to something else, and you should get the file not found error printed instead.

Challenges

Practice makes *permanent*. By completing these challenges, you'll practice what you've learned in this chapter and pick up a few more tidbits of knowledge about working with observables. A starter playground workspace as well as the finished version of it are provided for each challenge. Enjoy!

Challenge 1: Perform side effects

In the `never` operator example earlier, nothing printed out. That was before you were adding your subscriptions to dispose bags, but if you *had* added it to one, you would've been able to print out a message in `subscribe`'s `onDisposed` handler. There is another useful operator for when you want to do some side work that doesn't affect the observable you're working with.

The `do` operator allows you to insert *side effects*; that is, handlers to do things that will not change the emitted event in any way. `do` will just pass the event through to the next operator in the chain. `do` also includes an `onSubscribe` handler, something that `subscribe` does not.

The method for using the `do` operator is `do(onNext:onError:onCompleted:onSubscribe:onDispose)` and you can provide handlers for any or all of these events. Use Xcode's autocompletion to get the closure parameters for each of the events.

To complete this challenge, insert the `do` operator in the `never` example using the `onSubscribe` handler. Feel free to include any of the other handlers if you'd like; they work just like `subscribe`'s handlers do.

And while you're at it, create a dispose bag and add the subscription to it.

Don't forget you can always peek into the finished challenge playground for "inspiration."

Challenge 2: Print debug info

Performing side effects is one way to help debug your Rx code. But it turns out that there's even a better utility for that purpose: the `debug` operator, which will print information about every event for an observable. It has several optional parameters, perhaps the most useful being that you can include an identifier string that will be printed on each line. In complex Rx chains, where you might add `debug` calls in multiple places, this can really help differentiate the source of each printout.

Continuing to work in the playground from the previous challenge, complete this challenge by replacing the use of the `do` operator with `debug` and provide a string identifier to it as a parameter. Observe the debug output in Xcode's console.

Chapter 3: Subjects

By Scott Gardner

You've gotten a handle on what an observable is, how to create one, how to subscribe to it, and how to dispose of things when you're done. Observables are a fundamental part of RxSwift, but a common need when developing apps is to manually add new values onto an observable at runtime that will then be emitted to subscribers. What you want is something that can act as both an observable and as an *observer*. And that something is called a **Subject**.

In this chapter, you're going to learn about the different types of subjects in RxSwift, see how to work with each one and why you might choose one over another based on some common use cases.

Getting started

After running `pod install`, open the starter project for this chapter named **RxSwiftPlayground** and do a build. You'll start out with a quick example to prime the pump. Write the following code in your playground:

```
example(of: "PublishSubject") {
   let subject = PublishSubject<String>()
}
```

Here you create a `PublishSubject`. It's aptly named, because, like a newspaper publisher, it will receive information and then turn around and publish it to subscribers, possibly after modifying that information in some way first. It's of type `String`, so it can only receive and publish strings. After being initialized, it's ready to receive some.

Add the following code to the example:

```
subject.onNext("Is anyone listening?")
```

This puts a new string onto the subject. But nothing is printed out yet, because there are no observers. Create one by adding the following code to the example:

```
let subscriptionOne = subject
   .subscribe(onNext: { string in
      print(string)
   })
```

You created a subscription to `subject` just like in the last chapter, printing `.next` events. But still, nuthin' shows up in Xcode's output console. Ain't this fun? You're going to learn about the different subjects shortly.

What's happening here is that a `PublishSubject` only emits to *current* subscribers. So if you weren't subscribed when something was added to it previously, you don't get it when you do subscribe. Think of the tree falling analogy. If a tree falls and no one's there to hear it, does that make your illegal logging business a success?

To fix things, add this code to the end of the example:

```
subject.on(.next("1"))
```

Notice that, because you defined the publish subject to be of type `String`, only strings may be put onto it. Now, because `subject` *has* a subscriber, it will emit that text.

```
--- Example of: PublishSubject ---
1
```

In a similar fashion to the `subscribe` operators, `on(.next(_:))` is how you add a new `.next` event *onto* a subject, passing the element as the parameter. And just like `subscribe`, there's shortcut syntax for subjects. Add the following code to the example:

```
subject.onNext("2")
```

`onNext(_:)` does the same thing as `on(.next(_:))`. It's just a bit easier on the eyes. And now the 2 is printed as well.

```
--- Example of: PublishSubject ---
1
2
```

With that gentle intro, now it's time to learn all about subjects.

What are subjects?

Subjects act as both an observable and an observer. You saw earlier how they can receive events and also be subscribed to. The subject received `.next` events, and each time it received an event, it turned around and emitted it to its subscriber.

There are four subject types in RxSwift:

- `PublishSubject`: Starts empty and only emits new elements to subscribers.
- `BehaviorSubject`: Starts with an initial value and replays it or the latest element to new subscribers.
- `ReplaySubject`: Initialized with a buffer size and will maintain a buffer of elements up to that size and replay it to new subscribers.
- `Variable`: Wraps a `BehaviorSubject`, preserves its current value as state, and replays only the latest/initial value to new subscribers.

Taking on each of these in turn, you're going to learn a lot more about subjects and how to work with them next.

Working with publish subjects

Publish subjects come in handy when you simply want subscribers to be notified of new events from the point at which they subscribed, until they either unsubscribe, or the subject has terminated with a `.completed` or `.error` event.

In the following marble diagram, the top line is the publish subject and the second and third lines are subscribers. The upward-pointing arrows indicate subscriptions, and the downward-pointing arrows represent emitted events.

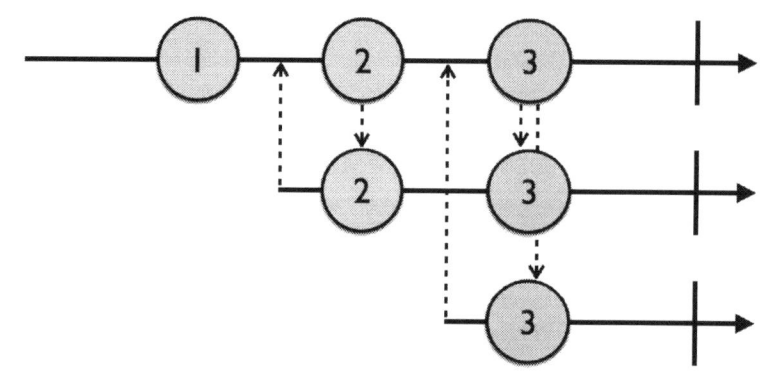

The first subscriber subscribes after 1), so it doesn't get receive that event. It does get 2) and 3), though. And because the second subscriber doesn't join in on the fun until after 2), it only gets 3).

Returning to the playground, add this code to the bottom of the same example:

```
let subscriptionTwo = subject
  .subscribe { event in
    print("2)", event.element ?? event)
  }
```

Events have an optional `element` property that will contain the emitted element for `.next` events. You use the nil-coalescing operator here to print the element if there is one; otherwise, you print the event.

As expected, `subscriptionTwo` doesn't print anything out yet because it subscribed after the 1 and 2 were emitted. Now enter this code:

```
subject.onNext("3")
```

The 3 is printed twice, once each for `subscriptionOne` and `subscriptionTwo`.

```
3
2) 3
```

Add this code to terminate `subscriptionOne` and then add another `.next` event onto the subject:

```
subscriptionOne.dispose()

subject.onNext("4")
```

The value 4 is only printed for subscription 2), because `subscriptionOne` was disposed.

```
2) 4
```

When a publish subject receives a `.completed` or `.error` event, also known as a *stop* event, it will emit that stop event to new subscribers and it will no longer emit `.next` events. However, it will *re-emit* its stop event to future subscribers. Add this code to the example:

```
// 1
subject.onCompleted()

// 2
subject.onNext("5")

// 3
subscriptionTwo.dispose()

let disposeBag = DisposeBag()

// 4
subject
  .subscribe {
    print("3)", $0.element ?? $0)
  }
  .disposed(by: disposeBag)

subject.onNext("?")
```

Here's what you did:

1. Put the `.completed` event onto the subject, using the convenience operator for `on(.completed)`. This effectively terminates the subject's observable sequence.

2. Add another element onto the subject. This won't be emitted and printed, though, because the subject has already terminated.

3. Don't forget to dispose of subscriptions when you're done!

4. Create a new subscription to the subject, this time adding it to a dispose bag.

Maybe the new subscriber 3) will kickstart the subject back into action? Nope, but you do still get the `.completed` event.

```
2) completed
3) completed
```

Actually, *every* subject type, once terminated, will re-emit its stop event to future subscribers. So it's a good idea to include handlers for stop events in your code, not just to be notified when it terminates, but also in case it is already terminated when you subscribe to it.

You might use a publish subject when you're modeling time-sensitive data, such as in an online bidding app. It wouldn't make sense to alert the user who joined at 10:01 am that at 9:59 am there was only 1 minute left in the auction. That is, of course, unless you like 1-star reviews to your bidding app.

Sometimes you want to let new subscribers know what the latest element value is, even though that element was emitted before the subscription. For that, you've got some options.

Working with behavior subjects

Behavior subjects work similarly to publish subjects, except they will *replay* the latest `.next` event to new subscribers. Check out this marble diagram:

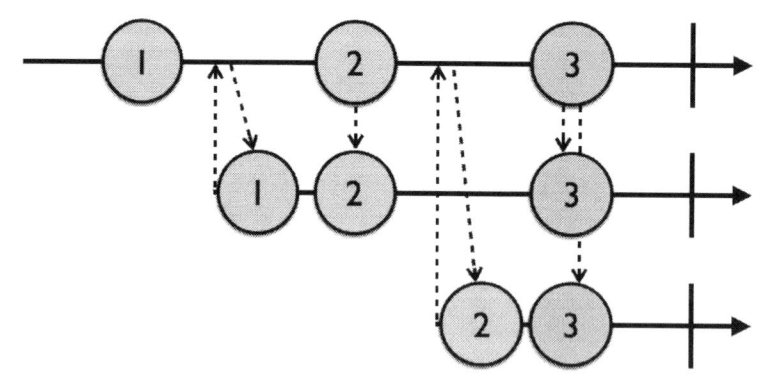

The first line from the top is the subject. The first subscriber on the second line down subscribes after 1) but before 2), so it gets 1) immediately upon subscription, and then 2) and 3) as they're emitted by the subject. Similarly, the second subscriber subscribes after 2) but before 3), so it gets 2) immediately and then 3) when it's emitted.

Add this new example to your playground:

```
// 1
enum MyError: Error {
    case anError
}

// 2
func print<T: CustomStringConvertible>(label: String, event: Event<T>) {
    print(label, event.element ?? event.error ?? event)
```

```
  }
  // 3
  example(of: "BehaviorSubject") {
    // 4
    let subject = BehaviorSubject(value: "Initial value")
    let disposeBag = DisposeBag()
  }
```

Here's the play-by-play:

1. Define an error type to use in upcoming examples.

2. Expanding upon the use of the ternary operator in the previous example, here you create a helper function that will print the element if there is one, or else an error if there is one of those, or else the event itself. How convenient!

3. Start a new example.

4. Create a new `BehaviorSubject` instance. Its initializer takes an initial value.

> **Note**: Since `BehaviorSubject` *always* emits the latest element, you can't create one without providing a default initial value. If you can't provide a default initial value at creation time, that probably means you need to use a `PublishSubject` instead.

Now add the following code to the example:

```
subject
  .subscribe {
    print(label: "1)", event: $0)
  }
  .disposed(by: disposeBag)
```

This creates a subscription to the subject, but the subscription was created *after* the subject was. No other elements have been added to the subject, so it replays the initial value to the subscriber.

```
--- Example of: BehaviorSubject ---
1) Initial value
```

Now insert the following code right *before* the previous subscription code, but *after* the definition of the subject:

```
subject.onNext("X")
```

The X is printed, because now *it's* the latest element when the subscription is made.

```
--- Example of: BehaviorSubject ---
1) X
```

Add the following code to the end of the example. But first, look it over and see if you can determine what will be printed:

```
// 1
subject.onError(MyError.anError)

// 2
subject
  .subscribe {
    print(label: "2)", event: $0)
  }
  .disposed(by: disposeBag)
```

Taking it section-by-section:

1. Add an error event onto the subject.

2. Create a new subscription to the subject.

Did you figure out that the error event will be printed twice, once for each subscription? If so, right on!

```
1) anError
2) anError
```

Behavior subjects are useful when you want to pre-populate a view with the most recent data. For example, you could bind controls in a user profile screen to a behavior subject, so that the latest values can be used to pre-populate the display while the app fetches fresh data.

But what if you wanted to show more than the latest value? For example, on a search screen, you may want to show the most recent five search terms used. This is where replay subjects come in.

Working with replay subjects

Replay subjects will temporarily cache, or *buffer*, the latest elements they emit, up to a specified size of your choosing. They will then replay that buffer to new subscribers.

The following marble diagram depicts a replay subject with a buffer size of 2. The first subscriber (middle line) is already subscribed to the replay subject (top line) so it gets elements as they're emitted. The second subscriber (bottom line) subscribes after 2), so it gets 1) and 2) replayed to it.

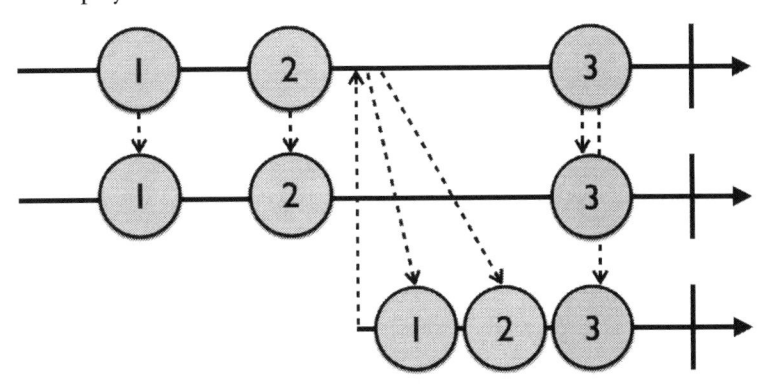

Keep in mind when using a replay subject that this buffer is held in memory. You can definitely shoot yourself in the foot here, such as if you set a large buffer size for a replay subject of some type whose instances each take up a lot of memory, like images. Another thing to watch out for is creating a replay subject of an *array* of items. Each emitted element will be an array, so the buffer size will buffer that many arrays. It would be easy to create memory pressure here if you're not careful.

Add this new example to your playground:

```
example(of: "ReplaySubject") {
  
  // 1
  let subject = ReplaySubject<String>.create(bufferSize: 2)
  
  let disposeBag = DisposeBag()
  
  // 2
  subject.onNext("1")
  
  subject.onNext("2")
  
  subject.onNext("3")
  
  // 3
  subject
    .subscribe {
      print(label: "1)", event: $0)
    }
    .disposed(by: disposeBag)
  
  subject
    .subscribe {
```

```
        print(label: "2)", event: $0)
    }
    .disposed(by: disposeBag)
}
```

From the top:

1. You create a new replay subject with a buffer size of 2. Replay subjects are initialized using the type method `create(bufferSize:)`.

2. Add three elements onto the subject.

3. Create two subscriptions to the subject.

The latest two elements are replayed to both subscribers. 1 never gets emitted, because 2 and 3 were added onto the replay subject with a buffer size of 2 before anything subscribed to it.

```
--- Example of: ReplaySubject ---
1) 2
1) 3
2) 2
2) 3
```

Now add the following code to the example:

```
subject.onNext("4")

subject
  .subscribe {
    print(label: "3)", event: $0)
  }
  .disposed(by: disposeBag)
```

With this code, you add another element onto the subject, and then create a new subscription to it. The first two subscriptions will receive that element as normal because they were already subscribed when the new element was added to the subject, while the new third subscriber will get the last two buffered elements replayed to it.

```
1) 4
2) 4
3) 3
3) 4
```

You're getting pretty good at this stuff by now, so there should be no surprises here. What would happen if you threw a wrench into the works here? Add this line of code right after adding 4 onto the subject, before creating the third subscription:

```
subject.onError(MyError.anError)
```

This *may* surprise you. And if so, that's OK. Life's full of surprises.

```
1) 4
2) 4
1) anError
2) anError
3) 3
3) 4
3) anError
```

What's going on here? The replay subject is terminated with an error, which it will re-emit to new subscribers as you've already seen subjects do. But the buffer is also still hanging around, so it gets replayed to new subscribers as well, before the stop event is re-emitted. Now add this line of code immediately after adding the error:

```
subject.dispose()
```

By explicitly calling `dispose()` on the replay subject beforehand, new subscribers will only receive an error event indicating that the subject was already disposed.

```
3) Object `RxSwift.ReplayMany<Swift.String>` was already
disposed.
```

Explicitly calling `dispose()` on a replay subject like this isn't something you generally need to do, because if you've added your subscriptions to a dispose bag (and avoided creating any strong reference cycles), then everything will be disposed of and deallocated when the owner (e.g., a view controller or view model) is deallocated. It's just good to be aware of this little gotcha for those edge cases.

> **Note:** In case you're wondering what is a `ReplayMany`, it's an internal type that is used to create replay subjects.

By using a publish, behavior, or replay subject, you should be able to model most any need. There may be times, though, when you simply want to go old-school and ask an observable type, "Hey, what's your current value?" Variables FTW here!

Working with variables

As mentioned earlier, a `Variable` wraps a `BehaviorSubject` and stores its current value as state. You can access that current value via its `value` property, and, unlike other subjects and observables in general, you also use that `value` property to set a new element onto a variable. In other words, you don't use `onNext(_:)`.

Because it wraps a behavior subject, a variable is created with an initial value, and it will replay its latest or initial value to new subscribers. In order to access a variable's underlying behavior subject, you call `asObservable()` on it.

Also unique to `Variable`, as compared to other subjects, is that it is *guaranteed* not to emit an error. So although you can listen for `.error` events in a subscription to a variable, you cannot add an `.error` event onto a variable. A variable will also automatically complete when it's about to be deallocated, so you do not (and in fact, cannot) manually add a `.completed` event to it.

Add this new example to your playground:

```
example(of: "Variable") {
    
    // 1
    let variable = Variable("Initial value")
    
    let disposeBag = DisposeBag()
    
    // 2
    variable.value = "New initial value"
    
    // 3
    variable.asObservable()
        .subscribe {
            print(label: "1)", event: $0)
        }
        .disposed(by: disposeBag)
}
```

Here's what you're doing this time:

1. Create a variable with an initial value. The variable's type is inferred, but you could have explicitly declared the type as `Variable<String>("Initial value")`.

2. Add a new element onto the variable.

3. Subscribe to the variable, first by calling `asObservable()` to access its underlying behavior subject.

The subscription gets the latest value.

```
--- Example of: Variable ---
1) New initial value
```

Now add this code to the example:

```
// 1
variable.value = "1"

// 2
variable.asObservable()
  .subscribe {
    print(label: "2)", event: $0)
  }
  .disposed(by: disposeBag)

// 3
variable.value = "2"
```

From the top:

1. Add a new element onto the variable.

2. Create a new subscription to the variable.

3. Add another new element onto the variable.

The existing subscription 1) receives the new value 1 added onto the variable. The new subscription receives that same value when it subscribes, because it's the latest value. And both subscriptions receive the 2 when it's added onto the variable.

```
1) 1
2) 1
1) 2
2) 2
```

There is no way to add an `.error` or `.completed` event onto a variable. Any attempts to do so will generate compiler errors (no need to add this code to your playground, it won't work).

```
// These will all generate errors
variable.value.onError(MyError.anError)

variable.asObservable().onError(MyError.anError)

variable.value = MyError.anError

variable.value.onCompleted()

variable.asObservable().onCompleted()
```

Variables are versatile. You can subscribe to them as observables to be able to react whenever a new `.next` event is emitted, just like any other subject. And they can accommodate one-off needs, such as when you just need to check the current value without subscribing to receive updates. You'll implement an example of this in the second challenge for this chapter.

Challenges

Put your new super subject skills to the test by completing these challenges. There are starter and finished versions for each challenge in the exercise files download.

Challenge 1: Create a blackjack card dealer using a publish subject

In the starter project, twist down the playground page and **Sources** folder in the **Project navigator**, and select the **SupportCode.swift** file. Review the helper code for this challenge, including a `cards` array that contains 52 tuples representing a standard deck of cards, `cardString(for:)` and `point(for:)` helper functions, and a `HandError` enumeration.

In the main playground page, add code right below the comment `// Add code to update dealtHand here` that will evaluate the result returned from calling `points(for:)`, passing the `hand` array. If the result is greater than 21, add the error `HandError.busted` onto the `dealtHand`. Otherwise, add `hand` onto `dealtHand` as a `.next` event.

Also in the main playground page, add code right after the comment `// Add subscription to dealtHand here` to subscribe to `dealtHand` and handle `.next` and `.error` events. For `.next` events, print a string containing the results returned from calling `cardString(for:)` and `points(for:)`. For an `.error` event, just print the error.

The call to `deal(_:)` currently passes 3, so three cards will be dealt each time you press the **Execute Playground** button in the bottom left corner of Xcode. See how many times you go bust versus how many times you stay in the game. Are the odds stacked up against you in Vegas or what?

The card emoji characters are pretty small when printed in the console. If you want to be able to make out what cards you were dealt, you can temporarily increase the font size of the **Executable Console Output** for this challenge. To do so, select **Xcode/Preferences.../Fonts & Colors/Console**, select **Executable Console Output**, and click the **T** button in the bottom right to change it to a larger font, such as 48.

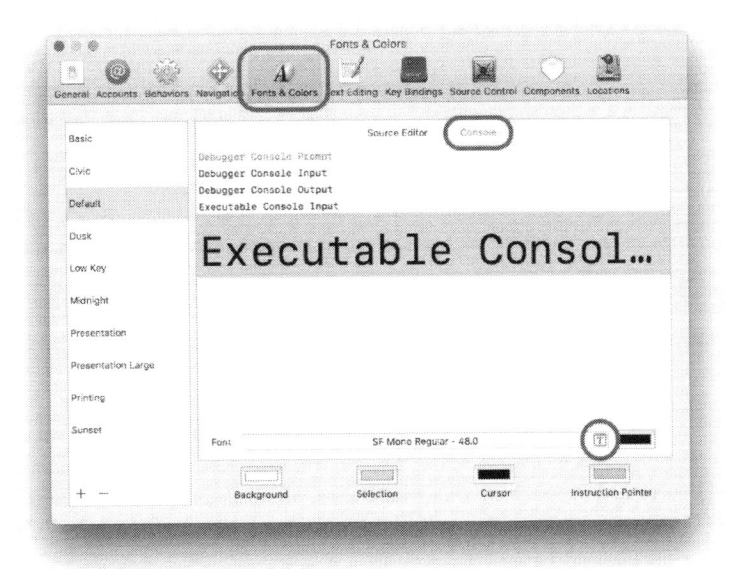

Challenge 2: Observe and check user session state using a variable

Most apps involve keeping track of a user session, and a variable can come in handy for such a need. You can subscribe to react to changes to the user session such as log in or log out, or just check the current value for one-off needs. In this challenge, you're going to implement examples of both.

Review the setup code in the starter project. There are a couple enumerations to model `UserSession` and `LoginError`, and functions to `logInWith(username:password:completion:)`, `logOut()`, and `performActionRequiringLoggedInUser(_:)`. There is also a `for-in` loop that attempts to log in and perform an action using invalid and then valid login credentials.

There are four comments indicating where you should add the necessary code in order to complete this challenge.

Chapter 4: Observables and Subjects in Practice

By Marin Todorov

By this point in the book, you understand how observables and different types of subjects work, and you've learned how to create and experiment with them in a Swift playground.

It could be a bit challenging, however, to see the practical use of observables in everyday development situations such as binding your UI to a data model, or presenting a new controller and getting output back from it.

It's okay to be a little unsure how to apply these newly acquired skills to the real world. In this book, you'll work through theoretical chapters such as Chapter 2, "Observables" and Chapter 3, "Subjects", as well as practical step-by-step chapters — just like this one!

In the "… *in practice*" chapters, you'll work on a complete app. The starter Xcode project will include all the non-Rx code. Your task will be to add the RxSwift framework and add other features using your newly-acquired reactive skills.

That doesn't mean to say you won't learn few new things along the way — *au contraire*!

In this chapter, you'll use RxSwift and your new observable superpowers to create an app that lets users create nice photo collages — the reactive way.

Getting started

Open the starter project for this chapter: **Combinestagram**. It takes a couple of tries to roll your tongue just right to say the name, doesn't it? It's probably not the most marketable name, but it will do.

Install all pods and open **Combinestagram.xcworkspace**. Refer to Chapter 1, "Hello RxSwift" for details on how to do that.

Select **Main.storyboard** and you'll see the interface of the app you will bring to life:

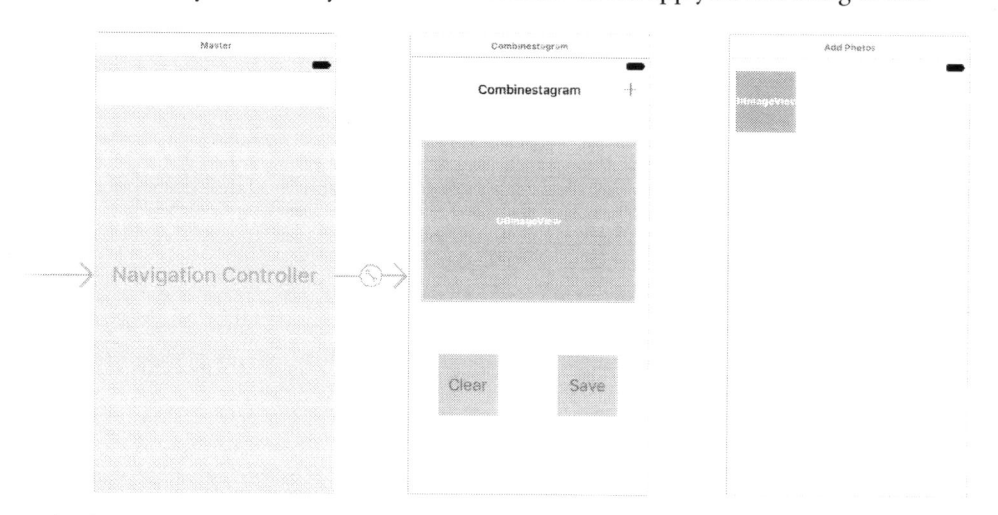

In the first screen, the user can see the current photo collage and has buttons to either clear the current list of photos or to save the finished collage to disk.

Additionally, when the user taps on the + button at the top right, they will be taken to the second view controller in the storyboard where they will see the list of photos in their Camera Roll. The user can add photos to the collage by tapping on the thumbnails.

The view controllers and the storyboard are already wired up, and you can also peek at **UIImage+Collage.swift** to see how the actual collage is put together.

In this chapter, you are going to focus on putting your new skills to practice. Time to get started!

Using a variable in a view controller

You'll start by adding a `Variable<[UIImage]>` property to the controller class and store the selected photos in its `value`. As you learned in Chapter 3, "Subjects", the `Variable` class works much like you're used to with plain variables: you can manually change the `value` property any time you want. You will start with this simple example and later move on to subjects and custom observables.

Open **MainViewController.swift** and add the following inside the body of `MainViewController`:

```
private let bag = DisposeBag()
private let images = Variable<[UIImage]>([])
```

Since no other class will use those two constants, you define them as `private`. Privacy FTW!

Since the dispose bag is owned by the view controller, as soon as the view controller is released all your observables will be disposed as well:

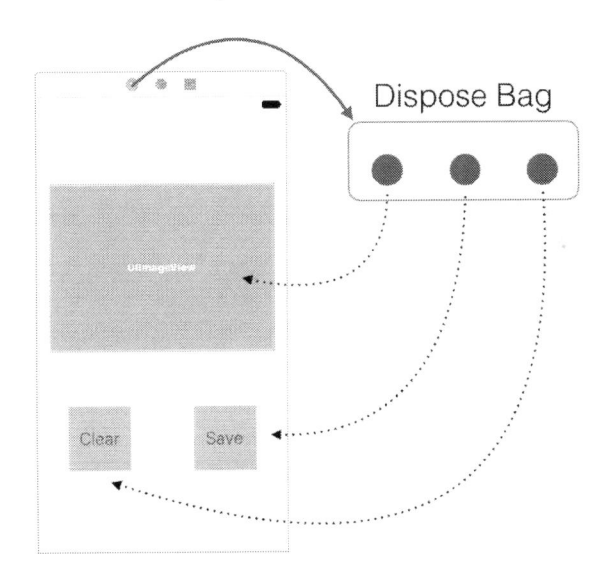

This makes Rx subscription memory management very easy: simply throw subscriptions in the bag and they will be disposed alongside the view controller's deallocation.

However, that won't happen for this specific view controller, since it's the root view controller and it isn't released before the app quits. You'll see the clever dispose-upon-deallocation mechanism at work later on in this chapter for the other controller in the storyboard.

At first, your app will always build a collage based on the same photo. No worries; it's a nice photo from the Barcelona country side, which is already included in **Assets.xcassets**. Each time the user taps + you will add that same photo, one more time, to images.

Find actionAdd() and add the following to it:

```
images.value.append(UIImage(named: "IMG_1907.jpg")!)
```

Notice that you alter the current value of images as you'd do with any plain old variable. The Variable class automatically produces an observable sequence of all the discrete values you are assigning to its value property. The initial value of the images Variable is an empty array, and every time the user hits the + button, the observable sequence produced by images emits a new .next event with the new array as an element.

To permit the user to clear the current selection, scroll up and add the following to actionClear():

```
images.value = []
```

With these few lines of code, you neatly handled the user input. You can now move on to observing images and displaying the result on screen.

Adding photos to the collage

Now that you have images wired up, you can observe for changes and update the collage preview accordingly.

In viewDidLoad(), create the following subscription to images. Don't forget that since it's a Variable you need to get its Observable in order to subscribe to it:

```
images.asObservable()
  .subscribe(onNext: { [weak self] photos in
    guard let preview = self?.imagePreview else { return }
    preview.image = UIImage.collage(images: photos,
      size: preview.frame.size)
  })
  .disposed(by: bag)
```

You subscribe for .next events emitted by images, and for each event you create a collage with the starter project function UIImage.collage(images:size:). Finally, you add this subscription to the view controller's dispose bag.

In this chapter, you are going to subscribe your observables in viewDidLoad(). Later in the book, you will look into extracting these into separate classes and, in the last chapter, into an MVVM architecture.

You now have your collage UI together; the user can update `images` by tapping the **+** bar item (or **Clear**) and you update the UI in turn.

Run the app and give it a try! If you add the photo four times, your collage will look like this:

Wow, that was easy!

Of course, the app is a bit boring right now, but don't worry — you will add the ability to select photos from Camera Roll in just a bit.

Driving a complex view controller UI

As you play with the current app, you'll notice the UI could be a bit smarter to improve the user experience. For example:

- You could disable the **Clear** button if there aren't any photos selected just yet, or in the event the user has just cleared the selection.
- Similarly, there's no need for the **Save** button to be enabled if there aren't any photos selected.
- You could also disable **Save** for an odd number of photos, as that would leave an empty spot in the collage.
- It would be nice to limit the amount of photos in a single collage to six, since more photos simply look a bit weird.
- Finally, it would be nice if the view controller title reflected the current selection.

If you take a moment to read through the list above one more time, you'll certainly see these modifications could be quite a hassle to implement the non-reactive way.

Thankfully, with RxSwift you simply subscribe to `images` one more time and update the UI from a single place in your code.

Add this subscription inside `viewDidLoad()`:

```
images.asObservable()
  .subscribe(onNext: { [weak self] photos in
      self?.updateUI(photos: photos)
  })
  .disposed(by: bag)
```

Each time there's a change to the photo selection, you call `updateUI(photos:)`. You don't have that method just yet, so add it anywhere inside the class body:

```
private func updateUI(photos: [UIImage]) {
  buttonSave.isEnabled = photos.count > 0 && photos.count % 2 == 0
  buttonClear.isEnabled = photos.count > 0
  itemAdd.isEnabled = photos.count < 6
  title = photos.count > 0 ? "\(photos.count) photos" : "Collage"
}
```

In the above code you update the complete UI according to the ruleset above. All of the logic is in a single place and easy to read through. Run the app again, and you will see all the rules kick in as you play with the UI:

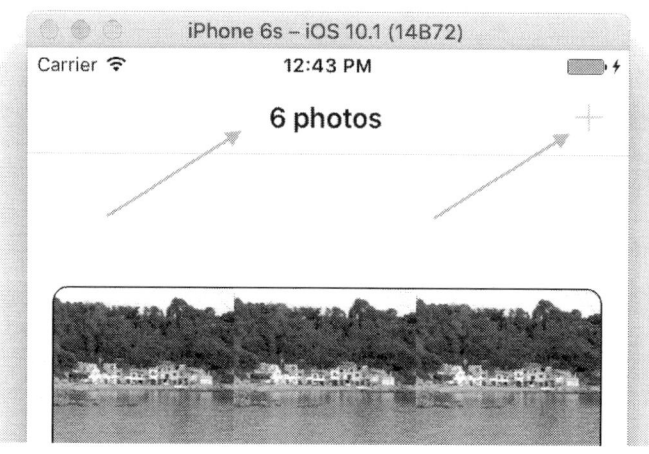

By now you're probably starting to see the real benefits of Rx when applied to your iOS apps. If you look through all the code you've written in this chapter, you'll see there are only a few simple lines that drive the whole UI!

Talking to other view controllers via subjects

In this section of the chapter, you will connect the `PhotosViewController` class to the main view controller in order to let the user select arbitrary photos from their Camera Roll. That will result in *far* more interesting collages!

First, you need to push `PhotosViewController` to the navigation stack. Open **MainViewController.swift** and find `actionAdd()`. Comment out the line that always uses the **IMG_1907.jpg** photo, and add this code in its place:

```
let photosViewController =
storyboard!.instantiateViewController(
   withIdentifier: "PhotosViewController") as!
PhotosViewController

navigationController!.pushViewController(photosViewController,
animated: true)
```

Above, you instantiate `PhotosViewController` from the project's storyboard and push it onto the navigation stack. Run the app and tap + to see the Camera Roll. The very first time you do this, you'll need to grant access to your Photo Library:

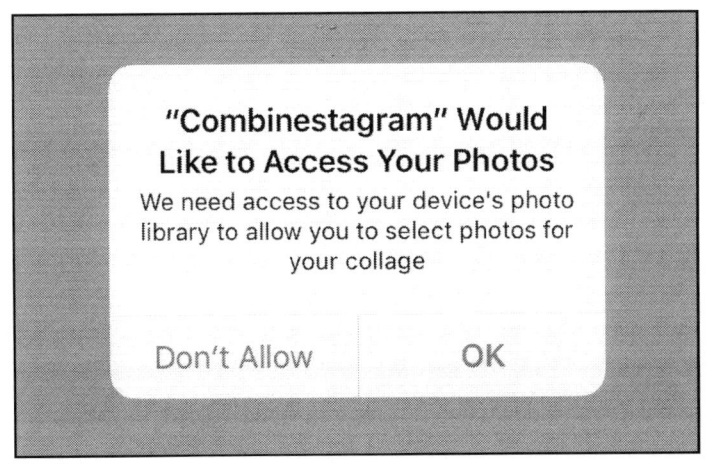

Once you tap **OK** you will see what the photos controller looks like. The actual photos might differ on your device, and you might need to go back and try again after granting access. The second time around, you should see the sample photos included with the iPhone Simulator.

If you were building an app using the established Cocoa patterns, your next step would be to add a delegate protocol so that the photos controller could talk back to your main controller (that is, the non-reactive way):

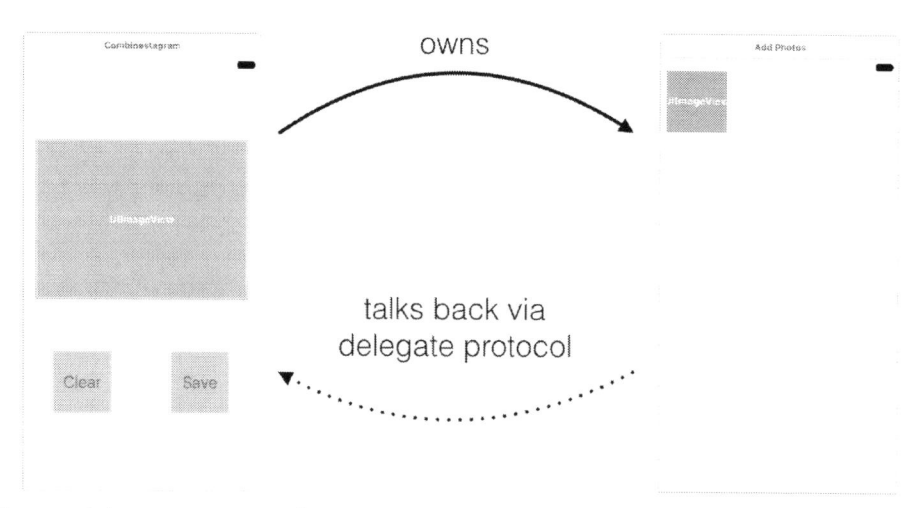

adopts delegate protocol   uses delegate protocol

With RxSwift, however, you have a universal way to talk between **any** two classes — an `Observable`! There is no need to define a special protocol, because an `Observable` can deliver any kind of message to any one or more interested parties — the observers.

Creating an observable out of the selected photos

You'll next add a subject to `PhotosViewController` that emits a `.next` event each time the user taps a photo from the Camera Roll. Open **PhotosViewController.swift** and add the following near the top:

```
import RxSwift
```

You'd like to add a `PublishSubject` to expose the selected photos, but you don't want the subject publicly accessible, as that would allow other classes to call `onNext(_)` and make the subject emit values. You might want to do that elsewhere, but not in this case.

Add the following properties to `PhotosViewController`:

```
private let selectedPhotosSubject = PublishSubject<UIImage>()
var selectedPhotos: Observable<UIImage> {
  return selectedPhotosSubject.asObservable()
}
```

Here you define both a private `PublishSubject` that will emit the selected photos and a public property named `selectedPhotos` that exposes the subject's observable. Subscribing to this property is how the main controller can observe the photo sequence, without being able to interfere with it.

`PhotosViewController` already contains the code to read photos from your Camera Roll and display them in a collection view. All you need to do is add the code to emit the selected photo when the user taps on a collection view cell.

Scroll down to `collectionView(_:didSelectItemAt:)`. The code inside fetches the selected image and flashes the collection cell to give the user a bit of a visual feedback.

Next, `imageManager.requestImage(...)` gets the selected photo and gives you `image` and `info` parameters to work with in its completion closure. In that closure, you'd like to emit a `.next` event from `selectedPhotosSubject`.

Inside the closure, just after the `guard` statement, add:

```
if let isThumbnail = info[PHImageResultIsDegradedKey as NSString] as? Bool, !isThumbnail {
  self?.selectedPhotosSubject.onNext(image)
}
```

You use the `info` dictionary to check if the image is the thumbnail or the full version of the asset. `imageManager.requestImage(...)` will call that closure once for each size. In the event you receive the full-size image, you call `onNext(_)` on your subject and provide it with the full photo.

That's all it takes to expose an observable sequence from one view controller to another. There's no need for delegate protocols or any other shenanigans of that sort. As a bonus, once you remove the protocols, the controllers relationship becomes very simple:

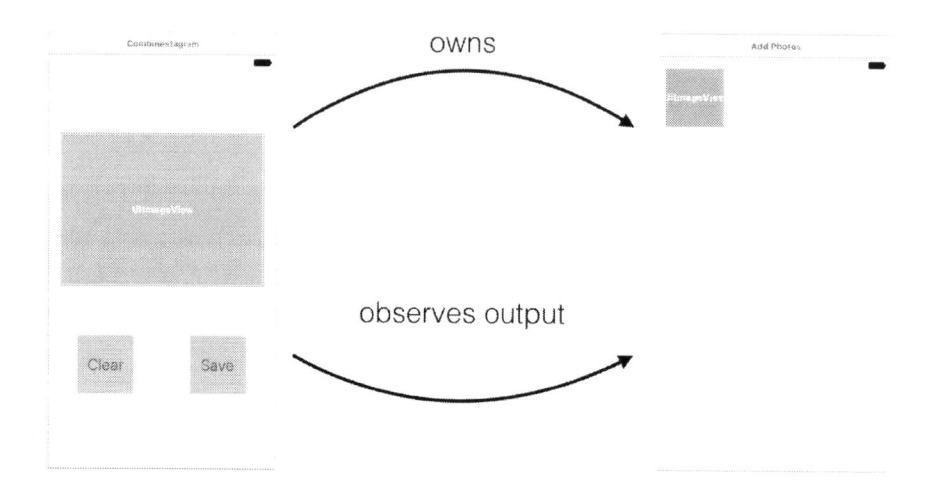

Observing the sequence of selected photos

Your next task is to return to **MainViewController.swift** and add the code to complete the last part of the schema above: namely, observing the selected photos sequence.

Find `actionAdd()` and add the following just before the line where you push the controller onto the navigation stack:

```
photosViewController.selectedPhotos
  .subscribe(onNext: { [weak self] newImage in

  }, onDisposed: {
     print("completed photo selection")
  })
  .disposed(by: bag)
```

Before you push the controller, you subscribe for events on its `selectedPhotos` observable. You are interested in two events: `.next`, which means the user has tapped a photo, and also when the subscription is disposed. You'll see why you need that in a moment.

Insert the following code inside the `onNext` closure to get everything working. It's the same code you had before, but this time it adds the photo from Camera Roll:

```
guard let images = self?.images else { return }
images.value.append(newImage)
```

Run the app, select a few photos from your Camera Roll, and go back to see the result. Cool!

Disposing subscriptions - review

The code seemingly works as expected, but try the following: add few photos to a collage, go back to the main screen and inspect the console.

Do you see a message saying "completed photo selection"? You added a `print` to your last subscription's `onDispose` closure, but it never gets called! That means the subscription is never disposed and never frees its memory!

How so? You subscribe an observable sequence and throw it in the main screen's dispose bag. This subscription (as discussed in previous chapters) will be disposed of either when the bag object is released, or when the sequence completes via an error or completed event.

Since you neither destroy the main view controller to release its `bag` property, nor complete the photos sequence, your subscription just hangs around for the lifetime of the app!

To give your observers some closure, you could emit a `.completed` event when that controller disappears from the screen. This would notify all observers that the subscription has completed to help with automatic disposal.

Open **PhotosViewController.swift** and add a call to your subject's `onComplete()` method in the controller's `viewWillDisappear(_:)`.

```
selectedPhotosSubject.onCompleted()
```

Perfect! Now you're ready for the last part of this chapter: taking a plain old boring function and converting it into a super-awesome and fantastical reactive class.

Creating a custom observable

So far, you've tried `Variable`, `PublishSubject`, and an `Observable`. To wrap up, you'll create your own custom `Observable` and turn a plain old Apple API into a reactive class. You'll use the `Photos` framework to save the photo collage — and since you're already an RxSwift veteran, you are going to do it the reactive way!

You could add a reactive extension on `PHPhotoLibrary` itself, but to keep things simple, in this chapter you will create a new custom class named `PhotoWriter`:

```
class PhotoWriter                           .next(assetID)
                                             .completed
   PHPhotoLibrary.requestChanges(…)  ·······················▶
                                             .error
```

Creating an `Observable` to save a photo is easy: if the image is successfully written to disk you will emit its asset ID and a `.completed` event, or otherwise an `.error` event.

Wrapping an existing API

Open **PhotoWriter.swift**, found in the Classes project folder. This file includes a couple of definitions to get you started. First, as always, import RxSwift:

```
import RxSwift
```

Then add a new static method to `PhotoWriter`, which will create the observable you will give back to code that wants to save photos:

```
static func save(_ image: UIImage) -> Observable<String> {
  return Observable.create({ observer in

  })
}
```

`save(_:)` will return an `Observable<String>`, because after saving the photo you will emit a single element: the unique local identifier of the created asset.

`Observable.create(_)` creates a new `Observable`, and you need to add all the meaty logic inside that last closure.

Add the following to the `Observable.create(_)` parameter closure:

```swift
var savedAssetId: String?
PHPhotoLibrary.shared().performChanges({

}, completionHandler: { success, error in

})
```

In the first closure parameter of `performChanges(_:completionHandler:)`, you will create a photo asset out of the provided image, and in the second one, you will emit either the asset ID or an `.error` event.

Add inside the first closure:

```swift
let request = PHAssetChangeRequest.creationRequestForAsset(from: image)
savedAssetId = request.placeholderForCreatedAsset?.localIdentifier
```

You create a new photo asset by using `PHAssetChangeRequest.creationRequestForAsset(from:)` and store its identifier in `savedAssetId`. Next insert into `completionHandler` closure:

```swift
DispatchQueue.main.async {
  if success, let id = savedAssetId {
    observer.onNext(id)
    observer.onCompleted()
  } else {
    observer.onError(error ?? Errors.couldNotSavePhoto)
  }
}
```

If you got a success response back and `savedAssetId` contains a valid asset ID, you emit a `.next` event and a `.completed` event. In case of an error, you emit either a custom or the default error.

With that, your observable sequence logic is completed.

As a last step, you need to return a `Disposable` out of that outer closure, so add one final line to `Observable.create({})`:

```swift
return Disposables.create()
```

That wraps up the class nicely. Xcode should finally be happy and all compile errors should disappear. The complete `save()` method should look like this:

```
static func save(_ image: UIImage) -> Observable<String> {
    return Observable.create({ observer in
        var savedAssetId: String?
        PHPhotoLibrary.shared().performChanges({
            let request = PHAssetChangeRequest.creationRequestForAsset(from: image)
            savedAssetId = request.placeholderForCreatedAsset?.localIdentifier
        }, completionHandler: { success, error in
            DispatchQueue.main.async {
                if success, let id = savedAssetId {
                    observer.onNext(id)
                    observer.onCompleted()
                } else {
                    observer.onError(error ?? Errors.couldNotSavePhoto)
                }
            }
        })
        return Disposables.create()
    })
}
```

If you've been paying attention, you might be asking yourself "Why do we need an `Observable` that emits just a single `.next` event?"

Take a moment to reflect on what you've learned in the previous chapters. For example, you can create an `Observable` by using any of the following:

- `Observable.never()`: Creates an observable sequences that never emits any elements.

- `Observable.just(_:)`: Emits one element and a `.completed` event.

- `Observable.empty()`: Emits no elements followed by a `.completed` event.

- `Observable.error(_)`: Emits no elements and a single `.error` event.

As you see, observables can produce any combination of zero or more `.next` events, possibly terminated by either a `.completed` or an `.error`.

In the particular case of `PhotoWriter`, you are only interested in one event since the save operation completes just once. You use `.next` + `.completed` for successful writes, and `.error` if a particular write failed.

You get a big bonus point if you're screaming *"But what about Single?"* about now. Indeed, what about `Single`?

RxSwift traits in practice

In Chapter 2, "Observables" you had the chance to learn about RxSwift traits: specialized variations of the `Observable` implementation that are very handy in certain cases.

In this chapter you're going to do a quick review and use some of the traits in the Combinestagram project! Let's start with `Single`:

Single

As you know from Chapter 2, `Single` is an `Observable` specialization. It represents a sequence, which can emit just once either a `.success(Value)` event or an `.error`. Under the hood, a `.success` is just `.next` + `.completed` pair.

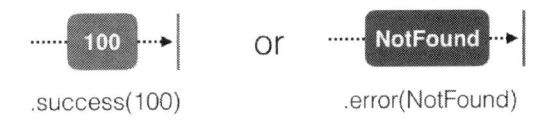

This kind of trait is useful in situations such as saving a file, downloading a file, loading data from disk., or basically any asynchronous operation that yields a value. You can categorize two distinct use-cases of `Single`:

1. For wrapping operations which emit exactly one element upon success, just as `PhotoWriter.save(_)` earlier in this chapter.

   You can directly create a `Single` instead of an `Observable`. In fact you will update the `save(_)` method in `PhotoWriter` to create a `Single` in one of this chapter's challenges.

2. To better express your intention to consume a single element from a sequence and ensure if the sequence emits more than one element the subscription will error out.

   To achieve this, you can subscribe to any observable and use `.asSingle()` to convert it to a `Single`. You'll try this just after you've finished reading through this section.

Maybe

`Maybe` is quite similar to `Single` with the only difference that the observable **may** not emit a value upon successful completion.

.success(100)   .completed   .error(NotFound)

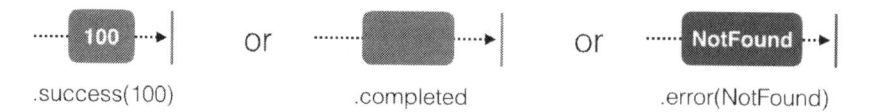

If we keep to the photograph-related examples imagine this use-case for `Maybe`, your app is storing photos in its own custom photo album. You persist the album identifier in UserDefaults and use that ID each time to "open" the album and write a photo inside. You would design a `open(albumId:) -> Maybe<String>` method to handle the following situations:

- In case the album with the given ID still exists, just emit a `.completed` event.
- in case the user has deleted the album in the meanwhile, create a new album and emit a `.next` event with the new ID so you can persist it in `UserDefaults`.
- in case something is wrong and you can't access the Photos library at all, emit an `.error` event.

Just like other traits, you can achieve the same functionality with using a "vanilla" `Observable`, but `Maybe` gives more context both to you as you're writing your code and to the programmers coming to alter the code later on.

Just as with `Single`, you can either create a `Maybe` directly by using `Maybe.create({ ... })` or by converting any observable sequence via `.asMaybe()`.

Completable

The final trait to cover is `Completable`. This variation of `Observable` allows only for a single `.completed` or `.error` event to be emitted before the subscription is disposed of.

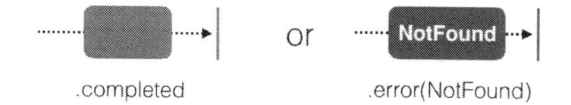

.completed   .error(NotFound)

One aspect to keep in mind is that you cannot covert an observable sequence to a completable once. Since the observable's contract allows for emitting value elements, you can't convert between the two.

You can only create a completable sequence by using `Completable.create({ ... })` with code very similar to that you'd use to create other observables or traits.

You might notice that `Completable` simply doesn't allow for emitting any values and wonder why would you need a sequence like that. You'd be surprised at the number of use-cases where you only need to know whether an async operation succeeded or not.

Let's look at an example before going back to `Combinestagram`. Let's say your app auto-saves the document while the user is working on it. You'd like to asynchronously save the document in a background queue, and when completed, show a small notification or an alert box onscreen if the operation fails.

Let's say you wrapped the saving logic into a function `saveDocument()` -> `Completable`. This is how easy it is then to express the rest of the logic:

```
saveDocument()
  .andThen(Observable.from(createMessage))
  .subscribe(onNext: { message in
    message.display()
  }, onError: {e in
    alert(e.localizedDescription)
  })
```

The `andThen` operator allows you to chain more completables or observables upon a success event and subscribe for the final result. In case any of them emits an error, your code will fall through to the final `onError` closure.

I'll assume you're delighted to hear that you will get to use `Completable` in two chapters from now. And now back to `Combinestagram` and the problem at hand!

Subscribing to the custom observable

The current feature — saving a photo to the Photos library — falls under one of those special use-cases for which there is a special trait. Your `PhotoWriter.save(_)` observable emits just once (the new asset ID), or it errors out, and is therefore a great case for a `Single`.

Now for the sweetest part of all: making use of your custom-designed `Observable` and kicking serious butt along the way!

Open **MainViewController.swift** and add the following inside the `actionSave()` action method for the **Save** button:

```
guard let image = imagePreview.image else { return }

PhotoWriter.save(image)
  .asSingle()
  .subscribe(onSuccess: { [weak self] id in
    self?.showMessage("Saved with id: \(id)")
    self?.actionClear()
  }, onError: { [weak self] error in
    self?.showMessage("Error", description:
  error.localizedDescription)
  })
  .disposed(by: bag)
```

Above you call `PhotoWriter.save(image)` to save the current collage. Then you convert the returned `Observable` to a `Single`, ensuring your subscription will get at most one element, and display a message when it succeeds or errors out. Additionally, you clear the current collage if the write operation was a success.

> **Note:** `asSingle()` ensures that you get at most one element by throwing an error if the source sequence emits more than one.

Give the app one last triumphant run, build up a nice photo collage, and save it to the disk.

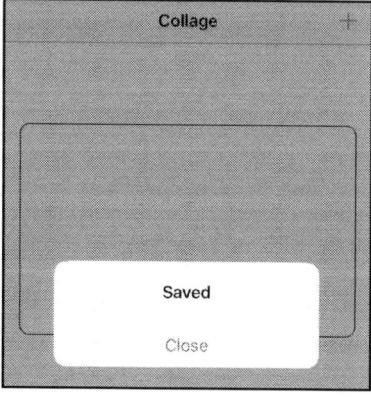

Don't forget to check your Photos app for the result!

With that, you've completed Section 1 of this book – congratulations!

You are not a young Padawan anymore, but an experienced RxSwift Jedi. However, don't be tempted to take on the dark side just yet. You will get to battle networking, thread switching, and error handling soon enough!

Before that, you must continue your training and learn about one of the most powerful aspects of RxSwift. In Section 2, "Operators and Best Practices", operators will allow you to take your `Observable` superpowers to a whole new level!

Challenges

Before you move on to the next section, there are two challenges waiting for you. You will once again create a custom `Observable` — but this time with a little twist.

Challenge 1: It's only logical to use a Single

You've probably noticed that you didn't gain much by using `.asSingle()` when saving a photo to the Camera Roll. The observable sequence already emits at most one element!

Well, you are right about that, but the point was to provide a gentle introduction to `.asSingle()`. Now you can improve the code on your own in this very challenge.

Open **PhotoWriter.swift** and change the return type of `save(_)` to `Single<String>`. Then replace `Observable.create` with `Single.create`.

This should clear most errors. There is one last thing to take care of: `Observable.create` receives an observer as parameter so you can emit multiple values and/or terminating events. `Single.create` receives as a parameter a closure, which you can use only once to emit either a `.success(T)` or `.error(E)` values.

Complete the conversion yourself and remember that the parameter is a closure not an observer object, so you call it like this: `single(.success(id))`.

Challenge 2: Add custom observable to present alerts

Open **MainViewController.swift** and scroll towards the bottom of the file. Find the `showMessage(_:description:)` method that came with the starter project.

The method shows an alert onscreen and runs a callback when the user taps the **Close** button to dismiss the alert. That does sound quite similar to what you've already done for `PHPhotoLibrary.performChanges(_)`, doesn't it?

To complete this challenge, code the following:

- Add an extension method to `UIViewController` that presents an alert onscreen with a given title and message and returns a `Completable`.

- Add a **Close** button to allow the user to close the alert.

- Dismiss the alert controller when the subscription is dismissed, so that you don't have any dangling alerts.

In the end, use the new completable to present the alert from within `showMessage(_:description:)`.

As always, if you run into trouble, or are curious to see the provided solution, you can check the completed project and challenge code in the **resources** folder for this chapter. You can peek in there anyway, but do give it your best shot first!

Section II: Operators and Best Practices

Operators are the building blocks of Rx, which you can use to transform, process, and react to events emitted by observables. Just as you can combine simple arithmetic operators like +, -, and / to create complex math expressions, you can chain and compose together Rx's simple operators to express complex app logic.

You are going to start by looking into filtering operators, which allow you to process some events but ignore others. Then you will move onto transforming operators, which allow you to create and express complex data transformations. You can for example start with a button event, transform that into some kind of input, process that and return some output to show in the app UI. You will also look into combining operators, which allow for powerful composition of most other operators.

Finally, you'll look into operators that allow you to do time based processing: delaying events, grouping events over periods of time, and more. Work though all the chapters, and by the end of this section you'll be able to write simple RxSwift apps!

Chapter 5: Filtering Operators

Chapter 6: Filtering Operators in Practice

Chapter 7: Transforming Operators

Chapter 8: Transforming Operators in Practice

Chapter 9: Combining Operators

Chapter 10: Combining Operators in Practice

Chapter 11: Time Based Operators

Chapter 5: Filtering Operators

By Scott Gardner

Learning a new technology stack is a bit like building a skyscraper. You've got to build a solid foundation before you can kiss the sky. By now you've established a solid RxSwift foundation, and it's time to start building up your knowledge base and skill set, one floor at a time.

This chapter will teach you about RxSwift's filtering operators that you can use to apply conditional constraints to `.next` events, so that the subscriber only receives the elements it wants to deal with. If you've ever used the `filter(_:)` method in the Swift standard library, you're already half way there. But if not, no worries; you're going to be an expert at this filtering business by the end of this chapter.

Getting started

The starter project for this chapter is named **RxSwiftPlayground**. Open it up, install the project pod dependencies as explained in Chapter 1, and give it a build.

Ignoring operators

Without further ado, you're going to jump right in and look at some useful filtering operators in RxSwift, beginning with `ignoreElements`. As depicted in the following marble diagram, `ignoreElements` will do that; ignore `.next` event elements. It will, however, allow through stop events, i.e., `.completed` or `.error` events. Allowing through stop events is usually implied in marble diagrams. It's just explicitly called out this time because that's *all* `ignoreElements` will let through.

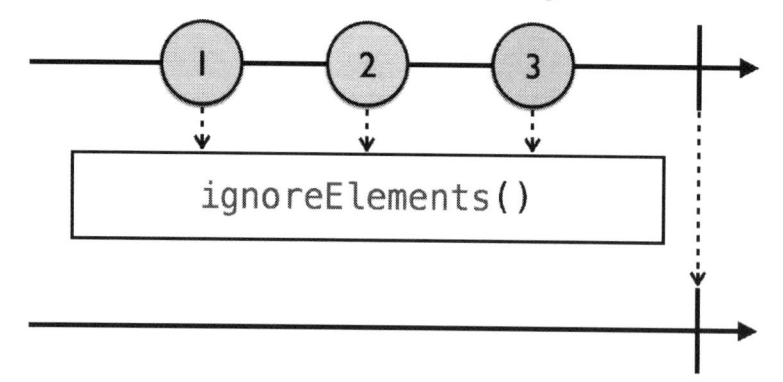

> **Note:** Up until now you've seen marble diagrams used for types. This type of marble diagram helps to visualize how *operators* work. The top line is the observable that is being subscribed to. The box represents the operator and its parameters, and the bottom line is the subscriber, or more specifically, what the subscriber will *receive* after the operator does its thing.

See one, now do one, by adding this example to your playground:

```
example(of: "ignoreElements") {
    
    // 1
    let strikes = PublishSubject<String>()
    
    let disposeBag = DisposeBag()
```

```
    // 2
    strikes
      .ignoreElements()
      .subscribe { _ in
        print("You're out!")
      }
      .disposed(by: disposeBag)
}
```

Here's what you're doing:

1. Create a `strikes` subject.
2. Subscribe to *all* `strikes`' events, but ignore all `.next` events by using `ignoreElements`.

`ignoreElements` is useful when you only want to be notified when an observable has terminated, via a `.completed` or `.error` event. Add this code to the example:

```
strikes.onNext("X")
strikes.onNext("X")
strikes.onNext("X")
```

Even though this batter can't seem to hit the broad side of a barn and has clearly struck out, nothing is printed, because you're ignoring all `.next` events. It's up to you to add a `.completed` event to this subject in order to let the subscriber be notified. Add this code to do that:

```
strikes.onCompleted()
```

Now the subscriber will receive the `.completed` event, and print that catchphrase *no* batter ever wants to hear.

```
--- Example of: ignoreElements ---
You're out!
```

> **Note:** If you don't happen to know much about strikes, batters, and the game of baseball in general, you can read up on those when you decide to take a little break from programming: https://simple.wikipedia.org/wiki/Baseball.

There may be times when you only want to handle the the *nth* (ordinal) element emitted by an observable, such as the third strike. For that you can use `elementAt`, which takes the index of the element you want to receive, and it ignores everything else. In the marble diagram, `elementAt` is passed an index of `1`, so it only allows through the second element.

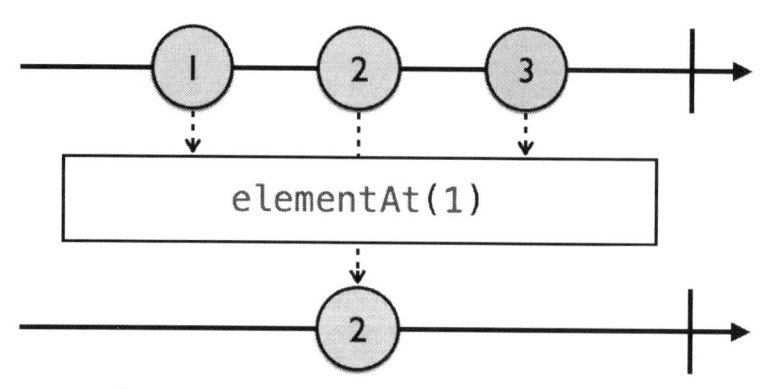

Add this new example:

```
example(of: "elementAt") {
    
    // 1
    let strikes = PublishSubject<String>()
    
    let disposeBag = DisposeBag()
    
    // 2
    strikes
        .elementAt(2)
        .subscribe(onNext: { _ in
            print("You're out!")
        })
        .disposed(by: disposeBag)
}
```

Here's the play-by-play:

1. You create a subject.

2. You subscribe to the `.next` events, ignoring all but the 3rd `.next` event (found at index 2).

Now you can simply add new strikes onto the subject, and your subscription will take care of letting you know when the batter has struck out. Add this code:

```
strikes.onNext("X")
strikes.onNext("X")
strikes.onNext("X")
```

"Hey batta, batta, batta, swing batta!"

```
--- Example of: elementAt ---
You're out!
```

`ignoreElements` and `elementAt` are filtering elements emitted by an observable. When your filtering needs go beyond all or one, there's `filter`. `filter` takes a predicate closure, which it applies to each element, allowing through only those elements for which the predicate resolves to `true`.

Check out this marble diagram, where only 1 and 2 are let through, because the filter's predicate only allows elements that are less than 3.

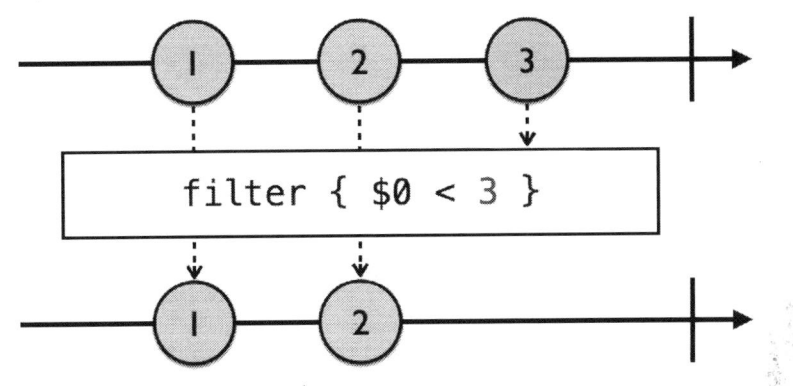

Add this example to your playground:

```
example(of: "filter") {
    let disposeBag = DisposeBag()
    // 1
    Observable.of(1, 2, 3, 4, 5, 6)
        // 2
        .filter { integer in
            integer % 2 == 0
        }
        // 3
        .subscribe(onNext: {
            print($0)
        })
        .disposed(by: disposeBag)
}
```

From the top:

1. You create an observable of some predefined integers.

2. You use the `filter` operator to apply a conditional constraint to prevent odd numbers from getting through. `filter` takes a predicate that returns a `Bool`. Return `true` to let the element through or `false` to prevent it. `filter` will filter elements for the life of the subscription.

3. You subscribe and print out the elements that passed the filter predicate.

The result of applying this filter is that only even numbers are printed.

```
--- Example of: filter ---
2
4
6
```

Skipping operators

It might be that you need to skip a certain number of elements. To continue with the weather forecast example, maybe you don't want to start receiving hourly forecast data until later in the day, because you're stuck in a cubicle until then anyway. The `skip` operator allows you to ignore from the 1st to the number you pass as its parameter. This marble diagram shows `skip` being passed 2, so it ignores the first 2 elements.

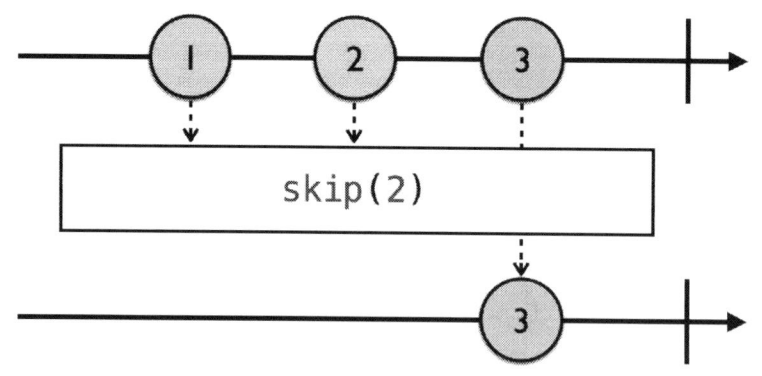

Enter this new example in your playground:

```
example(of: "skip") {
    
    let disposeBag = DisposeBag()
    
    // 1
    Observable.of("A", "B", "C", "D", "E", "F")
        // 2
        .skip(3)
        .subscribe(onNext: {
            print($0)
        })
        .disposed(by: disposeBag)
}
```

With this code, you:

1. Create an observable of letters.
2. Use `skip` to skip the first 3 elements and subscribe to `.next` events.

After skipping the first 3 elements, only D, E, and F are printed like so:

```
--- Example of: skip ---
D
E
F
```

There's a small family of `skip` operators. Like `filter`, `skipWhile` lets you include a predicate to determine what should be skipped. However, unlike `filter`, which will filter elements for the life of the subscription, `skipWhile` will only skip up until something is *not* skipped, and then it will let everything else through from that point on.

And with `skipWhile`, returning `true` will cause the element to be skipped, and returning `false` will let it through. It's the opposite of `filter`. In this marble diagram, 1 is prevented because 1 % 2 equals 1, but then 2 is allowed through because it fails the predicate, and 3 (and everything else going forward) gets through because `skipWhile` is no longer skipping.

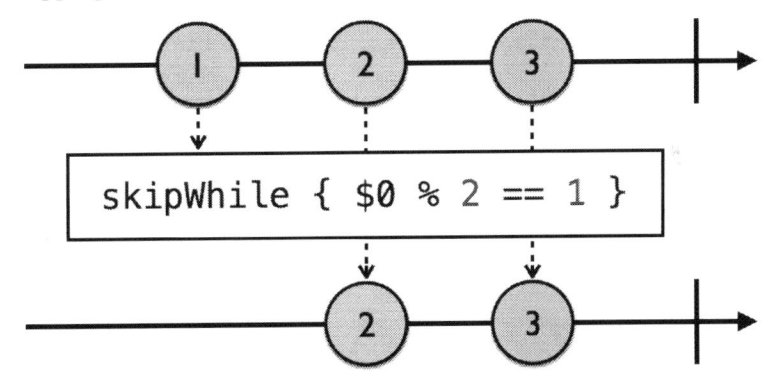

Add this new example to your playground:

```
example(of: "skipWhile") {
    let disposeBag = DisposeBag()
    
    // 1
    Observable.of(2, 2, 3, 4, 4)
        // 2
        .skipWhile { integer in
            integer % 2 == 0
        }
        .subscribe(onNext: {
```

```
        print($0)
    })
        .disposed(by: disposeBag)
}
```

Here's what you did:

1. Create an observable of integers.

2. Use `skipWhile` with a predicate that skips elements until an odd integer is emitted.

`skip` only skips elements up until the first element is let through, and then *all* remaining elements are allowed through.

```
--- Example of: skipWhile ---
3
4
4
```

If you were developing an insurance claims app, you could use `skipWhile` to deny coverage until the deductible is met. If only the insurance industry were that straightforward here in the United States.

So far, the filtering has been based on some static condition. What if you wanted to dynamically filter elements based on some other observable? There are a couple of operators that you'll learn about here that can do this. The first is `skipUntil`, which will keep skipping elements from the source observable (the one you're subscribing to) until some other *trigger* observable emits. In this marble diagram, `skipUntil` ignores elements emitted by the source observable (the top line) until the trigger observable (second line) emits a `.next` event. Then it stops skipping and lets everything through from that point on.

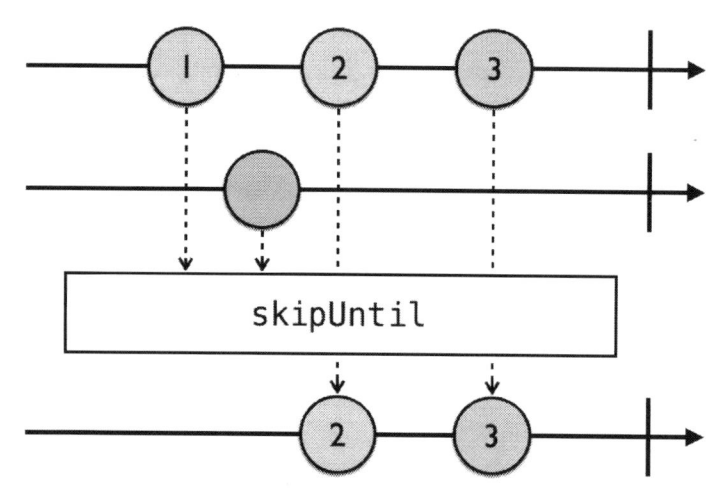

Add this example to see how `skipUntil` works in code:

```
example(of: "skipUntil") {
  let disposeBag = DisposeBag()

  // 1
  let subject = PublishSubject<String>()
  let trigger = PublishSubject<String>()

  // 2
  subject
    .skipUntil(trigger)
    .subscribe(onNext: {
      print($0)
    })
    .disposed(by: disposeBag)
}
```

In this code, you:

1. Create a subject to model the data you want to work with, and another subject to model a trigger to change how you handle things in the first subject.

2. Use `skipUntil`, passing the `trigger` subject. When `trigger` emits, `skipUntil` will stop skipping.

Add a couple of `.next` events onto `subject`:

```
subject.onNext("A")
subject.onNext("B")
```

Nothing is printed out, because you're skipping. Now add a new `.next` event onto `trigger`:

```
trigger.onNext("X")
```

Doing so causes `skipUntil` to stop skipping. From this point onward, all elements will be let through. Add another `.next` event onto subject:

```
subject.onNext("C")
```

Sure enough, it's printed out.

```
--- Example of: skipUntil ---
C
```

Taking operators

Taking is the opposite of skipping. When you want to take elements, RxSwift has you covered. The first taking operator you'll learn about is `take`, which as shown in this marble diagram, will take the first of the number of elements you specified.

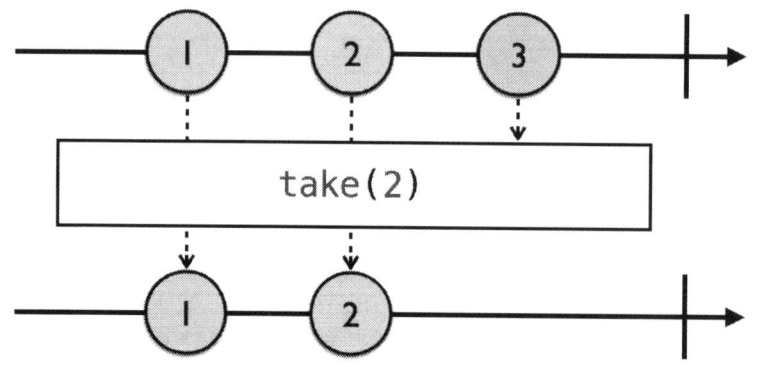

Add this example to your playground to explore the first of the `take` operators:

```
example(of: "take") {
    let disposeBag = DisposeBag()
    
    // 1
    Observable.of(1, 2, 3, 4, 5, 6)
        // 2
        .take(3)
        .subscribe(onNext: {
            print($0)
        })
        .disposed(by: disposeBag)
}
```

Here's what you did:

1. Create an observable of integers.

2. Take the first 3 elements using `take`.

What you take is what you get. The output this time is:

```
--- Example of: take ---
1
2
3
```

There's also a `takeWhile` operator that works similarly to `skipWhile`, except you're taking instead of skipping.

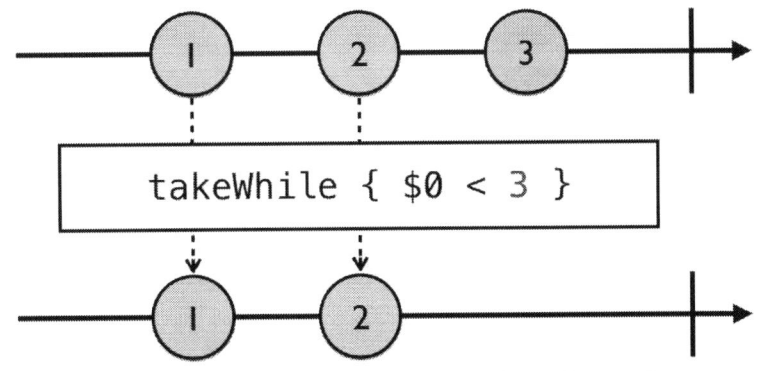

```
         1       2       3
         │       │       │
    ┌────────────────────────────┐
    │    takeWhile { $0 < 3 }    │
    └────────────────────────────┘
         │       │
         1       2
```

Sometimes you may also want to reference the index of the element being emitted. For that, you can use the `enumerated` operator, which yields tuples containing the index and element of each emitted element from an observable, similar to how the `enumerated` method in the Swift Standard Library works. Enter this new example in your playground:

```swift
example(of: "takeWhile") {

  let disposeBag = DisposeBag()

  // 1
  Observable.of(2, 2, 4, 4, 6, 6)
    // 2
    .enumerated()
    // 3
    .takeWhile { index, integer in
      // 4
      integer % 2 == 0 && index < 3
    }
    // 5
    .map { $0.element }
    // 6
    .subscribe(onNext: {
      print($0)
    })
    .disposed(by: disposeBag)
}
```

From the top:

1. Create an observable of integers.

2. Use the `enumerated` operator to get tuples containing the index and value of each element emitted.

3. Use the `takeWhile` operator, and decompose the tuple into individual values.
4. Pass a predicate that will take elements until the condition fails.
5. Use `map` (works just like the Swift Standard Library `map` but on observables) to reach into the tuple returned from `takeWhile` and get the `element`.
6. Subscribe to and print out `.next` event elements.

> **Note:** You'll work more with the `map` operator in chapter 7.

As a result, you only receive elements as long as the integers are even and up to when the element's index is 3 or greater.

```
--- Example of: takeWhile ---
2
2
4
```

Like `skipUntil`, there's also a `takeUntil` operator, shown in this marble diagram, taking from the source observable until the trigger observable emits an element.

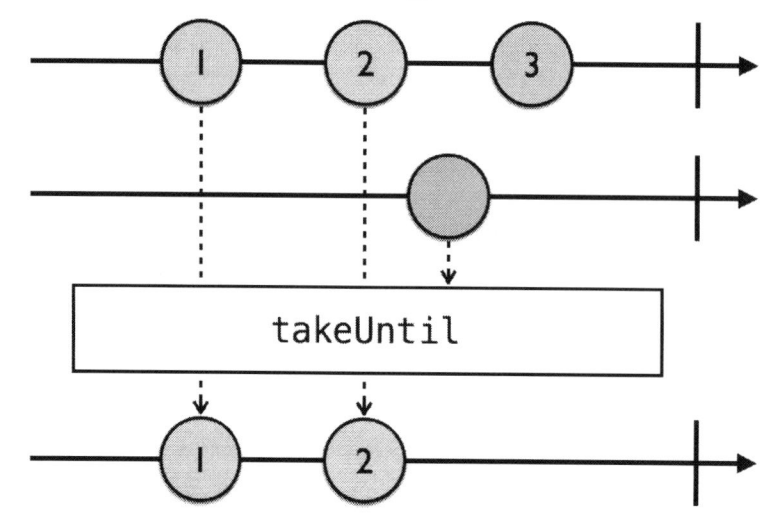

Add this new example, which is just like the `skipUntil` example you created earlier:

```
example(of: "takeUntil") {
    let disposeBag = DisposeBag()
    
    // 1
    let subject = PublishSubject<String>()
```

```
    let trigger = PublishSubject<String>()

    // 2
    subject
      .takeUntil(trigger)
      .subscribe(onNext: {
        print($0)
      })
      .disposed(by: disposeBag)

    // 3
    subject.onNext("1")
    subject.onNext("2")
}
```

Here's what you did:

1. Create a primary subject and a trigger subject.
2. Use `takeUntil`, passing the `trigger` that will cause `takeUntil` to stop taking once it emits.
3. Add a couple of elements onto `subject`.

Those elements are printed out, but `takeUntil` is in taking mode.

```
--- Example of: takeUntil ---
1
2
```

Now add an element onto `trigger`, followed by another element onto `subject`:

```
trigger.onNext("X")
```

```
subject.onNext("3")
```

The X stops the taking, so 3 is not allowed through and nothing more is printed.

Used in concert with API from the RxCocoa library (which you'll learn about later in the book), `takeUntil` can also be used to dispose of a subscription, instead of adding it to a dispose bag.

Playing if-then-but-what with observables and subscriptions is a sure-fire way to leak memory, or at least overly complicate your code. Simply adding a subscription to a dispose bag is a nice way to set it and forget it (for the most part).

For the sake of completeness, here's an example of how you would use `takeUntil` with RxCocoa (don't enter this into your playground, because it won't compile):

```
someObservable
```

```
    .takeUntil(self.rx.deallocated)
    .subscribe(onNext: {
        print($0)
    })
```

In the previous code, the trigger that will cause `takeUntil` to stop taking is the deallocation of `self`, which is typically a view controller or view model.

Distinct operators

Back to the regularly-scheduled show. The next couple of operators you're going to learn about let you prevent duplicate contiguous items from getting through. As shown in this marble diagram, `distinctUntilChanged` only prevents duplicates that are right next to each other, so the second 1 gets through.

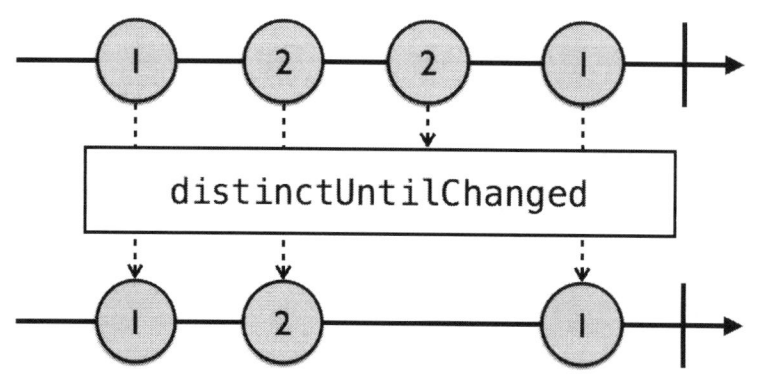

Add this new example to your playground:

```
example(of: "distinctUntilChanged") {

    let disposeBag = DisposeBag()

    // 1
    Observable.of("A", "A", "B", "B", "A")
        // 2
        .distinctUntilChanged()
        .subscribe(onNext: {
            print($0)
        })
        .disposed(by: disposeBag)
}
```

What you're doing here:

1. Create an observable of letters.
2. Use `distinctUntilChanged` to prevent sequential duplicates from getting through.

`distinctUntilChanged` only prevents contiguous duplicates. So the 2nd element is prevented because it's the same as the 1st, but the last item, also an A, *is* allowed through, because it comes after a different letter (B).

The resulting printout only includes the 1st A, 1st B, and then the A at the end.

```
--- Example of: distinctUntilChanged ---
A
B
A
```

These are strings, which conform to `Equatable`. So, these elements are compared for equality based on their implementation conforming to `Equatable`. However, you can provide your own custom comparing logic by using `distinctUntilChanged(_:)`, where the externally unnamed parameter is a comparer.

In the following marble diagram, objects with a property named `value` are being compared for distinctness based on `value`.

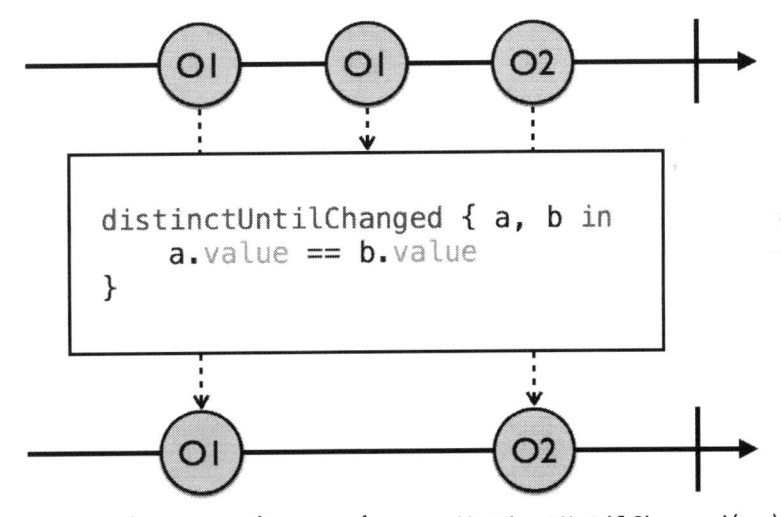

Add this new example to your playground to use `distinctUntilChanged(_:)` in a slightly more elaborate example:

```
example(of: "distinctUntilChanged(_:)") {
    let disposeBag = DisposeBag()
```

```
// 1
let formatter = NumberFormatter()
formatter.numberStyle = .spellOut

// 2
Observable<NSNumber>.of(10, 110, 20, 200, 210, 310)
  // 3
  .distinctUntilChanged { a, b in
    // 4
    guard let aWords = formatter.string(from: a)?.components(separatedBy: " "),
      let bWords = formatter.string(from: b)?.components(separatedBy: " ")
      else {
        return false
    }

    var containsMatch = false

    // 5
    for aWord in aWords {
      for bWord in bWords {
        if aWord == bWord {
          containsMatch = true
          break
        }
      }
    }

    return containsMatch
  }
  // 4
  .subscribe(onNext: {
    print($0)
  })
  .disposed(by: disposeBag)
}
```

From the top, you:

1. Create a number formatter to spell out each number.

2. Create an observable of `NSNumbers` (so that you don't have to convert integers when using the formatter next).

3. Use `distinctUntilChanged(_:)`, which takes a closure that receives each sequential pair of elements.

4. Use `guard` to conditionally bind the element's components separated by an empty space, or else return false.

1. Iterate over each pair of element's words in nested `for-in` loops and return the result of checking to see if the two elements contain any of the same words.
2. Subscribe and print out elements that are considered distinct based on the comparing logic you provided.

As a result, only the distinct integers are printed, taking into account that in each pair of integers, one does not contain any of the word components of the other.

```
--- Example of: distinctUntilChanged(_:) ---
10
20
200
```

`distinctUntilChanged(_:)` is also useful when you want to distinctly prevent duplicates for types that do not conform to `Equatable`.

Challenges

Challenges help harden the wet cement around what you just learned. There are starter and finished versions of the challenge in the exercise files download.

Challenge 1: Create a phone number lookup

Open the challenge starter project, install dependencies, and let's have a look at what's to be found inside!

Breaking down this challenge, you'll need to use several filter operators. Here are the requirements, along with a suggested operator to use:

1. Phone numbers can't begin with `0` — use `skipWhile`.
2. Each input must be a single-digit number — use `filter` to only allow elements that are less than `10`.
3. Limiting this example to U.S. phone numbers, which are 10 digits, take only the first `10` numbers input — use `take` and `toArray`.

Review the setup code in the starter project. There's a simple contacts dictionary:

```
let contacts = [
  "603-555-1212": "Florent",
  "212-555-1212": "Junior",
  "408-555-1212": "Marin",
  "617-555-1212": "Scott"
]
```

There's a utility function that will return a formatted phone number for the array of 10 values you pass to it:

```
func phoneNumber(from inputs: [Int]) -> String {
  var phone = inputs.map(String.init).joined()

  phone.insert("-", at: phone.index(
    phone.startIndex,
    offsetBy: 3)
  )

  phone.insert("-", at: phone.index(
    phone.startIndex,
    offsetBy: 7)
  )

  return phone
}
```

There's a publish subject to start you off:

```
let input = PublishSubject<Int>()
```

And there's a series of onNext calls to test that your solution works:

```
input.onNext(0)
input.onNext(603)

input.onNext(2)
input.onNext(1)

// Confirm that 7 results in "Contact not found," and then
change to 2 and confirm that Junior is found
input.onNext(7)

"5551212".characters.forEach {
  if let number = (Int("\($0)")) {
    input.onNext(number)
  }
}

input.onNext(9)
```

Because this challenge is focused on using the filter operators, here's code you can use in the subscription's .next event handler to take the result from phoneNumber(from:) and print out the contact if found or else "Contact not found":

```
if let contact = contacts[phone] {
  print("Dialing \(contact) (\(phone))...")
} else {
```

```
    print("Contact not found")
}
```

Add your code right below the comment `// Add your code here`.

Once you've implemented your solution, follow the instructions in the comment beginning `// Confirm that 7 results in...` to test that your solution works.

Chapter 6: Filtering Operators in Practice

By Marin Todorov

In the previous chapter, you began your introduction to the *functional* aspect of RxSwift. The first batch of operators you learned about helped you filter the elements of an observable sequence.

As explained previously, the operators are simply methods on the `Observable<E>` class, and some of them are defined on the `ObservableType` protocol, to which `Observable<E>` adheres.

The operators operate on the elements of their `Observable` class and produce a new observable sequence as a result. This comes in handy because, as you saw previously, this allows you to **chain** operators, one after another, and perform several transformations in sequence:

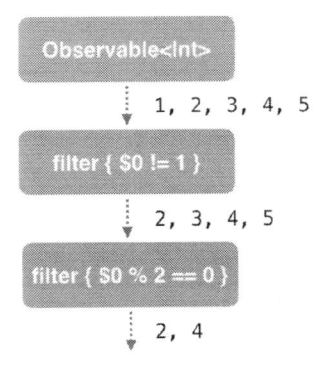

```
Observable<Int>
       |
       v  1, 2, 3, 4, 5
  filter { $0 != 1 }
       |
       v  2, 3, 4, 5
  filter { $0 % 2 == 0 }
       |
       v  2, 4
```

The preceding diagram definitely looks great in theory. In this chapter, you're going to try using the filtering operators in a real-life app. In fact, you are going to continue working on the Combinestagram app that you already know and love from Chapter 4, "Observables and Subjects in Practice".

> **Note:** In this chapter, you will need understand the theory behind the filtering operators in RxSwift. If you haven't worked through Chapter 5, "Filtering Operators", do that first and then come back to the current chapter.

Without further ado, let's have a look at putting `filter`, `take`, and company to work!

Improving the Combinestagram project

If you successfully completed the challenges from Chapter 4, "Observables and Subjects in Practice", re-open the project and keep working on it. Otherwise, you can use the starter project provided for this chapter.

It's important that you have a correct solution to the challenge in Chapter 4, since it plays a role in one of the tasks in this chapter. If you're in doubt, just consult **UIAlertViewController+Rx.swift** in the provided starter project and compare it to your own solution.

In this chapter, you are going to work through series of tasks, which (surprise!) will require you to use different filter operators. You'll use different ones and see how you can use counterparts like `skip` and `take`. You'll also learn how to achieve similar effect by using different operators, and finally, you will take care of a few of the issues in the current Combinestagram project.

> **Note:** Since this book has only covered a few operators so far, you will not write the "best possible" code. For this chapter, don't worry about best practices or proper architecture yet, but instead focus on truly understanding how to use the filtering operators. In this book, you're going to slowly build up towards writing good RxSwift code. It's a process!

Refining the photos sequence

Currently the main screen of the app looks like this:

The app works for the most part, but if you play with it for a while, you will certainly notice some shortcomings. And, honestly, it could do with some new and fresh features as well.

For example, once the user has added a batch of photos to their collage, you might want to do more than simply regenerate the preview each time. At the point when the photos observable completes, the user will be coming back to the main screen; there might be things to turn on or off, labels to update, or more. You'll take a look next at how to "do more things" by sharing a subscription to the same `Observable` instance.

Sharing subscriptions

Is there anything wrong with calling `subscribe(...)` on the same observable multiple times? Turns out there might be!

I've already mentioned that observables are lazy, pull-driven sequences. Simply calling a bunch of operators on an `Observable` doesn't involve any actual work. The moment you call `subscribe(...)` directly on an observable or on one of the operators applied to it, *that's* when the `Observable` livens up and starts producing elements.

To do that, the observable calls its `create` closure each time you subscribe to it. in some situations, this might produce some bedazzling effects!

Take a look at the code below; you can type it in a Playground if you want:

```
let numbers = Observable<Int>.create { observer in
    let start = getStartNumber()
    observer.onNext(start)
    observer.onNext(start+1)
    observer.onNext(start+2)
    observer.onCompleted()
    return Disposables.create()
}
```

The code creates an `Observable<Int>`, which produces a sequence of three numbers: `start, start+1, start+2`.

Now see what `getStartNumber()` looks like:

```
var start = 0
func getStartNumber() -> Int {
    start += 1
    return start
}
```

The function increments a variable and returns it; nothing can go wrong there. Or can it? Add a subscription to `numbers` and see for yourself:

```
numbers
    .subscribe(onNext: { el in
        print("element [\(el)]")
    }, onCompleted: {
        print("--------------")
    })
```

You will get the exact output you expected. Yay!

```
element [1]
element [2]
element [3]
--------------
```

Copy and paste the exact same subscription code one more time though, and this time the output is different.

```
element [1]
element [2]
element [3]
--------------
element [2]
element [3]
element [4]
--------------
```

The problem is that each time you call `subscribe(...)`, this creates a new `Observable` for that subscription — and each copy is not guaranteed to be the same as the previous. And even when the `Observable` *does* produce the same sequence of elements, it's overkill to produce those same duplicate elements for each subscription. There's no point in doing that.

To share a subscription, you can use the `share()` operator. A common pattern in Rx code is to create several sequences from the same source `Observable` by filtering out different elements in each of the results.

You'll use `share` in a practical example in Combinestagram to understand its purpose a bit better.

Open the project and select **MainViewController.swift**. Scroll to `actionAdd()` and **replace** the line `photosViewController.selectedPhotos` with:

```
let newPhotos = photosViewController.selectedPhotos
  .share()

newPhotos
  [ here the existing code continues: .subscribe(...) ]
```

Now, instead of each subscription creating a new `Observable` instance like so:

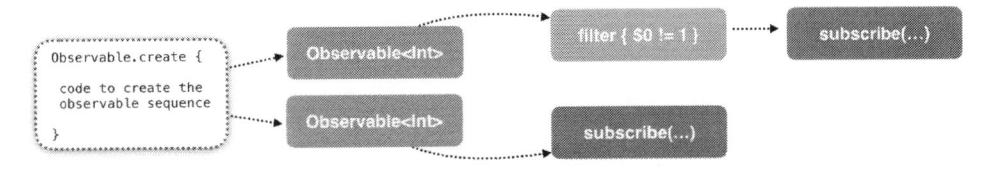

You allow for multiple subscriptions to consume the elements that a single `Observable` produces for all of them, like so:

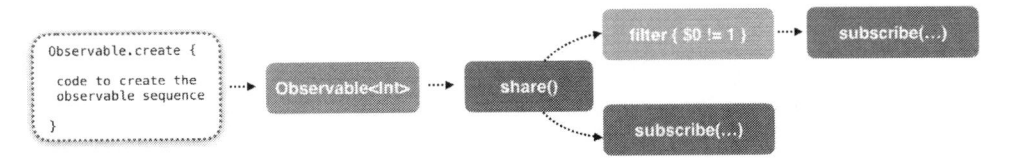

Now you can create a second subscription to `newPhotos` and filter out some of the elements you don't need.

Before moving on though, it's important to learn a bit more about how `share` works.

`share` (and its specializations via parameters) create a subscription only when the number of subscribers goes from 0 to 1 (e.g. when there isn't a shared subscription already). When a second, third and so on subscribers start observing the sequence, `share` uses the already created subscription to share with them. If all subscriptions to the shared sequence get disposed (e.g. there are no more subscribers), `share` will *dispose the shared sequence as well*. If another subscriber starts observing, `share` will create a *new* subscription for it just like described above.

> **Note:** `share()` does not provide any of the subscriptions with values emitted before the subscription takes effect. `share(replay:scope:)`, on the other hand, keeps a buffer of the last few emitted values and can provide them to new observers upon subscription.

The rule of thumb about sharing operators is that it's safe to use `share()` with observables that do not complete, or if you guarantee no new subscriptions will be made after completion. If you want piece of mind use `share(replay: 1)` - you'll learn more about this in Chapter 8, "Transforming Operators in Practice."

Ignoring all elements

You will start with the simplest filtering operator: the one that filters out all elements. No matter your value or type, `ignoreElements()` says "You shall not pass!"

Recall that `newPhotos` emits a `UIImage` element each time the user selects a photo. In this section, you are going to add a small preview of the collage in the top-left corner of the screen — a navigation icon, if you will.

Since you would like to update that icon only once, when the user returns to the main view controller, you need to ignore all `UIImage` elements and act only on a `.completed` event.

`ignoreElements()` is the operator that lets you do just that: it discards all elements of the source sequence and lets through only `.completed` or `.error`.

Inside `actionAdd()`, just under the last piece of code you added, insert the following:

```
newPhotos
  .ignoreElements()
  .subscribe(onCompleted: { [weak self] in
```

```
        self?.updateNavigationIcon()
    })
    .disposed(by: photosViewController.bag)
```

This subscription to `newPhotos` will ignore all images and will run the `onCompleted` closure when the user returns to the main view controller. To silence the Xcode error, add the missing method to the `MainViewController` class:

```
private func updateNavigationIcon() {
  let icon = imagePreview.image?
    .scaled(CGSize(width: 22, height: 22))
    .withRenderingMode(.alwaysOriginal)

  navigationItem.leftBarButtonItem = UIBarButtonItem(image: icon,
      style: .done, target: nil, action: nil)
}
```

Run the app, and make a new collage. Each time you come back from adding photos, your new subscription updates the mini-preview in the top-left corner.

Filtering elements you don't need

Of course, as great as `ignoreElements()` is, sometimes you will need to ignore just *some* of the elements — not all of them.

In those cases, you will use `filter(_:)` to let some elements through and discard others.

For example, you might have noticed that photos in portrait orientation do not fit very well in the collages in Combinestagram.

Of course, you could write smarter collage-building code... but in this chapter you're going to discard portrait photos and only include landscapes instead. That's one way to solve the issue. Pretend it's a feature, and not a bug! :]

Scroll to the top of `actionAdd()` and alter the first subscription to `newPhotos`. For the first operator, insert a `filter`:

```
newPhotos
  .filter { newImage in
    return newImage.size.width > newImage.size.height
  }
  [existing code .subscribe(...)]
```

Now each photo that `newPhotos` emits will have to pass a test before it gets to `subscribe(...)`. Your `filter` operator will check if the width of the image is larger than its height, and if so, it will let it through. Photos in portrait orientation will be discarded.

Run the app and try adding some photos from your device's Camera Roll. No matter how many times you tap on any photo in portrait orientation, it will not be added to the collage.

Implementing a basic uniqueness filter

Combinestagram, in its current form, has another controversial feature: you can add the same photo more than once. That doesn't make for very interesting collages, so in this section you'll add some advanced filtering to prevent the user from adding the same photo multiple times.

> **Note:** There are better ways to achieve the required result than what you are going to implement below. It is, however, a great exercise to build a solution with your current RxSwift skill set.

Observables don't provide a current state or a value history. Therefore, to check if emitted elements are unique, you need to somehow keep track of them yourself.

Keeping an index of emitted images is not going to help you, since two `UIImage` objects representing the same image aren't equal. The best method is to store a hash of the image data or the asset URL, but in this simple exercise, you are going to use the byte length of the image. This will not *guarantee* the uniqueness of the image's index, but it'll help you build a working solution without going too deep into the implementation details.

Add a new property to the `MainViewController` class:

```swift
private var imageCache = [Int]()
```

You will store the length in bytes of each image in this array, and will look it up for each incoming image. Scroll further down and insert another `filter`, just below the `filter` you added last:

```swift
[existing .filter {newImage in ... ]
.filter { [weak self] newImage in
    let len = UIImagePNGRepresentation(newImage)?.count ?? 0
    guard self?.imageCache.contains(len) == false else {
        return false
    }
    self?.imageCache.append(len)
    return true
}
[existing code .subscribe(...)]
```

Inside the `filter`'s closure you get the PNG data for the new image and store its byte count as the constant `len`. If `imageCache` contains a number with the same value, you assume the image is not unique and discard it by returning `false`.

If the image is unique for the collage, you store its byte length in `imageCache` and return `true`.

> **Note:** In this example, you introduce state (namely `imageCache`) in your otherwise very neat and lean code. Don't worry too much about it: in Chapter 9, "Combining Operators" you will learn about the `scan` operator, which helps you solve these kinds of situations.

To nicely wrap up this feature, add the following to `actionClear()`:

```
imageCache = []
```

This will clear your image cache and ensure the user can re-use the photos for their next collage.

Run the app and give your new feature a try by tapping few times on the same photo. You will see that the photo is added to the collage just once.

Congratulations — that was quite a complex filtering you just did!

Keep taking elements while a condition is met

One of the "best" bugs in Combinestagram is that the + button is disabled if you add six photos, which prevents you from adding any more images. But if you are in the photos view controller, you can add as many as you wish. There ought to be a way to limit those, right?

Well, believe it or not, you can easily filter all elements after a certain condition has been met by using the `takeWhile(_)` operator. You provide a Boolean condition, and `takeWhile(_)` discards all elements when this condition evaluates to `false`.

Scroll again towards the top of `actionAdd()`, find the line `newPhotos` of the first subscription and add the following code just below that line:

```
newPhotos
  .takeWhile { [weak self] image in
    return (self?.images.value.count ?? 0) < 6
  }
  [existing code: filter {...}]
```

`takeWhile(...)` will let photos through as long as the total number of images in the collage is less than 6. You use the `??` coalescing operator to default to `0` if `self` is `nil`. This is to satisfy the compiler and avoid force-unwrapping `self`.

Run the app and try to add lots photos to the collage. Once you add 6 photos, you won't be able to add any more. Mission accomplished! :]

> **Note:** In the code above you access a property of your view controller directly, which is a somewhat controversial practice in reactive programming. In Chapter 9 "Combining Operators" you will learn how to combine multiple observable sequences so that you don't have to use the view controller to keep state.

Improving the photo selector

In this section, you will move on to **PhotosViewController.swift**. First, you are going to build a new custom `Observable`, and then (*surprise!*) filter it in different ways to improve the user experience on that screen.

PHPhotoLibrary authorization observable

When you first ran Combinestagram, you had to grant it access to your photo library. Do you remember if the user experience was flawless in that moment? Probably not. You were probably overwhelmed at the time with operators, observable sequences, and the like.

The very first time your app tries to access the device's photo library, the OS will asynchronously ask for the user's permission. That happens just once: the very first time you run the app. Therefore, for this section you will need to reset the contents of your Simulator in order to recreate that first-run state for your app.

> **Note:** Be sure you don't need any of the contents of the Simulator before resetting it! If you aren't sure, work through the rest of the chapter without resetting your Simulator.

If you decide to follow the chapter exactly, do the following: bring the iPhone Simulator to the front. From its main menu, choose **Reset Content and Settings...**, then click **Reset**. This will restore your Simulator to its initial state. (In other words it will delete all the apps you were working on and revert to the default settings.)

Run Combinestagram and tap on +; the access alert box will pop up. When you tap **OK**, you'll see that the photos **don't** show up automatically. If you go back to the main view controller and tap + again, the photos appear. Hm...

Let's see what the problem is and how can you solve it. In `PhotosViewController`, you load all photos in a property named `photos`. There currently is no way to *reload* `photos` once the access has been granted.

Create a new source file and name it **PHPhotoLibrary+rx.swift**. Add the following inside:

```
import Foundation
import Photos
import RxSwift

extension PHPhotoLibrary {
  static var authorized: Observable<Bool> {
    return Observable.create { observer in

      return Disposables.create()
    }
  }
}
```

This adds a new `Observable<Bool>` property named `authorized` on `PHPhotoLibrary`. Nothing you haven't done before.

This observable can go two separate ways, depending on whether the user has already granted access:

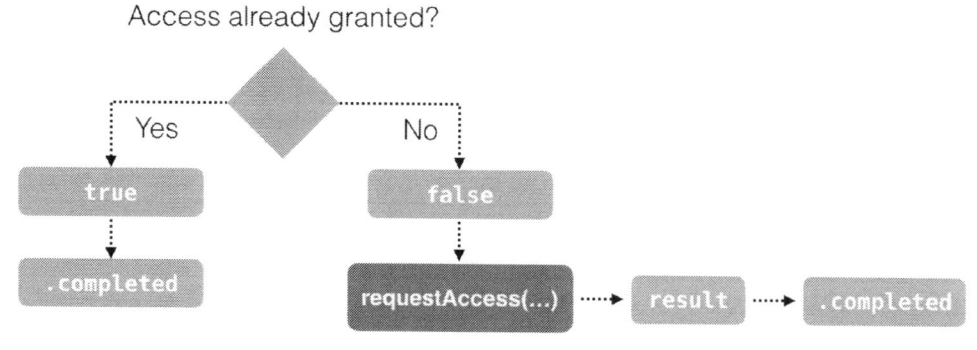

Let's recreate the logic from the flowchart above in code. Inside the `create` closure in your code, insert the following just above the line: `return Disposables.create()`:

```
DispatchQueue.main.async {
  if authorizationStatus() == .authorized {
    observer.onNext(true)
    observer.onCompleted()
  } else {
    observer.onNext(false)
    requestAuthorization { newStatus in
      observer.onNext(newStatus == .authorized)
      observer.onCompleted()
    }
  }
}
```

If the user has previously granted access, the code instantly emits a `true` value. Otherwise, the code asks for user permission and emits the result: `true` if access was granted, or `false` in any other case.

A note on the usage of `DispatchQueue.main.async {...}`: generally, your observables should not block the current thread because that could block your UI, prevent other subscriptions, or have other nasty consequences.

Now that you've built a fancy new observable sequence, it's time to divide and conquer... erm... I mean filter and observe.

Reload the photos collection when access is granted

You have two scenarios in which you end up having access to the photo library:

- On a first run of the app, the user taps **OK** in the alert box:

  .... `false` .... `true` ....▶ `.completed`

- On any subsequent run of the app if access has been previously granted:

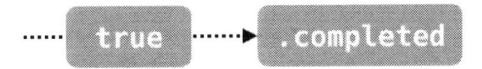

  .... `true` ....▶ `.completed`

The first thing you are going to do is subscribe to `PHPhotoLibrary.authorized`. `true` can only be the last element in that particular sequence, so whenever you get a `true` element that means you can reload the collection and display the Camera Roll photos onscreen.

Open **PhotosViewController.swift** and in `viewDidLoad()` add:

```
let authorized = PHPhotoLibrary.authorized
  .share()
```

Here you create a new shareable observable and name it `authorized`. You do this because you will create two separate subscriptions to that `Observable`.

As this section's task, you will wait for a `true` element. When you encounter one, you will reload the photos and the collection view. Add this code to `viewDidLoad()`:

```
authorized
  .skipWhile { $0 == false }
  .take(1)
  .subscribe(onNext: { [weak self] _ in
    self?.photos = PhotosViewController.loadPhotos()
```

```
    DispatchQueue.main.async {
      self?.collectionView?.reloadData()
    }
  })
  .disposed(by: bag)
```

In this code, you use two filtering operators one after another. First you use `skipWhile(_:)` to ignore all `false` elements. In case the user doesn't grant access, your subscription's `onNext` code will never get executed.

Secondly, you chain another operator: `take(1)`. Whenever a `true` comes through the filter, you take that one element and ignore everything else after it.

In this particular sequence, `true` is always the last element so there is no screaming need to use `take(1)`. But using a `take(1)` clearly expresses your intention, and if the permission mechanism changes later on, your subscription will still do exactly what you wanted: on the first `true` element, it will reload the collection view and ignore anything that comes afterwards.

Inside the `subscribe(...)` closure you switch to the main thread before reloading the collection view. Why do you need to do that? If you look up the source code for `PHPhotoLibrary.authorized`, here's where you emit the `true` value after the user has tapped **OK** to grant access:

```
requestAuthorization { newStatus in
  observer.onNext(newStatus == .authorized)
}
```

`requestAuthorization(_:)` doesn't guarantee on *which* thread your completion closure will be executed, so it might fall on a background thread. You call `onNext(_:)`, which invokes all the subscription code to the observable on the same thread. Finally, in your subscription you call `self?.collectionView?.reloadData()`, and if you're still on the background thread, UIKit will crash. When you update the UI, you need to be sure you're on the main thread.

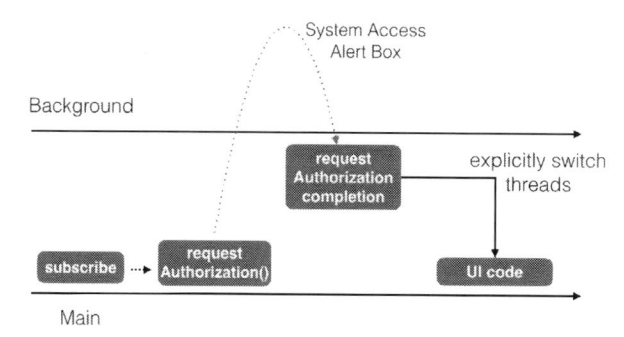

> **Note:** Threading is always important in asynchronous programming, and if anything, RxSwift makes it easier to tame your threads. In RxSwift code you aren't encouraged to use GCD to switch threads, you should use Schedulers instead. You will learn more about this in Chapter 15, "Intro to Schedulers and Threading in Practice".

Display an error message if the user doesn't grant access

So far, you have subscribed for the cases when the user has granted Combinestagram access to the photos library, but you don't do anything when they simply deny the app that right.

Here are all the possible outcomes when the app doesn't have access:

- On the first run of the app, the user taps on **Don't Grant** in the access alert box:

  `false` → `false` → `.completed`

- On any subsequent run if the user has previously denied access:

  `false` → `false` → `.completed`

The sequence elements are the same in both cases because they fall in the same code path. What you can see from the two sequences above is a pattern:

- You can always ignore the first element from the sequence, since it's never the final one.
- You then check if the last element in the sequence is `false`. In that case, show an error message.

It seems easy enough! Add the following code to `viewDidLoad()`:

```
authorized
  .skip(1)
  .takeLast(1)
  .filter { $0 == false }
  .subscribe(onNext: { [weak self] _ in
    guard let errorMessage = self?.errorMessage else { return }
    DispatchQueue.main.async(execute: errorMessage)
  })
  .disposed(by: bag)
```

> **Note:** There are different ways to write the same code. For example `filter { $0 == false }` could be written more concisely as `filter { !$0 }`. Or simply `filter(!)`. All of these achieve the same effect, but in this book we will use the easiest-to-read format to make it easier for beginners to parse the code.

Now you have a bit of an operator overkill! :] Using `skip`, `takeLast` and `filter` together expresses best what you intend to do. However, it feels a bit too much, given that in this particular situation you might not need all of them.

For example, if you are using `takeLast(1)`, doesn't that imply you are going to skip the first element anyway? And if you are using `filter` to check for a `false` element, is it really necessary to take the last one?

As with all big questions in life - the answer is "it depends" :trollface:

With the current implementation of `PHPhotosLibrary.authorized`, the code below will suffice:

```
authorized
  .skip(1)
  .filter { $0 == false }
```

You always know there will be maximum of two elements, so you skip the first and filter the following ones. But this code would also have been enough:

```
authorized
  .takeLast(1)
  .filter { $0 == false }
```

This way you ignore everything before the last element and check if that last one is `false`. This is also a fine solution.

You can even involve some other filtering operators; you can replace `skip` and `takeLast` with `distinctUntilChanged()`. For the given possible elements, you can do the following:

```
authorized
  .distinctUntilChanged()
  .takeLast(1)
  .filter { $0 == false }
```

With this, you will achieve exactly the same effect, given the order and possible values of the current sequence. For other sequences, all of the code examples above aren't guaranteed to produce the same result.

So in fact, you can shorten your subscription code quite a bit. But that's if you are *sure* the sequence logic will *never* change. What about when the next iOS version comes out? Can you guarantee that the logic behind `grant-access-alert-box` will not change? Probably you can't (except if you're on the UIKit team, and in that case - hello, we have to talk!)

So, keeping `skip`, `takeLast`, *and* `filter` might be the best way to ensure that the app logic isn't going to break after the next iOS version is released. Or you can keep it as-is, and make the logic of your `authorized` observable more deterministic so that the subscription code can be simpler.

As I said, it depends! ¯_(ツ)_/¯

But for now, let's focus on clearing that annoying error in Xcode that says `errorMessage` is not found. You can add that method anywhere in `PhotosViewController`:

```
private func errorMessage() {
  alert(title: "No access to Camera Roll",
     text: "You can grant access to Combinestagram from the Settings app")
    .subscribe(onDisposed: { [weak self] in
      self?.dismiss(animated: true, completion: nil)
      _ =
self?.navigationController?.popViewController(animated: true)
    })
    .disposed(by: bag)
}
```

You use `alert(title:description:)` from Challenge 1 of Chapter 4 to show an alert box. If you implemented `alert(title:description:)` as required, the resulting `Observable` will complete once the user taps the alert button. This will dispose the observable and hide the alert, and that ultimately will trigger your `onDisposed` code from above and pop out the photos controller.

You can try that new feature by doing the following: open the Settings app in your Simulator, scroll to the bottom, tap on Combinestagram, then turn off the Photos access switch.

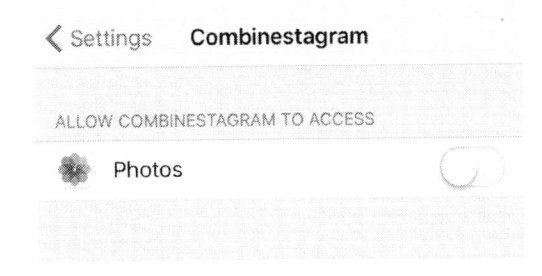

Then run the app again, and tap on the **+** button to trigger the complete sequence of checking for the current access authorization, invoking `requestAuthorization(_:)`, and ultimately popping that alert on screen:

> **No access to Camera Roll**
> You can grant access to Combinestagram from the Settings app
>
> Close

Isn't it fascinating that the complete logic of authorization checks and UI updates is made so simple through the use of observables? I certainly find it fascinating!

Trying out time based filter operators

You will learn more details about time-based operators in Chapter 11, "Time Based Operators". However, some of those operators are also filtering operators. That's why you are going to try using a couple of them in this chapter.

Time-based operators use something called a **Scheduler**. Schedulers are an important concept that you will learn about later in this book. For the examples below, you will use `MainScheduler.instance`, which is a shared scheduler object that will, alongside its other features, run your code on the main thread of your app.

Without going into more details, let's have a look at two short examples of filtering based on time.

Completing a subscription after given time interval

Right now if the user has denied access to their photo library they see the *No access* alert box and they have to tap on **Close** to go back.

It's a common pattern for messages that don't necessarily require user input to disappear on their own after a while. In this section, you are going to alter your code so that you show the alert box for a maximum of 5 seconds. If the user doesn't tap **Close** themselves within that time limit, you will automatically hide the alert and dispose of the subscription.

Open **PhotosViewController.swift** and scroll to that last method you added in there: `errorMessage()`. Directly after the line `alert(title: ..., description: ...)`, insert the following:

```
.take(5.0, scheduler: MainScheduler.instance)
[existing code: .subscribe(onDisposed: ...)]
```

`take(_:scheduler:)` is a filtering operator much like `take(1)` or `takeWhile(...)`. `take(_:scheduler:)` takes elements from the source sequence for the given time period. Once the time interval has passed, the resulting sequence completes.

Now your alert box observable is going to live, at most, for five seconds (if not less) and then it will complete, thus disposing of the subscription, hiding the alert box, and popping out the current controller as per your subscription code.

In the event the user taps **Close**, that will complete the sequence immediately without waiting for 5 seconds and will have the same effect: hide the alert and pop the current controller out.

Using throttle to reduce work on subscriptions with high load

Sometimes you are only interested in the current element of a sequence, and consider any previous values to be useless. For a real-life example, switch to **MainViewController.swift** and find `viewDidLoad()`.

Consider this part of the existing code:

```
images.asObservable()
  .subscribe(onNext: { [unowned self] photos in
    self.imagePreview.image = UIImage.collage(images: photos,
      size: self.imagePreview.frame.size)
  })
  .disposed(by: bag)
```

Each time the user selects a photo, the subscription receives the new photo collection and produces a collage. As soon as you receive the new photo collection, the previous one is useless. However, if the user taps on multiple photos quickly in succession, the subscriptions will produce a new collage for each incoming element nonetheless. Producing all those intermediate collages is wasted effort; each incoming element renders the work put into creating the preceding collage futile.

But how can you know if there will be a new element incoming shortly in the future or not?

You will be surprised how often you will find yourself in the situation where you need to solve this exact problem: "if there are many incoming elements one after the other, take only the last one." Since it's such a a common pattern of asynchronous programming, there is a special Rx operator for it.

Directly after `images.asObservable()` in the first subscription in `viewDidLoad()` insert the following:

```
.throttle(0.5, scheduler: MainScheduler.instance)
[existing code: .subscribe(onNext: ...]
```

`throttle(_:scheduler:)` filters any elements followed by another element within the specified time interval.

So if the user selects a photo and taps another one after 0.2 seconds, `throttle` will filter the first element out and only let the second one through. This will save you the work to build the first intermediate collage, which will be immediately outdated by the second one.

Of course, `throttle` also works for more than one element that comes in close succession. If the user selects five photos, tapping them quickly one after the other, `throttle` will filter the first four and let only the 5th element through, as long as there isn't another element following it in less than 0.5 seconds.

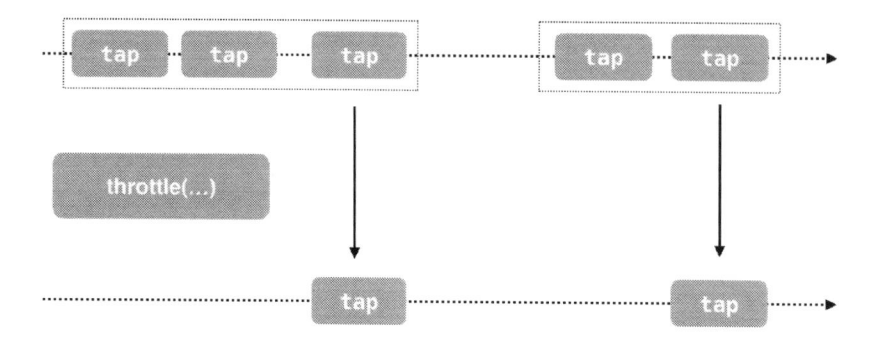

Here are just some of the many situations in which you can use `throttle`:

- You have a search text field subscription, which sends its current text to a server API. By using `throttle`, you can let the user quickly type in words and only send a request to your server after the user has finished typing.

- You present a modal view controller when the user taps a bar button. You can prevent double taps, which present the modal controller two times, by throttling the tap events by only accepting the last tap in double or triple tap sequences.

- The user is dragging their finger across the screen and you are interested only in the spots where they stop for a moment. You can throttle the current touch location and only consider only the elements where the current location stops changing.

`throttle(_:scheduler:)` is incredibly useful in situations when you are given too much input. I would love to have a `throttle` operator in real life, but I can dream, can't I?

With this last exercise, you have wrapped up development on Combinestagram and completed your introduction to filtering operators.

You also tapped a little bit into upcoming material in this book. You've seen that taming threads is a common pattern, and I'm sure you are looking forward to the operators that will allow you to switch threads as you work on your subscriptions.

Another topic you peeked into was time-based operators. No worries though; since RxSwift is an asynchronous event-based framework, time is always on your side. And you can do more with time operators than just filtering – but you will learn more about that soon enough.

Before moving on, take time to reflect on all the code you wrote in Combinestagram, and how it simplified some of the common asynchronous programming patterns you had to deal with.

Challenges

Challenge 1: Combinestagram's source code

Your challenge is to clean up the code in your project. For example, right in that last spot where you added code in **MainViewController.swift**'s `viewDidLoad()`, there are two subscriptions to the same observable. Clean that up by using a shared sequence.

Additionally, look at all subscriptions and decide if you want to replace some operators, or even remove some of them.

If you're feeling like taking on an extra task for desert, currently the navigation bar preview doesn't clear when you click the Clear button. Fix that any way you like.

Generally, take it easy and don't push yourself too hard. Operators can be overwhelming if you try to take them all in at once. When you feel ready, move on to the next chapter where you will be introduced to the poster-child of reactive programming `map` and its weird cousin `flatMap`.

Chapter 7: Transforming Operators

By Scott Gardner

Before you decided to buy this book and commit to learning RxSwift, you might have felt that RxSwift was some esoteric library; elusive, yet strangely compelling you to master it. And maybe that reminds you of when you first started learning iOS or Swift. Now that you're up to Chapter 7, you've come to realize that RxSwift isn't magic. It's a carefully constructed API that does a lot of heavy lifting for you and streamlines your code. You should be feeling good about what you've learned so far.

In this chapter, you're going to learn about one of the most important categories of operators in RxSwift: transforming operators. You'll use transforming operators all the time, to prep data coming from an observable for use by your subscriber. Once again, there are parallels between transforming operators in RxSwift and the Swift standard library, such as map(_:) and flatMap(_:). By the end of this chapter, you'll be transforming all the things!

Getting started

The starter project for this chapter is named **RxSwiftPlayground**. Once you've opened it and done an initial build, you're ready for action.

Transforming elements

Observables emit elements individually, but you will frequently want to work with collections, such as when you're binding an observable to a table or collection view, which you'll learn how to do later in the book. A convenient way to transform an observable of individual elements into an array of all those elements is by using `toArray`. As depicted in this marble diagram, `toArray` will convert an observable sequence of elements into an array of those elements, and emit a `.next` event containing that array to subscribers.

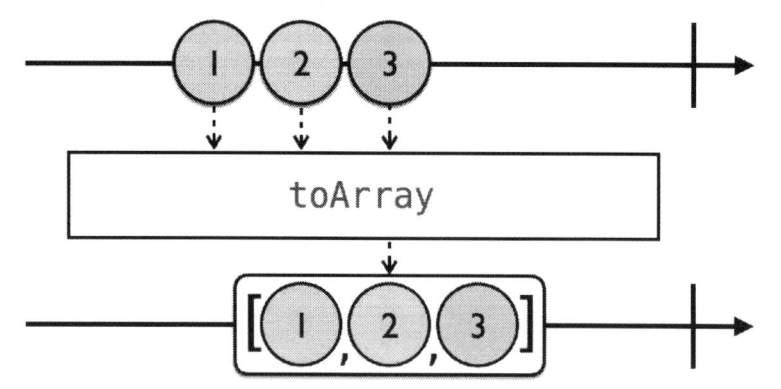

Add this new example to your playground:

```swift
example(of: "toArray") {

    let disposeBag = DisposeBag()

    // 1
    Observable.of("A", "B", "C")
        // 2
        .toArray()
        .subscribe(onNext: {
            print($0)
        })
        .disposed(by: disposeBag)
}
```

Here's what you just did:

1. Create an observable of letters.
2. Use `toArray` to transform the elements in an array.

An array of the letters is printed.

```
--- Example of: toArray ---
["A", "B", "C"]
```

RxSwift's `map` operator works just like Swift's standard `map`, except it operates on observables. In the marble diagram, `map` takes a closure that multiplies each element by 2.

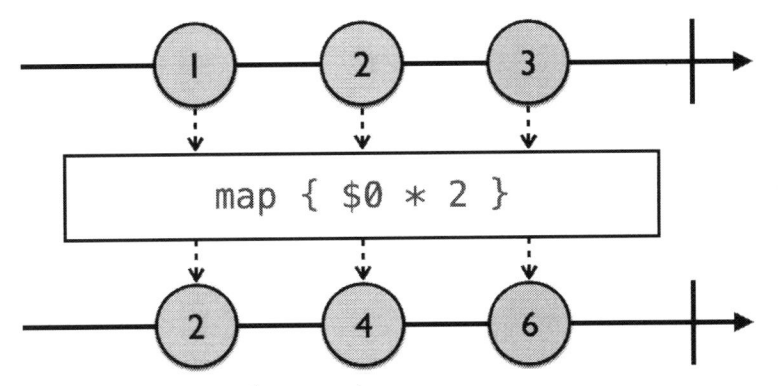

Add this new example to your playground:

```
example(of: "map") {
    
    let disposeBag = DisposeBag()
    
    // 1
    let formatter = NumberFormatter()
    formatter.numberStyle = .spellOut
    
    // 2
    Observable<NSNumber>.of(123, 4, 56)
        // 3
        .map {
            formatter.string(from: $0) ?? ""
        }
        .subscribe(onNext: {
            print($0)
        })
        .disposed(by: disposeBag)
}
```

Here's the play-by-play:

1. You create a number formatter to spell out each number.

2. You create an observable of `NSNumbers` so that you don't have to convert integers when using the formatter in the next step.

3. You use `map`, passing a closure that gets and returns the result of using the formatter to return the number's spelled out string or an empty string if that operation returns `nil`.

In Chapter 5, you learned about using `enumerated` and `map` with filtering operators. For the sake of completeness, you'll run through an example of using `enumerated` with `map` next. Add this code to your playground:

```
example(of: "enumerated and map") {
    let disposeBag = DisposeBag()
    
    // 1
    Observable.of(1, 2, 3, 4, 5, 6)
    // 2
    .enumerated()
    // 3
    .map { index, integer in
        index > 2 ? integer * 2 : integer
    }
    // 4
    .subscribe(onNext: {
        print($0)
    })
    .disposed(by: disposeBag)
}
```

Step by step:

1. Create an observable of integers.

2. Use `enumerated` to produce tuple pairs of each element and its index.

3. Use `map`, and decompose the tuple into individual values if the element's `index` is greater than 2, multiply it by 2 and return it; else, return it as is.

4. Subcribe and print elements as they're emitted.

Only the fourth element onward will be transformed and sent to the subscriber to be printed.

```
--- Example of: enumerated and map ---
1
2
```

```
3
8
10
12
```

You may have wondered at some point, "How do I work with observables that are properties of observables?" Enter the matrix.

Transforming inner observables

Add the following code to your playground, which you'll use in the upcoming examples:

```
struct Student {
    var score: BehaviorSubject<Int>
}
```

`Student` is structure that has a `score` property that is a `BehaviorSubject<Int>`. RxSwift includes a few operators in the `flatMap` family that allow you to reach into an observable and work with its observable properties. You're going to learn how to use the two most common ones here.

> **Note:** A heads up before you begin: These operators have elicited more than their fair share of questions (and groans and moans) from newcomers to RxSwift. They may seem complex at first, but you are going to walk through detailed explanations of each, so by the end of section you'll be ready to put these operators into action with confidence.

The first one you'll learn about is `flatMap`. The documentation for `flatMap` describes that it "Projects each element of an observable sequence to an observable sequence and merges the resulting observable sequences into one observable sequence." Whoa! That description, and the following marble diagram, may feel a bit overwhelming at first. Read through the play-by-play explanation that follows, referring back to the marble diagram.

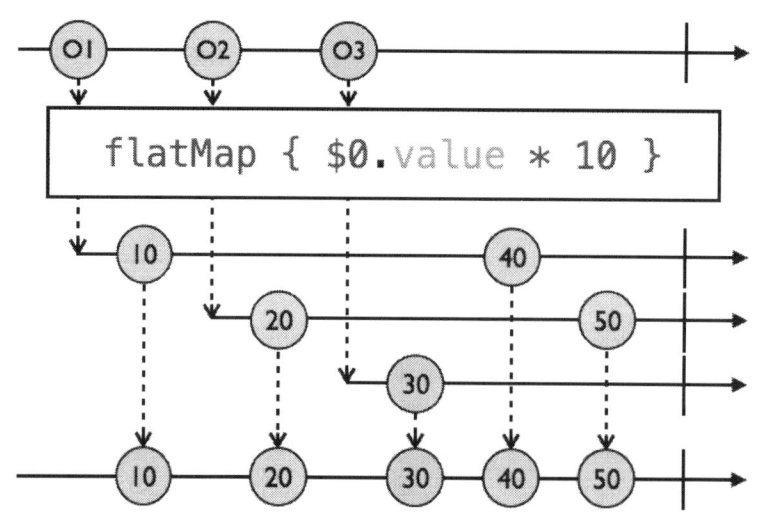

```
    ( O1 )    ( O2 )    ( O3 )
      ↓        ↓         ↓
┌─────────────────────────────────────┐
│     flatMap { $0.value * 10 }       │
└─────────────────────────────────────┘
      ↓        ↓         ↓
    ( 10 )              ( 40 )
             ( 20 )              ( 50 )
                      ( 30 )
      ↓        ↓        ↓       ↓       ↓
    ( 10 )-( 20 )-( 30 )-( 40 )-( 50 )
```

The easiest way to follow what's happening in this marble diagram is to take each path from the source observable (the top line) all the way through to the target observable that will deliver elements to the subscriber (the bottom line). The source observable is of an object type that has a `value` property that *itself* is an observable of type `Int`. It's `value` property's *initial* value is the number of the object, that is, `O1`'s initial `value` is 1, `O2`'s is 2, and `O3`'s is 3.

Starting with `O1`, `flatMap` receives the object and reaches in to access its `value` property and multiply it by `10`. It then projects the transformed elements from `O1` onto a new observable (the 1st line below `flatMap` just for `O1`), and that observable is flattened down to the target observable that will deliver elements to the subscriber (the bottom line).

Later, `O1`'s `value` property changes to 4, which is not visually represented in the marble diagram (otherwise the diagram would become even more congested). But the evidence that `O1`'s `value` has changed is that it is transformed, projected onto the existing observable for `O1` as `40`, and then flattened down to the target observable. This all happens in a time-linear fashion.

The next value in the source observable, `O2`, is received by `flatMap`, its initial value 2 is transformed to `20`, projected onto a new observable for `O2`, and then flattened down to the target observable. Later, `O2`'s `value` is changed to 5. It is transformed to `50`, projected, and flattened to the target observable.

Finally, `O3` is received by `flatMap`, its initial `value` of 3 is transformed, projected, and flattened.

flatMap projects and transforms an observable value *of* an observable, and then flattens it down to a target observable. Time to go hands-on with flatMap and really see how to use it. Add this example to your playground:

```
example(of: "flatMap") {

    let disposeBag = DisposeBag()

    // 1
    let ryan = Student(score: BehaviorSubject(value: 80))
    let charlotte = Student(score: BehaviorSubject(value: 90))

    // 2
    let student = PublishSubject<Student>()

    // 3
    student
        .flatMap {
            $0.score
        }
        // 4
        .subscribe(onNext: {
            print($0)
        })
        .disposed(by: disposeBag)
}
```

Here's the play-by-play:

1. You create two instances of Student, ryan and charlotte.

2. You create a source subject of type Student.

3. You use flatMap to reach into the student subject and access its score. You don't modify score in any way. Just pass it through.

4. You print out .next event elements in the subscription.

Nothing is printed yet. Add this code to the example:

```
student.onNext(ryan)
```

As a result, ryan's score is printed out.

```
--- Example of: flatMap ---
80
```

Now change ryan's score by adding this code to the example:

```
ryan.score.onNext(85)
```

ryan's new `score` is printed.

```
85
```

Next, add a different `Student` instance (`charlotte`) onto the source subject by adding this code:

```
student.onNext(charlotte)
```

`flatMap` does its thing and `charlotte`'s `score` is printed.

```
90
```

Here's where it gets interesting. Change `ryan`'s score by adding this line of code:

```
ryan.score.onNext(95)
```

`ryan`'s new `score` is printed.

```
95
```

This is because `flatMap` keeps up with each and every observable it creates, one for each element added onto the source observable. Now change `charlotte`'s `score` by adding the following code, just to verify that both observables are being monitored and changes projected:

```
charlotte.score.onNext(100)
```

Sure enough, her new `score` is printed out.

```
100
```

To recap, `flatMap` keeps projecting changes from each observable. There will be times when you want this behavior. And there will be times when you only want to keep up with the latest element in the source observable. So what do you think is the name of the `flatMap` operator that only keeps up with the *latest* element?

`flatMapLatest` is actually a combination of two operators, `map` and `switchLatest`. You're going to learn about `switchLatest` later in the book in the "Combining Operators" chapter, but you're getting a sneak peek here. `switchLatest` will produce values from the most recent observable, and unsubscribe from the previous observable.

So, `flatMapLatest` "Projects each element of an observable sequence into a new sequence of observable sequences and then transforms an observable sequence of observable sequences into an observable sequence producing values only from the most recent observable sequence." Wowza! Take a look at the marble diagram of `flatMapLatest`.

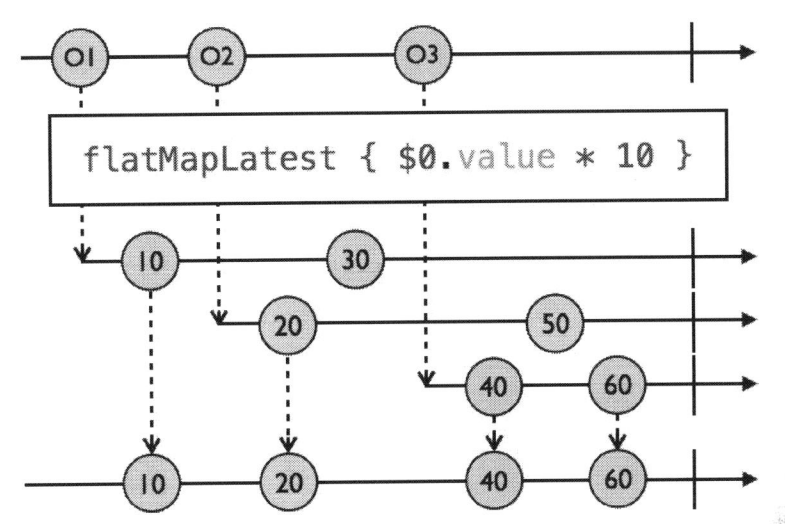

```
    O1      O2      O3
    │       │       │
┌───┼───────┼───────┼──────────────┐
│   flatMapLatest { $0.value * 10 }│
└───┼───────┼───────┼──────────────┘
    ▼       ┊       ┊
    10      30      ┊
            ▼       ┊
            20      50
                    ▼
                    40      60
    ▼       ▼       ▼       ▼
    10      20      40      60
```

`flatMapLatest` works just like `flatMap` to reach into an observable element to access its observable property, it applies a transform and projects the transformed value onto a new sequence for each element of the source observable. Those elements are flattened down into a target observable that will provide elements to the subscriber. What makes `flatMapLatest` different is that it will automatically *switch* to the latest observable and *unsubscribe* from the the previous one.

In the above marble diagram, `O1` is received by `flatMapLatest`, it transforms its `value` to `10`, projects it onto a new observable for `O1`, and flattens it down to the target observable. Just like before. But then `flatMapLatest` receives `O2` and it does its thing, switching to `O2`'s observable because *it's* now the latest.

When `O1`'s `value` changes, `flatMapLatest` actually still does the transform (something to be mindful of if your transform is an expensive operation), but then it ignores the result. The process repeats when `O3` is received by `flatMapLatest`. It then switches to its sequence and ignores the previous one (`O2`). The result is that the target observable only receives elements from the *latest* observable.

Add the following example to your playground, which is a copy/paste of the previous example except for changing `flatMap` to `flatMapLatest`:

```
example(of: "flatMapLatest") {
    
    let disposeBag = DisposeBag()
    
    let ryan = Student(score: BehaviorSubject(value: 80))
    let charlotte = Student(score: BehaviorSubject(value: 90))
```

```
    let student = PublishSubject<Student>()

    student
      .flatMapLatest {
        $0.score
      }
      .subscribe(onNext: {
        print($0)
      })
      .disposed(by: disposeBag)

  student.onNext(ryan)

  ryan.score.onNext(85)

  student.onNext(charlotte)

  // 1
  ryan.score.onNext(95)

  charlotte.score.onNext(100)
}
```

Only one thing to point out here that's different from the previous example of `flatMap`:

1. Changing `ryan`'s score here will have no effect. It will not be printed out. This is because `flatMapLatest` has already switched to the latest observable, for `charlotte`.

```
--- Example of: flatMapLatest ---
80
85
90
100
```

So you may be wondering when would you use `flatMap` for `flatMapLatest`? Probably the most common use case is using `flatMapLatest` with networking operations. You will go through examples of this later in the book, but for a simple example, imagine that you're implementing a type-ahead search. As the user types each letter, s, w, i, f, t, you'll want to execute a new search and ignore results from the previous one. `flatMapLatest` is how you do that.

Observing events

There may be times when you want to convert an observable into an observable of its events. One typical scenario where this is useful is when you do not have control over an observable that has observable properties, and you want to handle error events to avoid terminating outer sequences.

Enter this new example into the playground:

```
example(of: "materialize and dematerialize") {
    
    // 1
    enum MyError: Error {
        case anError
    }
    
    let disposeBag = DisposeBag()
    
    // 2
    let ryan = Student(score: BehaviorSubject(value: 80))
    let charlotte = Student(score: BehaviorSubject(value: 100))
    
    let student = BehaviorSubject(value: ryan)
}
```

Setting up this example, you:

1. Create an error type.

2. Create two instances of Student and a student behavior subject with the first student ryan as its initial value.

Similar to the previous two examples, you want to subscribe to the inner score property of Student. Add this code to the example:

```
// 1
let studentScore = student
    .flatMapLatest {
        $0.score
    }

// 2
studentScore
    .subscribe(onNext: {
        print($0)
    })
    .disposed(by: disposeBag)

// 3
ryan.score.onNext(85)

ryan.score.onError(MyError.anError)

ryan.score.onNext(90)
```

```
// 4
student.onNext(charlotte)
```

Continuing this example, you:

1. Create a `studentScore` observable using `flatMapLatest` to reach into the `student` observable and access its `score` observable property.
2. Subscribe and print out each `score` as it's emitted.
3. Add a score, error, and another score onto the current student.
4. Add the second student `charlotte` onto the `student` observable. Because you used `flatMapLatest`, this will switch to this new student and subscribe to her `score`.

This error is unhandled. As a result, the `studentScore` observable terminates, as does the outer `student` observable.

```
--- Example of: materialize and dematerialize ---
80
85
Received unhandled error: RxSwiftPlayground.playground:
150:__lldb_expr_171 -> anError
```

Using the `materialize` operator, you can wrap each event emitted by an observable *in* an observable.

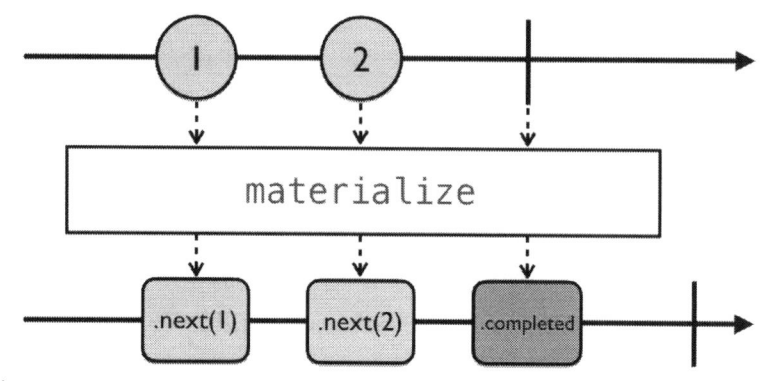

Change the `studentScore` implementation to the following:

```
let studentScore = student
  .flatMapLatest {
    $0.score.materialize()
  }
```

Option-click on `studentScore` and you'll see it is now an `Observable<Event<Int>>`. And the subscription to it now emits events. The error still causes the `studentScore` to terminate, but not the outer `student` observable, so when you switch to the new student, its `score` is successfully received and printed.

```
--- Example of: materialize and dematerialize ---
next(80)
next(85)
error(anError)
next(100)
```

However, now you're dealing with events, not elements. That's were `dematerialize` comes in. It will convert a materialized observable back into its original form.

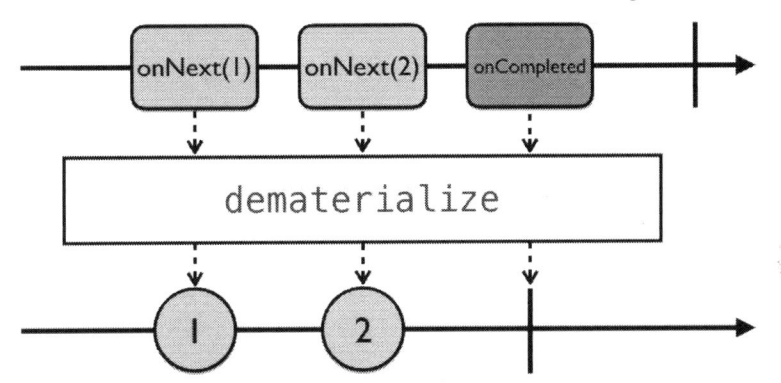

Change the subscription to the following:

```
studentScore
    // 1
    .filter {
        guard $0.error == nil else {
            print($0.error!)
            return false
        }

        return true
    }
    // 2
    .dematerialize()
    .subscribe(onNext: {
        print($0)
    })
    .disposed(by: disposeBag)
```

Wrapping things up:

1. You print and filter out any errors.

2. You use `dematerialize` to return the `studentScore` observable to its original form, emitting scores and stop events, not events of scores and stop events.

As a result, your `student` observable is protected by errors on its inner `score` observable. The error is printed and `ryan`'s `studentScore` is terminated, so adding a new score onto him does nothing. But when you add `charlotte` onto the `student` subject, her score is printed.

```
--- Example of: materialize and dematerialize ---
80
85
anError
100
```

Challenges

Completing challenges helps drive home what you learned in the chapter. There are starter and finished versions of the challenge in the exercise files download.

Challenge 1: Modify the challenge from Chapter 5 to take alpha-numeric characters

In Chapter 5's challenge, you created a phone number lookup using filtering operators. You added the code necessary to look up a contact based on a 10-digit number entered by the user.

```
input
  .skipWhile { $0 == 0 }
  .filter { $0 < 10 }
  .take(10)
  .toArray()
  .subscribe(onNext: {
    let phone = phoneNumber(from: $0)
    if let contact = contacts[phone] {
      print("Dialing \(contact) (\(phone))...")
    } else {
      print("Contact not found")
    }
  })
  .disposed(by: disposeBag)
```

Your goal for this challenge is to modify this implementation to be able to take *letters* as well, and convert them to their corresponding number based on a standard phone keypad (`abc` is 2, `def` is 3, and so on).

The starter project includes a helper closure to do the conversion:

```
let convert: (String) -> UInt? = { value in
  if let number = UInt(value),
    number < 10 {
    return number
  }

  let convert: [String: UInt] = [
    "abc": 2, "def": 3, "ghi": 4,
    "jkl": 5, "mno": 6, "pqrs": 7,
    "tuv": 8, "wxyz": 9
  ]

  let converted = keyMap
    .filter { $0.key.contains(value.lowercased()) }
    .map { $0.value }
    .first

  return converted
}
```

And there are closures to format and "dial" the contact if found (really, just print it out):

```
let format: ([UInt]) -> String = {
  var phone = $0.map(String.init).joined()

  phone.insert("-", at: phone.index(
    phone.startIndex,
    offsetBy: 3)
  )

  phone.insert("-", at: phone.index(
    phone.startIndex,
    offsetBy: 7)
  )

  return phone
}

let dial: (String) -> String = {
  if let contact = contacts[$0] {
    return "Dialing \(contact) (\($0))..."
  } else {
    return "Contact not found"
  }
}
```

These closures allow you to move the logic out of the subscription, where it really doesn't belong. So what's left to do then? You'll use multiple `map`s to perform each transformation along the way. You'll use `skipWhile` just like you did in Chapter 5 to skip `0`s at the beginning.

You'll also need to handle the optionals returned from `convert`. To do so, you can use a handy operator from the RxSwiftExt repo created by fellow author Marin: `unwrap`. RxSwiftExt includes useful operators that are not part of the core RxSwift library. The `unwrap` operator replaces the need to do this:

```
Observable.of(1, 2, nil, 3)
  .flatMap { $0 == nil ? Observable.empty() : Observable.just($0!) }
  .subscribe(onNext: {
    print($0)
  })
  .disposed(by: disposeBag)
```

With `unwrap`, you can just do this:

```
Observable.of(1, 2, nil, 3)
  .unwrap()
  .subscribe(onNext: {
    print($0)
  })
  .disposed(by: disposeBag)
```

The starter project also includes code to test your solution. Just add your solution right below the comment `// Add your code here`.

Chapter 8: Transforming Operators in Practice

By Marin Todorov

In the previous chapter, you learned about the real workhorses behind reactive programming with RxSwift: the `map` and `flatMap` dynamic duo. Of course, those aren't the only two operators you can use to transform observables, but a program can rarely do without using those two at least few times. The more experience you gain with these two, the better (and shorter) your code will be.

You already got to play around with transforming operators in the safety of a Swift playground, so hopefully you're ready to take on a real-life project. Like in other "... *in practice*" chapters, you will get a starter project, which includes as much non-Rx code as possible, and you will complete that project by working through a series of tasks. In the process, you will learn more about `map` and `flatMap`, and in which situations you should use them in your code.

> **Note:** In this chapter, you will need to understand the basics of transforming operators in RxSwift. If you haven't worked through Chapter 7, "Transforming Operators", do that first and then come back to this chapter.

Without further ado, it's time to get this show started!

Getting started with GitFeed

I wonder what the latest activity is on the RxSwift repository? In this chapter, you'll build a project to tell you this exact thing.

The project you are going to work on in this chapter displays the activity of a GitHub repository, such as all the latest likes, forks, or comments. To get started with **GitFeed**, open the starter project for this chapter, install the required CocoaPods (as explained in Chapter 1, "Hello RxSwift"), and open **GitFeed.xcworkspace**.

The app is a simple navigation controller project and features a single table view controller in which you will display the latest activity fetched from GitHub's JSON API.

> **Note:** The starter project is set to display the activity of `https://github.com/ReactiveX/RxSwift`, but if you'd like to change it to any other repository of your choice, feel free.

Run the app and you will see the empty default screen:

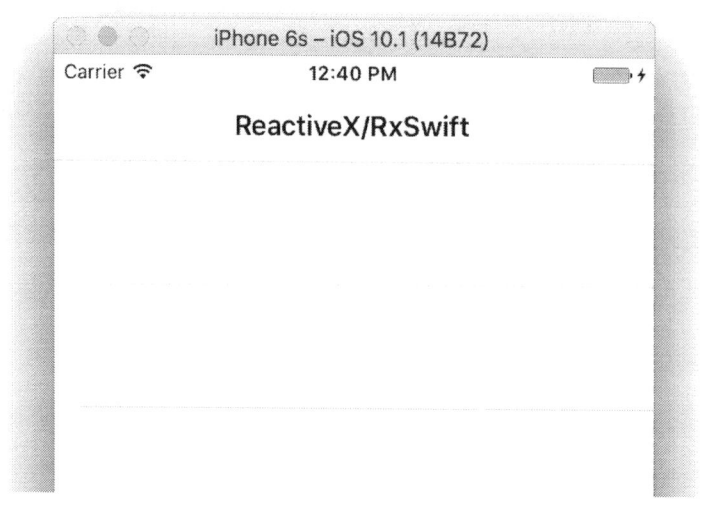

There's nothing too complex going on right now, but you'll soon have this whole setup ablaze!

The project will feature two distinct storylines:

- The main plot is about reaching out to GitHub's JSON API, receiving the JSON response, and ultimately converting it into a collection of objects.

- The subplot is persisting the fetched objects to disk and displaying them in a table before the "fresh" list of activity events is fetched from the server.

You will see that these two complement each other perfectly — and there are *plenty* of opportunities to use both `map` and `flatMap` to build what's required.

Fetching data from the web

Hopefully you've used the `URLSession` API before and have a general idea of its workflow. In summary: you create a `URLRequest` containing a web URL and parameters, then send it off to the Internet. After a bit, you receive the server response.

With your current knowledge of RxSwift, it won't be difficult to add a reactive extension to the `URLSession` class. Since you will specifically look as adding a proper reactive extension to `URLSession` in Chapter 17, "Creating a Custom Reactive Extension". In this chapter you will simply use a solution boxed with RxCocoa — RxSwift's companion library.

If you peek into **GitFeed**'s Podfile, you will notice that you import two different CocoaPods: `RxSwift` and `RxCocoa`. *What gives?*

RxCocoa is a library based on RxSwift, which implements many helpful APIs to aid with developing against RxSwift on Apple's platforms. In an effort to keep RxSwift itself as close as possible to the common Rx API shared between all implementations such as RxJS, RxJava, and RxPython, all "extra functionality" is separated into RxCocoa. You will learn about it in more detail in Chapters 12 and 13.

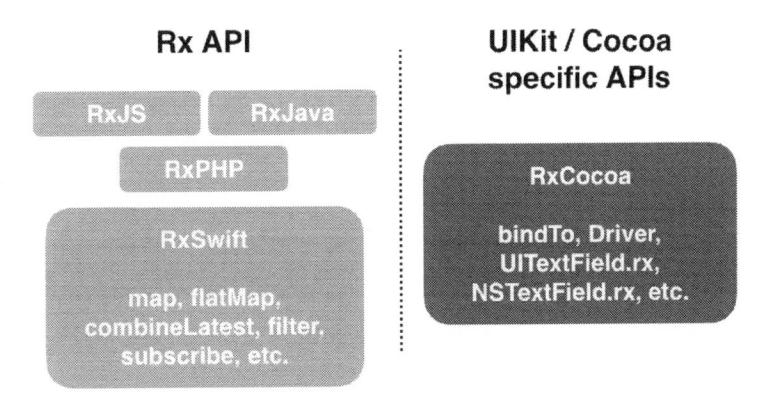

Rx API
- RxJS
- RxJava
- RxPHP
- RxSwift
  - map, flatMap, combineLatest, filter, subscribe, etc.

UIKit / Cocoa specific APIs
- RxCocoa
  - bindTo, Driver, UITextField.rx, NSTextField.rx, etc.

You will use the default RxCocoa `URLSession` extension to quickly fetch JSON from GitHub's API in this chapter.

Using map to build a request

The first task you will undertake is to build a `URLRequest` you will send off to GitHub's server. You will follow a reactive approach that might not make sense immediately, but don't worry — when you re-visit that part of the project later on, you will appreciate it!

Open **ActivityController.swift** and peek inside. You configure the view controller's UI in `viewDidLoad()`, and when you're finished, you call `refresh()`. `refresh()` in turn calls `fetchEvents(repo:)` and hands over to it the repo name `"ReactiveX/RxSwift"`.

It is in `fetchEvents(repo:)` where you will add most of your code in this section. To get started, add the following:

```
let response = Observable.from([repo])
```

To start building the web request, you begin with a simple string, which is the repository's full name. The idea to start with a string instead of directly building a `URLRequest` is to be flexible with the observable's input. This means you won't have a lot of issues if you decide to change which repo you work with — which is what you will do in the Challenges section.

Next, take the address string and create the fully qualified URL of the activity API endpoint:

```
.map { urlString -> URL in
  return URL(string: "https://api.github.com/repos/\(urlString)/events")!
}
```

You use a couple of shortcuts to create the full URL by using a hard-coded string and force unwrapping the result. You end up with the URL to access the latest events' JSON.

Have you noticed that you specified the closure's output type? Did you really have to do that? The obvious answer is *no*; usually you don't need to explicitly spell out closure input and output types. You can usually leave it to the compiler to figure those out.

However, especially in code where you have several `map` and/or `flatMap` operators chained together, you might need to help the compiler out. It will sometimes get lost in figuring out the proper types, but you can aid it by at least spelling out the output types. If you see an error about mismatched or missing types, you can add more type information to your closures and it'll probably fix the problem.

But enough about compiler woes — back to coding!

Now that you have a URL, you can move on to transforming it into a complete request. Chain to the last operator:

```
.map { url -> URLRequest in
  return URLRequest(url: url)
}
```

Easy enough: you use `map` to transform a `URL` to a `URLRequest` by using the provided web address.

Nice work! You've chained a couple of `map` operators to create a more complex transformation:

```
String  --map-->  URL  --map-->  URLRequest  -->
```

Now it's time to bring `flatMap` into play and fetch some JSON.

Using flatMap to wait for a web response

In the previous chapter, you learned that `flatMap` flattens out observable sequences. One of the common applications of `flatMap` is to add some asynchronicity to a transformation chain. Let's see how that works.

When you chain several transformations, that work happens synchronously. That is to say, all transformation operators immediately process each other's output:

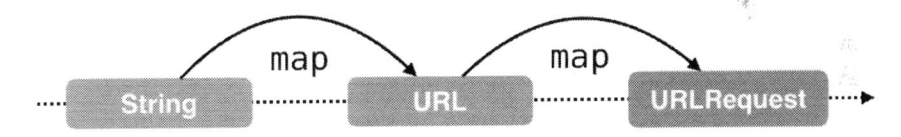

```
String  --map-->  URL  --map-->  URLRequest  -->
```

When you insert a `flatMap` in between, you can achieve different effects:

- You can flatten observables that instantly emit elements and complete, such as the `Observable` instances you create out of arrays of strings or numbers.

- You can flatten observables that perform some asynchronous work and effectively "wait" for the observable to complete, and only then let the rest of the chain continue working.

What you need to do in your **GitFeed** code is something like this:

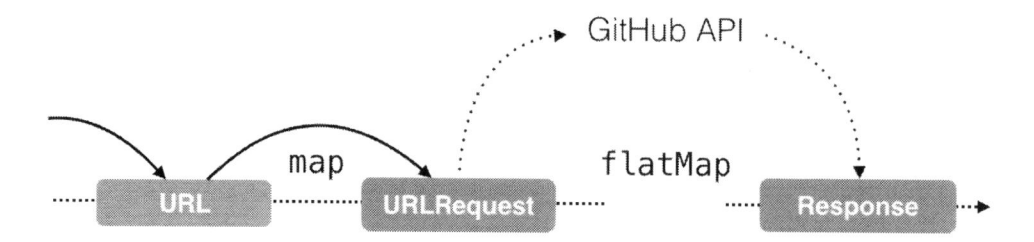

```
         map                    flatMap
URL  ─────────▶  URLRequest  ─────────▶  Response
                      ╲                    ╱
                       ╲─▶ GitHub API ◀───╱
```

To do that, append the following code to the operator chain that you have so far:

```
.flatMap { request -> Observable<(response: HTTPURLResponse,
    data: Data)> in
    return URLSession.shared.rx.response(request: request)
}
```

You use the RxCocoa `response(request:)` method on the shared `URLSession` object. That method returns an `Observable<(response: HTTPURLResponse, data: Data)>`, which completes whenever your app receives the full response from the web server. You will learn more about the RxCocoa `rx` extensions and how to extend Foundation and UIKit classes yourself later on in the book.

> **Note**: Since `response(request:)` can error out if there's no connectivity or the url is malformed, you should catch any errors inside the `flatMap` body. You will see how to do that in Chapter 14.

In the code you just wrote, `flatMap` allows you to send the web request and receive a response *without* the need of protocols and delegates. How cool is that? Freely mixing `map` and `flatMap` transformations (as above) enables the kind of linear yet asynchronous code you hopefully are starting to appreciate more and more in this book.

Finally, to allow more subscriptions to the result of the web request, chain one last operator. You will use `share(replay:, scope:)` to share the observable and keep in a buffer the last emitted event:

```
.share(replay: 1, scope: .whileConnected)
```

Unlike in Chapter 6, "Filtering Operators in Practice", this time you use `share(replay:, scope:)`. Let's shortly have a look why.

share vs. shareReplay

`URLSession.rx.response(request:)` sends your request to the server, and upon receiving the response, emits a `.next` event *just once* with the returned data, and then completes.

In this situation, if the observable completes and then you subscribe to it again, that will create a new subscription and will fire another identical request to the server.

To prevent situations like this, you use `share(replay:, scope:)`. This operator keeps a buffer of the last `replay` emitted elements and feeds them to any newly subscribed observer. Therefore if your request has completed and a new observer subscribes to the shared sequence (via `share(replay:, scope:)`), it will immediately receive the response from the server that's being kept in the buffer.

There are two scopes available to choose from: `.whileConnected` and `.forever`. The former will buffer elements up to the point where it has no subscribers, and the latter will keep the buffered elements forever. That sounds nice, but consider the implications on how much memory is used by the app.

Let's see how the app would behave when using either scope:

- `.forever`: the buffered network response is kept forever. New subscribers get the buffered response.
- `.whileConnected`: the buffered network response is kept until there are no more subscribers, and is then discarded. New subscribers get a fresh network response.

The rule of thumb for using `share(replay:, scope:)` is to use it on any sequences you expect to complete; this way you prevent the observable from being re-created. You can also use this if you'd like observers to automatically receive the last *n* emitted events.

Transforming the response

It will probably not come as a surprise that along with all the `map` transforms you did **before** sending the web request, you will need to do some more **after** you receive its response.

If you think about it, the `URLSession` class gives you back a `Data` object, and this is not an object you can work with right away. You need to transform it to JSON and then to a native object you can *safely* use in your code.

You'll now create a subscription to the `response` observable that converts the response data into objects. Just after that last piece of code you wrote, add the following code on a new line:

```
response
  .filter { response, _ in
    return 200..<300 ~= response.statusCode
  }
```

With the `filter` operator above, you easily discard all error response codes. Your filter will only let through responses having a status code between `200` and `300`, which is all the success status codes.

> **Note:** Interested in the HTTP response codes list? Check out this article on Wikipedia: https://en.wikipedia.org/wiki/List_of_HTTP_status_codes

What's with that pesky, built-in `~=` operator? It's one of the lesser-known Swift operators, and when used with a range on its left side, checks if the range includes the value on its right side.

Also note you're going to *ignore* the non-successful status codes, instead of having your observable send an error event. This is a stylistic choice meant to keep the code simple for now, but you'll see in later chapters how easy error propagation with Rx can be.

The data you receive will generally be a JSON-encoded server response containing a list of event objects. As your next task, you will try transforming the response data to an array of dictionaries.

Append another `map` to the last operator chain:

```
.map { _, data -> [[String: Any]] in
  guard let jsonObject = try? JSONSerialization.jsonObject(with: data, options: []),
    let result = jsonObject as? [[String: Any]] else {
      return []
  }
  return result
}
```

Let's deconstruct this piece of code:

- Unlike what you've done previously, you discard the response object and take only the response data.

- You aid the compiler by letting it know you will return an `Array<[String: Any]>`. This is what an array of JSON objects looks like.

- You proceed to use `JSONSerialization` as usual to try to decode the response data and return the result.

- In case `JSONSerialization` fails, you return an empty array.

It's really cool how RxSwift forces you to encapsulate these discrete pieces of work by using operators. And as an added benefit, you are always guaranteed to have the input and output types checked at compile time.

You are almost finished processing the API response. There's a couple of things left to do before updating the UI. First, you need to filter out any responses that do not contain any event objects. Append to the chain:

```
.filter { objects in
   return objects.count > 0
}
```

This will discard any error responses or any responses that do not contain new events since you last checked. You'll implement fetching only new events later in the chapter, but you can account for this now and help out your future self.

As a final transformation, you will convert the list of JSON objects to a collection of `Event` objects. Open **Event.swift** from the starter project and you will see that the class already includes the following:

- A handy `init` that takes a JSON object as a parameter.
- A dynamic property named `dictionary` that exports the event as a JSON object.

That's about everything you need this data entity class to do.

Switch back to **ActivityController.swift** and append this to the last operator chain inside `fetchEvents(repo:)`:

```
.map { objects in
   return objects.map(Event.init)
}
```

This final `map` transformation takes in a `[[String: Any]]` parameter and outputs an `[Event]` result. It does that by calling `map` on the array itself and transforming its elements one-by-one.

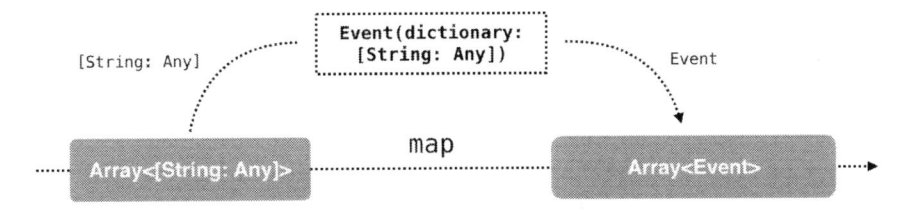

```
                    Event(dictionary:
  [String: Any]     [String: Any])        Event

  Array<[String: Any]>  ——— map ———→  Array<Event>
```

Bam! `map` just went meta! You're doing a `map` inside of a `map`.

I hope you noticed the difference between the two maps. One is a method on an `Observable<Array<[String: Any]>>` instance and is acting asynchronously on each emitted element. The second `map` is a method on an `Array`; this `map` synchronously iterates over the array elements and converts them using `Event.init`.

Finally, it's time to wrap up this seemingly endless chain of transformations and get to updating the UI. To simplify the code, you will write the UI code in a separate method. For now, simply append this code to the final operator chain:

```
.subscribe(onNext: { [weak self] newEvents in
   self?.processEvents(newEvents)
})
.disposed(by: bag)
```

Processing the response

Yes, it's finally time to perform some side effects. You started with a simple string, built a web request, sent it off to GitHub, and received an answer back. You transformed the response to JSON and then to native Swift objects. Now it's time to show the user what you've been cooking up behind the scenes all this time.

Add this code anywhere in `ActivityController`'s body:

```
func processEvents(_ newEvents: [Event]) {

}
```

In `processEvents(_:)`, you grab the last 50 events from the repository's event list and store the list into the `Variable` property `events` on your view controller. You'll do that manually for now, since you haven't yet learned how to directly bind sequences to variables or subjects.

Insert into `processEvents()`:

```
var updatedEvents = newEvents + events.value
if updatedEvents.count > 50 {
   updatedEvents = Array<Event>(updatedEvents.prefix(upTo: 50))
}

events.value = updatedEvents
```

You append the newly fetched events to the list in `events.value`. Additionally, you cap the list to 50 objects. This way you will show only the latest activity in the table view.

Finally, you set the value of `events` and are ready to update the UI. Since the data source code is already included in `ActivityController`, you simply reload the table view to display the new data.

To the end of the `processEvents` function, add the following line:

```
tableView.reloadData()
```

Run the app, and you should see the latest activity from GitHub. Yours will be different, depending on the current state of the repo in GitHub.

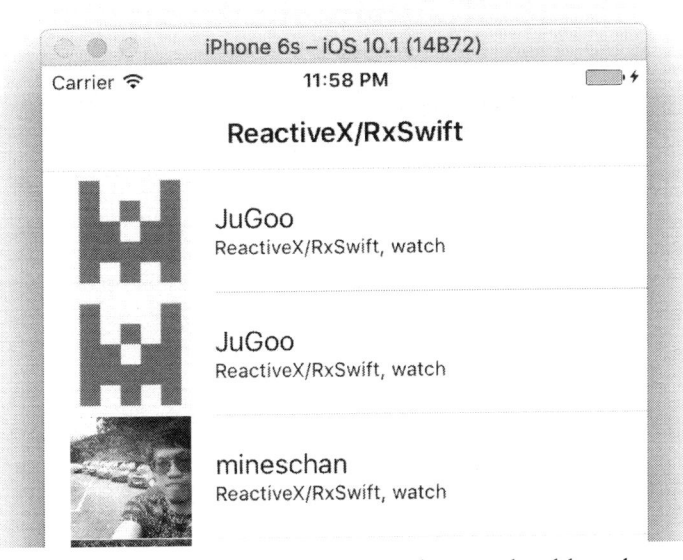

However, as soon as you see those avatars pop up, the app should crash pretty heavily and you will notice Xcode showing you the issue in the code editor:

```
tableView.reloadData()    UITableView.reloadData() must be used from main thread only
refreshControl?.endRefreshing()
```

Unfortunately, you still haven't looked into managing threads with RxSwift, so even though that's not the recommended way to do things, let's just use GCD to switch to the main thread and update the table. Wrap the call to `reloadData()` like so:

```
DispatchQueue.main.async {
  self.tableView.reloadData()
}
```

Since the code that came with the starter project in `viewDidLoad()` sets up a table refresh control, you can try to pull down the table. As soon as you pull far enough, the refresh control calls `refresh()` and reloads the events.

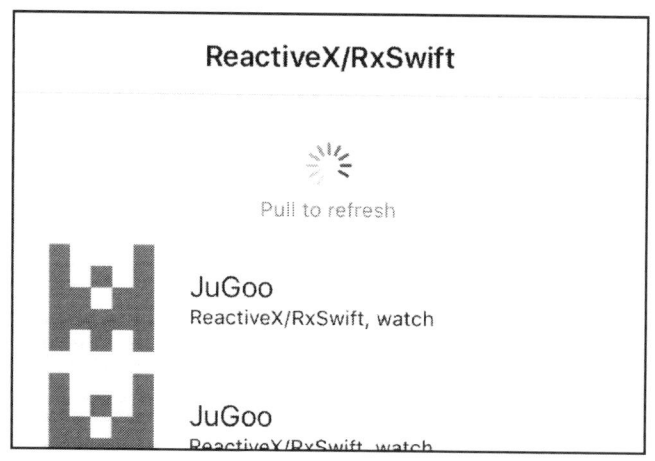

If someone forked or liked the repo since the last time you fetched the repo's events, you will see new cells appear on top.

There is a little issue when you pull down the table view: the refresh control never disappears, even if your app has finished fetching data from the API. To hide it when you've finished fetching events, add the following code just below `self.tableView.reloadData()`:

```
self.refreshControl?.endRefreshing()
```

`endRefreshing()` will hide the refresh control and reset the table view to its default state.

So far, you should have a good grasp of how and when to use `map` and `flatMap`. Throughout the rest of the chapter, you are going to tie off a few loose ends of the **GitFeed** project to make it more complete. In the challenges, you will again work through some tasks requiring smart observable sequence transformations.

Intermission: Handling erroneous input

The project as-is is pretty solid, at least in the perfect safety of a Swift Playground or in a step-by-step tutorial like this one. In this short intermission, you are going to look into some real-life server woes that your app might experience.

Switch to **Event.swift** and have a look at its `init`. What would happen if one of those objects coming from the server contained a key with a wrong name? Yes you guessed it

— your app would crash. The code of the `Event` class is written somewhat lazily, and it assumes the server will always return valid JSON.

Fix this quickly before moving on. First of all, you need to change the `init` to a failing initializer. Add a question mark right after the word `init` like so:

```
init?(dictionary: AnyDict)
```

This way, you can return `nil` from the initializer instead of crashing the app. Find the line `fatalError()` and replace it with the following:

```
return nil
```

As soon as you do that, you will see a few errors pop up in Xcode. The compiler complains that your subscription in `ActivityController` expects `[Event]`, but receives an `[Event?]` instead. Since some of the conversions from JSON to an `Event` object might fail, the result has now changed type to `[Event?]`.

Fear not! This is a perfect opportunity to exercise the difference between `map` and `flatMap` one more time. In `ActivityController`, you are currently converting JSON objects to events via `map(Event.init)`. The shortcoming of this approach is that you can't filter out `nil` elements and change the result, so to say, in mid-flight.

What you want to do is filter out any calls to `Event.init` that returned `nil`. Luckily, there's a function that can do this for you: `flatMap` — specifically, the `flatMap` on `Array` (not `Observable`).

Return to `ActivityController.swift` and scroll to `fetchEvents(repo:)`. Replace `.map(Event.init)` with:

```
objects.flatMap(Event.init)
```

To recap: any `Event.init` calls will return `nil`, and `flatMap` on those `objects` will remove any `nil` values, so you end up with an `Observable` that returns an array of `Event` objects (non-optional!). And since you removed the call to `fatalError()` in the `Event.init` function, your code is now safer.

Persisting objects to disk

In this section, you are going to work on the subplot as described in the introduction, where you will persist objects to disk, so when the user opens the app they will instantly see the events you last fetched.

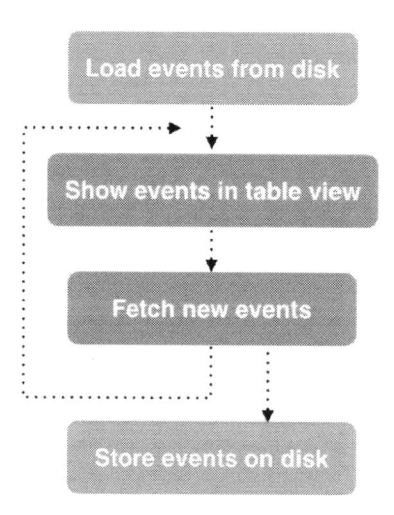

[Flowchart: Load events from disk → Show events in table view → Fetch new events → Store events on disk]

In this example, you are about to persist the events to a `.plist` file. The amount of objects you are about to store is small, so a `.plist` file will suffice for now. Later in the book, you will learn about other methods to persist data; for example, using the Realm Mobile Database in Chapter 21, "RxRealm".

First, add a new property to the `ActivityController` class:

```
private let eventsFileURL = cachedFileURL("events.plist")
```

`eventsFileURL` is the file URL where you will store the events file on your device's disk. It's time to implement the `cachedFileURL` function to grab a URL to where you can read and write files. Add this outside the definition of the view controller class:

```
func cachedFileURL(_ fileName: String) -> URL {
  return FileManager.default
    .urls(for: .cachesDirectory, in: .allDomainsMask)
    .first!
    .appendingPathComponent(fileName)
}
```

Add that function anywhere in the controller file. Now, scroll down to `processEvents(_:)` and append this to the bottom:

```
let eventsArray = updatedEvents.map{ $0.dictionary } as NSArray
eventsArray.write(to: eventsFileURL, atomically: true)
```

In this code, you convert `updatedEvents` to JSON objects (also a good format for saving in a `.plist` file) and store them in `eventsArray`, which is an instance of `NSArray`. Unlike a native Swift array, `NSArray` features a very simple and straightforward method to save its contents straight to a file.

To save the array, you call `write(to:atomically:)` and give it the URL of the file where you want to create the file or overwrite an existing one.

Cool! `processEvents(_:)` is the place to perform side effects, so writing the events to disk in that place feels right. But where can you add the code to read the saved events from disk?

Since you need to read the objects back from the file just once, you can do that in `viewDidLoad()`. This is where you will check if there's a file with stored events, and if so, load its contents into `events`.

Scroll up to `viewDidLoad()` and add this just above the call to `refresh()`:

```
let eventsArray = (NSArray(contentsOf: eventsFileURL)
    as? [[String: Any]]) ?? []
events.value = eventsArray.flatMap(Event.init)
```

This code works similarly to the one you used to save the objects to disk — but in reverse. You first create an `NSArray` by using `init(contentsOf:)`, which tries to load list of objects from a `plist` file and cast it as `Array<[String: Any]>`.

Then you do a little dance by using `flatMap` to convert the JSON to `Event` objects and filter out any failing ones. Even though you persisted them to disk, they all *should* be valid, but hey — safety first!

That should do it. Delete the app from the Simulator, or from your device if you're working there. Then run the app, wait until it displays the list of events, and then stop it from Xcode. Run the project a second time, and observe how the table view instantly displays the older data while the app fetches the latest events from the web.

Add a Last-Modified header to the request

To exercise `flatMap` and `map` one more time (yes, they simply are *that* important), you will optimize the current **GitFeed** code to request only events it hasn't fetched before. This way, if nobody has forked or liked the repo you're tracking, you will receive an empty response from the server and save on network traffic and processing power.

First, add a new property to `ActivityController` to store the file name of the file in question:

```
private let modifiedFileURL = cachedFileURL("modified.txt")
```

This time you don't need a `.plist` file, since you essentially need to store a single string like `Mon, 30 May 2017 04:30:00 GMT`. This is the value of a header named `Last-Modified` that the server sends alongside the JSON response. You need to send the same header back to the server with your next request. This way, you leave it to the server to figure out which events you last fetched and if there are any new ones since then.

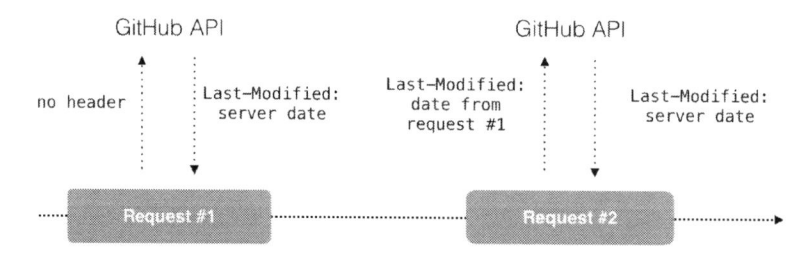

```
            GitHub API                    GitHub API
                ▲                             ▲
                │   Last-Modified:   Last-Modified:    Last-Modified:
  no header     │   server date      date from         server date
                │                    request #1
                ▼                             ▼
    ·········  Request #1  ···············  Request #2  ·········▶
```

As you did previously for the events list, you will use a `Variable` to keep track of the `Last-Modified` header. Add the following new property to `ActivityController`:

```
private let lastModified = Variable<NSString?>(nil)
```

You will work with an `NSString` object for the same reasons you used an `NSArray` before — `NSString` can easily read and write to disk, thanks to a couple of handy methods.

Scroll to `viewDidLoad()` and add this code above the call to `refresh()`:

```
lastModified.value = try? NSString(contentsOf: modifiedFileURL,
  usedEncoding: nil)
```

If you've previously stored the value of a `Last-Modified` header to a file, `NSString(contentsOf:usedEncoding:)` will create an `NSString` with the text; otherwise, it will return a `nil` value.

Start with filtering out the error responses. Move to `fetchEvents()` and create a second subscription to the `response` observable by appending the following code to the bottom of the method:

```
response
  .filter { response, _ in
    return 200..<400 ~= response.statusCode
  }
```

Next you need to:

- Filter all responses that do not include a `Last-Modified` header.
- Grab the value of the header.
- Convert it to an `NSString` value.
- Finally, filter the sequence once more, taking the header value into consideration.

It does sound like a lot of work, and you might be planning on using a `filter`, `map`, another `filter`, or more. In this section, you will use a single `flatMap` to easily filter the sequence.

You can use `flatMap` to filter the responses that don't feature a `Last-Modified` header.

Append this to the operator chain from above:

```
.flatMap { response, _ -> Observable<NSString> in
    guard let value = response.allHeaderFields["Last-Modified"]
  as? NSString else {
      return Observable.empty()
    }
    return Observable.just(value)
}
```

You use `guard` to check if the response contains an HTTP header by the name of `Last-Modified`, whose value can be cast to an `NSString`. If you can make the cast, you return an `Observable<NSString>` with a single element; otherwise, you return an `Observable`, which never emits any elements:

```
Observable<URLResponse, Data>

         Last-Modified != nil

   yes                      no

.next(Last-Modified)       never
   .completed
```

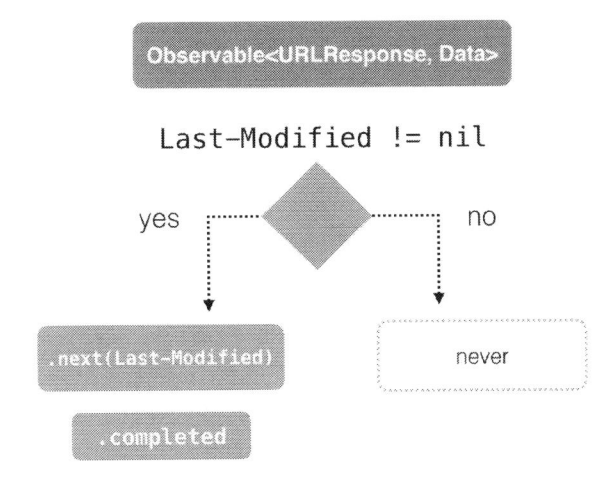

Now that you have the final value of the desired header, you can proceed to update the `lastModified` property and store the value to the disk. Add the following:

```
.subscribe(onNext: { [weak self] modifiedHeader in
  guard let strongSelf = self else { return }
  strongSelf.lastModified.value = modifiedHeader
  try? modifiedHeader.write(to: strongSelf.modifiedFileURL,
atomically: true,
    encoding: String.Encoding.utf8.rawValue)
})
.disposed(by: bag)
```

In your subscription's onNext closure, you update lastModified.value with the latest date and then call NSString.write(to:atomically:encoding) to save to disk. In the end, you add the subscription to the view controller's dispose bag.

To finish working through this part of the app, you need to use the stored header value in your request to GitHub's API. Scroll toward the top of fetchEvents(repo:) and find the particular map below where you create a URLRequest:

```
.map { url -> URLRequest in
  return URLRequest(url: url)
}
```

Replace the above code with this:

```
.map { [weak self] url -> URLRequest in
  var request = URLRequest(url: url)
  if let modifiedHeader = self?.lastModified.value {
    request.addValue(modifiedHeader as String,
      forHTTPHeaderField: "Last-Modified")
  }
  return request
}
```

In this new piece of code, you create a URLRequest just as you did before, but you add an extra condition: if lastModified contains a value, no matter whether it's loaded from a file or stored after fetching JSON, add that value as a Last-Modified header to the request.

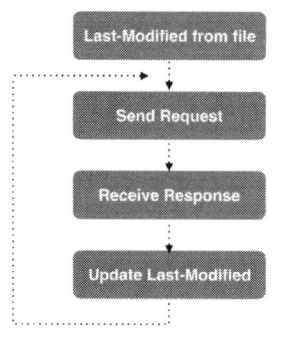

This extra header tells GitHub that you aren't interested in any events older than the header date. This will not only save you traffic, but responses which don't return any data won't count towards your GitHub API usage limit. Everybody wins!

In this chapter, you learned about different real-life use cases for `map` and `flatMap` — and built a cool project along the way, even though you still need to handle the results on the main thread (like the smart programmer you are).

But you can still do better! In the challenges section, you will work on adding threading strategy to the project so that you can do transformations on a background thread and switch to the main thread to do UI updates. This will keep your app snappy and responsive.

In a further challenge, you will see how you can easily extend the project by throwing even more `maps` and `flatMaps` into the mix.

Once you work through the challenges, you can move on to the next chapter, where you will finally learn about combining operators to greatly simplify more complex subscriptions.

Challenges

Challenge 1: Fetch top repos and spice up the feed

In this challenge, you will go through one more `map`/`flatMap` exercise. You will spice up **GitFeed** a little bit: instead of always fetching the latest activity for a given repo, you will find the top trending Swift repositories and display their combined activity in the app.

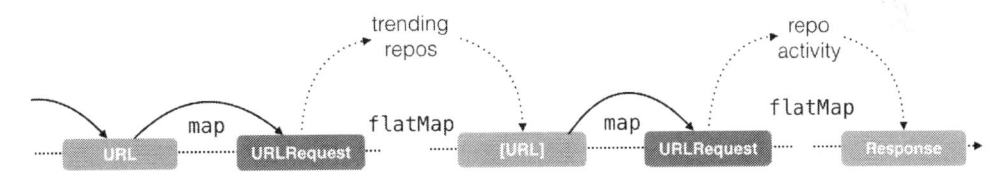

At first sight, this might look like a lot of work, but in the end you'll find it's only about a dozen lines of code.

To get started, replace `let response = Observable.from([repo])` in `fetchEvents(repo:)` with:

```
let response = Observable.from(["https://api.github.com/search/repositories?q=language:swift&per_page=5"])
```

This API endpoint will return a list of the top five popular Swift repositories. Since you don't specify an order parameter in that API call, GitHub will order the returned results by their "score", which is a secret magic GitHub computed property that has to do with each item's relevance to the search terms.

> **Note:** The GitHub JSON API is a great tool to play with. You can grab a bunch of very interesting data such as trending repositories, public activity, and more. If you are interested to learn more, visit the API homepage at https://developer.github.com/v3/.

Now proceed in exactly the same manner as you did in the chapter to transform that string into a URL and transform that in turn into a URLRequest. There's no need to include a Last-Modified header.

Since you don't need the response headers, you can use URLSession.shared.rx.json(request:), which is a method which directly returns the transformed JSON instead of raw data.

As the last step, you will need to get the JSON response as a [String: Any] dictionary and try grabbing its items key. items should contain a list of [String: Any] dictionaries, which represent each of the trending repos. You need the full_name of each of these.

This is the repo name that includes the user name and the repo name, such as icanzilb/EasyAnimation, realm/realm-cocoa, ReactiveX/RxSwift, and so on.

Use flatMap, and in case any of those assumptions fail, return Observable.empty() just as you did previously. If everything goes according to plan, return an Observable<String> created out of the list of the trending repos' full names.

Now you can chain the existing code to that flatMap like so:

```
let response = Observable.from(["https://api.github.com/search/repositories?q=language:swift&per_page=5"])

[map to convert to to URLRequest]

[flatMap to fetch JSON back]

[flatMap to convert JSON to list of repo names,
  and create Observable from that list]

[existing code follows below]

.map { urlString -> URL in
    return URL(string: "https://api.github.com/repos/\(urlString)/
```

```
events?per_page=5")!
}
.map { [weak self] url -> URLRequest in
  var request = URLRequest(url: url)
  ...
}
```

Now each time you start the app or pull down the table to refresh, the app will get the list of top five Swift repositories and then fire off five different requests to GitHub to fetch the events for each repo. If you end up seeing too many events from the same repository, you can cap the server response by adding a `per_page=5` query parameter to the URL. Then it will store the events locally and update the table with the latest data:

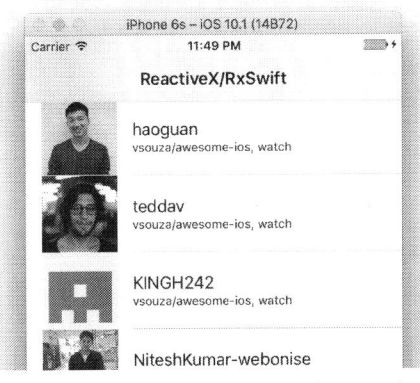

If you'd like to play around some more, you can sort the combined list of events by date and other interesting ways. What other types of sorting or filtering can you come up with?

If you wrapped up this challenge successfully, you can consider yourself a transformation pro! Oh... if you could only use a `map` in real life to turn lead into gold, that would really be something! But data transformation with RxSwift comes a close second — and that's great too.

Chapter 9: Combining Operators

By Florent Pillet

In earlier chapters, you learned how to create, filter and transform observable sequences. RxSwift filtering and transformation operators behave much like Swift's standard collection operators. You got a glimpse into the true power of RxSwift with `flatMap`, the workhorse operator that lets you perform a lot of tasks with very little code.

This chapter will show you several different ways to assemble sequences, and how to combine the data within each sequence. Some operators you'll work with are very similar to Swift collection operators. They help combine elements from asynchronous sequences, just as you do with Swift arrays.

Getting started

This chapter comes with an empty **RxSwiftPlayground**. Open the workspace with Xcode, then build the RxSwiftPlayground scheme. You will again use the example(of:) construct to wrap your code in distinct blocks. Remember to show the Debug Area in Xcode (under the **View** and **Debug Area** menus), as this is where playground print(_:) statements display their output.

RxSwift is all about working with and mastering asynchronous sequences. But you'll often need to make order out of chaos! There is a lot you can accomplish by combining observables.

Prefixing and concatenating

The first and most obvious need when working with observables is to guarantee that an observer receives an initial value. There are situations where you'll need the "current state" first. Good use cases for this are "current location" and "network connectivity status." These are some observables you'll want to prefix with the current state.

The diagram below should make it clear what this operator does:

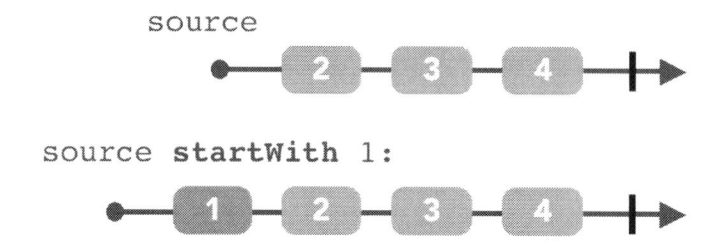

Add the following code to the playground:

```
example(of: "startWith") {
  // 1
  let numbers = Observable.of(2, 3, 4)
  
  // 2
  let observable = numbers.startWith(1)
  observable.subscribe(onNext: { value in
    print(value)
  })
}
```

The `startWith(_:)` operator prefixes an observable sequence with the given initial value. This value must be of the same type as the observable elements.

Here's what's going on in the code above:

1. Create a sequence of numbers.
2. Create a sequence starting with the value 1, then continue with the original sequence of numbers.

Don't get fooled by the position of the `startWith(_:)` operator! Although you chain it to the numbers sequence, the observable it creates emits the initial value, followed by the values from the numbers sequence.

Look at the debug area in the playground to confirm this:

```
--- Example of: startWith ---
1
2
3
4
```

This is a handy tool you'll use in many situations. It fits well in the deterministic nature of RxSwift and guarantees observers they'll get an initial value right away, and any updates later.

As it turns out, `startWith(_:)` is the simple variant of the more general **concat** family of operators. Your initial value is a sequence of one element, to which RxSwift appends the sequence that `startWith(_:)` chains to. The `Observable.concat(_:)` static function chains two sequences. Have a look:

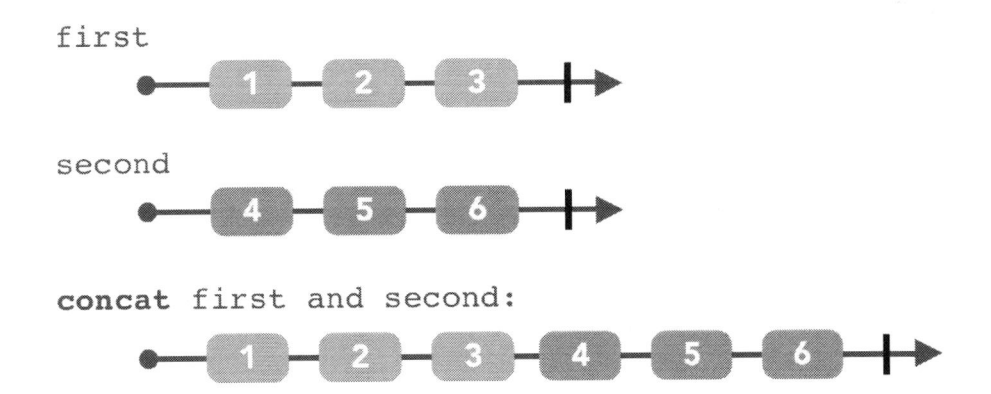

```
first
●——1——2——3——┤▶

second
●——4——5——6——┤▶

concat first and second:
●——1——2——3——4——5——6——┤▶
```

Add this code to the playground:

```
example(of: "Observable.concat") {
    // 1
    let first = Observable.of(1, 2, 3)
    let second = Observable.of(4, 5, 6)

    // 2
    let observable = Observable.concat([first, second])

    observable.subscribe(onNext: { value in
        print(value)
    })
}
```

Written this way, the concatenation order is more obvious to the untrained reader than when using `startWith(_:)`. Run the example to see elements from the first sequence: 1 2 3, followed by elements of the second sequence 4 5 6.

The `Observable.concat(_:)` static function takes an ordered collection of observables (i.e. an array). It subscribes to the first sequence of the collection, relays its elements until it completes, then moves to the next one. The process repeats until all the observables in the collection have been used. If at any point an inner observable emits an error, the concatenated observable in turn emits the error and terminates.

Another way to append sequences together is the `concat(_:)` operator (an instance method of `Observable`, not a class method). Add this code to the playground:

```
example(of: "concat") {
    let germanCities = Observable.of("Berlin", "München", "Frankfurt")
    let spanishCities = Observable.of("Madrid", "Barcelona", "Valencia")

    let observable = germanCities.concat(spanishCities)
    observable.subscribe(onNext: { value in
        print(value)
    })
}
```

This variant applies to an existing observable. It waits for the source observable to complete, then subscribes to the parameter observable. Aside from instantiation, it works just like `Observable.concat(_:)`. Check the playground output; you'll see a list of German cities followed by a list of Spanish cities.

> **Note:** Observable sequences are strongly typed. You can only concatenate sequences whose elements are of the same type!
>
> If you try to concatenate sequences of different types, brace yourself for compiler errors. The Swift compiler knows when one sequence is an `Observable<String>` and the other an `Observable<Int>` so it will not allow you to mix them up.

A final operator of interest is `concatMap(_:)`, closely related to `flatMap(_:)` which you learned about in Chapter 7, "Transforming Operators". The closure you pass to `flatMap(_:)` returns an `Observable` sequence which is subscribed to, and the emitted observables are all merged. `concatMap(_:)` guarantees that each sequence produced by the closure will run to completion before the next is subscribed to. `concatMap(_:)` is therefore a handy way to guarantee sequential order.

Try it in the playground:

```
example(of: "concatMap") {
  // 1
  let sequences = [
    "Germany": Observable.of("Berlin", "München", "Frankfurt"),
    "Spain": Observable.of("Madrid", "Barcelona", "Valencia")
  ]

  // 2
  let observable = Observable.of("Germany", "Spain")
    .concatMap { country in sequences[country] ?? .empty() }

  // 3
  _ = observable.subscribe(onNext: { string in
    print(string)
  })
}
```

This example:

1. Prepares two sequences producing German and Spanish city names.

2. Has a sequence emit country names which are map to sequences emitting city names for this country.

3. Outputs the full sequence for a given country before starting to consider the next one.

Now that you know how to *append* sequences together, it's time to move on to *combining* elements from multiple sequences.

Merging

RxSwift offers several ways to combine sequences. The easiest to start with is **merge**. Can you picture what it does from the diagram below?

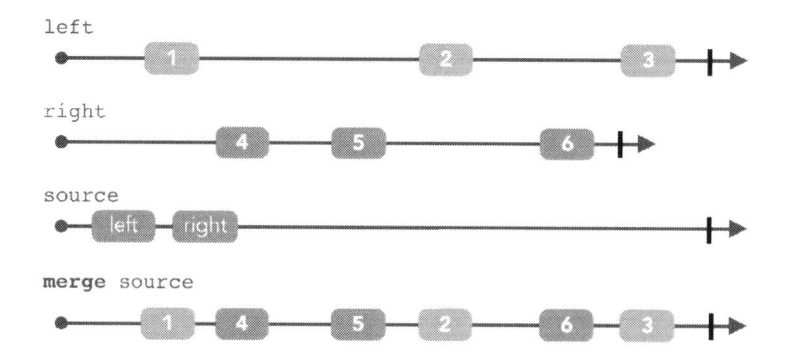

Switch to the playground; your task is to add a new `example(of:)` block, and prepare two subjects to which you can push values. You learned about `Subject` in Chapter 3, "Subjects".

```
example(of: "merge") {
  // 1
  let left = PublishSubject<String>()
  let right = PublishSubject<String>()
```

Now create a source observable of observables — it's like *Inception*! To keep things simple, make it a fixed list of your two subjects:

```
  // 2
  let source = Observable.of(left.asObservable(),
right.asObservable())
```

Next, create a merge observable from the two subjects, as well as a subscription to print the values it emits:

```
  // 3
  let observable = source.merge()
  let disposable = observable.subscribe(onNext: { value in
    print(value)
  })
```

Then you need to randomly pick and push values to either observable. The loop uses up all values from `leftValues` and `rightValues` arrays then exits.

```
// 4
var leftValues = ["Berlin", "Munich", "Frankfurt"]
var rightValues = ["Madrid", "Barcelona", "Valencia"]
repeat {
  if arc4random_uniform(2) == 0 {
    if !leftValues.isEmpty {
      left.onNext("Left:  " + leftValues.removeFirst())
    }
  } else if !rightValues.isEmpty {
    right.onNext("Right: " + rightValues.removeFirst())
  }
} while !leftValues.isEmpty || !rightValues.isEmpty
```

One last bit before you're done. Since `Subject` never completes, remember to call `dispose()` on the subscription so as not to create a memory leak!

```
  // 5
  disposable.dispose()
}
```

Whoa, that was a lot of code, so if you don't see any warnings, pat yourself on the shoulder — good job!

Run the code (it might have run automatically after you saved your work) and look at the debug output. Results will be different each time you run this code, but they should look similar to this:

```
--- Example of: merge ---
Right: Madrid
Left:  Berlin
Right: Barcelona
Right: Valencia
Left:  Munich
Left:  Frankfürt
```

A `merge()` observable subscribes to each of the sequences it receives and emits the elements as soon as they arrive — there's no predefined order.

You may be wondering when and how `merge()` completes. Good question! As with everything in RxSwift, the rules are well-defined:

- `merge()` completes after its source sequence completes **and** all inner sequences have completed.
- The order in which the inner sequences complete is irrelevant.
- If any of the sequences emit an error, the `merge()` observable immediately relays the error, then terminates.

Take a second to look at the code. Notice that `merge()` takes a *source* observable, which itself emits observables sequences of the element type. This means that you could send a *lot* of sequences for `merge()` to subscribe to!

To limit the number of sequences subscribed to at once, you can use `merge(maxConcurrent:)`. This variant keeps subscribing to incoming sequences until it reaches the `maxConcurrent` limit. After that, it puts incoming observables in a queue. It will subscribe to them in order, as soon as one of current sequences completes.

> **Note:** You might end up using this limiting variant less often than `merge()` itself. Keep it in mind, though, as it can be handy in resource-intensive situations. You could use it in scenarios such as making a lot of network requests to limit the number of concurrent outgoing connections.

Combining elements

An essential group of operators in RxSwift is the **combineLatest** family. They combine values from several sequences:

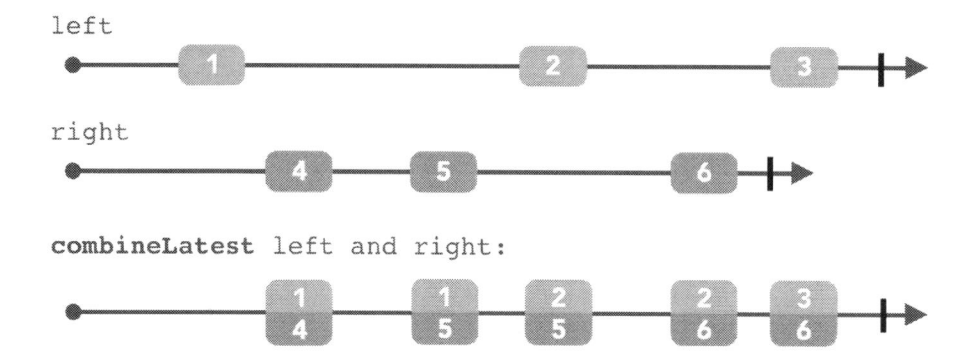

Every time one of the inner (combined) sequences emits a value, it calls a closure you provide. You receive the last value from each of the inner sequences. This has many concrete applications, such as observing several text fields at once and combining their value, watching the status of multiple sources, and so on.

Does this sound complicated? It's actually quite simple! You'll break it down by working through a few examples.

First, create two subjects to push values to:

```
example(of: "combineLatest") {
    let left = PublishSubject<String>()
    let right = PublishSubject<String>()
```

Next, create an observable that combines the latest value from both sources. Don't worry; you'll understand how the code exactly works once you've finished adding everything together.

```
// 1
let observable = Observable.combineLatest(left, right,
resultSelector: {
    lastLeft, lastRight in
    "\(lastLeft) \(lastRight)"
})
let disposable = observable.subscribe(onNext: { value in
    print(value)
})
```

Now add the following code to start pushing values to the observables:

```
// 2
print("> Sending a value to Left")
left.onNext("Hello,")
print("> Sending a value to Right")
right.onNext("world")
print("> Sending another value to Right")
right.onNext("RxSwift")
print("> Sending another value to Left")
left.onNext("Have a good day,")
```

Finally, don't forget to dispose your observable and close the `example(of:)` trailing closure. Remember that you're working with infinite sequences:

```
    disposable.dispose()
}
```

Run the complete example from above. You'll see three sentences show up in the debug output of the Playground, plus information about when you send values to the combined observable. These help make it clear as to when your closure receives values.

A few notable points about this example:

1. You **combine** observables using a closure receiving the latest value of each sequence as arguments. In this example, the combination is the concatenated string of both left and right values. It could be anything else that you need, as the **type** of the elements emitted by the combined observable is the return type of the closure. In

practice, this means you can combine sequences of heterogeneous types. It is the only core operator that permits this.

2. Nothing happens until each of the combined observables emits one value. After that, each time one emits a new value, the closure receives the **latest** value of each of the observable and produces its element.

> **Note:** Remember that `combineLatest(_:_:resultSelector:)` waits for all its observables to emit one element before starting to call your closure. It's a frequent source of confusion and a good opportunity to use the `startWith(_:)` operator to provide an initial value for the sequences, which could take time to update.

Like the `map(_:)` operator covered in Chapter 7, "Transforming Operators", `combineLatest(_:_:resultSelector:)` creates an observable whose type is the closure return type. This is a great opportunity to switch to a new type alongside a chain of operators!

A common pattern is to combine values to a tuple then pass them down the chain. For example, you'll often want to combine values and then call `filter(_:)` on them like so:

```
let observable = Observable
  .combineLatest(left, right) { ($0, $1) }
  .filter { !$0.0.isEmpty }
```

> **Note:** The example above use the trailing closure Swift syntax, which really makes the code look nice and polished.

There are several variants in the `combineLatest` family of operators. They take between two and eight observable sequences as parameters. As mentioned above, sequences don't need to have the same element type.

Let's look at another example. Add this code to the playground:

```
example(of: "combine user choice and value") {
    let choice : Observable<DateFormatter.Style> =
Observable.of(.short, .long)
    let dates = Observable.of(Date())

    let observable = Observable.combineLatest(choice, dates) {
        (format, when) -> String in
        let formatter = DateFormatter()
        formatter.dateStyle = format
        return formatter.string(from: when)
```

```
    }
    observable.subscribe(onNext: { value in
      print(value)
    })
}
```

This example demonstrates automatic updates of on-screen values when the user settings change. Think about all the manual updates you'll remove with such patterns!

A final variant of the **combineLatest** family takes a collection of observables and a combining closure, which receives latest values in an array. Since it's a collection, all observables carry elements of the same type. Although less flexible than the multiple parameter variants, it is seldom-used but still handy to know about.

The string observable in your first combineLatest(_:_:resultSelector:) example could be rewritten as:

```
// 1
let observable = Observable.combineLatest([left, right]) {
    strings in strings.joined(separator: " ")
}
```

> **Note:** Last but not least, combineLatest completes only when the last of its inner sequences completes. Before that, it keeps sending combined values. If some sequences terminate, it uses the last value emitted to combine with new values from other sequences.

Another combination operator is the **zip** family of operators. Like the combineLatest family, it comes in several variants:

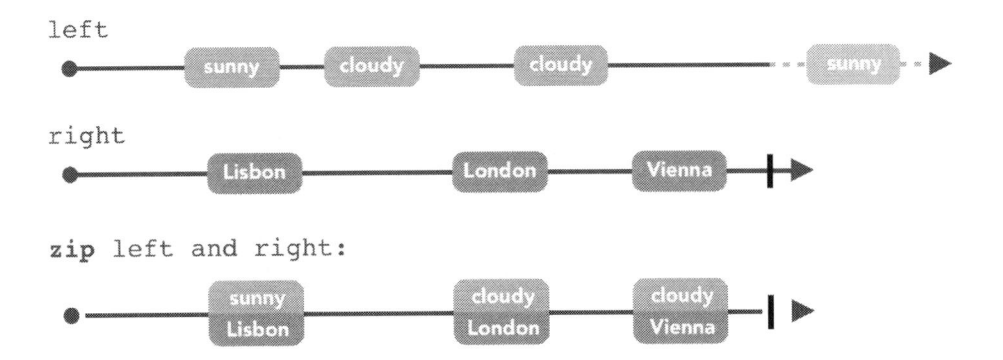

```
left
    ●────[sunny]───[cloudy]───────[cloudy]─────────[sunny]──▶

right
    ●────────[Lisbon]────────[London]─────[Vienna]──┤▶

zip left and right:
    ●──────────[sunny]─────────[cloudy]─────[cloudy]──┤▶
               [Lisbon]        [London]     [Vienna]
```

To get started, create a `Weather` enum and a couple of observables:

```
example(of: "zip") {
  enum Weather {
    case cloudy
    case sunny
  }
  let left: Observable<Weather> = Observable.of(.sunny, .cloudy,
.cloudy, .sunny)
  let right = Observable.of("Lisbon", "Copenhagen", "London",
"Madrid", "Vienna")
```

Then create a zipped observable of both sources. Note that you're using the `zip(_:_:resultSelector:)` variant. Use the shorter form as shown below, with the closure after the last parenthesis, for improved readability.

```
  let observable = Observable.zip(left, right) { weather, city in
    return "It's \(weather) in \(city)"
  }
  observable.subscribe(onNext: { value in
    print(value)
  })
}
```

Run the code and check the output:

```
--- Example of: zip ---
It's sunny in Lisbon
It's cloudy in Copenhagen
It's cloudy in London
It's sunny in Madrid
```

Here's what `zip(_:_:resultSelector:)` did for you:

- Subscribed to the observables you provided.

- Waited for each to emit a new value.

- Called your closure with both new values.

Did you notice how `Vienna` didn't show up in the output? Why is that?

The explanation lies in the way `zip` operators work. They wait until each of the inner observables emits a new value. If one of them completes, `zip` completes as well. It doesn't wait until all of the inner observables are done! This is called **indexed sequencing**, which is a way to walk though sequences in lockstep.

> **Note:** Swift also has a `zip(_:_:)` collection operator. It creates a new collection of tuples with items from both collections. But this is its only implementation. RxSwift offers variants for two to eight observables, plus a variant for collections, like **combineLatest** does.

Triggers

Apps have diverse needs and must manage multiple input sources. You'll often need to accept input from several observables at once. Some will simply trigger actions in your code, while others will provide data. RxSwift has you covered with powerful operators that will make your life easier. Well, your *coding* life at least!

You'll first look at `withLatestFrom(_:)`. Often overlooked by beginners, it's a useful companion tool when dealing with user interfaces, among other things.

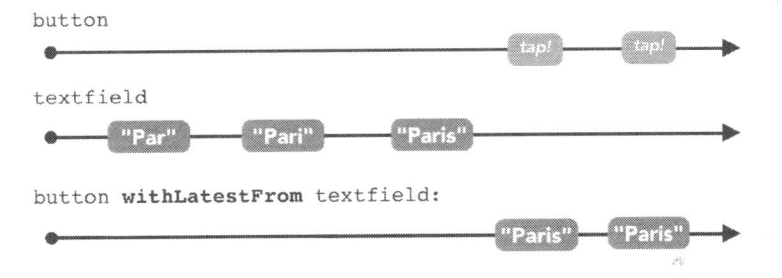

Add this code to the playground:

```
example(of: "withLatestFrom") {
  // 1
  let button = PublishSubject<Void>()
  let textField = PublishSubject<String>()

  // 2
  let observable = button.withLatestFrom(textField)
  _ = observable.subscribe(onNext: { value in
    print(value)
  })

  // 3
  textField.onNext("Par")
  textField.onNext("Pari")
  textField.onNext("Paris")
```

```
    button.onNext(())
    button.onNext(())
}
```

This example simulates a text field and a button. In Chapter 12, "Beginning RxCocoa", you'll learn about RxCocoa, a framework that helps bind your UI with RxSwift. The last two lines are duplicated on purpose!

Run this example and you'll see this output in the debug area:

```
Paris
Paris
```

Let's go through what you just did:

1. Create two subjects simulating button presses and text field input. Since the button carries no real data, you can use `Void` as an element type.

2. When `button` emits a value, ignore it but instead emit the latest value received from the simulated text field.

3. Simulate successive inputs to the text field, which is done by the two successive button presses.

Simple and straightforward! `withLatestFrom(_:)` is useful in all situations where you want the current (latest) value emitted from an observable, but only when a particular trigger occurs.

A close relative to `withLatestFrom(_:)` is the `sample(_:)` operator.

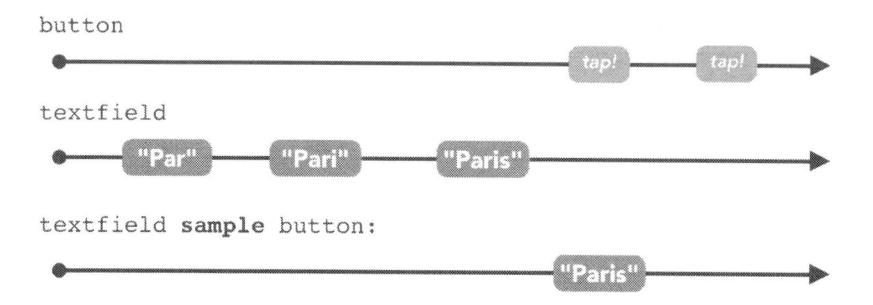

It does nearly the same thing with just one variation: each time the trigger observable emits a value, `sample(_:)` emits the latest value from the "other" observable, but only if it arrived since the last "tick". If no new data arrived, `sample(_:)` won't emit anything.

Try it in the playground. Replace `withLatestFrom(_:)` with `sample(_:)`:

```
// 2
let observable = textField.sample(button)
```

Notice that `"Paris"` now prints only once! This is because no new value was emitted by the text field between your two fake button presses. You could have achieved the same behavior by adding a `distinctUntilChanged()` to the `withLatestFrom(_:)` observable, but smallest possible operator chains are the Zen of Rx™.

> **Note:** Don't forget that `withLatestFrom(_:)` takes the data observable as a parameter, while `sample(_:)` takes the trigger observable as a parameter. This can easily be a source of mistakes — so be careful!

Waiting for triggers is a great help when doing UI work. In some cases your "trigger" may come in the form of a sequence of observables (I know, it's *Inception* once again). Or maybe you want to wait on a pair of observables and only keep one. No matter — RxSwift has operators for this!

Switches

RxSwift comes with two main so-called "switching" operators: `amb(_:)` and `switchLatest()`. They both allow you to produce an observable sequence by switching between the events of the combined or source sequences. This allows you to decide which sequence's events will the subscriber receive at runtime.

Let's look at `amb(_:)` first. Think of "amb" as in "ambiguous".

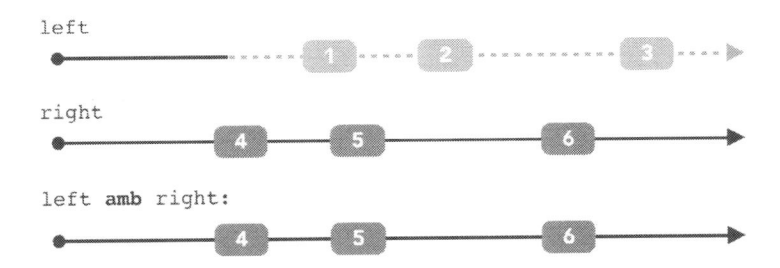

left
● - - - - - 1 - - - - 2 - - - - - - - 3 - - ▶

right
● ——— 4 —— 5 ————— 6 ——▶

left **amb** right:
● ——— 4 —— 5 ————— 6 ——▶

Add this code to the playground:

```
example(of: "amb") {
    let left = PublishSubject<String>()
    let right = PublishSubject<String>()
```

```
    // 1
    let observable = left.amb(right)
    let disposable = observable.subscribe(onNext: { value in
      print(value)
    })

    // 2
    left.onNext("Lisbon")
    right.onNext("Copenhagen")
    left.onNext("London")
    left.onNext("Madrid")
    right.onNext("Vienna")

    disposable.dispose()
}
```

You'll notice that the debug output only shows items from the `left` subject. Here's what you did:

1. Create an observable which resolves *ambiguity* between left and right.
2. Have both observables send data.

The `amb(_:)` operator subscribes to left and right observables. It waits for any of them to emit an element, then unsubscribes from the *other* one. After that, it only relays elements from the first active observable. It really does draw its name from the term *ambiguous*: at first, you don't know which sequence you're interested in, and want to decide only when one fires.

This operator is often overlooked. It has a few select practical applications, like connecting to redundant servers and sticking with the one that responds first.

A more popular option is the `switchLatest()` operator:

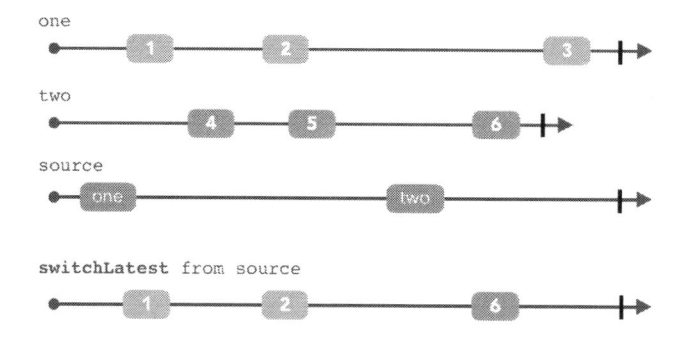

To try it out, first create three subjects and a source subject. You'll push observable sequences to this one.

```
example(of: "switchLatest") {
    // 1
    let one = PublishSubject<String>()
    let two = PublishSubject<String>()
    let three = PublishSubject<String>()

    let source = PublishSubject<Observable<String>>()
```

Next, create an observable with the `switchLatest()` operator and print its output.

```
    // 2
    let observable = source.switchLatest()
    let disposable = observable.subscribe(onNext: { value in
        print(value)
    })
```

Start feeding the source with observables, and feed observables with values.

```
    // 3
    source.onNext(one)
    one.onNext("Some text from sequence one")
    two.onNext("Some text from sequence two")

    source.onNext(two)
    two.onNext("More text from sequence two")
    one.onNext("and also from sequence one")

    source.onNext(three)
    two.onNext("Why don't you see me?")
    one.onNext("I'm alone, help me")
    three.onNext("Hey it's three. I win.")

    source.onNext(one)
    one.onNext("Nope. It's me, one!")
```

Finally dispose of the subscription when you're done.

```
    disposable.dispose()
}
```

> **Note:** It can be difficult to form a mental model of an observable of observables. Don't worry; you'll get used to it. Practice is key to a fluid understanding of sequences. Don't hesitate to review the examples as your experience grows! You'll learn more about putting this to good use in the next chapter.

The previous code produces this output:

```
--- Example of: switchLatest ---
Some text from sequence one
More text from sequence two
Hey it's three. I win.
Nope. It's me, one!
```

Notice the few output lines. Your subscription only prints items from the latest sequence pushed to the `source` observable. This is the purpose of `switchLatest()`.

> **Note:** Did you notice any similarity between `switchLatest()` and another operator? You learned about its cousin `flatMapLatest(_:)` in Chapter 7, "Transforming Operators". They do pretty much the same thing: `flatMapLatest` maps the latest value to an observable, then subscribes to it. It keeps only the latest subscription active, just like `switchLatest`.

Combining elements within a sequence

All cooks know that the more you reduce, the tastier your sauce will be. Although not aimed at chefs, RxSwift has the tools to reduce your sauce to its most flavorful components.

Through your coding adventures in Swift, you may already know about its `reduce(_:_:)` collection operator. If you don't, here's a great opportunity, as this knowledge applies to pure Swift collections as well.

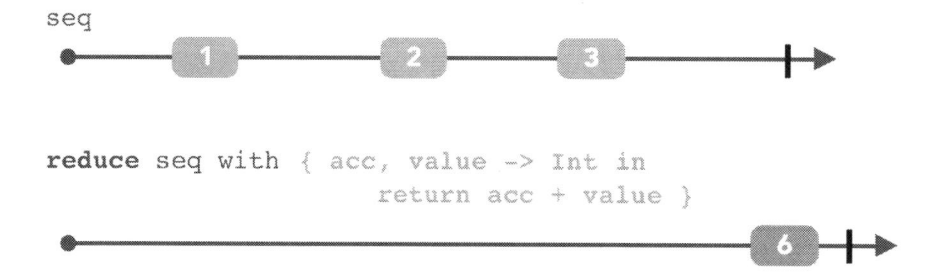

```
seq
●———[1]———————[2]———————[3]——————|▶

reduce seq with { acc, value -> Int in
                  return acc + value }

●——————————————————————————————[6]|▶
```

To get started, add this code to the playground:

```
example(of: "reduce") {
  let source = Observable.of(1, 3, 5, 7, 9)

  // 1
  let observable = source.reduce(0, accumulator: +)
  observable.subscribe(onNext: { value in
    print(value)
  })
}
```

This is much like what you'd do with Swift collections, but with observable sequences. The code above uses a shortcut form (using the + operator) to accumulate values. This by itself is not terribly self-explanatory. To get a grasp on how it works, replace the observable creation above with the following code:

```
  // 1
  let observable = source.reduce(0, accumulator: { summary, newValue in
    return summary + newValue
  })
```

The operator "accumulates" a summary value. It starts with the initial value you provide (in this example, you start with 0). Each time the source observable emits an item, `reduce(_:_:)` calls your closure to produce a new summary. When the source observable completes, `reduce(_:_:)` emits the summary value, then completes.

> **Note:** `reduce(_:_:)` produces its summary (accumulated) value only when the source observable completes. Applying this operator to sequences that never complete won't emit anything. This is a frequent source of confusion and hidden problems.

A close relative to `reduce(_:_:)` is the `scan(_:accumulator:)` operator. Can you spot the difference in the schema below, comparing to the last one above?

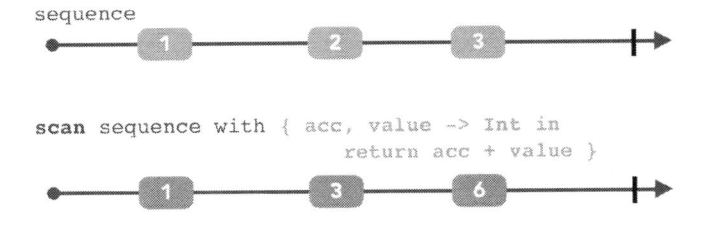

Add some code to the playground to experiment:

```
example(of: "scan") {
  let source = Observable.of(1, 3, 5, 7, 9)

  let observable = source.scan(0, accumulator: +)
  observable.subscribe(onNext: { value in
    print(value)
  })
}
```

Now look at the output:

```
--- Example of: scan ---
1
4
9
16
25
```

You get one output value per input value. As you may have guessed, this value is the running total accumulated by the closure. Each time the source observable emits an element, `scan(_:accumulator:)` invokes your closure. It passes the running value along with the new element, and the closure returns the new accumulated value. Like `reduce(_:_:)`, the resulting observable type is the closure return type.

The range of use cases for `scan(_:accumulator:)` is quite large; you can use it to compute running totals, statistics, states and so on. Encapsulating state information within a `scan(_:accumulator:)` observable is a good idea; you won't need to use local variables, and it goes away when the source observable completes. You'll see a couple of neat examples of `scan` in action in Chapter 20, "RxGesture".

Challenges

You learned a lot about many operators in this chapter. But there is so much more to learn (and more fun to be had) about sequence combination!

Challenge 1: The zip case

You've learned about the `zip` family of operators that lets you go through sequences in lockstep — it's time to start using it.

Take the code from the `scan(_:accumulator:)` example above and improve it so as to display both the current value and the running total at the same time.

There are several ways to do this — and not necessarily with `zip`. Bonus points if you can find more than one method.

The solutions to this challenge, found in the project files for this show two possible implementations. Can you find them both?

Chapter 10: Combining Operators in Practice

By Florent Pillet

In the previous chapter, you learned about combining operators and worked through increasingly more detailed exercises on some rather mind-bending concepts. Some operators may have left you wondering about the real-world application of these reactive concepts.

In this *"... in practice"* chapter, you'll have the opportunity to try some of the most powerful operators. You'll learn to solve problems similar to those you'll face in your own applications.

> **Note:** This chapter assumes you've already worked your way through Chapter 9, "Combining Operators". You should also be familiar with variables (covered in Chapter 3), filtering (Chapter 5) and transforming operators (Chapter 7). At this point in the book, it is important that you are familiar with these concepts, so make sure to review these chapters if necessary!

You'll start with a new project for this chapter and build a small application with an ambitious name: **Our Planet**.

Getting started

The project will tap into the wealth of public data exposed by NASA. You'll target EONET, NASA's *Earth Observatory Natural Event Tracker*. It is a near real-time, curated repository of natural events of all types occurring on the planet. Check out https://eonet.sci.gsfc.nasa.gov/ to learn more!

To get started with **Our Planet**, open the starter project for this chapter. Install the required CocoaPods (as explained in Chapter 1, "Hello RxSwift"), and open **OurPlanet.xcworkspace**.

Build and run the starter application; the default screen is an empty table view.

Your tasks with this application are as follows:

- Gather the event categories from the EONET public API https://eonet.sci.gsfc.nasa.gov/docs/v2.1 and display them on the first screen.
- Download events and show a count for each category.
- When user taps a category, display a list of events for this category.

You'll learn how useful `combineLatest` can be in several situations, but you'll also exercise `startWith`, `concat`, `merge`, `reduce` and `scan`. Of course, you'll also rely on operators you are already familiar with, like `map(_:)` and `flatMap(_:)`.

Preparing the web backend service

Good applications have a clear architecture with well-defined roles. The code that talks with the EONET API shouldn't live in any of the view controllers. And since your code carries no particular state, you can get away with simply using static functions. For clarity, you'll put the static functions in a class.

Let's call this the *EONET service*. It abstracts access to the data exposed by the EONET servers, providing them as a service to your application. You'll see that, combined with Rx, this pattern will find many applications. It lets you cleanly separate data *production* from *consumption* inside your application. You can easily replace or mock the production part, without any impact on the consumption side.

Expand the **Model** group in the **OurPlanet** project; the service data structures are ready for you to use. You'll find `EOCategory` and `EOEvent` structures that map to the content delivered by the API.

> **Note**: In Chapter 8, "Transforming Operators in Practice", you used a technique to deal with invalid JSON. You'll reuse this safe object initialization technique here. Did you spot it? It's the `init?(json:)` initializer you'll use with Swift's `flatMap` to drop invalid JSON objects. There shouldn't be any in this feed, but it's always better to be careful when dealing with network data.
>
> This will also shield your code against crashes in case the format changes in the back-end service.

Open **Model/EONET.swift**; it's already been fleshed out with the basic structure of the class, as well as API URLs and endpoints. It also provides a couple of helper functions you'll use later.

All EONET service APIs use a similar structure. You'll set up a general request mechanism to get data from EONET and reuse it to read both *categories* and *events*.

Generic request technique

You'll start by coding `request(endpoint:query:)`. Your goals with this crucial component of your EONET service are:

- Request data from the EONET API.
- Decode the response to a generic dictionary.
- Make sure all errors are taken care of.

It's always important to cover error cases. Don't let errors go silent, unless they're truly harmless! You want to handle programmer errors (yes, you'll make some), network errors and content errors.

Let's get started. Create a new `request(_:_:)` function:

```swift
static func request(endpoint: String, query: [String: Any] = [:]) -> Observable<[String: Any]> {
  do {
    guard let url = URL(string: API)?.appendingPathComponent(endpoint),
          var components = URLComponents(url: url, resolvingAgainstBaseURL: true) else {
      throw EOError.invalidURL(endpoint)
    }
```

Your parameters here are the endpoint name and optional query parameters. If the URL can't be constructed (i.e. you changed the service URL and mistyped it), it will throw an error. You'll catch all future errors in this function.

Once you have the URL, add the query parameters. You will use them later for event requests:

```
components.queryItems = try query.flatMap { (key, value) in
  guard let v = value as? CustomStringConvertible else {
    throw EOError.invalidParameter(key, value)
  }
  return URLQueryItem(name: key, value: v.description)
}
guard let finalURL = components.url else {
  throw EOError.invalidURL(endpoint)
}
```

The core processing part of this function uses an RxCocoa extension to `URLSession`. You learned about `rx.response` in Chapter 8, and will learn more about RxCocoa in Chapters 12 and 13.

Next, add the following code:

```
let request = URLRequest(url: finalURL)

return URLSession.shared.rx.response(request: request)
  .map { _, data -> [String: Any] in
    guard let jsonObject = try? JSONSerialization.jsonObject(with: data, options: []),
      let result = jsonObject as? [String: Any] else {
        throw EOError.invalidJSON(finalURL.absoluteString)
    }
    return result
  }
```

This is a structure you should now be familiar with. `URLSession`'s `rx.response` creates an observable from the result of a request. When the data comes back, the code deserializes it to an object, then casts to a `[String: Any]` dictionary.

Finally, close the function with a `catch` statement that simply ignores errors:

```
  } catch {
    return Observable.empty()
  }
}
```

Don't focus on the details of this right now; you'll learn the details of handling your errors in Chapter 14, "Error Handling in Practice".

You now have a solid mechanism to perform requests. Now you need to fetch the event categories.

Fetch categories

To get categories from EONET, you'll hit the `categories` API endpoint. Since these categories seldom change, you can make them a singleton. But you are fetching them asynchronously, so the best way to expose them is with an `Observable<[EOCategory]>`.

Add this code to the `EONET` class:

```
static var categories: Observable<[EOCategory]> = {
  return EONET.request(endpoint: categoriesEndpoint)
    .map { data in
      let categories = data["categories"] as? [[String: Any]] ?? []
      return categories
        .flatMap(EOCategory.init)
        .sorted { $0.name < $1.name }
    }
    .catchErrorJustReturn([])
    .share(replay: 1, scope: .forever)
}()
```

Here you apply techniques covered in previous chapters:

- Request data from the `categories` endpoint.
- Extract the `categories` array from the response.
- Map it to an array of `EOCategory` objects and sort them by name.
- If a network error occurs at this stage, output an empty array. You'll learn more about error handling in Chapter 14, Error Handling in Practice.

> **Note:** You may have noticed the use of the coalescing operator ?? above. It deals with potential errors in the JSON feed. A more appropriate behavior would be a `guard` statement that throws an error. You'll improve this pattern soon when working on the Events download code.

The interesting bit is the `.share(replay:,scope:)` at the end. Why would you do this here?

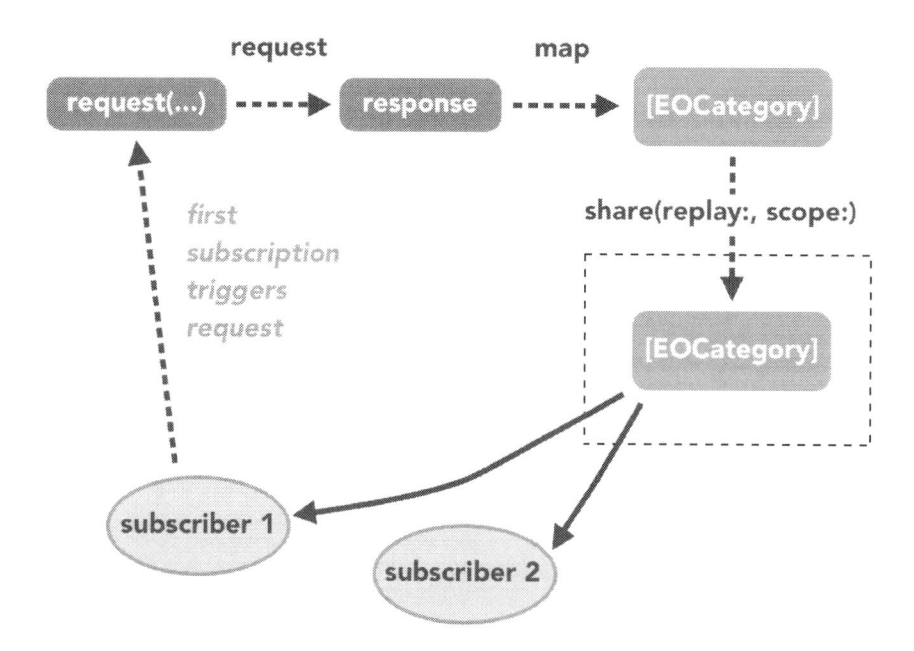

The `categories` observable you created is a singleton (`static var`). All subscribers will get the same one. Therefore:

- The first subscriber triggers the subscription to the `request` observable.
- The response maps to an array of categories.
- `share(replay: 1, scope: .forever)` relays all elements to the first subscriber.
- It then *replays* the last received element to any new subscriber, without re-requesting the data. It acts like a cache. This is the purpose of the `.forever` lifetime scope.

You're now ready to wire up the categories view controller!

Categories view controller

The categories view controller presents a sorted list of categories. Later on, you will spice things up by displaying the number of events in each category, as soon as events have been fetched. For now, let's keep it simple.

Open **CategoriesViewController.swift**.

You're displaying a `UITableViewController`, so you need to store the categories locally for display purposes. Start by adding a `Variable` to hold them, with the initial value as an empty array. Subscribing to it will trigger an update of the table view every time new data arrives.

Add the variable and a `DisposeBag` to hold your subscription disposables:

```
let categories = Variable<[EOCategory]>([])
let disposeBag = DisposeBag()
```

To get the number of table view items, pull the current contents from the `categories` variable. Update the code in `tableView(_:numberOfRowsInSection)`:

```
return categories.value.count
```

Note that you read the current value straight from the `categories` variable. Later on in the book, you'll learn about some better techniques using RxCocoa. For now, you'll keep things simple. Since `Variable` implements locking internally, you're safe even if updates come from a background thread.

Use the simple default cell to display categories. Insert the following inside `tableView(_:cellForRowAt:)`, just above the `return` statement:

```
let category = categories.value[indexPath.row]
cell.textLabel?.text = category.name
cell.detailTextLabel?.text = category.description
```

You're done with the basic setup. If you run the application, you won't see any categories yet as you first need to subscribe to the observable from the EONET service.

In the empty `startDownload()` function, add this code:

```
let eoCategories = EONET.categories
eoCategories
  .bind(to: categories)
  .disposed(by: disposeBag)
```

Nothing fancy here, since the EONET service is doing all the hard work. `bind(to:)` connects a source observable (`EONET.categories`) to an observer (the `categories` variable).

Finally, subscribe to the `Variable` to update the table view. Add this to `viewDidLoad()` before the line where you call `startDownload()`:

```
categories
  .asObservable()
  .subscribe(onNext: { [weak self] _ in
    DispatchQueue.main.async {
      self?.tableView?.reloadData()
    }
```

```
    })
    .disposed(by: disposeBag)
```

> **Note:** You're using a classic `DispatchQueue` technique to ensure the table view update occurs on the main thread. You'll learn to use schedulers and the `observeOn(_:)` operator in Chapter 15, "Intro to Schedulers/Threading in Practice".

Build and run the application and you'll see the categories show up.

Now you can move on to downloading the events, where the *real* Rx fun will happen!

Adding the event download service

The EONET API exposes two endpoints to download the events: all events, and events per category. Each also differentiates between *open* and *closed* events.

Open events are ongoing; for example, an ongoing flood or thunderstorm. *Closed* events have finished and are in the past. The actual EONET request parameters you're interested in are:

- The number of *days* to go back in time to find events.
- The *open* or *closed* status of the events.

The API requires that you download *open* and *closed* events separately. Still, you want to make them appear as one flow to subscribers. The initial plan involves making two requests and concatenating their result.

Add a private function to `EONET.swift` for requesting events with the appropriate parameters:

```
fileprivate static func events(forLast days: Int, closed: Bool)
  -> Observable<[EOEvent]> {
  return request(endpoint: eventsEndpoint, query: [
    "days": NSNumber(value: days),
    "status": (closed ? "closed" : "open")
  ])
    .map { json in
      guard let raw = json["events"] as? [[String: Any]] else {
        throw EOError.invalidJSON(eventsEndpoint)
      }
      return raw.flatMap(EOEvent.init)
    }
```

```
        .catchErrorJustReturn([])
    }
```

You're now familiar with JSON processing. The `request(_:_:)` function already decoded the JSON, so you just need to map the events array to an array of `EOEvent` objects.

Be careful when reading the code! You're using the RxSwift `map(_:)` to make an `[EOEvent]` observable out of a `[String: Any]` observable. But in the closure you're using a *Swift* `flatMap(_:)` to turn dictionaries into an array of events. This is a subtle distinction that may confuse you a few times before you get used to reading Rx code.

> **Note:** This time, you added proper error handling for invalid JSON. This `guard` statement that throws an error will propagate to an `Observable` error. You'll learn more about error handling in Chapter 14, "Error Handling in Practice". Now you can go back to the `categories` observable and fix it in the same way. Meanwhile, in this small application we simply catch errors and simply return empty data. More evolved strategies would involve retrying the request, then handling errors at the UI level to alert the user.

Finally, expose a new function in the EONET service to provide an `[EOEvent]` observable:

```
static func events(forLast days: Int = 360) ->
Observable<[EOEvent]> {
    let openEvents = events(forLast: days, closed: false)
    let closedEvents = events(forLast: days, closed: true)

    return openEvents.concat(closedEvents)
}
```

This is the function you'll call from view controllers to get events. Notice the `concat(_:)` operator? Here's what's going on:

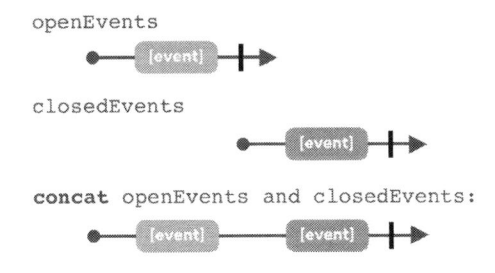

```
            openEvents
          •——[event]——▸|

            closedEvents
                        •——[event]——▸|

    concat openEvents and closedEvents:
          •——[event]————[event]——▸|
```

This is sequential processing. `concat` creates an observable that first runs its source observable (`openEvents`) to completion. It then subscribes to `closedEvents` and will complete along with it. It relays all events emitted by the first, and then the second observable. If either of those errors out, it immediately relays the error and terminates.

This is a good starter solution, but you'll improve on it later in this chapter.

You're now ready to add the events download feature to the categories view controller.

Getting events for categories

Head back to `CategoriesViewController.swift`. In `startDownload()`, you'll need a more elaborate categories download mechanism to download the events. You want to fill up each category with events, but downloading takes time. To provide the best user experience possible, you'll tackle this as follows:

- Download categories and display them first.
- Download all events for the past year.
- Update the category list to include a count of events in each category.
- Add a disclosure indicator.
- Push the events list view controller on selection.

Updating Categories with Events

You first need to replace the code in `startDownload()` with something more elaborate:

```
func startDownload() {
    let eoCategories = EONET.categories
    let downloadedEvents = EONET.events(forLast: 360)

}
```

You start by preparing two observables. `eoCategories` downloads the array of all categories. The new `downloadedEvents` calls into the `events` function you added to the EONET class, and downloads events for the past year.

Now what we need for this table view is a list of categories. Peek into the `EOCategory` model, and you'll see it has an `events` property. It's a `var` so you can add downloaded events to each category. How are you going to do this?

Add this code at the end of `startDownload()`:

```
let updatedCategories = Observable
    .combineLatest(eoCategories, downloadedEvents) {
        (categories, events) -> [EOCategory] in
```

There you go! You use `combineLatest(_:_:resultSelector:)` to combine the downloaded categories with the downloaded events and build an updated category list with events added. Your closure gets called with the latest categories array, from the `eoCategories` observable, and the latest events array, from the `downloadedEvents` observable. Its role is to combine them and produce an array of categories with their events.

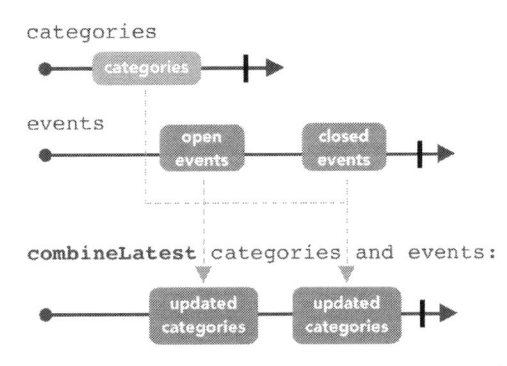

You can now add the guts of the combination closure:

```
return categories.map { category in
    var cat = category
    cat.events = events.filter {
        $0.categories.contains(category.id)
    }
    return cat
}
}
```

The `updatedCategories` observable will be of type `Observable<[EOCategory]>`. This is because the return type of the closure is `[EOCategory]`. It works with the `map` operator and lets you create a new Observable type.

The rest of the code above is regular Swift code. Events can belong to several categories, so it walks the category list and adds up all events matching the `id`.

Finally, bind to the `categories` Variable like so:

```
eoCategories
    .concat(updatedCategories)
```

```
    .bind(to: categories)
    .disposed(by: disposeBag)
```

This time you use the `concat(_:)` operator to bind items from the `eoCategories` observable and items from the `updatedCategories` observable. This will work just fine because `eoCategories` emits one element (an array of categories) then completes. This allows the `concat(_:)` operator to subscribe to the next observable, `updatedCategories`.

To recap, you've rewritten `startDownload()` to download the events and categories and combine the categories in one observable, with the events in another in order to add the events to the proper category. Now that you have the events for each category, you'll need to update your user interface to display that information.

Updating the display

Update `tableView(_:cellForRowAt:)` to display the number of events and a disclosure indicator. Change the cell's `textLabel` setup and add the disclosure indicator:

```
cell.textLabel?.text = "\(category.name) (\
(category.events.count))"
cell.accessoryType = (category.events.count >
0) ? .disclosureIndicator
   : .none
```

Build and run the application. You should see categories show up with a **(0)** event counter. After a while (have some patience here), you'll see them update with actual events count for the past year, as shown in the example below:

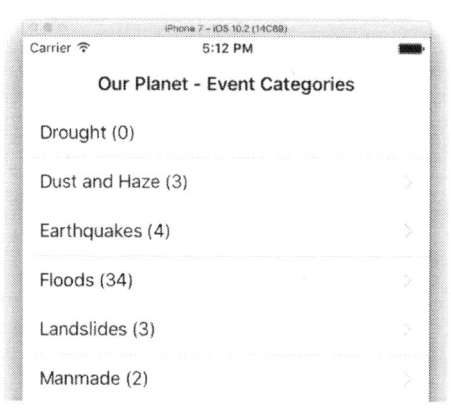

You'll notice quite a long delay between the time categories appear, and the time they get filled up with events. This is because updates from the EONET API can take some time. After all, you're requesting a full year of events! What can you do to improve this?

Downloading in parallel

Remember that the EONET API delivers *open* and *closed* events separately. Until now, you've been using `concat(_:)` to get them sequentially. It would be a good idea to download them in parallel instead. The cool thing with RxSwift is that you can make this change without any impact on UI code! Since your EONET service class exposes an observable of [EOEvent], it doesn't matter how many requests your code makes — it's transparent to the code consuming this observable.

Open the EONET.swift file again, then navigate to events(forLast:). Replace the return statement with the following:

```
return Observable.of(openEvents, closedEvents)
  .merge()
  .reduce([]) { running, new in
    running + new
  }
```

What's happening here?

- First, you created an observable of observables.

- Next, you merged them, just as you learned in the previous chapter. Remember, merge() takes an observable of observables. It subscribes to each observable emitted by the source observable and relays all emitted elements.

- Finally, you reduce the result to an array. You start with an empty array, and each time one of the observables delivers an array of events, your closure gets called. There you add the new array to the existing array and return it. This is your ongoing state that grows until all the observables complete. Once complete, reduce emits a single value (its current state) and completes.

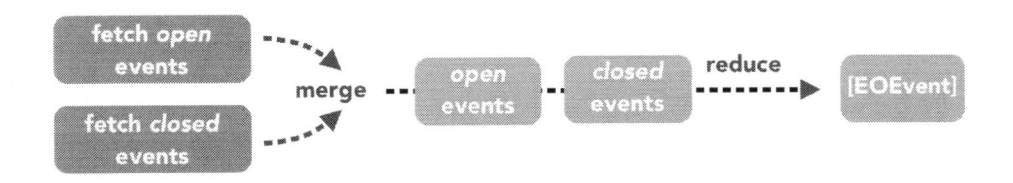

Build and run the application. You may notice a slight improvement in download time, although you'll soon learn that you can do even better.

Isn't it cool that you can change processing in your EONET service, without having to touch any of the UI code? This is one of the great benefits of Rx. A clean separation between producer and consumer gives you lots of flexibility.

Events view controller

You can now complete your UI by populating the Events view controller. Not only are you going to display events, but you'll also wire up a slider to control how much of the past year appears in the list. This is a good occasion to exercise some operators a bit more.

Open `EventsViewController.swift` and add the following variable to hold the events, as well as the always-useful `DisposeBag`:

```
let events = Variable<[EOEvent]>([])
let disposeBag = DisposeBag()
```

> **Note:** Tired of adding a `DisposeBag` everywhere? If your object is a subclass of `NSObject` (such as your view controllers) there's hope on the horizon! Look up the **NSObject+Rx** library on the **RxSwiftCommunity** GitHub organization. It provides a `DisposeBag` on demand for any `NSObject`!

In `viewDidLoad()`, add the following code to update the table view every time `events` gets a new value:

```
events.asObservable()
  .subscribe(onNext: { [weak self] _ in
    self?.tableView.reloadData()
  })
  .disposed(by: disposeBag)
```

It would also be wise to ensure the update happens on the main queue, since events may be emitted from a background queue. Unless otherwise specified, subscriptions receive elements on the thread which emitted them. You've seen this earlier in this chapter, and you'll apply the same technique here.

You can now update `tableView(_:numberOfRowsInSection:)`:

```
return events.value.count
```

In `tableView(_:cellForRowAt:)`, configure the cell as follows (above the `return` line at the bottom):

```
let event = events.value[indexPath.row]
cell.configure(event: event)
```

Finally you need to add selection handling to `CategoriesViewController`. This will push your events view controller:

```
func tableView(_ tableView: UITableView, didSelectRowAt
indexPath: IndexPath) {
  let category = categories.value[indexPath.row]
  if !category.events.isEmpty {
    let eventsController =
storyboard!.instantiateViewController(withIdentifier: "events")
as! EventsViewController
    eventsController.title = category.name
    eventsController.events.value = category.events
    navigationController!.pushViewController(eventsController,
animated: true)
  }
  tableView.deselectRow(at: indexPath, animated: true)
}
```

Easy enough; the `Variable<[EOEvent]>` in your Events view controller will hold the events. Setting this variable's value automatically triggers an update of the table view. Whether the view is already loaded or not is of no consequence, thanks to observables!

Build and run the application. You can now navigate to the events list of a category:

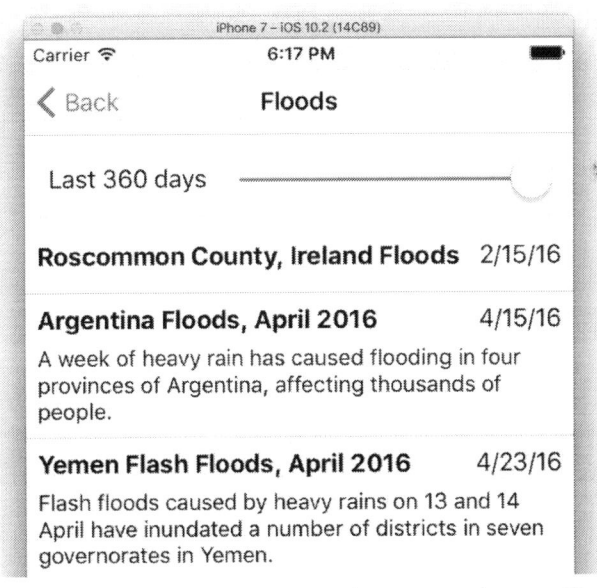

You're not done yet! The days selector is not wired up yet — but you'll see it's fairly easy to do.

Wiring the days selector

Here's the general approach you'll use to wire this one up:

- Bind the current slider value to a `Variable<Int>`.
- Combine the slider value with events to make a list of filtered events.
- Bind the table view to filtered events.

To get started, add the `days` and `filteredEvents` variables to `EventsViewController`:

```
let days = Variable<Int>(360)
let filteredEvents = Variable<[EOEvent]>([])
```

To filter the events, you need to take the latest value of `days` plus the `events` and filter them. You want to keep only the last *N* days you're interested in. Have you guessed which operator will come to the rescue?

Add this to `viewDidLoad()`:

```
Observable.combineLatest(days.asObservable(),
  events.asObservable()) { (days, events) -> [EOEvent] in
    let maxInterval = TimeInterval(days * 24 * 3600)
    return events.filter { event in
      if let date = event.closeDate {
        return abs(date.timeIntervalSinceNow) < maxInterval
      }
      return true
    }
}
```

It's your friend `combineLatest`! You should now recognize the structure of the operator call. You combine the `days` and `events` variables. The closure filters out events, keeping only those in the requested days range. Now that you have this observable, you can bind it to the `filteredEvents` variable:

```
.bind(to: filteredEvents)
.disposed(by: disposeBag)
```

Now you need to do two things:

- Bind the tableView to `filteredEvents`.
- Bind the slider to the `days` value.

The first step is easy. Change `events` to `filteredEvents` when subscribing in `viewDidLoad()` for table view updates:

```
filteredEvents.asObservable()
  .subscribe(onNext: { [weak self] _ in
    self?.tableView.reloadData()
  })
  .disposed(by: disposeBag)
```

Scroll down to `sliderAction(_:)` — the days slider in the storyboard is already wired to that action method. Insert the following code to update `days` any time the user moves the slider knob:

```
days.value = Int(slider.value)
```

Finally, update `tableView(_:numberOfRowsInSection:)` as well to return the number of filtered events instead of counting all of them:

```
return filteredEvents.value.count
```

Obviously, you'll have to also reflect that change in the other data source method as well. Find the line where you fetch the current event in `tableView(_:cellForRowAt:)` and replace it with:

```
let event = filteredEvents.value[indexPath.row]
```

Build and run the application, pick a category with lots of events, then play with the slider. You'll see the list shorten or lengthen as you drive the slider.

Oh — the label isn't updating. Add this to `viewDidLoad()` to fix that:

```
days.asObservable()
  .subscribe(onNext: { [weak self] days in
    self?.daysLabel.text = "Last \(days) days"
  })
  .disposed(by: disposeBag)
```

Now your application is complete. But downloading is still rather slow, and you don't see much progress while it's working. You'll take care of that next!

Splitting event downloads

Your last assignment in this chapter is to split downloads per category. The EONET API lets you either download all events at once, or by category. You'll download events by category, which will be a bit more complicated due to the simultaneous downloads — but you're quickly becoming an RxSwift pro and you know you can handle it.

Here's the strategy you'll use:

- First get the categories.
- Then request the events for each category.
- Each time a new event block arrives, update the categories and refresh the table view.
- Continue until you've obtained events for all categories.

You'll have to make some changes to `CategoriesViewController` and to the `EONET` service. Move to `EONET.swift` first.

Adding per-category event downloads to EONET

To download events by category, you'll need to be able to specify the endpoint to use on the API. Update the private `events(forLast:closed:)` method signature and the first line of code to take the endpoint as a parameter:

```
fileprivate static func events(forLast days: Int, closed: Bool,
  endpoint: String) -> Observable<[EOEvent]> {
    return request(endpoint: endpoint, query: [
```

To reflect the parameter name change, a little further down in that same method replace `throw EOError.invalidJSON(eventsEndpoint)` with:

```
throw EOError.invalidJSON(endpoint)
```

Now update the signature of the public `events(forLast:)` method. Change it to take a second parameter to set the category to fetch:

```
static func events(forLast days: Int = 360, category:
  EOCategory) -> Observable<[EOEvent]> {
```

You also need to update calls to build the *open* and *close* observables using the endpoint provided by the category. If you didn't notice it before, a category object initializes with an *endpoint* string. You can use that string to fetch events in this category from the API.

Replace the first two method lines with:

```
let openEvents = events(forLast: days, closed: false, endpoint:
  category.endpoint)
let closedEvents = events(forLast: days, closed: true, endpoint:
  category.endpoint)
```

With that last change you're done updating the service! Move to `CategoriesViewController` to add some interesting Rx action.

Incrementally updating the UI

Downloading events for each category revolves around using `flatMap` to produce as many event download observables as there are categories, then merge them. You've probably guessed where this is all going.

In `CategoriesViewController.swift` inside `startDownload()`, you should spot a line where Xcode complains about a missing parameter; replace the code that creates the `downloadedEvents` observable with the following:

```swift
let downloadedEvents = eoCategories.flatMap { categories in
  return Observable.from(categories.map { category in
    EONET.events(forLast: 360, category: category)
  })
}
.merge()
```

First, you get all the categories. You then call `flatMap` to transform them into an observable emitting one observable of events for each category. You then merge all these observables into a single stream of event arrays.

You need to replace the code that creates `updatedCategories` to make use of all the changes you're doing. Replace the whole piece of code inside `startDownload()` that sets `updatedCategories` with:

```swift
let updatedCategories = eoCategories.flatMap { categories in
  downloadedEvents.scan(categories) { updated, events in
    return updated.map { category in
      let eventsForCategory = EONET.filteredEvents(events: events, forCategory: category)
      if !eventsForCategory.isEmpty {
        var cat = category
        cat.events = cat.events + eventsForCategory
        return cat
      }
      return category
    }
  }
}
```

Remember the `scan(_:accumulator:)` operator from the previous chapter? For every element emitted by its source observable, it calls your closure and emits the accumulated value. In your case, this accumulated value is the updated list of categories.

So every time a new group of events arrives, `scan` emits a category update. Since the `updatedCategories` observable is bound to the `categories` variable, the table view updates.

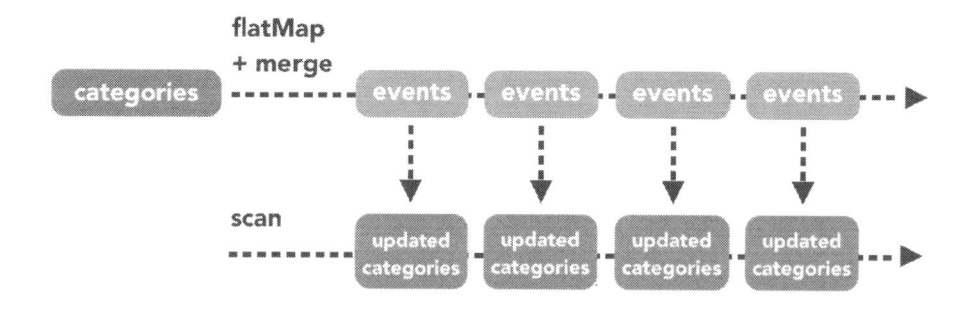

You have, in just a few lines of code, performed an elaborate sequence of API requests to produce timely updates.

But wait, there's...

Just one more thing

Say you have 25 categories, which trigger 2 API requests each. That's 50 API requests going out simultaneously to the EONET server. You want to limit the number of concurrent outgoing requests so you don't hit the free-use threshold of the APIs.

There's a simple but powerful change that completely turns your chain of operators into a threshold queue.

Replace the `merge()` call used when creating the `downloadedEvents` variable with:

```
.merge(maxConcurrent: 2)
```

This very simple change means that regardless of the number of event download observables `flatMap(_:)` pushes to its observable, only two will be subscribed to at the same time. Since each event download makes two outgoing requests (for *open* events and *closed* events), no more than four requests will fire at once. Others will be on hold until a slot is free.

Build and run the project and play around a bit — isn't reactive UI simply the best?

Hopefully you've seen the depth and power of RxSwift! It takes your code to a new level of abstraction, where you rely on powerful tools to express complex tasks with clarity.

Challenges

Challenge 1

Start from the final project in this chapter. Place an activity indicator in the navigation bar and start its spinning animation when you start fetching the events and hide the spinner once you've finished fetching all data from the network.

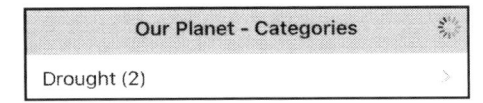

Our Planet - Categories	
Drought (2)	>

Challenge 2

The first challenge was cool, but you can do even better. Add a download progress indicator showing during the events download. You'll have to find the right spot to insert this in your code.

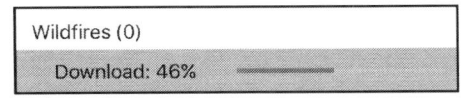

| Wildfires (0) |
| Download: 46% ――― |

You can complete this challenge in different ways so in the **challenge** folder for this chapter you will find two separate solutions. Did you come up with one of those on your own?

Chapter 11: Time Based Operators

By Florent Pillet

Timing is everything. The core idea behind reactive programming is to model asynchronous data flow *over time*. In this respect, RxSwift provides a range of operators that allow you to deal with time and the way that sequences react and transform over time. As you'll see throughout this chapter, managing the time dimension of your sequences is easy and straightforward.

To learn about time-based operators, you'll practice with an animated playground that demonstrates visually how data flows over time. This chapter comes with an empty **RxSwiftPlayground**, divided in several pages. You'll use each page to exercise one or more related operators. The playground also includes a number of ready-made classes that'll come in handy to build the examples.

Getting started

First prepare the workspace. Open Terminal, navigate to the root of the project and perform the classic `pod install` command. Once complete, open the `RxSwiftPlayground.xcworkspace` file that was just created and build the `RxSwiftPlayground` scheme.

You can keep the Debug Area visible, but what is most important is that you show the Assistant Editor. This will display a live view of the sequences you build in code. This is where the real action will happen! To display the Assistant Editor, click the middle button with two circles at top-right of the Xcode window, as shown below:

The Assistant Editor usually shows a "counterpart file". Make sure that you show the "timeline" for your current playground page, in case it is not visible:

Also make sure that anything you type automatically executes in the Assistant Editor's preview area. Long-click the blue arrow at the bottom of the editor (if it is currently set to run, it will be a square) and make sure **Automatically Run** is selected, as in the screenshot below:

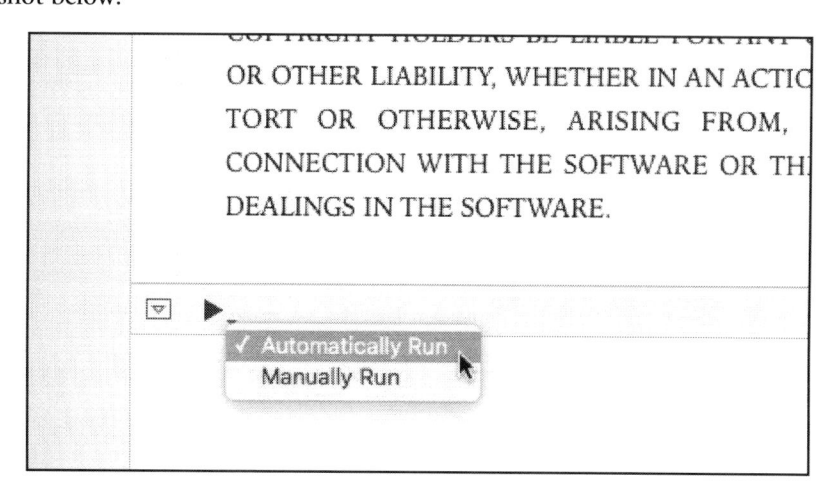

In the left Navigator pane, pick the first page named **replay**. You can then close the Navigator pane using its visibility control, which is the leftmost button at the top-right of the Xcode window.

Your layout should now look like this:

You're now all set! It's time to learn about the first group of time-based operators: **buffering operators**.

> **Note:** This playground uses advanced features of Xcode playgrounds. Xcode does not fully support importing linked frameworks from within files in the common `Sources` subfolder. Therefore, each playground page has to include a small bit of code (the part of `TimelineView` that depends on RxSwift) to function properly. Just ignore this code and leave it at bottom of the page.

Buffering operators

The first group of time-based operators deal with buffering. They will either replay past elements to new subscribers, or buffer them and deliver them in bursts. They allow you to control how and when past and new elements get delivered.

Replaying past elements

When a sequence emits items, you'll often need to make sure that a future subscriber receives some or all of the past items. This is the purpose of the replay(_:) and replayAll() operators.

To learn how to use them, you'll start coding in the **replay** page of the playground. To visualize what replay(_:) does, you'll display elements on a timeline. The playground contains custom classes to make it easy to display animated timelines.

Start by adding some definitions:

```
let elementsPerSecond = 1
let maxElements = 5
let replayedElements = 1
let replayDelay: TimeInterval = 3
```

You'll create an observable that emits elements at a frequency of elementsPerSecond. You'll also cap the total number of elements emitted, and control how many elements are "played back" to new subscribers. To build this emitting observable, use the Observable<T>.create function and some dispatch magic:

```
let sourceObservable = Observable<Int>.create { observer in
    var value = 1
    let timer = DispatchSource.timer(interval: 1.0 / Double(elementsPerSecond), queue: .main) {
```

The DispatchSource.timer function is an extension to DispatchSource defined in the playground Sources folder. It simplifies the creation of repeating timers. Add the code to emit elements:

```
        if value <= maxElements {
            observer.onNext(value)
            value = value + 1
        }
    }
    return Disposables.create {
        timer.suspend()
    }
}
```

Note that for the purpose of this example, you don't care about *completing* the observable. It simply emits as many elements as instructed and never completes.

Now add the replay functionality to the observable:

```
.replay(replayedElements)
```

This operator creates a new sequence which records the last `replayedElements` emitted by the source observable. Every time a new observer subscribes, it immediately receives the buffered elements (if any) and keeps receiving any new element like a normal subscription does.

To visualize the actual effect of `replay(_:)`, create a couple of `TimelineView` views. This class is defined at bottom of the playground page and relies on the `TimelineViewBase` class in the **Sources** group of the playground. It provides a live visualization of events emitted by an observable. Append, below the code you wrote previously:

```
let sourceTimeline = TimelineView<Int>.make()
let replayedTimeline = TimelineView<Int>.make()
```

You're going to use a `UIStackView` for convenience. It'll display the source (live) observable as viewed by an immediate subscriber, as well as another representation as viewed by a subscriber coming later. Create the stack view:

```
let stack = UIStackView.makeVertical([
  UILabel.makeTitle("replay"),
  UILabel.make("Emit \(elementsPerSecond) per second:"),
  sourceTimeline,
  UILabel.make("Replay \(replayedElements) after \(replayDelay) sec:"),
  replayedTimeline])
```

This looks complicated, but it's actually fairly straightforward. It simply creates a few vertically stacked views. The `UIStackView.makeVertical(_:)` and `UILabel.make(_:)` functions are convenience extensions local to this playground.

Now prepare an immediate subscriber and display what it receives in the top timeline:

```
_ = sourceObservable.subscribe(sourceTimeline)
```

The `TimelineView` class implements the `ObserverType` RxSwift protocol. Therefore, you can subscribe it to an observable sequence and it will receive the sequence's events. Every time a new event occurs (element emitted, sequence completed or errored out), `TimelineView` displays it on the timeline. Emitted elements are shown in green, completion in black and errors in red.

> **Note:** Did you notice that the code is ignoring the `Disposable` returned by the subscription? Good! This example code is not keeping them on purpose, as the playground page drops everything when refreshing. In your applications, remember to always keep long-running subscriptions in a `DisposeBag`!

Next, you want to subscribe again to the source observable, but with a slight delay:

```
DispatchQueue.main.asyncAfter(deadline: .now() + replayDelay) {
    _ = sourceObservable.subscribe(replayedTimeline)
}
```

This displays elements received by the second subscription in another timeline view. You'll see the timeline view shortly, I promise!

Now since `replay(_:)` creates a **connectable observable**, you need to connect it to its underlying source to start receiving items. If you forget this, subscribers will never receive anything.

> **Note:** Connectable observables are a special class of observables. Regardless of their number of subscribers, they won't start emitting items until you call their `connect()` method. While this is beyond the scope of this chapter, remember that a few operators return `ConnectableObservable<E>`, not `Observable<E>`. These operators are:
>
> `replay(_:)`
>
> `replayAll()`
>
> `multicast(_:)`
>
> `publish()`
>
> Replay operators are covered in this chapter. The last two operators are advanced, and only touched on briefly in this book. They allow sharing a single subscription to an observable, regardless of the number of observers.

So add this code to connect:

```
_ = sourceObservable.connect()
```

Finally, set up the host view in which the stack view will display. The playground has a utility function to keep your code simple:

```
let hostView = setupHostView()
hostView.addSubview(stack)
hostView
```

Once you save these source changes, Xcode will recompile the playground code and ... look at the Assistant Editor pane! Finally!

You'll see two timelines. The top timeline reflects an observer named `connect()` that subscribes before you. The bottom timeline is the one where subscription occurs after a delay. The source observable emits numbers for convenience. This way you can see the progress of emitted elements.

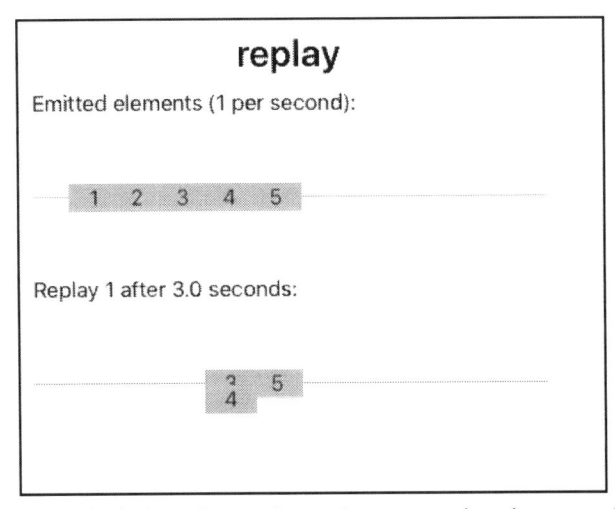

replay

Emitted elements (1 per second):

1 2 3 4 5

Replay 1 after 3.0 seconds:

3 5
4

You may need to wait a little bit after making changes to the playground to have the timeline view show up, especially on slower computers. Such is life with Xcode.

> **Note:** As exciting it is to see a live observable diagram. it might confuse at first. Static timelines usually have their elements aligned to the left, but if you think twice about it, they also have the most recent ones on the right side just as the animated diagrams you observe right now.

In the settings you used, `replayedElements` is equal to 1. It configures the `replay(_:)` operator to only buffer the last element from the source observable. The animated timeline shows that the second subscriber receives elements **3** and **4** in the same time frame. By the time it subscribes, it gets both the latest buffer element (**3**) and the one that happens to be emitted just right when subscription occurs. The timeline view shows them stacked up since the time they arrive is about the same (although not *exactly* the same).

> **Note:** You can now play with the `replayDelay` and `replayedElements` constants. Observe the effect of tweaking the number of replayed (buffered) elements. You can also tweak the total number of elements emitted by the source observable using `maxElements`. Set it to a very large value for continuous emission.

Unlimited replay

The second replay operator you can use is `replayAll()`. This one should be used with caution: only use it in scenarios where you know the total number of buffered elements will stay reasonable. For example, it's appropriate to use `replayAll()` in the context of HTTP requests. You know the approximate memory impact of retaining the data returned by a query. On the other hand, using `replayAll()` on a sequence that may not terminate and may produce a lot of data will quickly clog your memory. This could grow to the point where the OS jettisons your application!

To experiment with `replayAll()`, replace:

```
.replay(replayedElements)
```

with:

```
.replayAll()
```

Watch the effect on the timeline. You will see all buffered elements emitted instantly upon the second subscription.

Controlled buffering

Now that you touched on replayable sequences, you can look at a more advanced topic: controlled buffering. You'll first look at the `buffer(timeSpan:count:scheduler:)` operator. Switch to the second page in the playground called **buffer**. As in the previous example, you'll begin with some constants:

```
let bufferTimeSpan: RxTimeInterval = 4
let bufferMaxCount = 2
```

These constants define the behavior for the `buffer` operator you'll soon add to the code. For this example, you'll manually feed a subject with values. Add:

```
let sourceObservable = PublishSubject<String>()
```

You will push short strings (a single emoji) to this observable. Create the timeline visualizations and the stack to contain them just like before.

```
let sourceTimeline = TimelineView<String>.make()
let bufferedTimeline = TimelineView<Int>.make()

let stack = UIStackView.makeVertical([
  UILabel.makeTitle("buffer"),
  UILabel.make("Emitted elements:"),
  sourceTimeline,
  UILabel.make("Buffered elements (at most \(bufferMaxCount) every \(bufferTimeSpan) seconds):"),
  bufferedTimeline])
```

Subscribe to fill the top timeline with events, like you did in the **replay** playground page:

```
_ = sourceObservable.subscribe(sourceTimeline)
```

The buffered timeline will display the number of elements contained in each buffered array:

```
sourceObservable
    .buffer(timeSpan: bufferTimeSpan, count: bufferMaxCount,
  scheduler: MainScheduler.instance)
    .map { $0.count }
    .subscribe(bufferedTimeline)
```

What's happening here? Breaking it down:

- You want to receive arrays of elements from the source observable.
- Each array can hold **at most** `bufferMaxCount` elements.
- If that many elements are received before `bufferTimeSpan` expires, the operator will emit buffered elements and reset its timer.
- In a delay of `bufferTimeSpan` after the last emitted group, **buffer** will emit an array. If no element has been received during this timeframe, the array will be empty.

To activate your timeline views, set up the host view:

```
let hostView = setupHostView()
hostView.addSubview(stack)
hostView
```

Even though there is no activity on the source observable, you can witness empty buffers on the buffered timeline. The `buffer(_:scheduler:)` operators emits empty arrays at regular intervals if nothing has been received from its source observable. The `0`s mean that zero elements have been emitted from the source sequence.

You can start feeding the raw observable with data and observe the impact on the buffered observable. First, try pushing three elements over five seconds. Append:

```
DispatchQueue.main.asyncAfter(deadline: .now() + 5) {
  sourceObservable.onNext("🐱")
  sourceObservable.onNext("🐱")
  sourceObservable.onNext("🐱")
}
```

Can you guess what the effect will be? Look how the timeline moves:

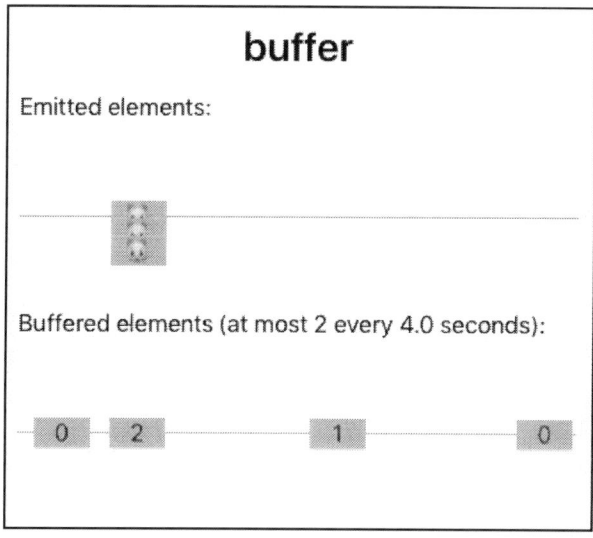

Each box shows the number of elements in each emitted array:

- At first the buffered timeline emits an empty array — there's no element in the source observable yet.

- Then you push three elements on the source observable.

- The buffered timeline immediately gets an array of two elements because it's the maximum count you specified (due to the `bufferMaxCount` constant).

- Four seconds elapse, and an array with just one element is emitted. This is the last of the three elements that have been pushed to the source observable.

As you can see, the buffer immediately emits an array of elements when it reaches full capacity, then waits for the specified delay, or until it's full again, before it emits a new array.

You can play a bit more with different buffering scenarios. Remove the `DispatchQueue` that emits elements, and add this instead:

```
let elementsPerSecond = 0.7
let timer = DispatchSource.timer(interval: 1.0 / Double(elementsPerSecond), queue: .main) {
  sourceObservable.onNext("🐱")
}
```

The timeline is very different! As before, you can tweak the constants (buffering time, buffering limit, elements per second) to see how grouping works.

Windows of buffered observables

A last buffering technique very close to `buffer(timeSpan:count:scheduler:)` is `window(timeSpan:count:scheduler:)`. It has roughly the same signature and nearly does the same thing. The only difference is that it emits an `Observable` of the buffered items, instead of emitting an array.

You're going to build a slightly more elaborate timeline view. Since windowed sequences emit multiple observables, it will be beneficial to visualize them separately. Get started in the **window** playground page:

```
let elementsPerSecond = 3
let windowTimeSpan: RxTimeInterval = 4
let windowMaxCount = 10
let sourceObservable = PublishSubject<String>()
```

You're going to look at how timed output is grouped in windowed observables by pushing strings to a subject. As usual, first add the stack view code:

```
let sourceTimeline = TimelineView<String>.make()

let stack = UIStackView.makeVertical([
  UILabel.makeTitle("window"),
  UILabel.make("Emitted elements (\(elementsPerSecond) per sec.):"),
  sourceTimeline,
  UILabel.make("Windowed observables (at most \(windowMaxCount) every \(windowTimeSpan) sec):")])
```

And this time add a timer to push elements to the source observable:

```
let timer = DispatchSource.timer(interval: 1.0 / Double(elementsPerSecond), queue: .main) {
  sourceObservable.onNext("🐱")
}
```

Then fill up the source timeline:

```
_ = sourceObservable.subscribe(sourceTimeline)
```

You're now at a point where you want to see each emitted observable separately. To this end, you'll insert a new timeline every time `window(timeSpan:count:scheduler:)` emits a new observable. Previous observables will move downwards. Append:

```
_ = sourceObservable
    .window(timeSpan: windowTimeSpan, count: windowMaxCount,
  scheduler: MainScheduler.instance)
```

This is your windowed observable. How can you handle emitted observables? Using your trusted `flatMap(_:)` operator of course! Chain this under the `window` operator:

```
.flatMap { windowedObservable -> Observable<(TimelineView<Int>,
  String?)> in
    let timeline = TimelineView<Int>.make()
    stack.insert(timeline, at: 4)
    stack.keep(atMost: 8)
    return windowedObservable
      .map { value in (timeline, value) }
      .concat(Observable.just((timeline, nil)))
}
```

Obviously this is the tricky part. Try to figure out the code yourself first, and then fall back on the following:

- Every time `flatMap(_:)` gets a new observable, you insert a new timeline view.

- You then map the observable of items to an observable of tuple. The goal is to transport both the value and the timeline in which to display it.

- Once this inner observable completes, you `concat(_:)` a single tuple so you can mark the timeline as complete.

- You `flatMap(_:)` the sequence of resulting observables of tuple to a single sequence of tuples.

- You subscribe to the resulting observable and fill up timelines as you receive tuples.

> **Note:** In trying to keep the code short, you're doing something that is generally not advisable in Rx code: you're adding side effects to an operator that's supposed to just be transforming data. The right solution would be to perform side effects using a `do(onNext:)` operator. This is left as an exercise in this chapter's challenges!

Finally, you need to subscribe and display elements in each timeline. Since you mapped the elements to the actual timeline they belong to, this becomes easy. Chain this code to the previous:

```
.subscribe(onNext: { tuple in
  let (timeline, value) = tuple
  if let value = value {
    timeline.add(.Next(value))
  } else {
    timeline.add(.Completed(true))
  }
})
```

The `value` in the tuple is a `String?`: the convention here is that if it is `nil`, it means the sequence completed. The code pushes either a `next` or a `completed` event to the timeline.

Finally, instantiate the host view as usual:

```
let hostView = setupHostView()
hostView.addSubview(stack)
hostView
```

Let the playground run. Things quickly get interesting, as `window(timeSpan:count:scheduler:)` emits new sequences:

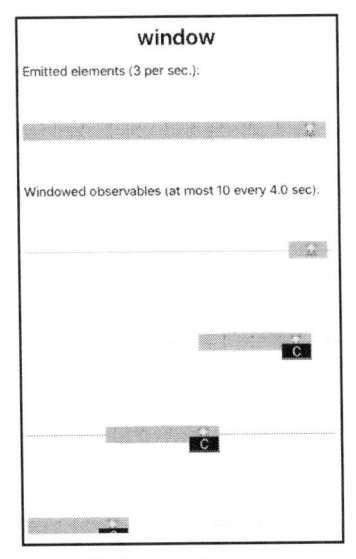

Starting from the second timeline, all the timelines you see are "most recent first". This screenshot was taken with a setting of five elements maximum per windowed observable, and a four second window. This means that a new observable is produced at least every four seconds. It will emit at most five elements before completing.

If the source observable emits more than four elements during the window time, a new observable is produced, and the cycle starts again.

Time-shifting operators

Every now and again, you need to travel in time. While RxSwift can't help with fixing your past relationship mistakes, it has the ability to freeze time for a little while to let you wait until self-cloning is available.

Next, you'll look into two time related operators. Open the **delay** playground page to get started.

Delayed subscriptions

You'll start with `delaySubscription(_:scheduler:)`. Since you are now used to creating animated timelines, this page comes with most of the setup code ready. Find the comment `Setup the delayed subscription` in the source and insert this code after it:

```
_ = sourceObservable
    .delaySubscription(RxTimeInterval(delayInSeconds), scheduler: MainScheduler.instance)
    .subscribe(delayedTimeline)
```

The idea behind the `delaySubscription(_:scheduler:)` is, as the name implies, to delay the time a subscriber starts receiving elements from its subscription. Run the example if it's not already running. In the right timeline view, you can observe that the second timeline starts picking up elements after the delay specified by `delayInSeconds`.

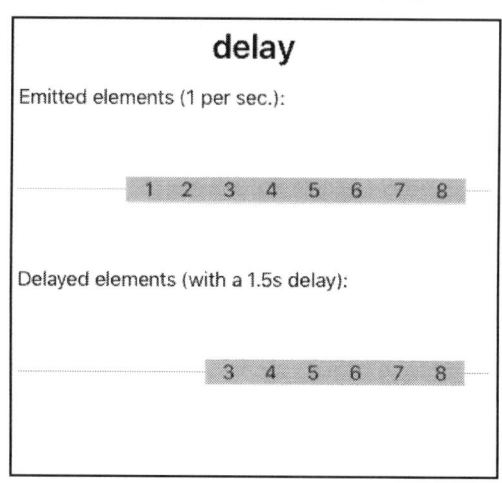

delay

Emitted elements (1 per sec.):

1 2 3 4 5 6 7 8

Delayed elements (with a 1.5s delay):

3 4 5 6 7 8

> **Note:** In Rx, some observables are called "cold" while others are "hot". Cold observables start emitting elements when you subscribe to them. Hot observables are more like permanent sources you happen to look at at some point (think of Notifications). When delaying a subscription, it won't make a difference if the observable is cold. If it's hot, you may skip elements, as in this example.
>
> Hot and cold observables are a tricky topic that can take some time getting your head around. Remember that cold observables emit events only when subscribed to, but hot observables emit events independent of being subscribed to.

Delayed elements

The other kind of delay in RxSwift lets you time-shift the whole sequence. Instead of subscribing late, the operator subscribes *immediately* to the source observable, but delays every emitted element by the specified amount of time. The net result is a concrete time-shift.

To try this out, stay in the **delay** playground page you just used. Replace the delayed subscription (that you just added) with:

```
_ = sourceObservable
  .delay(RxTimeInterval(delayInSeconds), scheduler: MainScheduler.instance)
  .subscribe(delayedTimeline)
```

As you can see the code is similar. You just replaced `delaySubscription(_:scheduler:)` with `delay(_:scheduler:)`. Look at the timelines. Can you spot the difference?

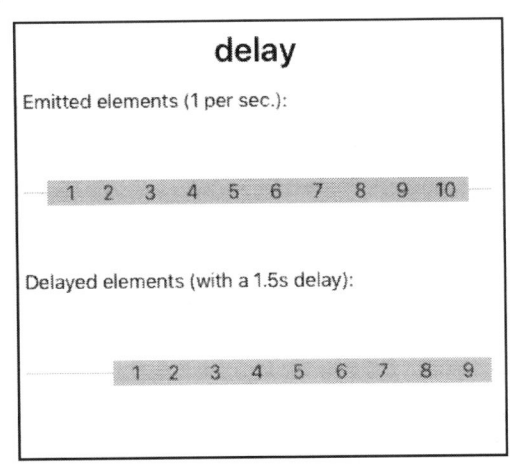

```
                        delay
Emitted elements (1 per sec.):

       1  2  3  4  5  6  7  8  9  10


Delayed elements (with a 1.5s delay):


                 1  2  3  4  5  6  7  8  9
```

In the previous example, delaying the subscription (with the default settings) made you miss the first two elements from the source observable. When using the `delay(_:scheduler:)` operator, you time-shift the elements and won't miss any. Again, the *subscription* occurs immediately. You simply "see" the items with a delay.

Timer operators

A common need in any kind of application is a *timer*. iOS and macOS come with several timing solutions. Historically, `NSTimer` did the job, but had a confusing ownership model that made it tricky to get just right. More recently, the `dispatch` framework offered timers through the use of dispatch sources. It's a better solution than `NSTimer`, but the API is still somewhat complicated unless you wrap it, like we did in this playground.

RxSwift provides a simple and efficient solution for both one-shot and repeating timers. It integrates perfectly with sequences and offers both cancellation and composability with other sequences.

Intervals

This chapter used `DispatchSource` several times to create interval timers through a handy custom function. You could replace these instances with RxSwift's `Observable.interval(_:scheduler:)` function. It produces an infinite observable sequence on `Int` values (effectively a counter) sent at the selected interval on the specified scheduler.

Go back to the **replay** playground page. Towards the beginning of the code, you created a source observable. You used `DispatchSource.timer(_:queue:)` to create a timer and feed observers with values.

Delete this code, starting at `let sourceObservable = Observable<Int>.create {...` and up to (and including) `replayAll();` and then insert instead:

```
let sourceObservable = Observable<Int>
   .interval(RxTimeInterval(1.0 / Double(elementsPerSecond)),
  scheduler: MainScheduler.instance)
   .replay(replayedElements)
```

And. That's. All.

Interval timers are incredibly easy to create with RxSwift. Not only that, but they are also easy to cancel: since `Observable.interval(_:scheduler:)` generates an observable sequence, subscriptions can simply `dispose()` the returned disposable to cancel the subscription and stop the timer. Very cool!

It is notable that the first value is emitted at the specified duration after a subscriber starts observing the sequence. Also, the timer won't start before this point. The subscription is the trigger that kicks it off.

> **Note:** As you can see in the timeline view, values emitted by `Observable.interval(_:scheduler:)` are signed integers starting from 0. Should you need different values, you can simply `map(_:)` them. In most real life cases, the value emitted by the timer is simply ignored. But it can make a convenient index.

One-shot or repeating timers

You may want a more powerful timer observable. You can use the `Observable.timer(_:period:scheduler:)` operator which is very much like `Observable.interval(_:scheduler:)` but adds the following features:

- You can specify a "due date" as the time that elapsed between the point of subscription and the first emitted value.

- The repeat period is *optional*. If you don't specify one, the timer observable will emit once, then complete.

Can you see how handy this can be? Give it a go. In the playground, open the **delay** page. Locate the place where you used the `delay(_:scheduler:)` operator. Replace the whole block of code with:

```
_ = Observable<Int>
    .timer(3, scheduler: MainScheduler.instance)
    .flatMap { _ in
        sourceObservable.delay(RxTimeInterval(delayInSeconds),
    scheduler: MainScheduler.instance)
    }
    .subscribe(delayedTimeline)
```

A timer triggering another timer? This *is* Inception! There are several benefits to using this over Dispatch:

- The whole chain is more readable (more "Rx-y").

- Since the subscription returns a disposable, you can cancel at any point before the first or second timer triggers with a single observable.
- Using the `flatMap(_:)` operator, you can produce timer sequences without having to jump through hoops with `Dispatch` asynchronous closures.

Timeouts

You'll complete this roundup of time-based operators with a special one: **timeout**. Its primary purpose is to semantically distinguish an actual timer from a timeout (error) condition. Therefore, when a timeout operator fires, it emits an `RxError.TimeoutError` error event; if not caught, it terminates the sequence.

Open the **timeout** playground page. Create a simple button:

```
let button = UIButton(type: .system)
button.setTitle("Press me now!", for: .normal)
button.sizeToFit()
```

You're going to use an extension from RxCocoa that turns button taps into an observable sequence. You'll learn more about RxCocoa in the following chapters. For now, the goal is to:

- Capture button taps.
- If the button is pressed within five seconds, print something and terminate the sequence.
- If the button is not pressed, print the error condition,

Prepare the timeline view and stack it up with the button:

```
let tapsTimeline = TimelineView<String>.make()

let stack = UIStackView.makeVertical([
  button,
  UILabel.make("Taps on button above"),
  tapsTimeline])
```

Setup the observable and connect it to the timeline view:

```
let _ = button
  .rx.tap
  .map { _ in "•" }
  .timeout(5, scheduler: MainScheduler.instance)
  .subscribe(tapsTimeline)
```

And as usual, add the stack to the host view to kick off the animation:

```
let hostView = setupHostView()
hostView.addSubview(stack)
hostView
```

If you click the button within five seconds (and within five seconds of subsequent presses), you'll see your taps on the timeline. Stop clicking, and five seconds after that, as the timeout fires, the timeline will stop with an Error.

An alternate version of `timeout(_:scheduler:)` takes an observable and, when the timeout fires, switches the subscription to this observable instead of emitting an error.

There are many uses for this form of timeout, one of which is to emit a value (instead of an error) then complete normally.

To try this, change the `timeout(_:scheduler:)` call in the playground to:

```
.timeout(5, other: Observable.just("X"), scheduler:
  MainScheduler.instance)
```

Now instead of the error indicator, you see the X element and a regular completion. Mission accomplished!

Challenges

Challenge 1: Circumscribe side effects

In the discussion of the `window(_:scheduler:)` operator, you created timelines on the fly inside the closure of a `flatMap(_:)` operator. While this was done to keep the code short, one of the guidelines of reactive programming is to "not leave the monad". In other words, avoid side effects except for specific areas created to apply side effects. Here, the "side effect" is the creation of a new timeline in a spot where only a transformation should occur.

Your task is to find an alternate way to do this. You can consider several approaches; try and pick the one that seems the most elegant to you. When finished, compare it with the proposed solution!

There are several possible approaches to tackle this challenge. The most effective will be to split the work into multiple observables then join them later.

Make the windowed observable a separate one that you use to produce two separate sequences: one that prepares the timeline views (remember that side effects can be performed with the `do(onNext:)` operator), and one that takes both the produced timeline view and the source sequence element (hint: use a combination of `zip` and `flatMap`) to generate a contextual value (timeline view and sequence) every time `window` emits a new sequence.

Section III: iOS Apps with RxCocoa

Since Rx is a multi-platform framework, it doesn't make any assumptions on which device your Rx powered app is running. RxSwift closely follows the general API design that RxPython, RxRuby, RxJS, and all other platforms conform to, so it does not include any specific features or integrations with UIKit or Cocoa to aid you in developing for iOS or macOS.

RxCocoa is a standalone library (though it's bundled with RxSwift) that allows you to use many prebuilt features to integrate better with UIKit and Cocoa.

RxCocoa will provide you with out-of-the-box classes to do reactive networking, react to user interactions, bind data models to UI controls, and more.

Chapter 12: Beginning RxCocoa

Chapter 13: Intermediate RxCocoa

Chapter 12: Beginning RxCocoa

By Junior Bontognali

In previous chapters, you were introduced to the basics of RxSwift, its functional parts and how to create, subscribe and dispose observables. It's important to understand these topics well in order to properly leverage RxSwift in your applications and to avoid unexpected side effects and unwanted results.

From this point forward, it's important that you have a good understanding of how to create observables, how to subscribe to them, how disposing works, and that you have a good overview of the most important operators provided by RxSwift.

In this chapter, you'll be introduced to another framework, which is part of the original RxSwift repository: **RxCocoa**.

RxCocoa works on all platforms, targeting the need of each one: iOS (iPhone, iPad, Apple Watch), Apple TV and macOS. Each platform has a set of custom wrappers, which provide a set of built-in extensions to many UI controls and other SDK classes. In this chapter, you will use the ones provided for iOS on the iPhone and iPad.

> **Note:** At present, the RxCocoa support in iOS is the most complete, followed by Apple Watch and macOS. The macOS implementation still lacks a few more advanced wrappers, but it includes all the basics to create a cross-platform solution sharing the logic underneath. You'll see how to do this in some of the later chapters in this book.

Getting started

The starter project for this chapter is an iOS application named **Wundercast**. As suggested by the name, it's a weather application using the current weather information provided by OpenWeatherMap http://openweathermap.org. The project has already been set up for you using CocoaPods and includes RxSwift, RxCocoa and SwiftyJSON for a better handling of the JSON data returned by the OpenWeatherMap API.

Before starting, open `Podfile` and check the project's dependencies to better understand what you will be using in this chapter. To install RxCocoa, you have an extra line to include the relevant CocoaPod:

```
`pod 'RxCocoa', '~> 3.0'`.
```

RxCocoa is released alongside RxSwift. Both frameworks share the same release schedule, so usually the latest RxSwift release has the same version number as RxCocoa.

Now, open Terminal and navigate to the root of the project. Perform the classic `pod install` command to pull in all dependencies so you're ready to compile and run the project.

At this point, RxCocoa is part of the project and the workspace has been correctly created. I recommend that you open the workspace, navigate the pod project and inspect what comes with RxCocoa. In this project, you'll use the two wrappers for `UITextField` and `UILabel` quite a bit, so it's a good idea to inspect these two files to understand how they work.

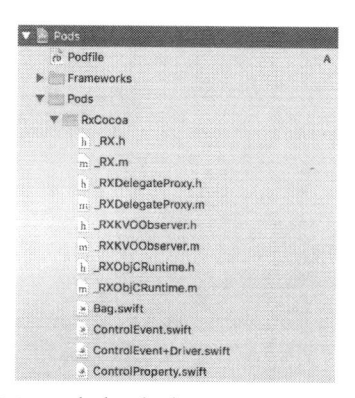

Open `UITextField+Rx.swift` and check the contents. You will immediately notice that the file is really short — less than 50 lines of code — and that the only property is a `ControlProperty<String?>` named `text`.

What's a `ControlProperty`, you say? Don't worry — you'll learn about this a bit later. What you need to know is that this type is a special kind of `Subject` that can be subscribed to and can have new values injected. The name of the property gives you a good idea about what can be observed: `text` means that the property is directly related to the text inside the `UITextField`.

Now open `UILabel+Rx.swift`. Here you can see two new properties: `text` and `attributedText`. As before, both names are related to the original `UILabel` implementation, so there are no name conflicts, and their purpose is clear. There's a new type used in both called `UIBindingObserver`.

This observer, similar to `ControlProperty`, is special and is dedicated to working with UI. `UIBindingObserver` is used to bind the UI with the underlying logic — and importantly, it can't bind errors. If an error is sent to an `UIBindingObserver`, this would call `fatalError()` when running a Debug schema in development, but will be added to the error log when running the app in production.

This short introduction to RxCocoa gave you a glimpse into what is it all about, but now it's time to get to work.

Configure the API key

OpenWeatherMap requires an API key to work, so sign up by following the instructions at https://home.openweathermap.org/users/sign_up.

Once you've signed up, navigate to the API key dedicated page https://home.openweathermap.org/api_keys and generate a new key to use in this project.

Copy the API key and paste it in **ApiController.swift** at the following spot:

```
private let apiKey = "[YOUR KEY]"
```

At this point, you're ready to proceed and receive data from the API.

Using RxCocoa with basic UIKit controls

First make sure you've completed the setup by building the project; you're now ready to input some data and ask the API to return the weather of a given city along with the temperature, humidity and the city name. The city name will give you some confirmation the data displayed actually belongs to the city you queried.

Displaying the data using RxCocoa

If you already ran the project, you're probably wondering why the app displays data before actually retrieving any from the API. The reason is simple: you can be sure that the manually injected data is correct, so if something fails you know it's somewhere in the API handling code — and not in your Rx logic and UI-related code.

In **ApiController.swift**, you'll see a `struct` which will be used as a data model to correctly map the JSON data structure to something more easily digested by Swift:

```swift
struct Weather {
  let cityName: String
  let temperature: Int
  let humidity: Int
  let icon: String
  ...
}
```

> **Note**: Using a `struct` here aids in creating cleaner code, since it requires all its properties to have a value at creation time. In case a value isn't available, you could always use `"N/A"` or a similar string.

Still in **ApiController.swift**, take a look at the following function:

```swift
func currentWeather(city: String) -> Observable<Weather> {
  // Placeholder call
  return Observable.just(
    Weather(
      cityName: city,
      temperature: 20,
      humidity: 90,
      icon: iconNameToChar(icon: "01d"))
  )
}
```

This function returns a fake city named `RxCity` and displays some dummy data, which you can use instead of real data until you retrieve real weather information from the server.

Having dummy data helps simplify the development process and gives you the chance to work with an actual data structure, even without a working internet connection.

Open `ViewController.swift`; this is the one single view controller present in this project. The main goal of this project is to connect this single view controller to `ApiController`, which is going to provide the data.

The result is a uni-directional data flow:

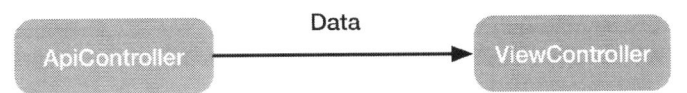

```
                    Data
   ApiController  ────────▶  ViewController
```

As explained in previous chapters, observables are entities capable of receiving data and letting all subscribers know that some data has arrived, pushing values to be processed.

For this reason, the correct place to subscribe to an observable while working in view controllers is inside `viewDidLoad`. This is because you need to subscribe as early as possible, but only after the view has been loaded.

Subscribing later might lead to missed events or parts of UI might be visible before you bind data to them.

Therefore you have to create all subscriptions *before* the application creates or requests data that needs to be processed and displayed to the user.

To retrieve the data, add the following code to the end of `viewDidLoad`:

```swift
ApiController.shared.currentWeather(city: "RxSwift")
  .observeOn(MainScheduler.instance)
  .subscribe(onNext: { data in
    self.tempLabel.text = "\(data.temperature)° C"
    self.iconLabel.text = data.icon
    self.humidityLabel.text = "\(data.humidity)%"
    self.cityNameLabel.text = data.cityName
  })
```

Build and run your app, and you should have the following result:

The application is correctly displaying the dummy data, but there are two problems:

1. There's a compiler warning
2. You still don't make use of the input text field.

The first problem is pointed out by the following warning displayed by Xcode:

> ⚠️ Result of call to 'subscribe(onNext:onError:onCompleted:onDisposed:)' is unused

As in previous chapters, a subscription returns a disposable object which will cancel the subscription when necessary. In this case, the subscription must be canceled when the view controller is dismissed. To achieve this, add the following property to the view controller class:

```
let bag = DisposeBag()
```

...and transform the previous code adding the correct `disposed(by:)` function at after the subscription:

```
ApiController.shared.currentWeather(city: "RxSwift")
  .observeOn(MainScheduler.instance)
  .subscribe(onNext: { data in
    self.tempLabel.text = "\(data.temperature)° C"
    self.iconLabel.text = data.icon
    self.humidityLabel.text = "\(data.humidity)%"
    self.cityNameLabel.text = data.cityName
  })
  .disposed(by:bag)
```

This will cancel and dispose the subscription whenever the view controller is released. This guards against wasting resources, but also avoids unexpected events or other side effects that can happen when a subscription isn't disposed.

You've solved the first issue, so you can turn your attention to the text field. As previously mentioned, RxCocoa adds a lot on top of Cocoa, so you can start using this functionality to achieve your ultimate goal. The framework uses the power of **protocol extensions** and adds the `rx` space to many of the UIKit components. This means you can type `searchCityName.rx.` to see the available properties and methods:

```
    searchCityName.rx.
e<KVORepresentable?> observeWeakly(type: KVORepresentable.Protc
e<KVORepresentable?> observeWeakly(type: KVORepresentable.Protc
e<RawRepresentable?> observeWeakly(type: RawRepresentable.Protc
e<RawRepresentable?> observeWeakly(type: RawRepresentable.Protc
    Observable<[Any]> sentMessage(selector: Selector)
rolProperty<String?> text
    TextInput<Base> textInput
rolProperty<String?> value
```

There's one you've already explored before: `text`. This function returns an observable that is a `ControlProperty<String?>`, which conforms to both `ObservableType` and `ObserverType` so you can subscribe to it and also emit new values (thus setting the field text).

Knowing the basics behind `ControlProperty`, you can improve the code to take advantage of the text field to display the city name in the dummy data. Add to `viewDidLoad()`:

```
searchCityName.rx.text
  .filter { ($0 ?? "").characters.count > 0 }
  .flatMap { text in
    return ApiController.shared.currentWeather(city: text ?? "Error")
      .catchErrorJustReturn(ApiController.Weather.empty)
  }
```

The above code will return a new observable with the data to display. `currentWeather` does not accept `nil` or empty values so you filter those out. Then you fetch the weather data by using the provided `ApiController` class. You've already completed similar tasks involving networking in the previous chapters so you won't go into more detail about that here.

Continue your previous block of code by switching to the correct thread and displaying the data:

```
  .observeOn(MainScheduler.instance)
  .subscribe(onNext: { data in
    self.tempLabel.text = "\(data.temperature)° C"
    self.iconLabel.text = data.icon
    self.humidityLabel.text = "\(data.humidity)%"
    self.cityNameLabel.text = data.cityName
  })
  .disposed(by: bag)
```

Once you have switched to `MainScheduler` and the main thread, you update all UI controls with the current weather data. The diagram below should help you visualize the flow of the code:

searchCityName --> filter { length > 0 } --> flatMap { currentWeather } --> subscribe(...)

At this point, whenever you change the input, the label will update with the name of the city — but right now it will always return your dummy data. You know the the application displays the dummy data correctly, so it's time to get the real data from the API.

> **Note**: The `catchErrorJustReturn` operator will be explained later in this book. It's required to prevent the observable from being disposed when you receive an error from the API. For instance, an invalid city name returns a 404 as an error for `NSURLSession`. In this case, you want to return an empty value so the app won't stop working if it encounters an error.

Retrieving data from the OpenWeather API

To retrieve live weather data from the API, you'll need an active internet connection. The API returns a structured JSON response, and the following are the useful bits:

```
{
  "weather": [
    {
      "id": 741,
      "main": "Fog",
      "description": "fog",
      "icon": "50d"
    }
  ],
}
```

The above data is related to the *current* weather; the `icon` elements is used to display the correct icon for the current conditions. The section below deals with the temperature and humidity data:

```
  "main": {
    "temp": 271.55,
    "pressure": 1043,
    "humidity": 96,
    "temp_min": 268.15,
    "temp_max": 273.15
  }
}
```

Don't freak out — those temperatures are in Kelvin, not Celsius or Fahrenheit! :]

Inside **ApiController.swift**, there's a function named `iconNameToChar` that takes a `String` (more precisely, the `icon` data from the JSON) and returns another `String`, which is the UTF-8 code of the weather icon that visually represents the current weather in your application. In the same file, there's a convenience function `buildRequest` to create network requests; this uses RxCocoa's wrapper for `NSURLSession` to perform network requests. This function is responsible for:

- Getting the base URL and appending the components to correctly build the GET (or POST) request

- Using the API key you generated at the beginning of this chapter
- Setting the content type of the request to `application/json`
- Asking for `metrics` as `units` (in this case, degrees Kelvin)
- Returning the data mapped as JSON objects

The last part is collapsed in a single `return` line:

```
//[...]
return session.rx.data(request: request).map { JSON(data: $0) }
```

This uses the `rx` extension of RxCocoa around `NSURLSession`, which uses the `data` function. This in turn returns an `Observable<Data>`. This data is used as the input to a `map` function used to transform the raw data into a SwiftyJSON data structure of type `JSON`.

It's always good to have a visualization when working with Rx in general, and an updated diagram with a bit more detail will probably help you understand what's happing inside the `ApiController`:

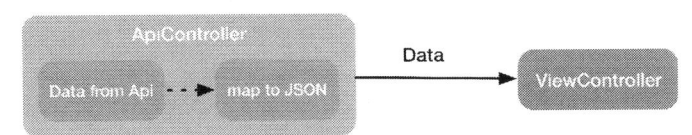

Switching from the dummy data to the actual data request is simple. You need to replace the `Observable.just([...])` call with a real data network request. The OpenWeatherMap API documentation http://openweathermap.org/current explains how to request the current weather for a given city name via `api.openweathermap.org/data/2.5/weather?q={city name}`.

In **ApiController.swift**, replace the dummy `currentWeather(city:)` method with:

```
func currentWeather(city: String) -> Observable<Weather> {
  return buildRequest(pathComponent: "weather", params: [("q", city)])
    .map { json in
      return Weather(
        cityName: json["name"].string ?? "Unknown",
        temperature: json["main"]["temp"].int ?? -1000,
        humidity: json["main"]["humidity"].int ?? 0,
        icon: iconNameToChar(icon: json["weather"][0]["icon"].string ?? "e")
      )
    }
}
```

The request returns a `JSON` object, which can be converted with some fallback values to the `Weather` data structure expected by your user interface.

Build and run, and enter **London** for the city. You should receive the following result:

Your app now correctly displays the data retrieved from the server. You've used a couple of RxCocoa features so far but you're going to see the real benefits when you move on to RxCocoa's more advanced features in the next section.

> **Note**: If you like going the extra mile, remove the `catchErrorJustReturn` operator inside `flatmap`. As soon as you receive a 404 due to an invalid city name, (you'll see this in the logs), the application will stop working correctly because your observable has errored out and is then disposed.

Binding observables

Binding is somewhat controversial — for example, Apple never released their binding system, named Cocoa Bindings, on iOS, even though it had been an important part of macOS for a long time. The Mac bindings are very advanced and somewhat too coupled with the specific Apple-provided class in the macOS SDK.

RxCocoa offers a somewhat simpler solution, which depends only on few types included with the framework. Since you're already feeling comfortable with RxSwift code, you'll figure bindings out very quickly.

An important thing to know here is that in RxCocoa, a binding is a **unidirectional** stream of data. This greatly simplifies data flow in the app, so you won't cover bi-directional bindings in this book.

What are binding observables?

The easiest way to understand binding is to think of the relationship as a connection between two entities:

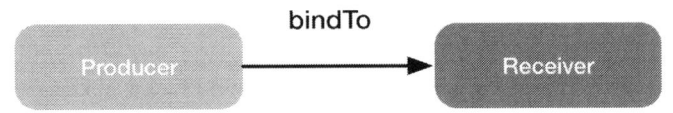

- A producer, which produces the value
- A receiver, which processes the values from the producer

A receiver cannot return a value. This is a general rule when using bindings of RxSwift.

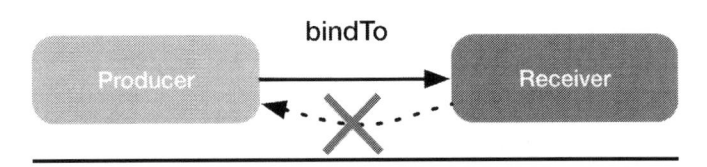

> **Note**: If you later want to experiment with bidirectional bindings (for example between a data model property and a text field), this could be modeled by using four of these entities: two producers, and two receivers. This, as you can imagine, increases the code complexity considerably — still, if you're in the mood to play around, it can be fun.

The fundamental function of binding is `bind(to:)`, and to bind an observable to another entity it's required that the receiver conforms to `ObserverType`. In previous chapters, this entity has been already explained as a `Subject` which can process values, but can also be manually written. `Subjects` are extremely important to work with the imperative nature of Cocoa, considering that the fundamental components like UILabel, UITexField, UIImageView, etc... have mutable data that can be set or get.

It's important to remember that `bind(to:)` can be used also for other purposes, not just to bind user interfaces to the underlaying data. You can for example use `bind(to:)` to create dependent processes, so a certain observable will trigger a subject performing some background tasks without having something displayed on the screen.

To summarize, the function `bind(to:)` is a special and tailored version of function `subscribe()`; there are no side effects or special cases when calling `bind(to:)`

Using binding observables to display data

Now that you know what bindings are, you can start to integrate them into your app. In the process, you'll make the whole code a little more elegant and turn the search result into a reusable data source.

The first change to apply is to refactor the long observable that assigns the data to the correct `UILabel` with `subscribe(onNext:)`. Open **ViewController.swift** and in `viewDidLoad()` replace the complete subscription code to `searchCityName` with:

```
let search = searchCityName.rx.text
    .filter { ($0 ?? "").characters.count > 0 }
    .flatMapLatest { text in
        return ApiController.shared.currentWeather(city: text ?? "Error")
            .catchErrorJustReturn(ApiController.Weather.empty)
    }
    .shareReplay(1)
    .observeOn(MainScheduler.instance)
```

This change, specifically `flatMapLatest`, makes the search result reusable and transforms a single-use data source into a multi-use `Observable`. The power of this change will be covered later in the chapter dedicated to MVVM, but for now simply realize that observables can be heavily reusable entities in Rx, and the correct modeling can make a long, difficult-to-read, single-use observer into a multi-use and easy to understand observer instead.

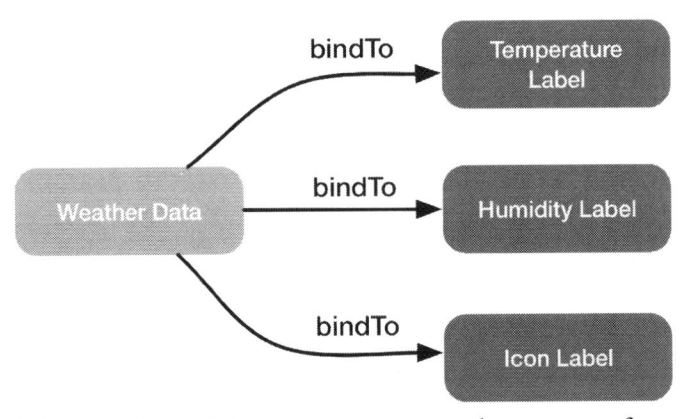

With this small change, it's possible to process every single parameter from a different subscription, mapping the value required to be displayed. For example, here's how to get the temperature as a string out of the shared data source observable:

```
search.map { "\($0.temperature)° C" }
```

This will create an observable which returns the required string to be displayed as temperature. To try creating your first binding, use `bindTo` to connect the original data source to the temperature label. Add to `viewDidLoad()`:

```
search.map { "\($0.temperature)° C" }
  .bind(to:tempLabel.rx.text)
  .disposed(by:bag)
```

Build and run to display the temperature using this new and shiny RxCocoa powered binding:

Now the application only displays the temperature, but you can restore the previous functionality by simply applying the same pattern to the rest of the labels.

```
search.map { $0.icon }
  .bind(to:iconLabel.rx.text)
  .disposed(by:bag)
```

```
search.map { "\($0.humidity)%" }
  .bind(to:humidityLabel.rx.text)
  .disposed(by:bag)

search.map { $0.cityName }
  .bind(to:cityNameLabel.rx.text)
  .disposed(by:bag)
```

Now the application displays the data you request from the server, using a single source observable named `search`, and binds different pieces of the data to each label on the screen.

Improving the code with Traits

RxCocoa offers even more advanced features to make working with Cocoa and UIKit a breeze. Beyond `bindTo`, it offers also a special implementation of observables, which have been exclusively created to be used with UI: **Traits**. Traits are a group of classes, which are specialized observables that help create straightforward, easy-to-write code, especially when working with UI. Let's have a look!

> **Note:** Very much like RxSwift traits you learned about in section one of this book, the RxCocoa traits are specializations that are helpful to use but optional if you prefer to stick to the observables you already know so well.

What are ControlProperty and Driver?

Traits are described as the following in the official documentation:

> *Traits...help communicate and ensure observable sequence properties across interface boundaries.*

It might be confusing at first, but the rules of using traits make the whole concept a little easier to understand:

- Traits can't error out.
- Traits are observed on main scheduler.
- Traits subscribe on main scheduler.
- Traits share side effects.

These entities ensure something is always displayed in the user interface and that they are always able to be handled by the user interface.

The main components part of the Traits framework are:

- `ControlProperty` and `ControlEvent`
- `Driver`

`ControlProperty` is not new; you used it just a little while ago to bind the data to the correct user interface component using the dedicated `rx` extension.

`ControlEvent` is used to *listen* for a certain event of the UI component, like the press of the "Return" button on the keyboard while editing a text field. A control event is available if the component uses `UIControlEvents` to keep track of its current status.

`Driver` is a special observable with the same constraints as explained before, so it can't error out. All processes are ensured to execute on the main thread, which avoids making UI changes on background threads.

Traits in general are an optional part of the framework; you're not forced to use them. Feel free to stick to observables and subjects, while making sure you are creating the right task in the right scheduler. But if you want some checks while compiling, and predictable rules when dealing with the UI, these components can be extremely powerful and save you time. It's easy to forget to call `.observeOn(MainScheduler.instance)` and end up creating UI processes on a background thread.

Don't worry if `Driver` and `ControlProperty` seem confusing right now. Like a lot of things in Rx, they will make more sense once you dive into the code.

Improving the project with Driver and ControlProperty

After some theory, it's time to apply all those nice concepts to your the application, make sure all the tasks are performed in the right thread, and that nothing will error out and stop subscriptions from delivering results.

The first step is to transform the weather data observable into a driver. Find where you define the `search` constant in `viewDidLoad()`, and replace the code with:

```
let search = searchCityName.rx.text
    .filter { ($0 ?? "").characters.count > 0 }
    .flatMapLatest { text in
      return ApiController.shared.currentWeather(city: text ?? "Error")
        .catchErrorJustReturn(ApiController.Weather.empty)
    }
    .asDriver(onErrorJustReturn: ApiController.Weather.empty)
```

The key line of code here is the one at the bottom: `.asDriver(...)`. This is the method that converts your observable into a `Driver`. the `onErrorJustReturn` parameter specifies a default value to be used in case the observable errors out — thus eliminating the possibility for the driver itself to emit an error.

You might have also noticed that auto completion offers also other variants to `asDriver(onErrorJustReturn:)`:

- **asDriver(onErrorDriveWith:)**: With this function, you can handle the error manually and return a new sequence generated for this purpose only.

- **asDriver(onErrorRecover:)**: Can be used alongside another existing `Driver`. This will come in play to recover the current `Driver` that just encountered an error.

But wait! The application doesn't build anymore because `bindTo` doesn't exist for `Driver`. What to do?

There's a similar function named `drive`, so you can replace all the `bindTo` calls with `drive`. You just need to replace the name `bindTo` with `drive` in all four subscriptions.

```
search.map { "\($0.temperature)° C" }
    .drive(tempLabel.rx.text)
    .disposed(by: bag)

search.map { $0.icon }
    .drive(iconLabel.rx.text)
    .disposed(by: bag)

search.map { "\($0.humidity)%" }
    .drive(humidityLabel.rx.text)
    .disposed(by: bag)
```

```
search.map { $0.cityName }
  .drive(cityNameLabel.rx.text)
  .disposed(by: bag)
```

This will restore the correct UI behavior of the application, while taking advantage of the power of `Driver`. `drive` works quite similarly to `bindTo`; the difference in the name better expresses the intent while using RxCocoa's Traits.

At this point, the application takes advantage of a lot of the shiny parts of RxCocoa, but there's still something you can improve. The application uses way too many resources and makes too many API requests because it fires a request each time you type a character. A bit of overkill, don't you think?

Find this line:

```
let search = searchCityName.rx.text
```

...and replace it with:

```
let search =
searchCityName.rx.controlEvent(.editingDidEndOnExit).asObservable()
  .map { self.searchCityName.text }
```

It's a good idea to make sure the input is valid, so you need to skip empty strings and filter the `search` observable. Then the chained code continues as usual:

```
  .flatMap { text in
    return ApiController.shared.currentWeather(city: text ?? "Error")
  }
  .asDriver(onErrorJustReturn: ApiController.Weather.empty)
```

Now the application retrieves the weather only when the user hits the "Search" button. You're not making unnecessary network requests, and the code is controlled at compile time by Traits. You also removed the `catchErrorJustReturn()` call to the observable returned by `currentWeather(city:)`.

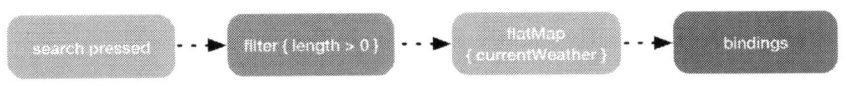

search pressed --▶ filter { length > 0 } --▶ flatMap { currentWeather } --▶ bindings

The original schema used a single observable that updated the entire UI; through a breakdown of multiple blocks, you've switched from `subscribe` to `bindTo` and reused the same observables across the view controller. This approach makes the code quite reusable and easy to work with.

For example, if you wanted to add the current barometric pressure to the user interface, all you would have to do is to add the property to the structure, map the JSON value, then add another `UILabel` and map that property to the new label. Easy!

Disposing with RxCocoa

The last topic of this chapter goes beyond the project and is pure theory. As explained at the beginning of the chapter, there's a `bag` inside the main view controller that takes care of disposing all the subscriptions when the view controller is released. But in this example, there's no usage of `weak` or `unowned` in all closures. Why?

The answer is simple: this application is a single view controller and the main view controller is always on screen while the application is running — so there's no need to guard against retain cycles or wasted memory.

unowned vs weak with RxCocoa

When dealing with RxCocoa or RxSwift with Cocoa, it might be hard to understand when to use `weak` or `unowned`. You'd use `weak` when a closure can be called at some point in the future when the current `self` object has already been released. For this reason, `self` becomes an Optional. `unowned` is used to avoid the Optional `self`. But the code has to be sure the object will never be released before the closure gets called — otherwise, the app will crash.

In RxSwift – and especially with RxCocoa – there are some good guidelines to follow when choosing to use `weak`, `unowned` or nothing at all:

- **nothing**: Inside singletons or a view controller which are never released (e.g. the root view controller).

- **unowned**: Inside all view controllers which are released after the closure task is performed.

- **weak**: Any other case.

These rules prevent against the classic `EXC_BAD_ACCESS` error. If you always respect these rules, it's unlikely you will have any trouble with memory management. And if you want to be extra safe, the raywenderlich.com Swift Guidelines https://github.com/raywenderlich/swift-style-guide#extending-object-lifetime recommend against using `unowned` at all.

Where to go from here?

In this chapter, you received a gentle introduction to RxCocoa, which is a really big framework. You saw only a small part of RxCocoa, but this should serve as a good foundation.

In the next chapter, you will see how to improve this application, add dedicated functionality to extend RxCocoa, and how to add more advanced features using RxSwift and RxCocoa.

Before proceeding, take some time to play around with RxCocoa and the .rx extension. Considering this framework has 32 extensions available, it's a good idea to look at a couple of examples first.

UIActivityIndicatorView

`UIActivityIndicatorView` is definitely one of the most used UIKit components. This extension has the following property available:

```
public var isAnimating: UIBindingObserver<Base, Bool>
```

Again, the name is self explanatory and is related to the original `isAnimating` property. Just like with `UILabel`, the property is of type `UIBindingObserver` and the result is that it can be bound to an observable to notify a background activity. You saw this used in the challenges of Chapter 10.

UIProgressView

`UIProgressView` is a less common component, but it's also covered in RxCocoa and uses the following property:

```
public var progress: UIBindingObserver<Base, Float>
```

As for all the other similar components, the `UIProgressBar` can be bound to an observable. For example, assume an `uploadFile()` function is producing an observable of a task uploading a file to a server, providing intermediate events with bytes sent and total bytes. This code could look much like this:

```
let progressBar = UIProgressBar()
let uploadFileObs = uploadFile(data: fileData)
uploadFileObs.map { sent, totalToSend in
    return sent / totalToSend
  }
  .bind(to:progressBar.rx.progress)
  .disposed(by:bag)
```

The result is that the progress bar is updated every single time an intermediate value is provided, and the user has some visual indication of the upload's progress.

At this point, it's your turn. The more time you spend playing with these extensions, the more you will be comfortable using them in the next chapter — and in future applications.

> **Note:** RxCocoa is a constantly improving framework. If you think any controls or extensions are missing, you can create them and submit a pull request to the official repository. Contributions are welcomed (and encouraged!) by the growing community.

Challenges

Challenge 1: Switch from Celsius to Fahrenheit

Your challenge in this chapter is to add a switch to change from Celsius to Fahrenheit. This task can be achieved in different ways:

- Change the API request from Metric to Imperial
- Map the Celsius value with the mathematical conversion: `temperature * 1.8 + 32`

Technically, each solution has its own obstacles to overcome. The first approach requires a change in **ApiController.swift** with an addition of a `Subject` to process the change right away and request the new data.

The second approach is shorter and probably easier. You can achieve this by combining the search observable with the control property of `UISwitch`. This solution is the recommended one for this chapter, especially when you consider that more advanced usages and architectures will be explained later in this book.

Generally, try to be as pragmatic as possible and don't over-engineer this solution. In the next chapter, you will see more advanced usages of RxCocoa, so take some time to play with the basics of this framework first.

Chapter 13: Intermediate RxCocoa

By Junior Bontognali

In the previous chapter, you were gently introduced to RxCocoa, the official RxSwift Cocoa extension. If you haven't gone through that chapter, it would be a good idea to read through it so you're ready to tackle this one.

In this chapter, you'll learn about some advanced RxCocoa integrations and how to create custom wrappers around existing UIKit components.

> **Note:** This chapter won't discuss RxSwift architecture, nor will it cover the best way to structure a RxSwift/RxCocoa project. This will be covered in Chapter 23, "MVVM with RxSwift".

Getting started

This chapter continues on from the previous project. To set up the project, you will need a valid OpenWeatherMap http://openweathermap.org key. If you already have one, simply skip ahead to the **Installing project dependencies** section below.

If you don't have a key, you can create one at https://home.openweathermap.org/users/sign_up.

Once you've completed the signup process, visit the dedicated page for API keys at https://home.openweathermap.org/api_keys and generate a new key.

Open the file `ApiController.swift` and copy the newly generated key into the correct place:

```
private let apiKey = "[YOUR KEY]"
```

Installing project dependencies

Open Terminal, navigate to the root of the project and perform the requisite `pod install` command. Once that's completed, you can build and run the application. Make sure the application compiles and that you get valid readings back from the OpenWeatherMap API when you enter a valid city in the search field.

Showing an activity while searching

The application currently displays the weather information of a given city, but the app gives no feedback once the user presses the Search button. It's a good practice to display an activity indicator while the app is busy making network requests.

When you're finished with this task, the app logic will look like this:

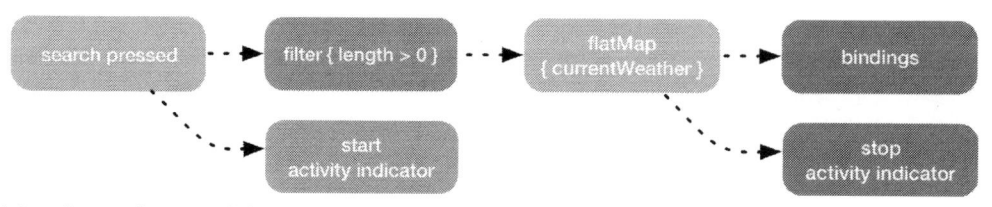

search pressed → filter { length > 0 } → flatMap { currentWeather } → bindings

search pressed → start activity indicator

flatMap { currentWeather } → stop activity indicator

To achieve this, you'll have to make some changes in the current code to decomposing the original events stream into smaller ones, so that you're notified when a user presses the button, and when the data has arrived from the server.

Open **ViewController.swift**. Go to `viewDidLoad()` and add the following code to the top of the function, below the call to `style()`:

```
let searchInput =
searchCityName.rx.controlEvent(.editingDidEndOnExit).asObservabl
e()
    .map { self.searchCityName.text }
    .filter { ($0 ?? "").count > 0 }
```

The `searchInput` observable will provide the text for a search when the input string is not empty and the user presses the Search button.

Now you can modify the `search` observable to use the `searchInput` observable instead of creating things from scratch. Modify `search` as follows:

```
let search = searchInput.flatMap { text in
    return ApiController.shared.currentWeather(city: text ??
"Error")
        .catchErrorJustReturn(ApiController.Weather.dummy)
    }
    .asDriver(onErrorJustReturn: ApiController.Weather.dummy)
```

Now you have two observables that indicate when the application is busy making requests to the API. One option is to bind both observables, correctly mapped, to the `isAnimating` property of `UIActivityIndicatorView` and do the same for all the labels with the `isHidden` property. This solution seems convenient enough, but in Rx there's a far more elegant way to accomplish this.

The two observables `searchInput` and `search` can be merged into a single observable having the value of either `true` or `false` depending on whether or not they are receiving events. The result is an observable describing whether the application is currently requesting data from the server or not.

Below the code block you just added, append this:

```
let running = Observable.from([
    searchInput.map { _ in true },
    search.map { _ in false }.asObservable()
])
    .merge()
    .startWith(true)
    .asDriver(onErrorJustReturn: false)
```

The combination of these two observables has this result:

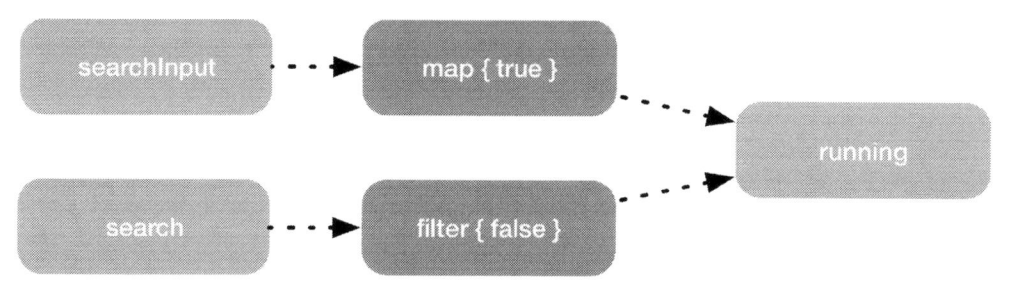

[Diagram: searchInput → map { true } → running; search → filter { false } → running]

The `.asObservable()` call is necessary on one of the array elements to help out Swift's type inferrer. You then merge the two observables. `.startWith(true)` is an extremely convenient call to avoid having to manually hide all the labels at application start.

At this point, the bindings will be very straightforward to create. You can place them before or after the bindings to the labels as it makes no difference which way you do it:

```
running
  .skip(1)
  .drive(activityIndicator.rx.isAnimating)
  .disposed(by: bag)
```

You have to remember that the first value is injected manually, so you have to skip the first value or else the activity indicator will display immediately once the application has been opened.

Then add the following to hide and show the labels according to their status:

```
running
  .drive(tempLabel.rx.isHidden)
  .disposed(by: bag)

running
  .drive(iconLabel.rx.isHidden)
  .disposed(by: bag)

running
  .drive(humidityLabel.rx.isHidden)
  .disposed(by: bag)

running
  .drive(cityNameLabel.rx.isHidden)
  .disposed(by: bag)
```

After applying this change, the application now should look like the following when it's making an API request:

Here is what things should look like immediately after it opens. All labels should be hidden, but the activity indicator should not display:

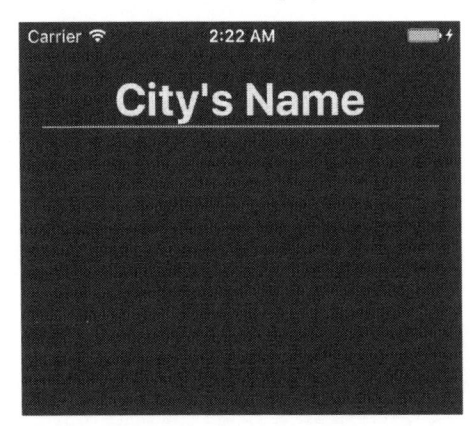

Nice job! Now you can add some new features to the app.

Extending CLLocationManager

RxCocoa is not only about UI components; it comes with some convenient classes to wrap the official Apple frameworks in a simple, customizable and powerful way.

A weather application that doesn't know its current location is a bit odd, to say the least. You can fix this by using some of the components provided in RxCocoa.

Creating the extension

The first step to integrate the `CoreLocation` framework is to create the necessary wrapper around it. Open the file under `Extensions` named `CLLocationManager+Rx.swift`. This is the file where the extension will be created.

All the other extensions are behind the `.rx` namespace. For `CLLocationManager`, the goal is to follow the same pattern. This smart behavior is achieved by using the `Reactive` proxy provided by RxSwift.

Navigate to the RxSwift library inside the Pod project and find a file named `Reactive.swift`. Open the file and you'll find a `struct` named `Reactive<Base>`, a protocol `ReactiveCompatible` and an extension `ReactiveCompatible`, which has the variable to create the namespace `rx`.

The last line is:

```
/// Extend NSObject with `rx` proxy.
extension NSObject: ReactiveCompatible { }
```

This is how every class inheriting from `NSObject` gets an `rx` namespace. Your job is to create the dedicated `rx` extensions for the class `CLLocationManager` and expose them for other classes to use.

Navigate into the **RxCocoa** folder inside the dedicated Pod project and you'll find some Objective-C files named `_RxDelegateProxy.h` and `_RxDelegateProxy.m` as well as `DelegateProxy.swift` and `DelegateProxyType.swift`. These files contain the implementation of a rather clever solution to bridge RxSwift with any framework that uses delegates (data sources) as the main resource for providing data.

The `DelegateProxy` object creates a *fake* delegate object, which will proxy all the data received into dedicated observables.

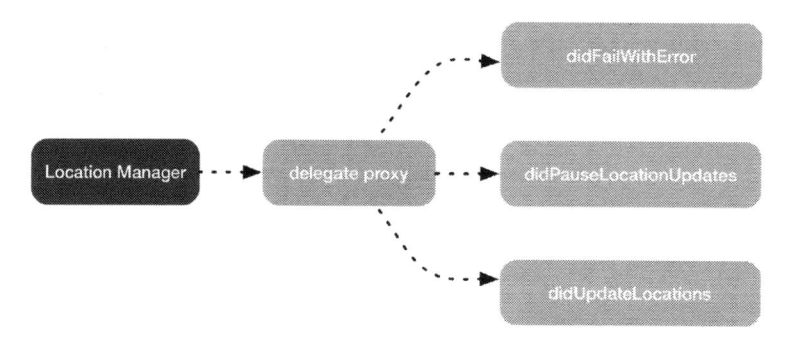

The combination of `DelegateProxy` and the right usage of `Reactive` will make your `CLLocationManager` extensions look just like all the other RxCocoa extensions already available. Neat!

`CLLocationManager` requires a delegate, and for this reason you need to create the necessary proxy to drive all the data from the necessary location manager delegates to the dedicated observables. The mapping is a simple one-to-one relationship, so a single protocol function will correspond to a single observable that returns the given data.

Navigate to `CLLocationManager+Rx.swift` and add the following code:

```
extension CLLocationManager: HasDelegate {
  public typealias Delegate = CLLocationManagerDelegate
}

class RxCLLocationManagerDelegateProxy:
DelegateProxy<CLLocationManager, CLLocationManagerDelegate>,
DelegateProxyType, CLLocationManagerDelegate {

}
```

`RxCLLocationManagerDelegateProxy` is going to be your proxy that attaches to the `CLLocationManager` instance right after an observable is created and has a subscription. This is simplified by the `HasDelegate` protocol.

At this point, you need to add an initializer for the proxy delegate and a reference to it.

First add the following init to the class:

```
public weak private(set) var locationManager: CLLocationManager?

public init(locationManager: ParentObject) {
  self.locationManager = locationManager
  super.init(parentObject: locationManager, delegateProxy: RxCLLocationManagerDelegateProxy.self)
}
```

And then a method to register the proper implementations:

```
static func registerKnownImplementations() {
  self.register
  { RxCLLocationManagerDelegateProxy(locationManager: $0) }
}
```

By using these two functions, you can initialize the delegate and register all implementations, which will be the proxy used to drive the data from the `CLLocationManager` instance to the connected observables. This is how you expand a class to use the delegate proxy pattern from RxCocoa.

Now create the observables to observe the change of location, using the proxy delegate you just created. Add in the same file:

```
extension Reactive where Base: CLLocationManager {
  public var delegate: DelegateProxy<CLLocationManager,
CLLocationManagerDelegate> {
    return RxCLLocationManagerDelegateProxy.proxy(for: base)
  }
}
```

Using the `Reactive` extension will expose the methods within that extension in the `rx` namespace for an instance of `CLLocationManager`. You now have an exposed extension `rx` available for every `CLLocationManager` instance, but unfortunately you have no real observables to get the real data.

Fix this by adding the following to the extension you just created:

```
var didUpdateLocations: Observable<[CLLocation]> {
  return
delegate.methodInvoked(#selector(CLLocationManagerDelegate.locat
ionManager(_:didUpdateLocations:)))
    .map { parameters in
      return parameters[1] as! [CLLocation]
    }
}
```

With this function, the delegate used as the proxy will listen to all the calls of `didUpdateLocations`, getting the data and casting it to an array of `CLLocation`. `methodInvoked(_:)` is part of the Objective-C code present in RxCocoa and is basically a low-level observer for delegates.

`methodInvoked(_:)` returns an observable that sends `next` events whenever the specified method is invoked. The elements included in those events are an array of the parameters the method was invoked with. You access this array with `parameters[1]` and cast it to an array of `CLLocation`.

Now you are ready to integrate this extension in the application.

Using the button to get the current position

Now that you've created the extension, you'll be able to use the location button in the bottom left corner:

Switch to ViewController.swift to work on the app UI. Before proceeding with the button logic, there are a few things to take care of. First, import the `CoreLocation` framework at the top of the file (but still after all other imports):

```
import CoreLocation
```

Next, add a location manager to the view controller:

```
let locationManager = CLLocationManager()
```

Perfect — your project is now ready to handle the location manager and retrieve the user's location.

> **Note:** Declaring a location manager instance inside `viewDidLoad()` would cause a release of the object and the subsequent weird behavior of the alert being displayed and immediately removed once `requestWhenInUseAuthorization()` was called.

Now you need to make sure the application has sufficient rights to access the user's location. Since iOS 8, the operating system must ask for the user's permission before making geolocation data available to the application. Therefore, the first thing you need to do when the user taps the current position button is to ask for permission to use the current location data and then update the data.

To achieve this, add the following code inside `viewDidLoad()`:

```
geoLocationButton.rx.tap
  .subscribe(onNext: { _ in
    self.locationManager.requestWhenInUseAuthorization()
    self.locationManager.startUpdatingLocation()
  })
  .disposed(by: bag)
```

To test that the application is actually receiving the user's location, add this temporary snippet:

```
locationManager.rx.didUpdateLocations
  .subscribe(onNext: { locations in
    print(locations)
  })
  .disposed(by: bag)
```

When you build and run the project you should see output in the console similar to this:

```
[<+37.32641795,-122.02626072> +/- 5.00m (speed 3.83 mps / course 310.70) @ 1/8/17, 11:07:20 AM Central European Standard Time]
[<+37.32641795,-122.02626072> +/- 5.00m (speed 3.83 mps / course 310.70) @ 1/8/17, 11:07:16 AM Central European Standard Time]
[<+37.32641795,-122.02626072> +/- 5.00m (speed 3.83 mps / course 310.70) @ 1/8/17, 11:07:20 AM Central European Standard Time]
[<+37.32852455,-122.02685257> +/- 6.00m (speed 3.84 mps / course 1.33) @ 1/8/17, 11:08:28 AM Central European Standard Time]
[<+37.32856216,-122.02685211> +/- 5.00m (speed 3.85 mps / course 0.46) @ 1/8/17, 11:08:29 AM Central European Standard Time]
```

> **Note:** When using the simulator, you can fake the location under **Debug ▸ Location** and select one of the simulated locations.

At this point, assuming the user gave permission for the app to access their location, the app can use that location data to retrieve the local weather. There's a dedicated function inside `ApiController.swift` to retrieve the data from the server based on the user's latitude and longitude:

```swift
func currentWeather(lat: Float, lon: Float) ->
Observable<Weather>
```

This function will return a `Weather` instance from geographical coordinates. You can use this to get the necessary data form the server.

Inside `viewDidLoad()`, create an observable that returns the last valid location:

```swift
let currentLocation = locationManager.rx.didUpdateLocations
  .map { locations in
    return locations[0]
  }
  .filter { location in
    return location.horizontalAccuracy <
kCLLocationAccuracyHundredMeters
  }
```

`didUpdateLocations` emits an array of fetched locations but you only need one to work with; that's why you use `map` to get only the first location. Then you use `filter` to prevent working with completely disparate data and to make sure the location is accurate to within a hundred meters.

Update the weather with the current data

You have an observable returning the user's location, and you have a mechanism to get the weather based on latitude and longitude. A natural combination of this in RxSwift would be this:

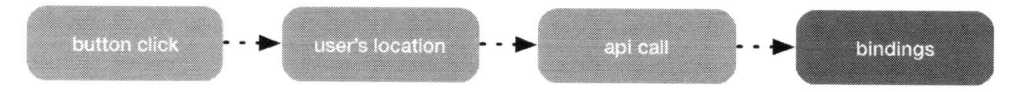

button click ┈▶ user's location ┈▶ api call ┈▶ bindings

To model the required observables, replace the existing `geoLocationButton.rx.tap` code with the following:

```
let geoInput = geoLocationButton.rx.tap.asObservable()
  .do(onNext: {
    self.locationManager.requestWhenInUseAuthorization()
    self.locationManager.startUpdatingLocation()
  })

let geoLocation = geoInput.flatMap {
  return currentLocation.take(1)
}
```

This makes sure the location manager is updating and providing information about the current location, and that only a single value is forwarded. This prevents the application from updating every single time a new value arrives from the location manager.

Next create a new observable to retrieve the weather data:

```
let geoSearch = geoLocation.flatMap { location in
  return ApiController.shared.currentWeather(lat: location.coordinate.latitude, lon: location.coordinate.longitude)
    .catchErrorJustReturn(ApiController.Weather.dummy)
}
```

This makes `geoSearch` an observable of type `Weather`, which is the same result of the call made by using the city name as input. Two observables, returning the same `Weather` type, performing the same task... it sounds this code needs a bit of refactoring!

Yes, this functionality can be merged with the observable which takes the city name as input. This gives you the same result, without having to refactor the entire application for this new feature.

The goal is to keep `search` as a `Driver` of `Weather`, and `running` as observable of the current state of the application. To achieve the first goal, **delete** the current `search` observable and create an intermediate one, right after the spot where you declare `searchInput`.

```
let textSearch = searchInput.flatMap { text in
  return ApiController.shared.currentWeather(city: text ?? "Error")
    .catchErrorJustReturn(ApiController.Weather.dummy)
}
```

Now you can combine `textSearch` with `geoSearch` to create a new `search` observable. Append after the previous block:

```
let search = Observable.from([
    geoSearch, textSearch
])
    .merge()
    .asDriver(onErrorJustReturn: ApiController.Weather.dummy)
```

This will deliver a `Weather` object to the UI regardless of the source, which can be either the city name or the user's current location. The last step is to provide feedback and make sure the search displays the activity indicator correctly, hiding it after the request has been completed.

Now jump to the definition of the `running` observable. Change first line of the code so that it includes `geoInput` as one of the sources, like so:

```
let running = Observable.from([
    searchInput.map { _ in true },
    geoInput.map { _ in true },
    search.map { _ in false }.asObservable()
])
```

Now, whether the user searches for the city or taps on the location button, the behavior of the application will be exactly the same.

You expanded the capability of the application adding a single extra source using the `merge` operator, which transformed your flat, single-flow stream, into a multi-source one:

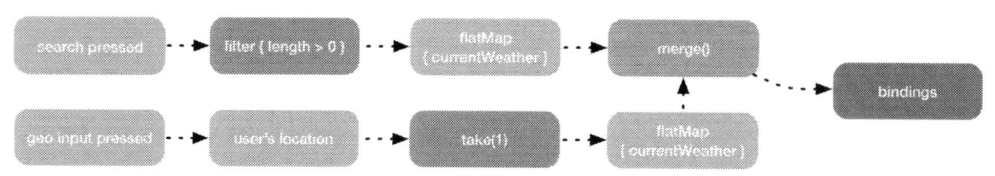

There are also some changes for the running status:

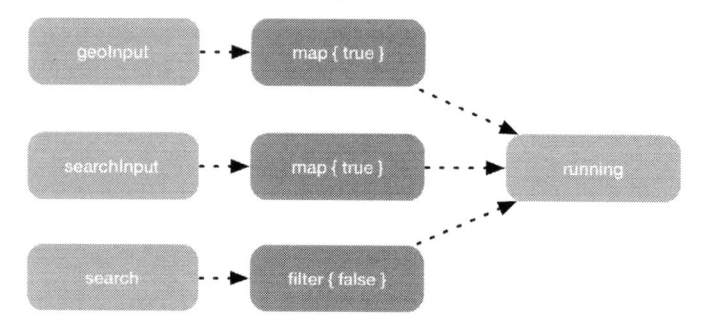

You've created a fairly advanced app: you started with a single text source, and you now have two data sources using the very same logic as you coded in the previous chapter.

How to extend a UIKit view

Now it's time to explore how to extend a UIKit component and go beyond what RxCocoa offers.

The application currently displays the weather of the user's location, but it would be nice to explore the surrounding weather on a map, while scrolling and navigating around.

This sounds like you will be creating new reactive extension, this time to the `MKMapView` class.

Extend UIKit views using MKMapView

To start extending `MKMapView`, you will start with exact same pattern you used to extend `CLLocationManager`: create a delegate proxy `RxMKMapViewDelegateProxy` and extend `Reactive` for the `MKMapView` base class.

Open `MKMapView+Rx.swift`, found in the **Extensions** directory, and create the base of the extension:

```
extension CLLocationManager: HasDelegate {
  public typealias Delegate = CLLocationManagerDelegate
}

class RxCLLocationManagerDelegateProxy:
DelegateProxy<CLLocationManager, CLLocationManagerDelegate>,
DelegateProxyType, CLLocationManagerDelegate {
}

extension Reactive where Base: CLLocationManager {
}
```

Inside `RxMKMapViewDelegateProxy`, create the initializer and the necessary reference in order to have the proxy in place:

```
public weak private(set) var locationManager: CLLocationManager?

public init(locationManager: ParentObject) {
  self.locationManager = locationManager
  super.init(parentObject: locationManager, delegateProxy:
RxCLLocationManagerDelegateProxy.self)
}
```

After this, add the method to register the implementations:

```
static func registerKnownImplementations() {
  self.register
{ RxCLLocationManagerDelegateProxy(locationManager: $0) }
}
```

Next, create the proxy by adding the following to the `Reactive` extension:

```
public var delegate: DelegateProxy<CLLocationManager,
CLLocationManagerDelegate> {
  return RxCLLocationManagerDelegateProxy.proxy(for: base)
}
```

You've created the proxy. Now you can extend `MKMapView` to proxy the delegate methods to observables.

Before extending `MKMapView`, it's a good idea to make sure the current project is showing the map view correctly.

There's already a button for this in the bottom right corner of the view controller:

Now add the code to `viewDidLoad()` to display or hide the map view when the button is pressed:

```
mapButton.rx.tap
  .subscribe(onNext: {
    self.mapView.isHidden = !self.mapView.isHidden
  })
  .disposed(by: bag)
```

Build and run the project and tap repeatedly the map button to see the map show and hide:

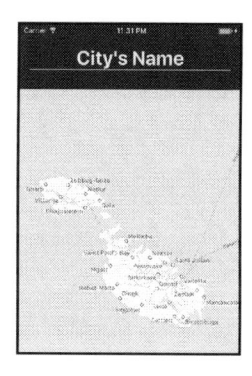

Display overlays in the map

The map is now ready to receive and display data, but you'll need to do a bit of work first to add the weather overlays. To add overlays to the map, you'll implement one of the delegate methods:

```
func mapView(_ mapView: MKMapView, rendererFor overlay:
  MKOverlay) -> MKOverlayRenderer
```

Wrapping a delegate that has a return type in Rx is a very hard task, for two reasons:

- Delegate methods with a return type are not meant for observation, but for customization of the behavior.
- Defining an automatic default value which would work in any case is a non-trivial task.

You *could* observe the value using a `Subject`, but in this case it would provide very little value.

Considering all these points, the best solution is to forward this call to a classic implementation of the delegate.

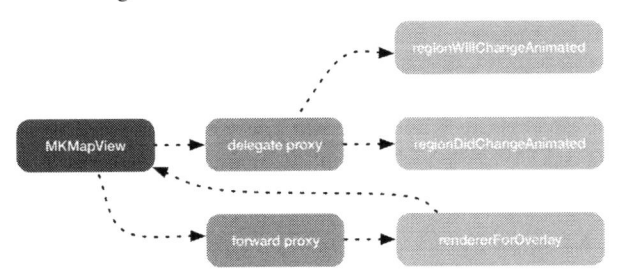

You're basically getting the best of both worlds: you want the practicality of conforming to delegate methods with return values as you do with normal UIKit development, but you also want the ability to use observables from delegate functions. This time, for once, you *can* have it both ways!

`MKMapViewDelegate` is not the only protocol that has delegate functions requiring a return type, so there's already a method which will help you out:

```
public static func installForwardDelegate(_ forwardDelegate:
  AnyObject, retainDelegate: Bool, onProxyForObject object:
  AnyObject) -> Disposable
```

If you want to check the implementation of the function, look for `DelegateProxyType.swift` in RxCocoa.

You want to forward the delegate methods that don't have a wrapper in the Rx proxy. Add the following to the `Reactive` extension for `MKMapView`:

```
public func setDelegate(_ delegate: MKMapViewDelegate) ->
Disposable {
  return RxMKMapViewDelegateProxy.installForwardDelegate(
    delegate,
    retainDelegate: false,
    onProxyForObject: self.base
  )
}
```

With this function, you can now install a forwarding delegate which will forward the calls and also provide the return value if necessary.

Add the following to the end of `viewDidLoad()` to set the view controller as the delegate that will receive all the non-handled calls from your `RxProxy`:

```
mapView.rx.setDelegate(self)
  .disposed(by: bag)
```

With this change, the compiler will raise the familiar error about the protocol not being implemented. To fix this, scroll to the end of the file and add the following:

```
extension ViewController: MKMapViewDelegate {
    func mapView(_ mapView: MKMapView, rendererFor overlay: MKOverlay) -> MKOverlayRenderer {
        if let overlay = overlay as? ApiController.Weather.Overlay {
            let overlayView = ApiController.Weather.OverlayView(overlay: overlay, overlayIcon: overlay.icon)
            return overlayView
        }
        return MKOverlayRenderer()
    }
}
```

`OverlayView` is the type required by the `MKMapView` instance to render the information over the map. The goal here is to simply display the weather icon over the map — without providing any extra information. Later in this section, you'll revisit `OverlayView` in detail.

You're almost done here: you solved the problem of the returning type of the delegate, created a forwarding proxy, and set up the overlay to display. Now it's time to process those overlays with RxSwift.

Navigate back to `MKMapView+Rx.swift` and add the following binding observer to the `Reactive` extension, which will take all the instances of `MKOverlay` and inject them into the current map:

```
var overlays: Binder<[MKOverlay]> {
  return Binder(self.base){ mapView, overlays in
    mapView.removeOverlays(mapView.overlays)
    mapView.addOverlays(overlays)
  }
}
```

Using `Binder` gives you the opportunity to use the `bind` or `drive` functions — very convenient!

Inside the `overlays` binding observable, the previous overlays will be removed and re-created every single time an array is sent to the `Subject`.

Considering the scope of the application, there's no need of any optimization here. It's unlikely there will be more than 10 overlays at a time, so removing everything and adding new ones is a fair compromise. If there's a need to process more, you could use a *diff algorithm* to improve performance and reduce overhead.

Use the created binding

It's now time to use the new binding property you've created. I'll bet you can't wait to see it in action!

Open **ApiController.swift** and check the content of the `Weather` structure. There are two nested classes: `Overlay` and `OverlayView`.

`Overlay` is a subclass of `NSObject` and implements the `MKOverlay` protocol. This is the information object you will pass to `OverlayView` to render the actual data over the map. You only need to know that `Overlay` holds just the information necessary to display the icons in the map: the coordinates, the rectangle in which to display the data, and the actual icon to use.

`OverlayView` is responsible for rendering the overlay. To avoid importing images, `imageFromText` will convert text into an image, so the icon can be displayed easily as an overlay on the map. `OverlayView` simply requires the original overlay instance and the icon string to create a new instance.

Inside the `Weather` structure, you'll see a convenience function that converts the structure into a valid `Overlay`:

```
func overlay() -> Overlay { ... }
```

Switch back to **ViewController.swift** and add the following code to `viewDidLoad()`:

```
search.map { [$0.overlay()] }
    .drive(mapView.rx.overlays)
    .disposed(by: bag)
```

This binds the newly-arrived data to the overlays subject you created previously, and maps the `Weather` structure to the correct overlay.

Build and run, search for a city, then open the map and scroll to the city. You should see something like the following:

The result looks great, and the icon is displayed at the location of the city you searched for.

Observing for map scroll events

After extending `MKMapView` with a binding property, it's time to see how to implement the more conventional notification mechanism for delegates. There's nothing different than what you did for `CLLocationManager`, so you can simply follow the same pattern.

In this occasion, the goal is to listen for user drag events and other navigation events from the map view. Once the user stops navigating around, you'll update the weather condition for the middle of the map and display it.

To observe this change, `MKMapViewDelegate` provides the following method:

```
func mapView(_ mapView: MKMapView, regionDidChangeAnimated
animated: Bool)
```

When you implement this delegate method, it is called each time the user drags the map to a new region. This is a perfect opportunity to create a reactive extension. In **MKMapView+Rx.swift**, add the following inside the extension:

```
public var regionDidChangeAnimated: ControlEvent<Bool> {
  let source = delegate
    .methodInvoked(#selector(MKMapViewDelegate.mapView(_:regionD
idChangeAnimated:)))
    .map { parameters in
      return (parameters[1] as? Bool) ?? false
    }
  return ControlEvent(events: source)
}
```

In case the cast fails, the method will fall back to `false`, just to be safe.

React to regionDidChangeAnimated events

The information about the dragging is provided, and an observation mechanism using RxSwift is in place. The only missing part is to actually use the previously created `ControlEvent`.

Switch to `ViewController.swift`, where you will make the following changes:

- Create a `mapInput`, which will use the previously created observable.
- Create a `mapSearch`, which will fire the search for the location.
- Update the `search` observable to handle the result of the `mapSearch`.
- Update the `running` observable to correctly handle the map events and weather result.

The first change is pretty straightforward and has to be done right after the `let textSearch = ...` line.

```
let mapInput = mapView.rx.regionDidChangeAnimated
  .skip(1)
  .map { _ in self.mapView.centerCoordinate }
```

`skip(1)` prevents the application from firing a search right after the `mapView` has initialized.

Next use `mapInput` to create a `mapSearch` observable that fetches the map weather data:

```
let mapSearch = mapInput.flatMap { coordinate in
    return ApiController.shared.currentWeather(lat:
coordinate.latitude, lon: coordinate.longitude)
        .catchErrorJustReturn(ApiController.Weather.dummy)
}
```

You've created two new observables, and the only thing left to do is update the `search` result observable and the `running` status observable.

Proceed with the first change, refactoring `search` as follows:

```
let search = Observable.from([geoSearch, textSearch, mapSearch])
```

You don't need to change any of the code; the only addition is adding `mapSearch` at the end of the array. The final change is to modify the observable called `running` in the following way:

```
let running = Observable.from([searchInput.map { _ in true },
                               geoInput.map { _ in true },
                               mapInput.map { _ in true},
                               search.map { _ in
false }.asObservable()])
```

As before, simply add `mapInput.map { _ in true}` to the array without changing the chained code.

Build and run your app, and navigate around the map to see a weather icon displaying the local weather conditions after each scroll!

One more thing: a signal!

RxSwift 4.0 introduces a new trait: `Signal`. This trait represents an observable sequence with following features:

- It can't fail
- Events are sharing only when connected
- All events are delivered in the main scheduler

You might consider this trait as an alternative to `Driver`, but there's an important detail you have to consider first: *there's no replay of the last event after subscription.*

The difference between `Driver` and `Signal` is a bit like between `BehaviorSubject` and `PublishSubject`. After you've written RxSwift code for a while, you usually figure out the nuances of when to use which.

To help you decide which to use, simply ask yourself: *"Do I need a replay of the last event when I connect to the resource?"*

If your answer is *no*, then `Signal` is a good option; otherwise, `Driver` is the solution.

Conclusions about RxCocoa

In these two chapters on RxCocoa, you got a glimpse of some of the most interesting parts of this amazing extension on top of RxSwift. RxCocoa isn't mandatory, and you still can write your applications without using it at all — but I suspect you already have seen how it can be useful in your own apps.

Here's a quick list of the big advantages of RxCocoa:

- It already integrates a lot of extensions for the most frequently-used components.
- It goes beyond basic UI components.
- It makes your code safer using Traits.
- It's easy to use with `bind` or `drive`
- It provides all the mechanisms to create your own custom extensions.

Before moving on to the next chapter, play around with RxCocoa a bit to gain some confidence in using the more common extensions, as later chapters will use them fairly extensively.

Challenges

Challenge 1: Add a binding property to focus the map on a given point

Your first challenge is to modify the behavior of the application when the user uses the text field or the localization button. In its current state, the application doesn't move the map correctly.

Take this challenge in two steps:

- Create a binding property which will take a coordinate object and update the map to move to the given position.
- Then bind the result of `geoSearch` and `textSearch` to the new binding property.

Be sure to not create any loops that will cause the application to update infinitely!

When you've finished this challenge, each time you receive a text or geolocation input, the map will correctly focus on the given position.

Challenge 2: Use the MKMapView to navigate a location and display the surrounding weather conditions

Your second challenge is a little bit harder. Navigating the map while scrolling returns only a single location and a single overlay in the map.

The goal for this challenge is to change this behavior and display the weather condition of the surroundings once the user has completed their interaction with the map.

Take this challenge in three steps:

- Create a new `currentWeatherAround` that takes a coordinate and returns an array of observables of requests for surrounding locations.
- Merge these requests using the correct operator, making sure the application is still responsive when the merge is taking place, and that the running status is still updated.
- Bind the result of the observables to the `.rx.overlays`.

Once done, the results will be shown in multiple overlays on the map, displaying the current weather condition of the various map regions.

Section IV: Intermediate RxSwift/RxCocoa

Once you start writing complete apps with RxSwift and RxCocoa, you will also need to take care of more intermediate topics than simply observing for events and processing them with Rx.

In a full production-quality app, you will need to build an error handling strategy, do more advanced multi-threading processing, create a solid test suite, and more.

In this part of the book, you will work through four challenging chapters, which will lift your Rx status from a rookie level to a battle-tested warrior.

Chapter 14: Error Handling in Practice

Chapter 15: Intro To Schedulers

Chapter 16: Testing with RxTest

Chapter 17: Creating Custom Reactive Extensions

Chapter 14: Error Handling in Practice

By Junior Bontognali

Life would be great if we lived in a perfect world, but unfortunately things frequently don't go as expected. Even the best RxSwift developers can't avoid encountering errors, so they need to know how to deal with them gracefully and efficiently. In this chapter, you'll learn how to deal with errors, how to manage error recovery through retries, or just surrender yourself to the universe and let the errors go.

Getting started

This application is a continuation of the one you worked on in Chapter 12, "Beginning RxCocoa". In this version of the application, you can retrieve the user's current position and look up weather for that position, but also request a city name and see the weather in that locaiton. The app also has an activity indicator to give the user some visual feedback.

Before continuing, make sure you have a valid OpenWeatherMap API Key http://openweathermap.org. If you don't already have a key, you can sign up for one at https://home.openweathermap.org/users/sign_up.

Once you've completed the signup process, visit the dedicated page for API keys at https://home.openweathermap.org/api_keys and generate a new one.

Open **ApiController.swift**, take the key you generated above and replace the placeholder in the following location:

```
let apiKey = BehaviorSubject(value: "[YOUR KEY]")
```

Once that's done, use Terminal to navigate to the root of the project and perform the necessary `pod install`. Once the pods have been installed, make sure that the application compiles and that you can retrieve the weather when you search for a city.

If that all looks good, then you can proceed right into the next section!

Managing errors

Errors are an inevitable part of any application. Unfortunately, no one can guarantee an application will never error out, so you will always need some type of error-handling mechanism.

Some of the most common errors in applications are:

- **No internet connection**: This is quite common. If the application needs an internet connection to retrieve and process the data, but the device is offline, you need to be able to detect this and respond appropriately.

- **Invalid input**: Sometimes you require a certain form of input, but the user might enter something entirely different. Perhaps you have a phone number field in your app, but the user ignores that requirement and enters letters instead of digits.

- **API error or HTTP error**: Errors from an API can vary widely. They can arrive as a standard HTTP error (response code from 400 to 500), or as errors in the response, such as using the `status` field in a JSON response.

In RxSwift, error handling is part of the framework and can be handled in two ways:

- **Catch**: Recover from the error with a default value.

Observable ⋯▶ Catch ⋯▶ Subscriptions

- **Retry**: Retry for a limited (or unlimited!) number of times.

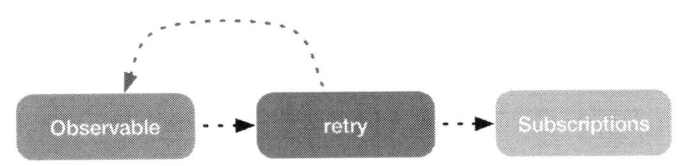

Observable ⋯▶ retry ⋯▶ Subscriptions

The starter version of this chapter's project doesn't have any real error handling. All the errors are caught with a single `catchErrorJustReturn` that returns a dummy version. This might sound like a handy solution, but there are better ways to handle this in RxSwift. A consistent and informative error-handling approach is expected in any top-notch application.

Throwing errors

A good place to start is by handling RxCocoa errors, which wrap the system errors returned by the underlying Apple frameworks. RxCocoa errors provide more details on the kind of error you've encountered, and also make your error handling code easier to write.

To see how the RxCocoa wrapper works under the hood, drill down in the Project Navigator in Pods project and then into **Pods/RxCocoa/URLSession+Rx.swift**. Search for the following method:

```
public func data(request: URLRequest) -> Observable<Data> {...}
```

This method returns an observable of type `Data`, created by a given `NSURLRequest`. The important part to look at is the bit of code that returns the error:

```
if 200 ..< 300 ~= response.statusCode {
  return data
} else {
  throw RxCocoaURLError.httpRequestFailed(response: response, data: data)
}
```

These five lines are a perfect example of how an observable can emit an error — specifically, a custom-tailored error, which you'll cover later in this chapter.

Note there's no `return` for the error in this closure. When you want to error out inside a `flatMap` operator, you should use `throw` as in regular Swift code. This is a great example of how RxSwift lets you write idiomatic Swift code where necessary, and RxSwift-style error handling where appropriate.

Handle errors with catch

After explaining how to throw errors, it's time to see how to handle errors. The most basic way is to use `catch`. The `catch` operator works much like the `do-try-catch` flow in plain Swift. An observable is performed, and if something goes wrong, you return an event that wraps an error.

In RxSwift there are two main operators to catch errors. The first:

```
func catchError(_ handler:) -> RxSwift.Observable<Self.E>
```

This is a general operator; it takes a closure as parameter and gives the opportunity to return a completely different observable. If you can't quite see where you'd use this option, think about a caching strategy that returns a previously cached value if the observable errors out. With this operator you can then achieve the following flow:

The `catchError` in this case returns values which were previously available and that, for some reason, aren't available anymore.

The second operator is:

```
func catchErrorJustReturn(_ element:) ->
  RxSwift.Observable<Self.E>
```

You saw this one used in the two earlier chapters covering RxCocoa — it ignores errors and just returns a pre-defined value. This operator is much more limited than the previous one as it's not possible to return a value for a given type of error — the same value is returned for any error, no matter what the error is.

A common pitfall

Errors are propagated through the observables chain, so an error that happens at the beginning of an observable chain will be forwarded to the final subscription if there aren't any handling operators in place.

What does this mean exactly? When an observable errors out, error subscriptions are notified and all subscriptions are then disposed. So when an observable errors out, the observable is essentially terminated and any event following the error will be ignored. This is a rule of the observable contract.

You can see this plotted below on a timeline. Once the network produces an error and the observable sequences errors out, the subscription updating the UI will stop working, effectively preventing future updates:

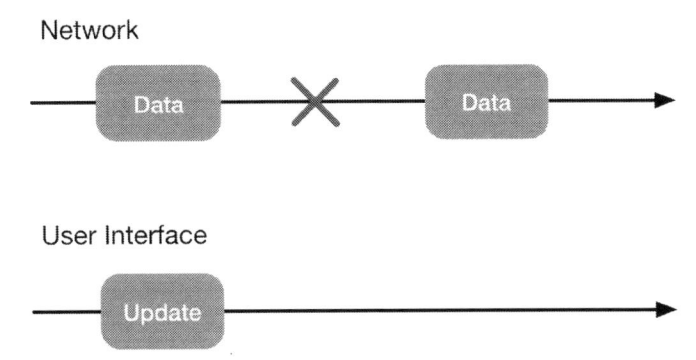

To translate this into the actual application, remove the `.catchErrorJustReturn(ApiController.Weather.empty)` line inside the `textSearch` observable, fire up the application and type random characters in the city search field until the API replies with a 404 error code. In this case the 404 means that the city you are looking for was not found.

You should see something similar to this in the console:

```
"http://api.openweathermap.org/data/2.5/weather?
q=goierjgioerjgioej&appid=[API-KEY]&units=metric" -i -v
Failure (207ms): Status 404
```

You will also notice that the search stops working after that 404 response! Not exactly the best user experience, is it?

Catching errors

Now that you've covered some theory, you can move on to writing code and updating the current project. Once you're finished, the application will recover from an error by returning an empty type of `Weather` so the application flow won't be interrupted.

The workflow this time, with included error handling, will look like this:

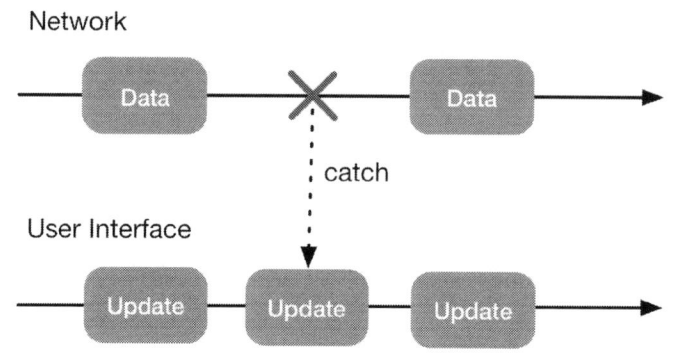

This is good enough, but it would be nice if the app could return cached data if available.

To start open **ViewController.swift** in the main project and create a simple dictionary to cache weather data, adding it as property of the view controller:

```
var cache = [String: Weather]()
```

This will temporarily store the cached data. Scroll down within the `viewDidLoad()` method and search for the line where you create the `textSearch` observable. Now populate the cache by changing the `textSearch` observable via adding `do(onNext:)` to the code chain:

```
let textSearch = searchInput.flatMap { text in
    return ApiController.shared.currentWeather(city: text ?? "Error")
        .do(onNext: { data in
            if let text = text {
                self.cache[text] = data
            }
        })
        .catchErrorJustReturn(ApiController.Weather.empty)
}
```

With this change, every valid weather response will be stored in the dictionary. Now — how to reuse the cached results?

To return a cached value in the event of an error,
replace `.catchErrorJustReturn(ApiController.Weather.empty)` with:

```
.catchError { error in
  if let text = text, let cachedData = self.cache[text] {
    return Observable.just(cachedData)
  } else {
    return Observable.just(ApiController.Weather.empty)
  }
}
```

To test this, input three or four various cities such as "London", "New York", "Amsterdam" and load the weather for these cities. After that, disable your internet connection and perform a search for a different city, such as "Barcelona"; you should receive an error. Leave your internet connection disabled and search for one of the cities you just retrieved data for, and the application should return the cached version.

This is a very common usage of `catch`. You can definitely extend this to make it a general and powerful caching solution.

Retrying on error

Catching an error is just one way errors are handled in RxSwift. You can also handle errors with `retry`.

When a `retry` operator is used and an observable errors out, the observable will repeat itself. It's important to remember that `retry` means repeating the *entire* task inside the observable.

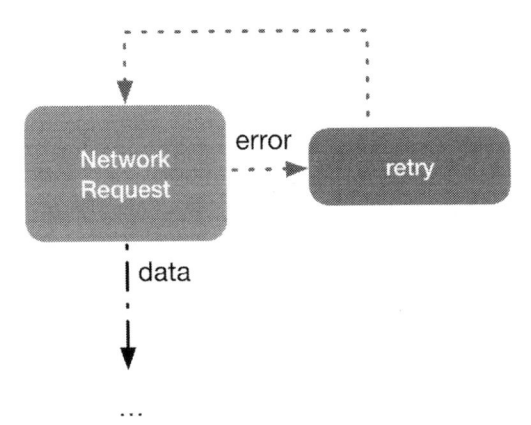

This is one of the main reasons it's recommended to avoid side effects that change the user interface inside an observable, as you can't control who will retry it!

Retry operators

There are three types of `retry` operators. The first one is the most basic:

```
func retry() -> RxSwift.Observable<Self.E>
```

This operator will repeat the observable an unlimited number of times until it returns successfully. For example, if there's no internet connection, this would continuously retry until the connection was available. This might sound like a robust idea, but it's resource-heavy, and it's seldom recommended to `retry` for an unlimited number of times if there's no valid reason for doing it.

To test this operator, comment the complete `catchError` block:

```
//.catchError { error in
//    if let text = text, let cachedData = self.cache[text] {
//        return Observable.just(cachedData)
//    } else {
//        return Observable.just(ApiController.Weather.empty)
//    }
//}
```

In its place, insert a simple `retry()`. Next, run the app, disable the internet connection and try to perform a search. You'll see a lot of output in the console, showing the app is trying to make the requests. After a few seconds, re-enable the internet connection and you'll see the result displayed once the application has successfully processed the request.

The second operator lets you vary the number of retries:

```
func retry(_ maxAttemptCount:) -> Observable<E>
```

With this variation, the observable is repeated for a specified number of times. To give it a try, do the following:

- Remove the `retry()` operator you just added
- Uncomment the previously commented code block
- Just before `catchError`, insert a `retry(3)`

The complete code block should now look like this:

```
return ApiController.shared.currentWeather(city: text ?? "Error")
    .do(onNext: { data in
        if let text = text {
            self.cache[text] = data
        }
    })
```

```
    .retry(3)
    .catchError { error in
      if let text = text, let cachedData = self.cache[text] {
        return Observable.just(cachedData)
      } else {
        return Observable.just(ApiController.Weather.empty)
      }
    }
```

If the observable is producing errors, it will be retried three times in succession. If it errors a fourth time, that error will not be handled and execution will move on to the `catchError` operator.

Advanced retries

The last operator, `retryWhen`, is suited for advanced retry situations. This error handling operator is considered one of the most powerful:

```
func retryWhen(_ notificationHandler:) -> Observable<E>
```

The important thing to understand is that `notificationHandler` is of type `TriggerObservable`. The trigger observable can be either a plain `Observable` or a `Subject` and is used to trigger the retry at arbitrary times.

This is the operator you will include in the current application, using a smart trick to retry if the internet connection is not available, or if there's an error from the API. The goal is to implement an incremental back-off strategy if the original search errors out. The desired result is as follows:

```
subscription -> error
delay and retry after 1 second

subscription -> error
delay and retry after 3 seconds

subscription -> error
delay and retry after 5 seconds

subscription -> error
delay and retry after 10 seconds
```

It's a smart yet complex solution. In regular imperative code, this would imply the creation of some abstractions, perhaps wrapping the task in `NSOperation`, or creating a tailored wrapper around Grand Central Dispatch — but with RxSwift, the solution is a short block of code.

Before creating the final result, consider what the inner observable (the trigger) should return, taking in consideration that the type can be ignored, and that the trigger can be of any type.

The goal is to retry four times with a given sequence of delays. First, inside `ViewController.swift`, just before the subscription to `ApiController.shared.currentWeather` sequence, define the maximum number of attempts before the `retryWhen` operator:

```
let maxAttempts = 4
```

After this many retries, the error should be forwarded on. Then replace `.retry(3)` with:

```
.retryWhen { e in
    // flatMap source errors
}
```

This observable has to be combined with the one that returns errors from the original observable. So when an error arrives as event, the combination of these observables will also receive the current index of the event.

You can achieve this by calling `enumerated()` on the observable and then using `flatMap`. The `enumerated()` method returns a new observable that sends tuples of the original observable's values and their index. Replace the comment `// flatMap source errors` with:

```
e.enumerated().flatMap { (attempt, error) -> Observable<Int> in
    // attempt few times
}
```

Now the original error observable, and the one defining how long the delay should be before retrying, are combined.

Now combine that code with a `timer`, taking only the first delayed event. Adjust the code from above to look like this:

```
e.enumerated().flatMap { (attempt, error) -> Observable<Int> in
    if attempt >= maxAttempts - 1 {
        return Observable.error(error)
    }
    return Observable<Int>.timer(Double(attempt + 1), scheduler:
MainScheduler.instance).take(1)
}
```

The completed block of code, including `retryWhen`, looks now like this:

```
.retryWhen { e in
    return e.enumerated().flatMap { (attempt, error) ->
Observable<Int> in
       if attempt >= maxAttempts - 1 {
          return Observable.error(error)
       }
       return Observable<Int>.timer(Double(attempt + 1), scheduler:
MainScheduler.instance).take(1)
    }
}
```

To log when the new retry is fired, add the following code before the second `return` in the `flatMap` operator:

```
print("== retrying after \(attempt + 1) seconds ==")
```

Now build and run, disable your internet connection and perform a search. You should see the following result in the log:

```
== retrying after 1 seconds ==
... network ...
== retrying after 2 seconds ==
... network ...
== retrying after 3 seconds ==
... network ...
```

Here's a good visualization of what's going on:

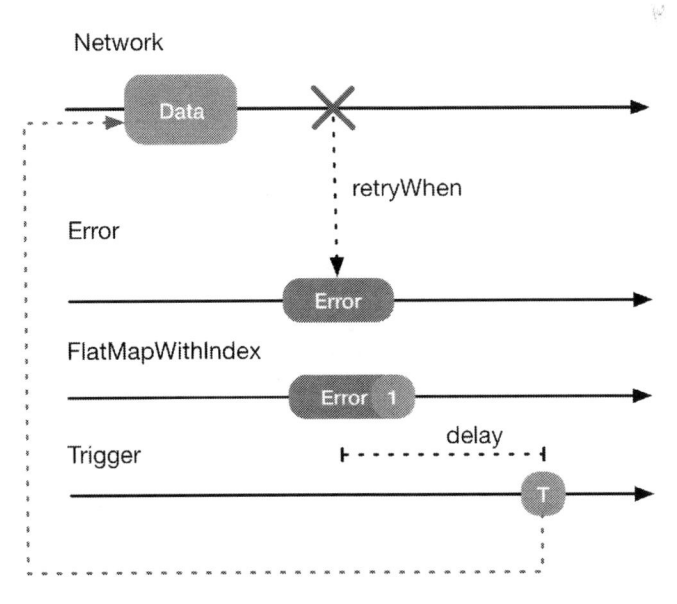

The trigger can take the original error observable into consideration to achieve quite complex back-off strategies. This shows how you can create complex error-handling strategies using only a few lines of RxSwift code.

Custom errors

Creating custom errors follows the general Swift principle, so there's nothing here that a good Swift programmer wouldn't already know, but it's still good to see how to handle errors and create tailored operators.

Creating custom errors

The errors returned from RxCocoa are quite general, so an HTTP 404 error (page not found) is pretty much treated like a 502 (bad gateway). These are two completely different errors, so it would be good to be able to handle them differently.

If you dig into **ApiController.swift**, you'll see there are two error cases already included that you can use to error handle different HTTP responses:

```
enum ApiError: Error {
    case cityNotFound
    case serverFailure
}
```

You'll use this error type inside `buildRequest(...)`. The last line of that method returns an observable of data, which is then mapped to a JSON object structure. This is where you have to inject the check and return the custom error you created. The `.data` convenience of RxCocoa already takes care of creating the custom error object.

Replace the code found inside the block of the last `flatMap` in the `buildRequest(...)` method:

```
return session.rx.response(request: request).map() { response, data in
    if 200 ..< 300 ~= response.statusCode {
        return JSON(data: data)
    } else if 400 ..< 500 ~= response.statusCode {
        throw ApiError.cityNotFound
    } else {
        throw ApiError.serverFailure
    }
}
```

Using this method, you can create custom errors and even add more advanced logic, such as when the API provides a response message inside the JSON. You could get the

JSON data, process the `message` field and encapsulate it into the error to throw. Errors are extremely powerful in Swift, and can be made even more powerful in RxSwift.

Using custom errors

Now that you're returning your custom error, you can do something constructive with it.

Before proceeding, back in **ViewController.swift** comment out the `retryWhen { ... }` operator. You want the error to go through the chain and be threaded by the observable.

There's a convenience view named `InfoView` that flashes a small view on the bottom of the application with the given error message. The usage is pretty simple, and is done with a single line of code like this one (you don't need to enter this right now):

```
InfoView.showIn(viewController: self, message: "An error occurred")
```

Errors are usually handled with retry or catch operators, but what if you want to perform a side effect and display the message on the user interface? To achieve this, there's the `do` operator. In the same subscription where you commented `retryWhen`, you've used a `do` to implement caching:

```
.do(onNext: { data in
    if let text = text {
        self.cache[text] = data
    }
})
```

Add a second parameter to that same method call so that you perform side effects in case of an error event. The complete block should look like so:

```
.do(onNext: { data in
    if let text = text {
        self.cache[text] = data
    }
}, onError: { [weak self] e in
    guard let strongSelf = self else { return }
    DispatchQueue.main.async {
        InfoView.showIn(viewController: strongSelf, message: "An error occurred")
    }
})
```

The dispatch is necessary because the sequence is observed in a background thread; otherwise, UIKit will complain about the UI being modified by a background thread. Build and run, try to search on a random string and the error will show up.

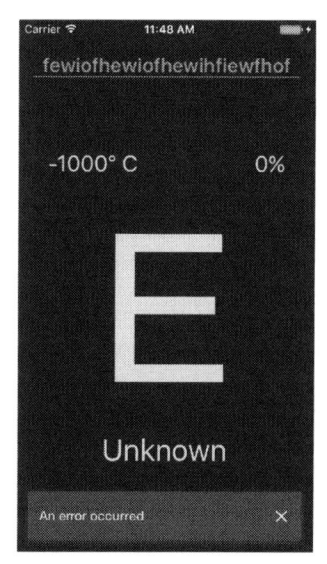

Well, the error is rather general. But you can easily inject some more information in there. RxSwift handles this just as Swift would, so you can check for the error case and display different messages. To make the code a bit tidier, add this new method to the view controller class:

```swift
func showError(error e: Error) {
  if let e = e as? ApiController.ApiError {
    switch (e) {
    case .cityNotFound:
      InfoView.showIn(viewController: self, message: "City Name is invalid")
    case .serverFailure:
      InfoView.showIn(viewController: self, message: "Server error")
    }
  } else {
    InfoView.showIn(viewController: self, message: "An error occurred")
  }
}
```

Then go back to the `do(onNext:onError:)` and replace the line `InfoView.showIn(...)` with:

```swift
strongSelf.showError(error: e)
```

This should provide more context about the error to the user.

Advanced error handling

Advanced error cases can be tricky to implement. There's no general rule about what to do when the API returns an error, besides show a message to the user.

Let's assume you want to add authentication to the current application. The user has to be authenticated and authorized to request a weather condition. This would imply the creation of a session, which will make sure the user is logged in and authorized correctly. But what do you do if the session has expired? Return an error, or return an empty value alongside a message string?

There's no silver bullet in this case. Both solutions apply here, but it's always useful to know more about the error, so you'll go that route.

In this case, the recommended method is to perform a side effect and retry right after the session has been correctly created.

You can use the subject called `apiKey` that contains your API key to simulate this behavior.

This API key subject can be used to trigger a retry in the `retryWhen` closure. A missing API key is definitely an error, so add the following extra error case in the `ApiError` enum:

```
case invalidKey
```

This error must be thrown when the server returns a `401` code. Throw that error in the `builderRequest(...)` function, right after the first if `if 200 ..< 300`:

```
else if response.statusCode == 401 {
  throw ApiError.invalidKey
}
```

That new error requires also a new handler. Update the `switch` inside `showError(error:)` method back in **ViewController.swift**, to include that new case:

```
case .invalidKey:
  InfoView.showIn(viewController: self, message: "Key is invalid")
```

Now you can go back to `viewDidLoad()` and re-implement the error handling code. Since you've commented out the current `retryWhen {...}` code, you can start building your error handling anew.

Above the subscription to `searchInput`, create a dedicated closure, outside of the observer chain, that will serve as an error handler:

```
let retryHandler: (Observable<Error>) -> Observable<Int> = { e
in
   return e.enumerated().flatMap { (attempt, error) ->
Observable<Int> in
      //error handling
   }
}
```

You'll copy some of the code you had before in that new error handling closure. Replace the `//error handling` comment with:

```
if attempt >= maxAttempts - 1 {
  return Observable.error(error)
} else if let casted = error as? ApiController.ApiError, casted
== .invalidKey {
  return ApiController.shared.apiKey
    .filter {$0 != ""}
    .map { _ in return 1 }
}
print("== retrying after \(attempt + 1) seconds ==")
return Observable<Int>.timer(Double(attempt + 1), scheduler:
MainScheduler.instance)
  .take(1)
```

The return type in the `invalidKey` case isn't important, but you have to be consistent. Before, it was an `Observable<Int>`, so you should stick with that return type. For this reason, you've used `{ _ in return 1 }`.

Now scroll to the commented `retryWhen {...}` and replace it with:

```
retryWhen(retryHandler)
```

The final step is to use the subject of the API key. There's already a method in **ViewController.swift** named `requestKey()`, which opens an alert view with a text field. The user then could type in the key (or paste it inside) to emulate a login functionality. You do that for testing purposes here; in a real-life app, the user would enter their credentials to get a key from your server.

Switch to **ApiController.swift**. Remove the API key in the `apiKey` subject and set it to an empty string. You might want to keep the key somewhere handy, as you will need it again in a second.

```
let apiKey = BehaviorSubject(value: "")
```

Build and run the application, try to perform a search and you'll receive an error:

Tap the key button in the bottom-right corner:

The application will then open the alert asking for the API key:

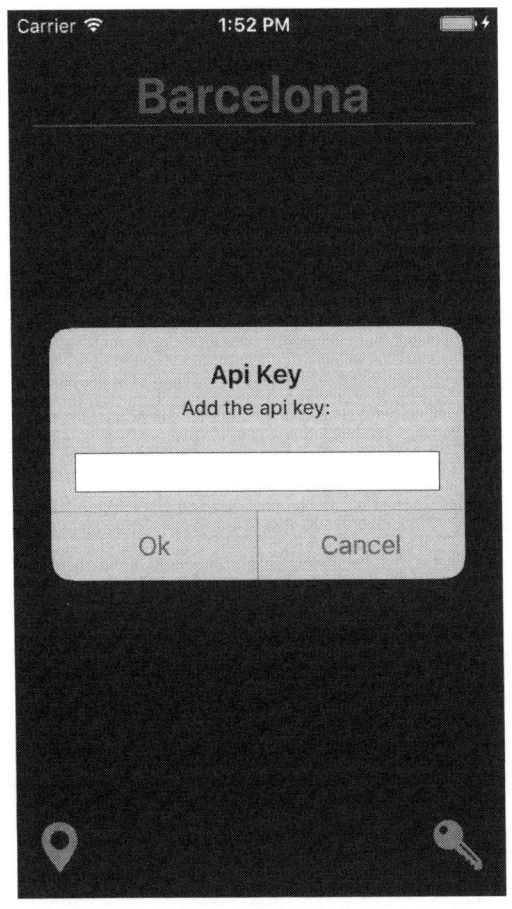

Paste the API key in the field and tap **OK**. The application will repeat the whole observable sequence, returning the correct information if the input is valid. If the input isn't valid, you'll end up on a different error path.

Materialize and dematerialize

Error handling can be be a difficult task to achieve, and sometimes it's necessary to debug a sequence which is failing by decomposing it to better understand the flow. Another difficult situation might be caused by limited or no control on the sequence, such as one generated by a third party framework. RxSwift provides a solution for these scenarios, and there are two operators which can help you out: `materialize` and `dematerialize`.

You've been introduced to the `Event` enum earlier in this book and are already aware of how important it is. It's one of the foundational elements of RxSwift, but it's rare that you'll use it directly. The `materialize` operator lets you transform any sequence into a sequence of `Event<T>` enums.

This process transforms the original sequence into a sequence of notifications:

Using this operator, you are able to transform implicit sequences, which are manipulated with proper operators and multiple handlers, into an explicit one, so the handler for `onNext`, `onError` and `onCompleted` can be a single function.

To reverse a sequence of notifications, you can use `dematerialize`:

This will transform a sequence of notifications into a regular `Observable` with all the original contracts in place.

You can use these two operators in combination to create advanced and custom event loggers:

```
observableToLog.materialize()
  .do(onNext: { (event) in
    myAdvancedLogEvent(event)
  })
  .dematerialize()
```

With this approach, you can then create a custom operator using `materialize` and `dematerialize` and perform advanced tasks on the `Event` enumerator.

> **Note:** `materialize` and `dematerialize` are usually used together, and have the power to completely break the original Observable contract. Use them carefully, and only when necessary, when there are no other options to handle a particular situation.

Where to go from here?

In this chapter, you were introduced to error handling using `retry` and `catch`. The way you handle errors in your app really depends on what kind of project you're building. When handling errors, design and architecture come in play, and creating the wrong handling strategy might compromise your project and result in re-writing portions of your code.

I'd also recommend spending some time playing with `retryWhen`. It's a non-trivial operator, so the more you play with it, the more you'll feel comfortable using it in your applications.

Challenges

Challenge 1: Use retryWhen on restored connectivity

In this challenge you need to handle the condition of an unavailable internet connection.

To start, take a look at the reachability service inside `RxReachability.swift`. Modify the code so it correctly delivers the notifications when the internet connection returns.

You can start monitoring the device connectivity by adding in the view controller's `viewDidLoad()` method:

```
_ = RxReachability.shared.startMonitor("openweathermap.org")
```

Once that's done, extend the `retryWhen` handler to handle the "no internet connection available" error. Remember that when the internet connection is up, you have to fire a retry.

To achieve this, add another `if` in your `.enumerated().flatMap()` operator where you check what kind of error has been returned. Try casting `error` as `NSError`, and if its `code` equals `-1009`, that means the network connection is out. In that case, return `RxReachability.shared.status` and filter it to let through only `.online` values, and just as you did in the other `if` statement, map to `1`.

The final goal is to have the system automatically retry once the internet is back, if the previous error was due to the device being offline.

As always, you can peek into the challenges folder and see the solution provided.

Chapter 15: Intro To Schedulers

By Junior Bontognali

Until now, you've managed to work with schedulers, while avoiding any explanation about how they handle threading or concurrency. In earlier chapters, you used methods which implicitly used some sort of concurrency/threading level, such as `buffer`, `delaySubscription` or `interval` operators.

You probably have a feeling that schedulers have some sort of magic under the hood, but before you understand schedulers, you'll also need to understand what those `observeOn` functions are all about.

This chapter is going to cover the beauty behind schedulers, where you'll learn why the Rx abstraction is so powerful and why working with asynchronous programming is far less painful than using locks or queues.

> **Note:** Creating custom schedulers is beyond of the scope of this book. Keep in mind that the schedulers and initializers provided by RxSwift, RxCocoa and RxBlocking generally cover 99% of cases. Always try to use the built-in schedulers.

What is a Scheduler?

Before getting your hands dirty with schedulers, it's important to understand what they are — and what they are not. To summarize, a scheduler is a context where a process takes place. This context can be a thread, a dispatch queue or similar entities, or even an `NSOperation` which is used inside the `OperationQueueScheduler`.

Here's a good example as to how schedulers can be used:

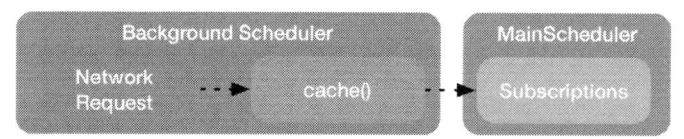

In this diagram, you have the concept of a cache operator. An observable makes a request to a server and retrieves some data. This data is processed by a custom operator named `cache`, which stores the data somewhere. After this, the data is passed to all subscribers in a different scheduler, most likely the `MainScheduler` which sits on top of the main thread, making the update of the UI possible.

Demystifying the scheduler

One common misconception about schedulers is that they are equally related to threads. And that might seem logical at first — after all, schedulers do work similarly to the GCD dispatch queues.

But this isn't the case at all. If you were writing a custom scheduler, which again is not a recommended approach, you could create multiple schedulers using the very same thread, or a single scheduler on top of multiple threads. That would be weird — but it would work!

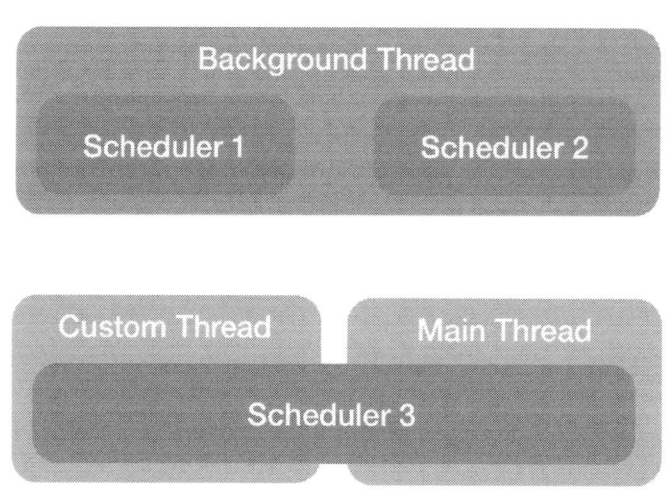

The important thing to remember is that schedulers are *not* threads, and they *don't* have a one-to-one relationship with threads. Always check the context in which the scheduler is performing an operation — not the thread. Later in this chapter, you'll encounter some good examples to help you understand this.

Setting up the project

Time to write some code! In this project, you are going to create a simple command-line tool for macOS. Why a command-line tool? Since you are playing with threads and concurrency, plain-text output will be easier to understand than any visual elements you could create in an app.

Install the CocoaPods dependencies for this chapter's project, as described in Chapter 1, "Hello RxSwift." (By now you definitely know how to do it by heart, but one never knows how many chapters you skipped through.)

Once finished, open the workspace, build and run, and the debugger console should show the following:

```
===== Schedulers =====
00s | [D] [dog] received on Main Thread
00s | [S] [dog] received on Main Thread
Program ended with exit code: 0
```

Before proceeding, open **Utils.swift** and take a look at the implementation of `dump()` and `dumpingSubscription()`.

The first method dumps the element and the current thread information inside a `do(onNext:)` operator using the `[D]` prefix. The second does the same using the `[S]` prefix, but calls `subscribe(onNext:)`. Both methods indicate the elapsed time, so the `00s` above stand for "0 seconds elapsed".

You have two different ways to inject the side-effect of printing info to the console, so you can chain them with `do(onNext:)` and eventually cap the chain by subscribing to it with `subscribe(onNext:)`. In the next section, you'll see how easy it is for a chain of observables to switch between schedulers.

Switching schedulers

One of the most important things in Rx is the ability to switch schedulers at any time, without any restrictions except for ones imposed by the inner process generating events.

> **Note:** An example of that type of restriction is if the observable emits non-thread safe objects, which cannot be sent across threads. In that case, RxSwift will allow you to switch schedulers, but you would be violating the logic of the underlying code.

To understand how schedulers behave, you'll create a simple observable to play with that provides some fruit.

Add the following code to the bottom of **main.swift**:

```
let fruit = Observable<String>.create { observer in
  observer.onNext("[apple]")
  sleep(2)
  observer.onNext("[pineapple]")
  sleep(2)
  observer.onNext("[strawberry]")
  return Disposables.create()
}
```

This observable features a `sleep` function. While this is not something you'd usually see in real applications, in this case it will help you understand how subscriptions and observations work.

Add the following code to subscribe to the observable you created:

```
fruit
  .dump()
  .dumpingSubscription()
  .disposed(by: bag)
```

Build and run, and check out the logging in the console:

```
00s | [D] [dog] received on Main Thread
00s | [S] [dog] received on Main Thread
00s | [D] [apple] received on Main Thread
00s | [S] [apple] received on Main Thread
02s | [D] [pineapple] received on Main Thread
02s | [S] [pineapple] received on Main Thread
04s | [D] [strawberry] received on Main Thread
04s | [S] [strawberry] received on Main Thread
```

Here you have the original subject, followed by a fruit every two seconds after that.

The fruit is generated on the main thread, but it would be nice to move it to a background thread. To create the fruit in a background thread, you'll have to use `subscribeOn`.

Using subscribeOn

In some cases you might want to change on which scheduler the observable *computation* code runs — *not* the code in any of the subscription operators, but the code that is actually emitting the observable events.

> **Note:** For the custom observable that you have created, the code that emits events is the one you supply as the trailing closure for `Observable.create { ... }`.

The way to set the scheduler for that *computation* code is to use `subscribeOn`. It might sound like a counterintuitive name at first glance, but after thinking about it for a while, it starts to make sense. When you want to actually *observe* an observable, you *subscribe* to it. This determines where the original processing will happen. If `subscribeOn` is not called, then RxSwift automatically uses the current thread:

This process is creating events on the main thread using the main scheduler. The `MainScheduler` you've used sits on top of the main thread. All the tasks you want to perform on the main thread have to use this scheduler, which is why you used it in previous examples when working with the UI. To switch schedulers, you'll use `subscribeOn`.

In **main.swift**, there's a pre-defined scheduler named `globalScheduler` that uses a background queue. This scheduler is created using the global dispatch queue, which is a concurrent queue:

```
let globalScheduler = ConcurrentDispatchQueueScheduler(queue:
DispatchQueue.global())
```

So, as the name of the class suggests, all tasks to be computed by this scheduler will be dispatched and handled by the global dispatch queue.

To use this scheduler, replace the previous subscription to `fruits` you created with this new one:

```
fruit
  .subscribeOn(globalScheduler)
  .dump()
  .dumpingSubscription()
  .disposed(by: bag)
```

Now add the following line to the end of the file:

```
RunLoop.main.run(until: Date(timeIntervalSinceNow: 13))
```

This is, admittedly, a hack; it prevents Terminal from terminating once all operations have completed on the main thread, which would kill your global scheduler and observable. In this case, Terminal will remain alive for 13 seconds.

> **Note**: 13 seconds might be overkill for this example, but as you move through the chapter, your app will need this length of time to finish. So feel free to stop the application once all the observables have completed.

Now that your new scheduler is in place, build and run and check the result:

```
00s | [D] [dog] received on Main Thread
00s | [S] [dog] received on Main Thread
00s | [D] [apple] received on Anonymous Thread
00s | [S] [apple] received on Anonymous Thread
02s | [D] [pineapple] received on Anonymous Thread
02s | [S] [pineapple] received on Anonymous Thread
04s | [D] [strawberry] received on Anonymous Thread
04s | [S] [strawberry] received on Anonymous Thread
```

The global queue uses a thread that doesn't have a name, so in this case `Anonymous Thread` is the global thread.

Now both the observable and the subscribed observer are processing data in the same thread.

That's cool, but what can you do if you want to change where the observer performs the code of your operators? You have to use `observeOn`.

Using observeOn

Observing is one of the three fundamental concepts of Rx. It involves an entity producing events, and an observer for those events. In this case, and in opposition to `subscribeOn`, the operator `observeOn` changes the scheduler where the *observation* happens.

So once an event is pushed by an `Observable` to all the subscribed observers, this operator will ensure that the event is correctly handled in the correct scheduler.

To switch from the current global scheduler to the main thread, you need to call `observeOn` before subscribing. One more time, replace your `fruits` subscription code:

```
fruit
  .subscribeOn(globalScheduler)
  .dump()
  .observeOn(MainScheduler.instance)
  .dumpingSubscription()
  .disposed(by: bag)
```

Build and run, and check the console output once more (you will need to wait a few seconds until the program stops printing in the console):

```
00s | [D] [dog] received on Main Thread
00s | [S] [dog] received on Main Thread
00s | [D] [apple] received on Anonymous Thread
00s | [S] [apple] received on Main Thread
02s | [D] [pineapple] received on Anonymous Thread
02s | [S] [pineapple] received on Main Thread
04s | [D] [strawberry] received on Anonymous Thread
04s | [S] [strawberry] received on Main Thread
```

You've achieved the result you wanted: All the events are now processed on the correct thread. The main observable is processing and generating events on the background thread, and the subscribing observer is doing its job on the main thread.

This is a very common pattern. You've used a background process to retrieve data from a server and process the data received, only switching to the `MainScheduler` to process the final event and display the data in the user interface.

Pitfalls

The ability to switch schedulers and threads looks amazing, but it comes with some pitfalls. To see why, you'll push some events to the subject using a new thread. Since you need to track on which thread the computation takes place, a good solution is to use `Thread` (or `NSThread` in Objective-C).

Right after the `fruit` observable, add the following code to generate some animals:

```
let animalsThread = Thread() {
  sleep(3)
  animal.onNext("[cat]")
  sleep(3)
  animal.onNext("[tiger]")
  sleep(3)
  animal.onNext("[fox]")
  sleep(3)
  animal.onNext("[leopard]")
}
```

Then name the thread so you will be able to recognize it, and start it up:

```
animalsThread.name = "Animals Thread"
animalsThread.start()
```

Build and run; you should see your new thread in action:

```
...
03s | [D] [cat] received on Animals Thread
03s | [S] [cat] received on Animals Thread
04s | [D] [strawberry] received on Anonymous Thread
04s | [S] [strawberry] received on Main Thread
06s | [D] [tiger] received on Animals Thread
06s | [S] [tiger] received on Animals Thread
09s | [D] [fox] received on Animals Thread
09s | [S] [fox] received on Animals Thread
12s | [D] [leopard] received on Animals Thread
12s | [S] [leopard] received on Animals Thread
```

Perfect — you have animals created on the dedicated thread. Next - process the result on the global thread.

> **Note:** It might seem repetitive to keep adding code and then replacing it with something else, but the goal here is to compare the differences between the various schedulers.

Replace the original subscription to the animal subject with the following code:

```
animal
  .dump()
  .observeOn(globalScheduler)
  .dumpingSubscription()
  .disposed(by: bag)
```

Build and run, and the new result is as follows:

```
...
03s | [D] [cat] received on Animals Thread
03s | [S] [cat] received on Anonymous Thread
04s | [D] [strawberry] received on Anonymous Thread
04s | [S] [strawberry] received on Main Thread
06s | [D] [tiger] received on Animals Thread
06s | [S] [tiger] received on Anonymous Thread
09s | [D] [fox] received on Animals Thread
09s | [S] [fox] received on Anonymous Thread
12s | [D] [leopard] received on Animals Thread
12s | [S] [leopard] received on Anonymous Thread
```

Now you're switching threads and nearly running into that 13-second limit!

What if you want the observation process on the global queue, but you want to handle the subscription on the `Main Thread`? For the first case, the `observeOn` is already correct, but for the second it's necessary to use `subscribeOn`.

Replace the `animal` subscription, this time with the following:

```
animal
    .subscribeOn(MainScheduler.instance)
    .dump()
    .observeOn(globalScheduler)
    .dumpingSubscription()
    .disposed(by: bag)
```

Build and run, and you'll get the following result:

```
03s | [D] [cat] received on Animals Thread
03s | [S] [cat] received on Anonymous Thread
04s | [D] [strawberry] received on Anonymous Thread
04s | [S] [strawberry] received on Main Thread
06s | [D] [tiger] received on Animals Thread
06s | [S] [tiger] received on Anonymous Thread
09s | [D] [fox] received on Animals Thread
09s | [S] [fox] received on Anonymous Thread
12s | [D] [leopard] received on Animals Thread
12s | [S] [leopard] received on Anonymous Thread
```

Wait?! What? Why isn't the computation happening on the correct scheduler? This is a common and dangerous pitfall that comes from thinking of Rx as asynchronous or multi-threaded by default — which isn't the case.

Rx and the general abstraction is free-threaded; there's no magic thread switching taking place when processing data. The computation is always performed on the original thread if not specified otherwise.

> **Note:** Any thread switching happens after an explicit request by the programmer using the operators `subscribeOn` and `observeOn`.

Thinking Rx does some thread handling by default is a common trap to fall into. What's happening above is a misuse of the `Subject`. The original computation is happening on a specific thread, and those events are pushed in that thread using `Thread() { ... }`. Due to the nature of `Subject`, Rx has no ability to switch the original computation scheduler and move to another thread, since there's no direct control over where the subject is pushed.

Why does this work with the fruit thread though? That's because using `Observable.create` puts Rx in control of what happens inside the `Thread` block so you can more finely customize thread handling.

This unexpected outcome is commonly known as the "Hot and Cold" observables problem.

In the case above, you are dealing with a **hot** observable. The observable doesn't have any side-effect during subscription, but it does have its own context in which events are generated and RxSwift can't control it (namely, it sports its own `Thread`).

A **cold** observable in contrast doesn't produce any elements before any observers subscribe to it. That effectively means it doesn't have its own context until, upon subscription, it creates some context and starts producing elements.

Hot vs. cold

The section above touched on the topic of hot and cold observables. The topic of hot and cold observables is quite opinionated and generates a lot of debate, so let's briefly look into it here. The concept can be reduced to a very simple question:

Observable — Is there any side effect performed upon subscription?

- NO (shared) → Hot
- YES (not shared) → Cold

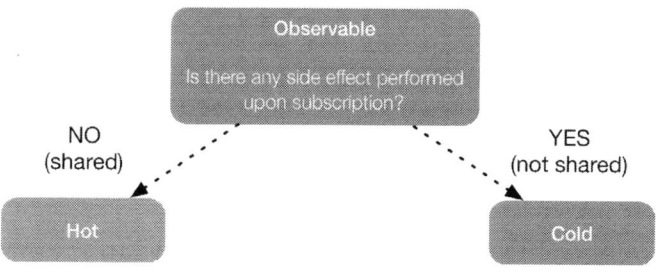

Some examples of side effects are:

- Fire a request to the server
- Edit the local database

- Write to the file system
- Launch a rocket

The world of side effects is endless, so you need to determine whether your `Observable` instance is performing side effects upon subscription. If you can't be certain about that, then perform more analysis or dig further into the source code. Launching a rocket on every subscription might *not* be what you're looking to achieve...

Another common way to describe this is to ask whether or not the `Observable` shares side-effects. If you're performing side effects upon subscription, it means that the side effect is *not* shared. Otherwise, the side effects are shared with all subscribers.

This is a fairly general rule, and applies to any `ObservableType` object like a subject and related subtypes.

As you've certainly noticed, we haven't spoken much about hot and cold observables so far in the book. It's a common topic in reactive programming, but in Rx you encounter the concept only in specific cases like the `Thread` example above or when you need greater control, such as when you run tests.

Keep this section as a point of reference, so in case you need to approach a problem in terms of hot or cold observables, you can quickly open the book to this point and refresh yourself on the concept.

Best practices and built-in schedulers

Schedulers are a non-trivial topic, so they come with some best practices for the most common use cases. In this section, you'll get a quick introduction to serial and concurrent schedulers, learn how they process the data and see which type works better for a particular context.

Serial vs concurrent schedulers

Considering that a scheduler is simply a context, which could be anything (dispatch queue, thread, custom context), and that all operators transforming sequences need to preserve the implicit guarantees, you need to be sure you're using the right scheduler.

- If you're using a serial scheduler, Rx will do computations serially. For a serial dispatch queue, schedulers will also be able to perform their own optimizations underneath.

- In a concurrent scheduler, Rx will try running code simultaneously, but `observeOn` and `subscribeOn` will preserve the sequence in which tasks need to be executed, and ensure that your subscription code ends up on the correct scheduler.

MainScheduler

`MainScheduler` sits on top of the main thread. This scheduler is used to process changes on the user interface and perform other high-priority tasks. As a general practice when developing applications on iOS, tvOS or macOS, long-running tasks should not be performed using this scheduler, so avoid things like server requests or other heavy tasks.

Additionally, if you perform side effects that update the UI, you must switch to the `MainScheduler` to guarantee those updates make it to the screen.

The `MainScheduler` is also used to perform all the computations when using `Units`, and more specifically, `Driver`. As discussed in an earlier chapter, `Driver` ensures the computation is always performed in the `MainScheduler` to give you the ability to bind data directly to the user interface of your application.

SerialDispatchQueueScheduler

`SerialDispatchQueueScheduler` manages to abstract the work on a serial `DispatchQueue`. This scheduler has the great advantage of several optimizations when using `observeOn`.

You can use this scheduler to process background jobs which are better scheduled in a serial manner. For example, if you have an application talking with a single endpoint of a server (as in a Firebase or GraphQL application), you might want to avoid dispatching multiple, simultaneous requests, which would put too much pressure on the receiving end. This scheduler is definitely the one you would want for any jobs that should advance much like a serial task queue.

ConcurrentDispatchQueueScheduler

`ConcurrentDispatchQueueScheduler`, similar to `SerialDispatchQueueScheduler`, manages to abstract work on a `DispatchQueue`. The main difference this time is that instead of a serial queue, the scheduler uses a concurrent one.

This kind of scheduler isn't optimized when using `observeOn`, so remember to account for that when deciding which kind of scheduler to use.

A concurrent scheduler might be a good option for multiple, long-running tasks that need to end simultaneously. Combining multiple observables with a blocking operator, so all results are combined together when ready, can prevent serial schedulers from performing at their best. Instead, a concurrent scheduler could perform multiple concurrent tasks and optimize the gathering of the results.

OperationQueueScheduler

`OperationQueueScheduler` is similar to `ConcurrentDispatchQueueScheduler`, but instead of abstracting the work over a `DispatchQueue`, it performs the job over an `NSOperationQueue`. Sometimes you need more control over the concurrent jobs you are running, which you can't do with a concurrent `DispatchQueue`.

If you need to fine-tune the maximum number of concurrent jobs, this is the scheduler for the job. You can define `maxConcurrentOperationCount` to cap the number of concurrent operations to suit your application's needs.

TestScheduler

`TestScheduler` is a special kind of beast. It's meant only to be used in testing, so try not to use this scheduler in production code. This special scheduler simplifies operator testing; it's part of the `RxTest` library. You will have a look into using this scheduler in the dedicated chapter about testing, but let's have a quick look since you're doing the grand tour of schedulers.

A good use case for this scheduler is provided by the test suite of RxSwift. Open the dedicated file for testing the `delay` operator **Observable+TimeTest.swift** and search for the single test case named `testDelaySubscription_TimeSpan_Simple`. Inside this test case, you have the initialization of the scheduler:

```
let scheduler = TestScheduler(initialClock: 0)
```

Following this initialization, you have the definition of the observable to test:

```
let xs = scheduler.createColdObservable([
    next(50, 42),
    next(60, 43),
    completed(70)
])
```

And just before the definition of the expectations, you have the declaration of how to get the results:

```
let res = scheduler.start {
    xs.delaySubscription(30, scheduler: scheduler)
}
```

`res` will be created by the scheduler using the previously defined `xs` observable. This result contains all the information about the events sent as well as the time tracked by the test scheduler.

With this, you could write a test case like so:

```
XCTAssertEqual(res.events, [
  next(280, 42),
  next(290, 43),
  completed(300)
])
```

Wondering why the event happens at 280, and not at 80 (considering the original 50, plus 30 for the delay)? This is due to the nature of `testScheduler`, which starts all subscriptions to `ColdObservable` after 200. This trick ensures that a cold observable won't start at an unpredictable time — which would make testing a nightmare!

The same thing doesn't apply to a `HotObservable`, so a `HotObservable` will start pushing events right away.

As you're testing a `delaySubscription` operator, just the information about the events sent and their time won't be enough to work with. You'll need extra information about the time of the subscription to ensure everything is working as expected.

With `xs.subscriptions`, you can get the list of the subscriptions to make the final part of the test:

```
XCTAssertEqual(xs.subscriptions, [
  Subscription(230, 300)
])
```

The first number defines the starting time of the first subscription. The second one defines when the subscription will be disposed. In this case, the second number matches the `completed` event because completion will dispose of all subscriptions.

Where to go from here?

Schedulers are a non-trivial topic in the Rx space; they're responsible for computing and performing all tasks in RxSwift. The golden rule of a `Scheduler` is that it can be *anything*. Keep this in mind, and you'll get along just fine when working with observables and using and changing schedulers.

As explained earlier, a scheduler can sit on top of a `DispatchQueue`, a `NSOperationQueue`, a `NSThread` or even perform the task immediately on the current thread. There's no hard rule about this, so make sure you know what scheduler you're using for the job at hand. Sometimes, using the wrong scheduler can have a negative impact on performance, while a well-chosen scheduler can have great performance returns.

Before proceeding, invest some time in playing around with the current example and test some schedulers to see what impact they have on the final result. Understanding schedulers will make life easier with RxSwift, and will improve your confidence when using `subscribeOn` and `observeOn`.

Chapter 16: Testing with RxTest

By Scott Gardner

👆 💯 🚀

👆 That's for you, for *not* skipping this chapter. Studies show that there are two reasons why developers skip writing tests:

1. They write bug-free code.
2. Writing tests isn't fun.

If the first reason is all you, you're hired! And if you agree with the second reason, well, let me introduce you to my little friend: RxTest. For all the reasons why you started reading this book and are excited to begin using RxSwift in your app projects, RxTest (and RxBlocking) may very soon have you excited to write tests against your RxSwift code, too. They provide an elegant API that makes writing tests easy and fun.

This chapter will introduce you to RxTest, and later, RxBlocking, by writing tests against several RxSwift operations and also writing tests against production RxSwift code.

Getting started

The starter project for this chapter is named **Testing**, and it contains a handy app to give you the red, green, and blue values and color name (if available) for the hex color code you enter. After running `pod install`, open up the project workspace and run it. You will see the app starts off with `rayWenderlichGreen`, but you can enter any hex color code and get the rgb and name values.

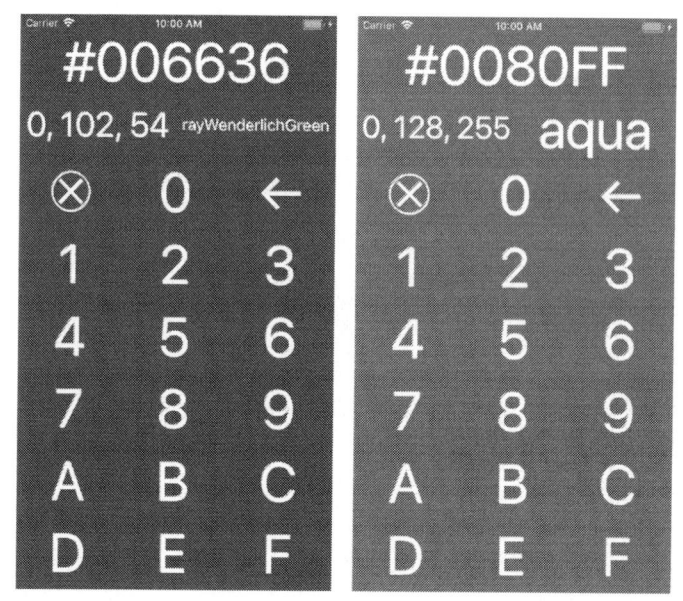

This app is organized using the MVVM design pattern, which you'll learn all about in the **MVVM** chapter. Suffice it to say that the view model is where the logic is housed that the view controller will use to control the view. And aside from an enumeration to model popular color names, the entire app runs on this logic, which you'll write tests against later in the chapter:

```
// Convert hex text to color
color = hexString.asObservable()
  .map { hex in
    guard hex.count == 7 else { return .clear }
    let color = UIColor(hex: hex)
    return color
  }
  .asDriver(onErrorJustReturn: .clear)

// Convert the color to an rgb tuple
rgb = color.asObservable()
  .map { color in
    var red: CGFloat = 0.0
```

```
    var green: CGFloat = 0.0
    var blue: CGFloat = 0.0

    color.getRed(&red, green: &green, blue: &blue, alpha: nil)
    let rgb = (Int(red * 255.0), Int(green * 255.0), Int(blue * 255.0))
    return rgb
  }
  .asDriver(onErrorJustReturn: (0, 0, 0))

// Convert the hex text to a matching name
colorName = hexString.asObservable()
  .map { hexString in
    let hex = String(hexString.dropFirst())

    if let color = ColorName(rawValue: hex) {
      return "\(color)"
    } else {
      return "--"
    }
  }
  .asDriver(onErrorJustReturn: "")
```

Before diving into testing *this* code, it would be helpful to learn about RxTest by writing a couple tests against RxSwift operators.

> **Note:** This chapter presumes you are familiar with writing unit tests in iOS using XCTest. If you're new to this, check out our video course, Beginning iOS Unit and UI Testing at https://videos.raywenderlich.com/courses/57-beginning-ios-unit-and-ui-testing/lessons/1.

Testing operators with RxTest

RxTest is a separate library from RxSwift. It's hosted within the RxSwift repo but requires a separate pod install and import. RxTest provides many useful additions for testing RxSwift code, such as `TestScheduler`, which is a virtual time scheduler that gives you granular control over testing time-linear operations, and methods including `next(_:_:)`, `completed(_:_:)`, and `error(_:_:)` that enable adding these events onto observables at specified times in your tests. It also adds hot and cold observables that you can think of as hot and cold sandwiches. No, not really.

What are hot and cold observables?

RxSwift goes to great lengths to streamline and simplify your Rx code, and there are circles of thought that feel the differences between hot and cold, when it comes to observables, in RxSwift can be thought of more as a trait of the observable instead of concrete types.

This is somewhat of an implementation detail, but worth being aware of because you won't see much talk about hot and cold observables in RxSwift outside of testing.

Hot observables:

- Use resources whether or not there are subscribers.
- Produce elements whether or not there are subscribers.
- Are primarily used with stateful types such as `Variable`.

Cold observables:

- Only consume resources upon subscription.
- Only produce elements if there are subscribers.
- Are primarily used for async operations such as networking.

You'll be using hot observables in the unit tests you'll soon be writing. But it's good to know the difference in case your needs call for using one over the other.

Open up **TestingOperators.swift** in the **TestingTests** group. At the top of the `class TestingOperators` definition, there are a couple of properties defined:

```
var scheduler: TestScheduler!
var subscription: Disposable!
```

`scheduler` is an instance of the `TestScheduler` that you'll use in each test, and `subscription` will hold your subscription in each test. Change the definition of `setUp()` to match the following:

```
override func setUp() {
  super.setUp()

  scheduler = TestScheduler(initialClock: 0)
}
```

In the `setUp()` method, which is called before each test case begins (e.g., the set of tests included in `TestingOperators` in your case), you initialize a new scheduler with an `initialClock` value of `0`. This means you want to start the test scheduler at the beginning time of the test. This will make more sense shortly.

Now change the `tearDown()` definition to match this code:

```
override func tearDown() {
  scheduler.scheduleAt(1000) {
    self.subscription.dispose()
  }

  super.tearDown()
}
```

`tearDown()` is called at the completion of each test. In it, you schedule disposal of the test's `subscription` at `1000` milliseconds. Each of the tests you'll write will run for less than 1 second, so it is safe to dispose of the test's subscription at 1 second.

And now friends, it's time to write a test! Add this new test to `TestingOperators` after the definition of `tearDown()`:

```
func testAmb() {

  // 2
  let observer = scheduler.createObserver(String.self)
}
```

Here's what you did:

1. As with all tests using XCTest, the method name must begin with `test`. You stub out a new test here of the `amb` operator.
2. You create an `observer` using the `scheduler`'s `createObserver(_:)` method, with a type hint of `String`.

`observer` will record and timestamp every event it receives, kind of like the `debug` operator in RxSwift, except it doesn't print anything out. You learned about the `amb` operator in the **Combining Operators** chapter. `amb` is used between two observables, and it will propagate events emitted by whichever observable emits first. In order to test `amb`, you'll need to create two observables. Add this code to test to do that:

```
// 1
let observableA = scheduler.createHotObservable([
  // 2
  next(100, "a"),
  next(200, "b"),
  next(300, "c")
])

// 3
let observableB = scheduler.createHotObservable([
  // 4
  next(90, "1"),
```

```
  next(200, "2"),
  next(300, "3")
])
```

With this code, you:

1. Create an `observableA` using the `scheduler`'s `createHotObservable(_:)` method.

2. Use `next(_:_:)` to add `.next` events onto `observableA` at the designated times (in milliseconds) with the value passed as the second parameter.

3. Create `observableB` hot observable.

4. Add `.next` events to `observableB` at the designated times and with the specified values.

Understanding that `amb` will propagate events emitted by the observable that emits first, you can guess that your test will confirm that using `amb` between these two observables should result in `observableB`'s elements being received.

In order to test this, add the following code to use the `amb` operator and assign the result to a local constant:

```
let ambObservable = observableA.amb(observableB)
```

Option-click on `ambObservable` and you will see that it is of type `Observable<String>`.

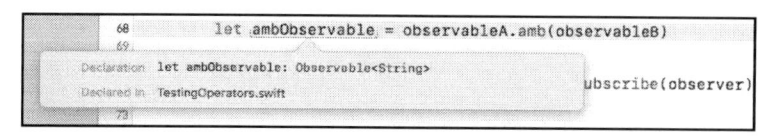

> **Note:** If Xcode is on the fritz again, you might see `<<error type>>` instead. Don't worry; Xcode will figure things out when you run the test.

Next, you'll need to tell the `scheduler` to schedule an action at a specific time. Add this code:

```
scheduler.scheduleAt(0) {
    self.subscription = ambObservable.subscribe(observer)
}
```

Here you schedule the ambObservable to subscribe to the observer at 0 time, and assign that subscription to the subscription property. In doing this, tearDown() will dispose of the subscription.

In order to actually kick off the test and then verify the results, add the following code:

```
scheduler.start()
```

This starts the virtual time scheduler, and observer will receive the .next events you specified via the amb operation.

Now you can collect and analyze the results. Enter this code:

```
let results = observer.events.map {
  $0.value.element!
}
```

You use map on the observer's events property to access each event's element. Now you can assert that these actual results match your expected results by adding this code:

```
XCTAssertEqual(results, ["1", "2", "3"])
```

Click the diamond button in the gutter to the left of func testAmb() to execute this test.

After Xcode builds and runs this test, you should see that it succeeded, or *passed*.

Normally you would create a negative test to complement this one, such as to test that the results received do not match what you know they should not be. You've many more tests to write before this chapter is done, so to quickly check that your test is working, change the assertion to match the following:

```
XCTAssertEqual(results, ["1", "2", "No you didn't!"])
```

Run the test again to verify that it failed with this error message:

```
XCTAssertEqual failed: ("["1", "2", "3"]") is not equal to
 ("["1", "2", "No you didn't!"]")
```

Undo that change and run the test again, and confirm it passes again.

You spent a whole chapter learning about filtering operators, so why not test one out? Add this test to `TestingOperators`, which follows the exact same format as `testAmb()`:

```
func testFilter() {

  // 1
  let observer = scheduler.createObserver(Int.self)

  // 2
  let observable = scheduler.createHotObservable([
    next(100, 1),
    next(200, 2),
    next(300, 3),
    next(400, 2),
    next(500, 1)
  ])

  // 3
  let filterObservable = observable.filter {
    $0 < 3
  }

  // 4
  scheduler.scheduleAt(0) {
    self.subscription = filterObservable.subscribe(observer)
  }

  // 5
  scheduler.start()

  // 6
  let results = observer.events.map {
    $0.value.element!
  }

  // 7
  XCTAssertEqual(results, [1, 2, 2, 1])
}
```

From the top, you:

1. Create an `observer`, this time type-hinting `Int`.

2. Create a hot observable that schedules a `.next` event every second for 5 seconds.

3. Create the `filterObservable` to hold the result of using `filter` on `observable` with a predicate that requires the element value to be less than 3.

4. Schedule the subscription to start at time `0` and assign it to the `subscription` property so it will be disposed of in `tearDown()`.

5. Start the scheduler.
6. Collect the results.
7. Assert that the results are what you expected.

Click the diamond in the gutter for this test to run it, and you should get a green checkmark indicating that the test succeeded.

These tests have been synchronous. When you want to test asynchronous operations, you have a couple choices. You'll learn the easiest way first, using RxBlocking.

Using RxBlocking

RxBlocking is another library housed within the RxSwift repo that, like RxTest, has its own pod and must be separately imported. Its primary purpose is to convert an observable to a `BlockingObservable` via its `toBlocking(timeout:)` method. What *this* does is block the current thread until the observable terminates, or if you specify a value for `timeout` (it is `nil` by default), and that `timeout` is reached before the observable terminates, it will throw an `RxError.timeout` error. This essentially turns an asynchronous operation into a synchronous one, making testing much easier.

Add this test to `TestingOperators` to test the `toArray` operator in three lines of code using RxBlocking:

```
func testToArray() {

  // 1
  let scheduler =
ConcurrentDispatchQueueScheduler(qos: .default)

  // 2
  let toArrayObservable = Observable.of(1,
2).subscribeOn(scheduler)

  // 3
  XCTAssertEqual(try! toArrayObservable.toBlocking().toArray(),
[1, 2])
}
```

What you just did:

1. Create a concurrent scheduler to run this asynchronous test, with the default quality of service.

2. Create an observable to hold the result of subscribing to an observable of two integers on the `scheduler`.

3. Use `toArray` on the result of calling `toBlocking()` on `toArrayObservable`, and assert that the return value from `toArray` equals the expected result.

`toBlocking()` converts `toArrayObservable` to a blocking observable, blocking the thread spawned by the scheduler until it terminates. Run the test and you should see it succeed. Three lines of code to test an asynchronous operation — woot! You'll work more with RxBlocking shortly, but now it's time to move away from testing operators and write some tests against the app's production code.

RxBlocking also has a `materialize` operator that can be used to examine the result of a blocking operation. It will return a `MaterializedSequenceResult`, which is an enum with two cases with associated values. From the documentation:

```
public enum MaterializedSequenceResult<T> {
  case completed(elements: [T])
  case failed(elements: [T], error: Error)
}
```

If the observable terminates successfully, the `.completed` case will associate an array of elements emitted from the underlying observable. And if it fails, the `.failed` case will associate both the elements array and the error. Add this new example to the playground, which reimplements the previous test of `toArray` using `materialize`:

```
func testToArrayMaterialized() {

  // 1
  let scheduler =
ConcurrentDispatchQueueScheduler(qos: .default)

  let toArrayObservable = Observable.of(1,
2).subscribeOn(scheduler)

  // 2
  let result = toArrayObservable
    .toBlocking()
    .materialize()

  // 3
  switch result {
  case .completed(elements: let elements):
    XCTAssertEqual(elements, [1, 2])
  case .failed(_, error: let error):
    XCTFail(error.localizedDescription)
  }
}
```

Step by step, you:

1. Create a scheduler and observable to test, the same as in the previous test.
2. Call `toBlocking` and `materialize` on the observable, and assign the result to a local constant `result`.
3. Switch on `result` and handle each case.

Run the tests again and confirm all tests succeed. As you can see, the usage of `materialize` in RxBlocking differs from RxSwift, but they are conceptually similar. The RxBlocking version goes the extra step of modeling the result as an enum to make examining it more robust and explicit. And if you were thinking, hey, that looks a lot like a `Single`, bravo!

Testing RxSwift production code

Start by opening **ViewModel.swift** in the **Testing** group (the app's main group). At the top, you'll see these property definitions:

```
let hexString = Variable<String>("")
let color: Driver<UIColor>
let rgb: Driver<(Int, Int, Int)>
let colorName: Driver<String>
```

`hexString` receives input from the view controller. `color`, `rgb`, and `colorName` are output that the view controller will bind to views. In the initializer for this view model, each output observable is initialized by transforming another observable and returning the result as a `Driver`. This is the code displayed at the beginning of the chapter.

Below the initializer is an enumeration definition to model common color names.

```
enum ColorName: String {
    case aliceBlue = "F0F8FF"
    case antiqueWhite = "FAEBD7"
    case aqua = "0080FF"
    // And many more...
```

Now open **ViewController.swift** and focus on the the `viewDidLoad()` implementation.

```
override func viewDidLoad() {
    super.viewDidLoad()

    configureUI()

    guard let textField = self.hexTextField else { return }
```

```swift
    textField.rx.text.orEmpty
      .bindTo(viewModel.hexString)
      .disposed(by: disposeBag)

    for button in buttons {
      button.rx.tap
        .bind {
          var shouldUpdate = false

          switch button.titleLabel!.text! {
          case "⊗":
            textField.text = "#"
            shouldUpdate = true
          case "←" where textField.text!.count > 1:
            textField.text = String(textField.text!.dropLast())
            shouldUpdate = true
          case "←":
            break
          case _ where textField.text!.count < 7:
            textField.text!.append(button.titleLabel!.text!)
            shouldUpdate = true
          default:
            break
          }

          if shouldUpdate {
            textField.sendActions(for: .valueChanged)
          }
        }
        .disposed(by: disposeBag)
    }

    viewModel.color
      .drive(onNext: { [unowned self] color in
        UIView.animate(withDuration: 0.2) {
          self.view.backgroundColor = color
        }
      })
      .disposed(by: disposeBag)

    viewModel.rgb
      .map { "\($0.0), \($0.1), \($0.2)" }
      .drive(rgbTextField.rx.text)
      .disposed(by: disposeBag)

    viewModel.colorName
      .drive(colorNameTextField.rx.text)
      .disposed(by: disposeBag)
}
```

From the top:

1. Bind the text field's text (or an empty string) to the view model's `hexString` input observable.
2. Loop over the buttons outlet collection, binding taps and switching on the button's title to determine how to update the text field's text, and if the text field should send the `.valueChanged` control event.
3. Use the view model's `color` driver to update the `view`'s background color.
4. Use the view model's `rgb` driver to update the `rgbTextField`'s text.
5. Use the view model's `colorName` driver to update the `colorNameTextField`'s text.

Open **TestingViewModel.swift** in the **TestingTests** group, and change the implementation of `setUp()` to match the following:

```
override func setUp() {
  super.setUp()

  viewModel = ViewModel()
  scheduler = ConcurrentDispatchQueueScheduler(qos: .default)
}
```

Here, you assign `viewModel` an instance of the app's `ViewModel` class and `scheduler` an instance of a concurrent scheduler with default quality of service.

Now you are ready to write tests against the app's view model. To begin, you'll write an asynchronous test using the traditional XCTest API with expectations. Add this test of the view model's `color` driver (using the traditional approach) to `TestingViewModel`:

```
func testColorIsRedWhenHexStringIsFF0000_async() {

  let disposeBag = DisposeBag()

  // 1
  let expect = expectation(description: #function)

  // 2
  let expectedColor = UIColor(red: 1.0, green: 0.0, blue: 0.0, alpha: 1.0)

  // 3
  var result: UIColor!
}
```

Here's what you did:

1. Create an expectation to be fulfilled later.
2. Create the expected test result `expectedColor` as equal to a red color.
3. Define the result to be later assigned.

This is just setup code. Now add the following code to the test to subscribe to the view model's `color` driver:

```
// 1
viewModel.color.asObservable()
  .skip(1)
  .subscribe(onNext: {
    // 2
    result = $0
    expect.fulfill()
  })
  .disposed(by: disposeBag)

// 3
viewModel.hexString.value = "#ff0000"

// 4
waitForExpectations(timeout: 1.0) { error in
  guard error == nil else {
    XCTFail(error!.localizedDescription)
    return
  }

  // 5
  XCTAssertEqual(expectedColor, result)
}
```

With this code, you:

1. Create a subscription to the view model's `color` driver. Notice that you skip the first one because Driver will replay the initial element upon subscription.
2. Assign the `.next` event element to `result` and call `fulfill()` on the expectation.
3. Add a new value onto the view model's `hexString` input observable (a `Variable`).
4. Wait for the expectation to fulfill with a 1 second timeout. In the closure, you guard for an error and then assert that the expected color equals the actual result.

Easy peasy, but a bit verbose. Run that test just to make sure it passes.

Now add the following test which accomplishes the same thing by using RxBlocking:

```
func testColorIsRedWhenHexStringIsFF0000() {

    // 1
    let colorObservable =
viewModel.color.asObservable().subscribeOn(scheduler)

    // 2
    viewModel.hexString.value = "#ff0000"

    // 3
    do {
        guard let result = try colorObservable.toBlocking(timeout:
1.0).first() else { return }

        XCTAssertEqual(result, .red)
    } catch {
        print(error)
    }
}
```

Here's the play-by-play:

1. Create the `colorObservable` to hold on to the observable result of subscribing on the concurrent scheduler.

2. Add a new value onto the view model's `hexString` input observable.

3. Use `guard` to optionally bind the result of calling `toBlocking()` with a 1 second timeout, catching and printing an error if thrown, and then asserting that the actual result matches the expected one.

Run the test to confirm it succeeds. This is essentially the same test as the previous one. You just didn't have to work as hard.

Next, add this code to test that the view model's `rgb` driver emits the expected red, green, and blue values for the given `hexString` input:

```
func testRgbIs010WhenHexStringIs00FF00() {

    // 1
    let rgbObservable =
viewModel.rgb.asObservable().subscribeOn(scheduler)

    // 2
    viewModel.hexString.value = "#00ff00"

    // 3
    let result = try! rgbObservable.toBlocking().first()!
```

```
        XCTAssertEqual(0 * 255, result.0)
        XCTAssertEqual(1 * 255, result.1)
        XCTAssertEqual(0 * 255, result.2)
    }
```

From the top:

1. Create `rgbObservable` to hold the subscription on the scheduler.

2. Add a new value onto the view model's `hexString` input observable.

3. Retrieve the first result of calling `toBlocking` on `rgbObservable` and then assert that each value matches expectations.

The conversion from 0-to-1 to 0-to-255 was just to match the test name and make things easier to follow. Run this test and it should succeed.

One more driver to test. Add this test to `TestingViewModel`, which tests that the view model's `colorName` driver emits the correct element for the given `hexString` input:

```
func testColorNameIsRayWenderlichGreenWhenHexStringIs006636() {
    
    // 1
    let colorNameObservable =
  viewModel.colorName.asObservable().subscribeOn(scheduler)
    
    // 2
    viewModel.hexString.value = "#006636"
    
    // 3
    XCTAssertEqual("rayWenderlichGreen", try!
  colorNameObservable.toBlocking().first()!)
}
```

The above code is fairly straightforward:

1. Create the observable.

2. Add the test value.

3. Assert that the actual result matching the expected result.

The phrase "rinse and repeat" comes to mind, but in a good way. Writing tests should *always* be this easy. Press **Command-U** to run all the tests in this project, and everything should pass with flying colors — or at least with the only color you want to see here: green.

Writing tests using RxText and RxBlocking is akin to writing data and UI binding code using RxSwift and RxCocoa (et al). There are no challenges for this chapter, because you will be doing more view model testing in the **MVVM** chapter. Happy testing!

Chapter 17: Creating Custom Reactive Extensions

By Junior Bontognali

After being introduced to RxSwift, RxCocoa, and learning how to create tests, you have yet to see how to create extensions using RxSwift on top of frameworks created by Apple or by third parties. Wrapping an Apple or third party framework's component was introduced in the chapter about RxCocoa, so you'll extend your learning as you work your way through this chapter's project.

In this chapter, you will create an extension to NSURLSession to manage the communication with an endpoint, as well as managing the cache and other things which are commonly part of a regular application. This example is pedagogical; if you want to use RxSwift with networking, there are several libraries available to do this for you, including RxAlamofire, which we also cover in this book.

Getting started

To start, you'll need a beta key for Giphy https://giphy.com, one of the most popular GIF services on the web. To get the beta key, navigate to the official docs https://developers.giphy.com/docs/.

When you create an app on that page (via the "Create an App" button) you will get a development key, which will suffice to work through this chapter. The API key is displayed under the name of your newly created app like so:

Your Apps

RxBook app

Api Key:
K64WzT0wyxvGV9oxN1oqkmIP

Request a production key

Open **ApiController.swift** and copy the key into the correct place:

```
private let apiKey = "[YOUR KEY]"
```

At this point, you can proceed with the CocoaPods installation process. Open Terminal, navigate to the root of the project and perform the necessary `pod install` command. Once you've completed this step, you will have all the necessary dependencies installed so you can build and run the application. Once you're sure the project builds without issues, you can proceed!

How to create extensions

Creating an extension over a Cocoa class or framework might seem like a non-trivial task; you will see that the process can be tricky and your solution might require some up-front thinking before continuing.

The goal here is to extend `URLSession` with the `rx` namespace, isolating the RxSwift extension, and making sure collisions are nearly impossible if you (or your team) need to extend this class further.

How to extend URLSession with .rx

To enable the `.rx` extension for `URLSession`, open **URLSession+Rx.swift** and add the following:

```
extension Reactive where Base: URLSession {
}
```

The `Reactive` extension, through a very clever protocol extension, exposes the `.rx` namespace over `URLSession`. This is the first step in extending `URLSession` with RxSwift. Now it's time to create the real wrapper.

How to create wrapper methods

You've exposed the `.rx` namespace over `NSURLSession`, so now you can create some wrapper functions to return an `Observable` of the type of the data you want to expose.

APIs can return various types of data, so it's a good idea to have some checks on the type of data your app expects. You want to create the wrappers for handling the following types of data:

- Data: just plain data
- String: data as text
- JSON: an instance of a JSON object
- Image: an instance of image

These wrappers are going to ensure the type you expect will be the one delivered. Otherwise, an error will be sent and the application will error out without crashing.

This wrapper, and one that will be used to create all the others, is the one that returns the `HTTPURLResponse` and the result `Data`. Your goal is to have an `Observable<Data>`, which will be used to create the remaining three operators:

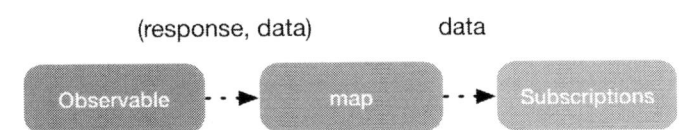

Observable --(response, data)--> map --data--> Subscriptions

Start by creating the skeleton of the main response function, so you know what to return. Add inside the extension you just created:

```
func response(request: URLRequest) ->
Observable<(HTTPURLResponse, Data)> {
    return Observable.create { observer in
```

```
    // content goes here
    return Disposables.create()
  }
}
```

It's pretty clear what this extension should return. The `URLResponse` is the part you will check to ensure the request has been successfully processed, while `Data` is, of course, the actual data returned by it.

`URLSession` is based on callbacks and tasks. For example the built-in method that sends a request and receives back the server response is `dataTask(with:completionHandler:)`. This function uses a callback to manage the result, so the logic of your observable has to be managed inside the required closure.

To do that add the following inside `Observable.create`:

```
let task = self.base.dataTask(with: request) { (data, response, error) in

}
task.resume()
```

The created task must be resumed (or started), so the `resume()` function will trigger the request. The result is then appropriately handled by the callback.

> **Note:** The use of the `resume()` function is what is known as "Imperative Programming". You'll see exactly what this means later on.

Now that the task is in place, there's a change to perform before proceeding. In the previous block, you were returning a `Disposable.create()`, which would simply do nothing if the `Observable` was disposed. It's better to cancel the request so that you don't waste any resources.

To do this, replace `return Disposables.create()` with:

```
return Disposables.create(with: task.cancel)
```

Now that you have the `Observable` with the correct lifetime strategy, it's time to make sure the data is correctly returned before sending any event to this instance.

To achieve this, add the following to your task closure just above `task.resume()`:

```
guard let response = response, let data = data else {
  observer.on(.error(error ?? RxURLSessionError.unknown))
  return
```

```
}
guard let httpResponse = response as? HTTPURLResponse else {
  observer.on(.error(RxURLSessionError.invalidResponse(response: response)))
    return
}
```

Both `guard` statements confirm the request has been successfully performed before notifying all the subscriptions. After ensuring the request has been correctly completed, this observable needs some data. Add the following code immediately after the code you added above:

```
observer.onNext((httpResponse, data))
observer.on(.completed)
```

This sends the event to all subscriptions followed immediately by the completion. Firing a request and receiving its response is a single usage `Observable`. It wouldn't make sense to keep the observable alive and perform other requests, which is more appropriate for things such as socket communication.

This is the most basic operator to wrap `URLSession`. You'll need to wrap a few more things to make sure the application is dealing with the correct kind of data. The good news is that you can reuse this method to build the rest of the convenience methods.

Start by adding the one returning a `Data` instance:

```
func data(request: URLRequest) -> Observable<Data> {
  return response(request: request).map { (response, data) -> Data in
      if 200 ..< 300 ~= response.statusCode {
        return data
      } else {
        throw RxURLSessionError.requestFailed(response: response, data: data)
      }
    }
}
```

The `Data` observable is the root of all the others. Data can be converted to a `String`, `JSON` object or `UIImage`. Add the following to return a `String`:

```
func string(request: URLRequest) -> Observable<String> {
   return data(request: request).map { d in
     return String(data: d, encoding: .utf8) ?? ""
   }
}
```

A `JSON` data structure is a simple structure to work with, so a dedicated conversion is more than welcomed. Add:

```
func json(request: URLRequest) -> Observable<JSON> {
  return data(request: request).map { d in
    return try JSON(data: d)
  }
}
```

Finally, implement the last one to return an instance of `UIImage`:

```
func image(request: URLRequest) -> Observable<UIImage> {
  return data(request: request).map { d in
    return UIImage(data: d) ?? UIImage()
  }
}
```

When you modularize an extension like you just did, you allow for better composability. For example, the last observable can be visualized in the following way:

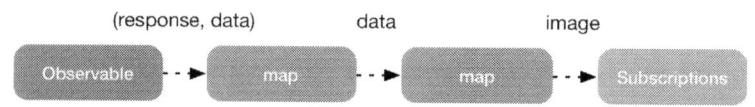

Some of RxSwift's operators, such as `map`, can be smartly assembled to avoid processing overhead so a multiple chain of maps will be optimized into a single call. Don't worry about chaining them or including too much in the closures.

How to create custom operators

In the chapter about RxCocoa you created a function to cache data. This looks like a good approach here, considering the size of some GIFs. As well, a good application should minimize loading times as much as possible.

A good approach in this case is to create a special operator to cache data that is only available for observables of type (`HTTPURLResponse, Data`). The goal is to cache as much as possible, so it sounds reasonable to create this operator only for observables of type (`HTTPURLResponse, Data`) and use the response object to retrieve the absolute URL of the request and use it as a key in the dictionary.

The caching strategy will be a simple `Dictionary`; you can later extend this basic behavior to persist the cache and reload it when reopening the app, but this goes beyond the current project scope.

Create the cache dictionary at the top, before the `RxURLSessionError`'s definition:

```
fileprivate var internalCache = [String: Data]()
```

Then create the extension which will target only observables of Data type:

```
extension ObservableType where E == (HTTPURLResponse, Data) {

}
```

Inside this extension, you can create the cache() function as shown:

```
func cache() -> Observable<E> {
   return self.do(onNext: { (response, data) in
      if let url = response.url?.absoluteString, 200 ..< 300 ~=
response.statusCode {
         internalCache[url] = data
      }
   })
}
```

To use the cache, make sure to modify the data(request:)'s return statement to cache the response before returning its own result. You can simply insert only the .cache() part:

```
return response(request: request).cache().map { (response, data)
-> Data in
   //...
}
```

To check if the data is already available, instead of firing a network request every time, add the following to the top of data(request:), before the return:

```
if let url = request.url?.absoluteString, let data =
internalCache[url] {
   return Observable.just(data)
}
```

You now have a very basic caching system that extends only a certain type of Observable:

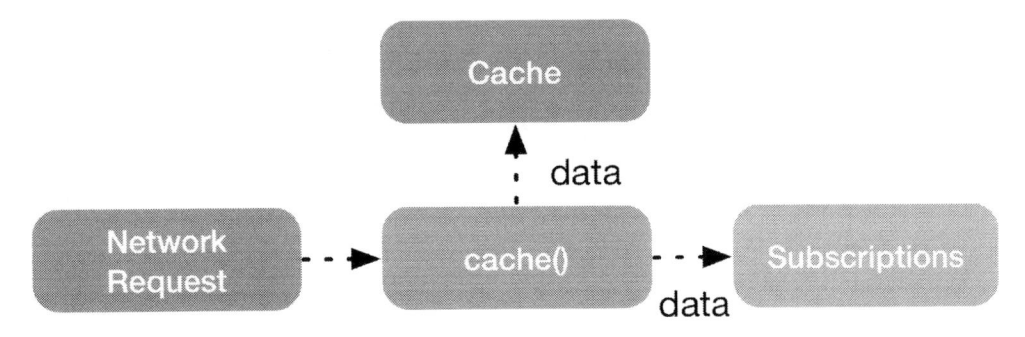

You can reuse the same procedure to cache other kinds of data, considering this is an extremely generic solution.

Use custom wrappers

You've created some wrappers around `URLSession`, as well as some custom operators targeting only some specific type of observables. Now it's time to fetch some results and display some funny cat GIFs.

The current project already has the batteries included, so the only thing you need to provide is a a list of `JSON` structures coming from the Giphy API.

Open **ApiController.swift** and have a look at the `search()` method. The code inside prepares a proper request to the Giphy API, but at the very bottom it doesn't make a network call, but just returns an empty observable instead (since this is placeholder code).

Now that you've completed your `URLSession` reactive extension, you can make use of it to get data from the network in the bespoke method. Modify the `return` statement like so:

```
return URLSession.shared.rx.json(request: request).map() { json in
    return json["data"].array ?? []
}
```

This will handle the request for a given query string, but the data is still not displayed. There's one last step to be performed before the GIF actually pops up on screen.

Add the following to **GifTableViewCell.swift**, right at the end of `downloadAndDisplay(gif stringUrl:)`:

```
let s = URLSession.shared.rx.data(request: request)
    .observeOn(MainScheduler.instance)
    .subscribe(onNext: { imageData in
        self.gifImageView.animate(withGIFData: imageData)
        self.activityIndicator.stopAnimating()
    })
disposable.setDisposable(s)
```

The usage of `SingleAssignmentDisposable()` is mandatory to keep things performing well. When a download of a GIF starts, you should make sure it's been stopped if the user scrolls away and doesn't wait for the rendering of the image.

To correctly balance this, `prepareForReuse()` has the following two lines already included in the starter code:

```
disposable.dispose()
disposable = SingleAssignmentDisposable()
```

The `SingleAssignmentDisposable()` will ensure only one subscription is ever alive at a given time for every single cell so you won't bleed resources.

Build and run, type something in the search bar and you'll see the app come alive.

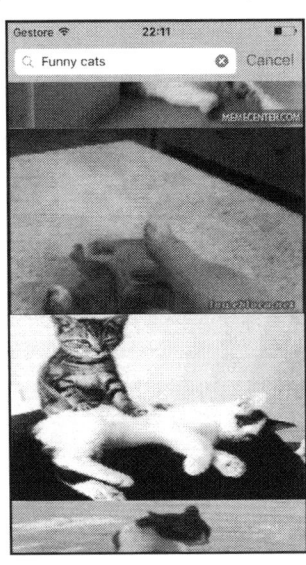

Testing custom wrappers

Although everything seems to be working properly, it's a good habit to create some tests and ensure everything keeps working correctly, especially when wrapping third party frameworks.

Test suites ensure the wrapper around a framework stays in good shape, and will help you find where the code is failing due to a breaking change or a bug.

How to write tests for custom wrappers

You were introduced to testing in the previous chapter; in this chapter you'll use a common library used to write tests on Swift called **Nimble**, along with its wrapper **RxNimble**.

RxNimble makes tests easier to write and helps your code be more concise. Instead of writing the classic:

```
let result = try! observabe.toBlocking().first()
expect(result).first != 0
```

You can write the much shorter:

```
expect(observable) != 0
```

Open the test file **iGifTests.swift**. Checking the import section, you can see the `Nimble`, `RxNimble`, `OHHTTPStubs` used to stub network requests and `RxBlocking` necessary to convert an asynchronous operation into a blocking ones.

At the end of the file, you can also find a short extension for `BlockingObservable` with a single function:

```
func firstOrNil() -> E? {}
```

This would avoid abusing the `try?` method all through the test file. You'll see this in use shortly.

At the top of the file, you'll find a dummy JSON object to test with:

```
let obj = ["array": ["foo", "bar"], "foo": "bar"] as [String: Any]
```

Using this predefined data makes it easier to write tests for `Data`, `String` and `JSON` requests.

The first test to write is the one for the data request. Add the following test to the test case class to check that a request is not returning `nil`:

```
func testData() {
    let observable = URLSession.shared.rx.data(request: self.request)
    expect(observable.toBlocking().firstOrNil()).toNot(beNil())
}
```

As soon as you wrap up typing in the method, Xcode will display a diamond shaped button in the editor gutter much like this (the line number might differ for you):

◇42

Click on the button and run the test. If the test succeeds, the button will turn green; if it fails, it will turn red. Hopefully you typed in all the code correctly, and you will see the button turn into a green checkmark.

Once the observable returning `Data` is tested and works correctly, the next one to test is the observable that handles `String`. Considering that the original data is a JSON representation, and considering that keys are sorted, the expected result should be:

```
{"array":["foo","bar"],"foo":"bar"}
```

The test is then really straightforward to write. Add the following, taking in consideration that the JSON string has to be escaped:

```
func testString() {
    let observable = URLSession.shared.rx.string(request: self.request)
    let string = "{\"array\":[\"foo\",\"bar\"],\"foo\":\"bar\"}"
    expect(observable.toBlocking().firstOrNil()) == string
}
```

Press the test button for that new test, and once finished, move on to testing JSON parsing. The test requires a `JSON` data structure to compare with. Add the following code to convert the string version to `Data` and process it as `JSON`:

```
func testJSON() {
    let observable = URLSession.shared.rx.json(request: self.request)
    let string = "{\"array\":[\"foo\",\"bar\"],\"foo\":\"bar\"}"
    let json = try? JSON(data: string.data(using: .utf8)!)
    expect(observable.toBlocking().firstOrNil()) == json
}
```

The last test is to make sure that errors are returned properly. Comparing two errors is a rather uncommon procedure, so it doesn't make sense to have an equal operator for an error. Therefore the test should use `do`, `try` and `catch` for the `unknown` error.

Add the following:

```
func testError() {
    var erroredCorrectly = false
    let observable = URLSession.shared.rx.json(request: self.errorRequest)
    do {
        let _ = try observable.toBlocking().first()
        assertionFailure()
    } catch (RxURLSessionError.unknown) {
        erroredCorrectly = true
    } catch {
        assertionFailure()
    }
    expect(erroredCorrectly) == true
}
```

At this point your project is complete. You've created your own extensions on top of `URLSession`, and you also created some cool tests which will ensure your wrapper is behaving correctly. Testing wrappers like the one you've built is extremely important because Apple frameworks and other third party frameworks can feature breaking changes in major releases — so you should be prepared to act fast if a test breaks and the wrapper stops working.

Common available wrappers

The RxSwift community is very active, and there are a lot of extensions and wrappers already available. Some are based on Apple components, while some others are based on widely-used, third-party libraries found in many iOS and macOS projects.

You can find a list of up-to-date wrappers at http://community.rxswift.org.

Here's a quick overview of the most common wrappers at present:

RxDataSources

`RxDataSources` is a `UITableView` and `UICollectionView` data source for RxSwift with some really nice features such as:

- $O(n)$ algorithm for calculating differences
- Heuristics to send the minimal number of commands to the sectioned view
- Support for extending already implemented views
- Support for hierarchical animations

These are all important features, but my favorite is the $O(n)$ algorithm to differentiate between two data sources: it ensures the application isn't performing unnecessary calculations when managing table views.

Consider the code you write with the built-in RxCocoa table binding:

```
let data = Observable<[String]>.just(
  ["1st place", "2nd place", "3rd place"]
)

data.bindTo(tableView.rx.items(cellIdentifier: "Cell")) { index,
model, cell in
  cell.placeLabel.text = model
}
.disposed(by:disposeBag)
```

This works perfectly with simple data sets, but lacks animations, support for multiple sections, and doesn't extend very well.

With `RxDataSource` correctly configured, the code becomes more robust:

```
//configure sectioned data source
let dataSource =
RxTableViewSectionedReloadDataSource<SectionModel<String,
String>>()
Observable.just([SectionModel(model: "Position", items: ["1st",
"2nd", "3rd"])])
  .bindTo(tableView.rx.items(dataSource: dataSource))
  .disposed(by: disposeBag)
```

And the minimal configuration of the data source that needs to be done in advance looks like so:

```
dataSource.configureCell = { dataSource, tableView, indexPath,
item in
  let cell = tableView.dequeueReusableCell(
    withIdentifier: "Cell", for: indexPath)
  cell.placeLabel.text = item
  return cell
}
dataSource.titleForHeaderInSection = { dataSource, index in
  return dataSource.sectionModels[index].header
}
```

Since binding table and collection views is an important every day task, you'll look into `RxDataSources` in more detail in a dedicated cookbook-style chapter later in this book.

RxAlamofire

RxAlamofire is a wrapper around the elegant Swift HTTP networking library Alamofire. Alamofire is one of the most popular third-party frameworks.

`RxAlamofire` features the following convenience extensions:

```
func data(_ method:_ url:parameters:encoding:headers:)
  -> Observable<Data>
```

This method combines all the request details into one call and returns the server response as `Observable<Data>`.

Further, the library offers:

```
func string(_ method:_ url:parameters:encoding:headers:)
  -> Observable<String>
```

This one returns an `Observable` of the content response as `String`.

Last, but no less important:

```
func json(_ method:_ url:parameters:encoding:headers:)
  -> Observable<Any>
```

This returns an instance of an object. It's important to know that this method doesn't return a `JSON` object like the one you created before.

Other than this, RxAlamofire also includes convenience functions to create observables to download or upload files and to retrieve progress information.

RxBluetoothKit

Working with Bluetooth can be complicated. Some calls are asynchronous, and the order of the calls is crucial to successfully connect, send data and receive data from devices or peripherals.

RxBluetoothKit abstracts some of the *most* painful parts of working with Bluetooth and delivers some cool features:

- `CBCentralManger` support
- `CBPeripheral` support
- Scan sharing and queueing

To start using RxBluetoothKit, you have to create a manager:

```
let manager = BluetoothManager(queue: .main)
```

The code to scan for peripherals looks something along the lines of:

```
manager.scanForPeripherals(withServices: [serviceIds])

.flatMap { scannedPeripheral in
    let advertisement = scannedPeripheral.advertisement
}
```

And to connect to one:

```
manager.scanForPeripherals(withServices: [serviceId])
    .take(1)
    .flatMap { $0.peripheral.connect() }
    .subscribe(onNext: { peripheral in
        print("Connected to: \(peripheral)")
    })
```

It's also possible to observe the current state of the manager:

```
manager.rx_state
    .filter { $0 == .poweredOn }
    .timeout(1.0, scheduler)
    .take(1)
    .flatMap { manager.scanForPeripherals(withServices:
[serviceId]) }
```

In addition to the manager, there are also super-convenient abstractions for characteristics and peripherals. For example, to connect to a peripheral you can do the following:

```
peripheral.connect()
    .flatMap { $0.discoverServices([serviceId]) }
    .subscribe(onNext: { service in
        print("Service discovered: \(service)")
})
```

And if you want to discover a characteristic:

```
peripheral.connect()
    .flatMap { $0.discoverServices([serviceId]) }
    .flatMap { $0.discoverCharacteristics([characteristicId])}
    .subscribe(onNext: { characteristic in
        print("Characteristic discovered: \(characteristic)")
})
```

RxBluetoothKit also features functions to properly perform connection restorations, to monitor the state of Bluetooth and to monitor the connection state of single peripheral.

Where to go from here?

In this chapter, you saw how to implement and wrap an Apple framework. Sometimes, it's very useful to abstract an official Apple Framework or third party library to better connect with RxSwift. There's no real written rule about when an abstraction is necessary, but the recommendation is to apply this strategy if the framework meets one or more of these conditions:

- Uses callbacks with completion and failure information
- Uses a lot of delegates to return information asynchronously
- Needs to inter-operate with other RxSwift parts of the application

You also need to know if the framework has restrictions on which thread the data must be processed. For this reason, it's a good idea to read the documentation thoroughly before creating a RxSwift wrapper. And don't forget to look for existing community extensions — or, if you've written one, consider sharing it back with the community!

Challenges

Challenge 1: Add processing feedback

In this challenge you're asked to add some information about the processing of `JSON` and `UIImage`. In the current state, the application receives an empty string or image when the data can't be processed.

Take a moment to review the code, remove the default, empty objects and make the code raise an error if the type conversion doesn't work out. The `RxURLSessionError` enum in URLSession+Rx.swift already includes a case called `deserializationFailed` — throw it when type conversion fails.

Before starting, try to understand where this has to be raised and when. Sending an error to an observable is a termination, so make sure you are sending the error in the correct case.

If you can't wrap up with this on your own, no worries — there's a solution provided along with this chapter.

Section V: RxSwift Community Cookbook

RxSwift's popularity keeps growing every day. Thanks to the friendly and creative community that formed around this library, a lot of community-driven Rx projects are being released on GitHub.

The advantage of the community-built libraries that use RxSwift is that unlike the main repository, which needs to follow the Rx standard, these libraries can afford to experiment and explore different approaches, provide non multi-platform specializations, and more.

In this section you are going to look into just a few of the many community open source projects. The section contains five short cookbook-style chapters that look briefly into five community projects that help you with binding table views, handling user gestures, persisting data with the Realm database, and talking to your server with Alamofire.

Chapter 18: Table and collection views

Chapter 19: Action

Chapter 20: RxGesture

Chapter 21: RxRealm

Chapter 22: RxAlamofire

Chapter 18: Table and Collection Views

By Florent Pillet

The most frequent requirement for iOS applications is to display content in table or collection views. A typical implementation features two or more dataSource and delegate callbacks, although you often end up with more. RxSwift not only comes with the tools to perfectly integrate observable sequences with tables and collections views, but also reduces the amount of boilerplate code by quite a large amount.

Basic support for `UITableView` and `UICollectionView` is present in the RxCocoa framework you were introduced to in previous chapters.

In this chapter, you'll learn how to quickly wire up tables and collections with just the built-in framework tools. Extended support for things such as sections and animations comes with **RxDataSources** https://github.com/RxSwiftCommunity/RxDataSources, an advanced framework found under the umbrella of RxSwiftCommunity organization.

The examples below are for `UITableView`, but the same patterns work for `UICollectionView` as well.

Basic table view

In a typical scenario, you want to display a list of items of the same type: for example, a list of cities, as you saw in previous chapters. Using standard cells to display them requires nearly zero setup. Consider a single observable list:

```
@IBOutlet var tableView: UITableView!

func bindTableView() {
  let cities = Observable.of(["Lisbon", "Copenhagen", "London", "Madrid", "Vienna"])
```

```
    cities
      .bind(to: tableView.rx.items) {
        (tableView: UITableView, index: Int, element: String) in
          let cell = UITableViewCell(style: .default,
reuseIdentifier: "cell")
          cell.textLabel?.text = element
          return cell
      }
      .disposed(by: disposeBag)
}
```

And. That's. All. You don't even need to set your `UIViewController` as a `UITableViewDataSource`. Wow!

This deserves a quick overview of what's going on:

- `tableView.rx.items` is a binder function operating on observable sequences of elements (like `Observable<[String]>`).

- The binding creates an invisible `ObserverType` object which subscribes to your sequence, and sets itself as the `dataSource` and `delegate` of the table view.

- When a new array of elements is delivered on the observable, the binding reloads the table view.

- To obtain the cell for each item, RxCocoa calls your closure with details (and date) for the row being reloaded.

This is straightforward to use. But what if you want to capture the user selection? Again, the framework is here to help:

```
tableView.rx
  .modelSelected(String.self)
  .subscribe(onNext: { model in
    print("\(model) was selected")
  })
  .disposed(by: disposeBag)
```

The `modelSelected(_:)` extension returns an observable which emits the model object (the element represented by the cell) every time the user selects it. A variant (`itemSelected()`) transports the `IndexPath` of the selected item.

RxCocoa offers a number of observables:

- `modelSelected(_:)`, `modelDeselected(_:)`, `itemSelected`, `itemDeselected` fire on item selection

- `itemAccessoryButtonTapped` fire on accessory button tap

- `itemInserted`, `itemDeleted`, `itemMoved` fire on events callbacks in table edit mode
- `willDisplayCell`, `didEndDisplayingCell` fire every time related `UITableViewDelegate` callbacks fire.

These are all simple wrappers around equivalent `UITableViewDelegate` callbacks.

Multiple cell types

It's nearly as easy to deal with multiple cell types. From a model standpoint, the best way to handle it is to use an `enum` with associated data as the element model. This way you can handle as many different cell types as you need while binding the table to an observable of arrays of the `enum` type.

To build a table with cells of just strings, or custom cells with two images, first define a data model with an enum then create an observable of arrays of this model:

```
enum MyModel {
  case text(String)
  case pairOfImages(UIImage, UIImage)
}

let observable = Observable<[MyModel]>.just([
  .textEntry("Paris"),
  .pairOfImages(UIImage(named: "EiffelTower.jpg")!, UIImage(named: "LeLouvre.jpg")!),
  .textEntry("London"),
  .pairOfImages(UIImage(named: "BigBen.jpg")!, UIImage(named: "BuckinghamPalace.jpg")!)
])
```

To bind it to the table, use a slightly different closure signature, and load a different cell class depending on the element emitted. The idiomatic code looks like this:

```
observable.bind(to: tableView.rx.items) {
  (tableView: UITableView, index: Int, element: MyModel) in
  let indexPath = IndexPath(item: index, section: 0)
  switch element {
  case .textEntry(let title):
    let cell = tableView.dequeueReusableCell(withIdentifier: "titleCell", for: indexPath) as! TextCell
    cell.titleLabel.text = title
    return cell
  case .pairOfImages(let firstImage, let secondImage):
    let cell = tableView.dequeueReusableCell(withIdentifier: "pairOfImagesCell", for: indexPath) as! ImagesCell
    cell.leftImage.image = firstImage
    cell.rightImage.image = secondImage
```

```
        return cell
    }
}
.disposed(by: disposeBag)
```

This is not much more code than before. The only complexity is dealing with multiple data types in the observable of arrays of objects, which you can elegantly solve using an enum. Isn't Swift great?

Providing additional functionality

Even though RxCocoa-driven table views and collection views don't need you to set up your view controller as a delegate, you can do so to provide complementary functionality not managed by RxCocoa extensions. In the case of `UICollectionView`, you may want to leave your `UIViewController` as the `UICollectionViewDelegate`. If you bind this in a nib or storyboard, RxCocoa will do the right thing: it will set itself as the actual delegate, then forward callbacks your view controller implements.

For example when using `UICollectionView` with manual sizing, you often need to implement `collectionView(_:layout:sizeForItemAt:)` to compute correct item sizes. If you wired up your collection view with your view controller as its delegate, then later use RxCocoa binding to manage the content, you have nothing special to do. RxCocoa takes care of the details.

If you have already bound your collection view with RxCocoa and want to add your view controller as the collection view delegate, you can simply use this idiom:

```
tableView.rx.setDelegate(myDelegateObject)
```

The table reactive extension will do the "right thing" and correctly forward your object all delegate methods it implements. Do *not* directly set your object as the table view or collection view delegate after binding it with RxCocoa. This would prevent some or all of the bindings from working correctly.

RxDataSources

RxCocoa handles the table and collection view needs of many apps. However you might want to implement many advanced features like animated insertions and deletions, sectioned reloading and partial (diff) updates, all with editing support for both `UITableView` and `UICollectionView`.

Using RxDataSources requires more work to learn its idioms, but offers more powerful, advanced features. Instead of a simple array of data, it requires you to provide contents using objects which conform to the `SectionModelType` protocol. Each section itself contains the actual objects. For sections with multiple object types, use the `enum` technique shown above to differentiate the types.

The power of RxDataSources lies in the diff algorithm it uses to determine what's changed in a model update, and optionally animate the changes. By adopting the `AnimatableSectionModelType` protocol, your section model can provide details on the animations it wants to perform for insertions, deletions and updates.

Look up the repository at https://github.com/RxSwiftCommunity/RxDataSources and the included examples to learn more about this advanced framework!

Chapter 19: Action

By Florent Pillet

A project living under the RxSwiftCommunity https://github.com/RxSwiftCommunity organization, **Action** is an important building block for reactive applications. Thinking about what *actions* are in your code, the definition is along the lines of:

- A *trigger event* signals that it's time to do something.
- A task is performed.
- Immediately, later (or maybe never!), some value results from performing this task.

Notice a pattern? The trigger event can be represented as an observable sequence of something, such as button taps, timer ticks, or gestures, which may or may not convey data, but always signals work to be done. The result of each action can therefore be seen as a sequence of results, one result for each piece of work performed.

In the middle sits the `Action` object. It does the following:

- Provides an `inputs` observer to bind observable sequences to. You can also manually trigger new work.
- Can observe an `Observable<Bool>` to determine its "enabled" status (in addition to whether it's currently executing).
- Calls your factory closure which performs / starts the work and returns an observable of results.
- Exposes an `elements` observable sequence of all work results (a `flatMap` of all work observables).
- Gracefully handles errors emitted by work observables.

`Action` exposes observables for errors, the current execution status, an observable of each work observable, guarantees that no new work starts when the previous has not completed, and it's generally such a cool class that you don't want to miss it!

Last but not least, Action defines a **contract**, where you provide some or no data, some work is done and you may later get resulting data. How this contract is implemented doesn't matter to the code using the action. You can replace real actions with mock ones for testing without impacting the code at all, as long as the mock respects the contract.

Creating an Action

`Action` is a generic class defined as `class Action<Input, Element>`. `Input` is the type of the input data provided to your factory worker function. `Element` is the type of element emitted by the observable your factory function returns.

The simplest example of an action takes no input, performs some work and completes without producing data:

```
let buttonAction: Action<Void, Void> = Action {
  print("Doing some work")
  return Observable.empty()
}
```

This is dead simple. Now what about an action which takes credentials, performs a network request and returns a "logged in" status?

```
let loginAction: Action<(String, String), Bool> = Action
{ credentials in
  let (login, password) = credentials
  // loginRequest returns an Observable<Bool>
  return networkLayer.loginRequest(login, password)
}
```

> **Note:** Each action executed is considered complete when the observable returned by your factory closure completes or errors. This prevents starting multiple long-running actions. This behavior is handy with network requests, as you'll see below.

`Action` looks cool but it might not be immediately obvious how useful it is in a variety of contexts, so let's have a look at few practical examples.

Connecting buttons

`Action` comes with reactive extensions for `UIButton` and several other UIKit components. It also defines `CocoaAction`, a `typealias` for `Action<Void, Void>` — perfect for buttons which don't expect an output.

To connect a button, simply do the following:

```
button.rx.action = buttonAction
```

Every time user presses the button, the action executes. If the action from the previous press is not complete, the tap is dismissed. Remove the action from the button by setting it to `nil`:

```
button.rx.action = nil
```

Composing behavior

Let's consider `loginAction` again from the *Creating an Action* example above. Connect it to your UI like this:

```
let loginPasswordObservable =
Observable.combineLatest(loginField.rx.text,
passwordField.rx.text) {
   ($0, $1)
}
loginButton
   .withLatestFrom(loginPasswordObservable)
   .bind(to: loginAction.inputs)
   .disposed(by: disposeBag)
```

Every time user presses the Login button, the latest value of the login and password text fields is emitted to the `inputs` observer of `loginAction`. If the action is not already executing (such as if a previous login attempt isn't ongoing), the factory closure is executed, a new login request is initiated and the resulting observable will deliver either a `true` or `false` value, or it will error out.

Now you can subscribe to the action's `elements` observable and get notified when the login is successful:

```
loginAction.elements
   .filter { $0 } // only keep "true" values
   .take(1)      // just interested in first successful login
   .subscribe(onNext: {
```

```
    // login complete, push the next view controller
  })
  .disposed(by: disposeBag)
```

Errors get a special treatment to avoid breaking your subscriber sequences. There are two kinds of errors:

- `notEnabled` - the action is already executing or disabled, and
- `underlyingError(error)` - an error emitted by the underlying sequence.

Handle them this way:

```
loginAction
  .errors
  .subscribe(onError: { error in
    if case .underlyingError(let err) = error {
      // update the UI to warn about the error
    }
  })
  .disposed(by: disposeBag)
```

Passing work items to cells

Action helps solve a common problem: how to connect buttons in table view cells. `Action` to the rescue! When configuring a cell, you assign an action to a button. This way you don't need to put actual work inside your cell subclasses, helping enforce a clean separation — even more important so if you're using an MVVM architecture.

Reusing an example from the previous cookbook chapter, here's how simple it is to bind a button:

```
observable.bind(to: tableView.rx.items) {
  (tableView: UITableView, index: Int, element: MyModel) in
  let cell = tableView.dequeueReusableCell(withIdentifier:
"buttonCell", for: indexPath)
  cell.button.rx.action = CocoaAction { [weak self] in
    // do something specific to this cell here
    return .empty()
  }
  return cell
}
.disposed(by: disposeBag)
```

Of course you could set an existing action instead of creating a new one. The possibilities are endless!

Manual execution

To manually execute an action, call its `execute(_:)` function, passing it an element of the action's `Input` type:

```
loginAction
  .execute(("john", "12345"))
  .subscribe(onNext: {
    // handle return of action execution here
  })
  .disposed(by: disposeBag)
```

Perfectly suited for MVVM

If you're using MVVM (see Chapter 24, "MVVM with RxSwift" and Chapter 25, "Building a complete RxSwift app") you may have figured out by now that RxSwift is very well-suited for this architectural pattern. Action is a perfect match too! It nicely complements the separation between your View Controller and View Model. Expose your data as observable and all actionable functionality as `Action` to achieve MVVM nirvana!

Chapter 20: RxGesture

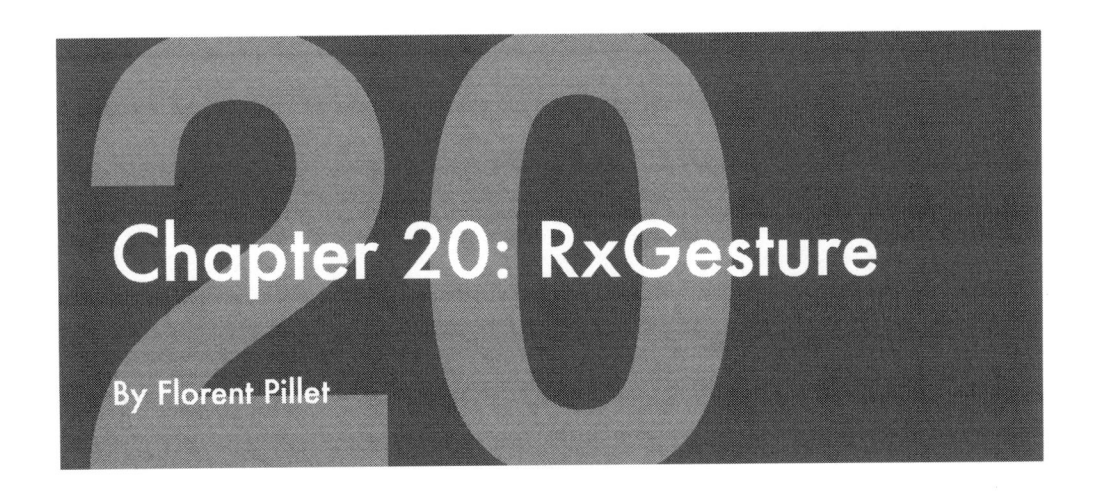

By Florent Pillet

Gesture processing is a good candidate for reactive extensions. Gestures can be viewed as a stream of events, either discrete or continuous. Working with gestures normally involves using the *target-action* pattern, where you set some object as the gesture target and create a function to receive updates.

At this point, you can appreciate the value of turning as much as of your data and event sources as possible into observable sequences. Enter **RxGesture**, https://github.com/RxSwiftCommunity/RxGesture, a project living under the RxSwiftCommunity at https://github.com/RxSwiftCommunity. It's cross-platform and works on both iOS and macOS.

In this chapter, you'll focus on the iOS implementation of RxGesture.

Attaching gestures

RxGesture makes it dead simple to attach a gesture to a view:

```
view.rx.tapGesture()
  .when(.recognized)
  .subscribe(onNext: { _ in
    print("view tapped")
  })
  .disposed(by: disposeBag)
```

In this example, RxGesture creates a `UITapGestureRecognizer`, attaches it to the view and emits an event every time the gesture is recognized. When you want to get rid of the recognizer, simply call `dispose()` on the `Disposable` object returned by the subscription.

You can also attach multiple gestures at once:

```
view.rx.anyGesture(.tap(), .longPress())
  .when(.recognized)
  .subscribe(onNext: { [weak view] gesture in
    if let tap = gesture as? UITapGestureRecognizer {
      print("view was tapped at \(tap.location(in: view!))")
    } else {
      print("view was long pressed")
    }
  })
  .disposed(by: disposeBag)
```

The event the subscription emits is the gesture recognizer object which changed state. The `when(_:...)` operator above lets you filter events based on the recognizer state to avoid processing events you're not interested in.

Supported gestures

RxGesture works with all iOS and macOS built-in gesture recognizers. You can use it with your own gesture recognizers, but that's beyond the scope of this chapter.

When you need a single gesture, use its reactive extension directly to attach it to the view. When you need multiple gestures at once, use the `anyGesture(_:...)` operator along with one of the supported functions. As seen in the examples above, you can either use `view.tapGesture()` or `view.anyGesture(.tap())`.

On iOS, the gesture extensions of `UIView` are `rx.tapGesture()`, `rx.swipeGesture(_:)`, `rx.longPressGesture()`, `rx.screenEdgePanGesture(edges:)`, `rx.pinchGesture()`, `rx.panGesture()` and `rx.rotationGesture()`. Swipe and Screen Edge Pan gestures require you to provide parameters to indicate the expected swipe direction or the screen edge for the recognizer to detect the gesture:

```
view.rx.screenEdgePanGesture(edges: [.top, .bottom])
  .when(.recognized)
  .subscribe(onNext: { recognizer in
    // gesture was recognized
  })
  .disposed(by: disposeBag)
```

On macOS, the gesture extensions of `NSView` are `rx.clickGesture()`, `rx.rightClickGesture()`, `rx.pressGesture()`, `rx.rotationGesture()` and `rx.magnificationGesture()`.

Each function that creates a gesture observable can take a configuration closure; this allows you to further tweak the gesture to your needs. For example, if you're writing an iPad Pro application and want to detect a swipe with the stylus only, you could do the following:

```
let observable = view.rx.swipeGesture(.left, configuration:
{ recognizer in
    recognizer.allowedTouchTypes = [NSNumber(value:
UITouchType.stylus.rawValue)]
})
```

Current location

Any gesture observable can be transformed to an observable of the location in the view of your choice with `asLocation(in:)`, saving you from doing it manually:

```
view.rx.tapGesture()
    .when(.recognized)
    .asLocation(in: .window)
    .subscribe(onNext: { location in
        // you now directly get the tap location in the window
    })
    .disposed(by: disposeBag)
```

Pan gestures

When creating a pan gesture observable with the `rx.panGesture()` reactive extension, use the `asTranslation(in:)` operator to transform events and obtain a tuple of current translation and velocity. The operator lets you specify which of the gestured view, superview, window or any other views you want to obtain the relative translation for. You'll get an `Observable<(translation: CGPoint, velocity: CGPoint)>` in return:

```
view.rx.panGesture()
    .asTranslation(in: .superview)
    .subscribe(onNext: { translation, velocity in
        print("Translation=\(translation), velocity=\(velocity)")
    })
    .disposed(by: disposeBag)
```

Rotation gestures

Similarly to pan gestures, rotation gestures created with the `rx.rotationGesture()` extension can be further transformed with the `asRotation()` operator. It creates an `Observable<(rotation: CGFloat, velocity: CGFloat)>`.

```
view.rx.rotationGesture()
  .asRotation()
  .subscribe(onNext: { rotation, velocity in
    print("Rotation=\(rotation), velocity=\(velocity)")
  })
  .disposed(by: disposeBag)
```

Automated view transform

More complex interactions, such as the pan/pinch/rotate combination gesture in `MapView`, can be fully automated with the help of the `transformGestures()` reactive extension of `UIView`:

```
view.rx.transformGestures()
  .asTransform()
  .subscribe(onNext: { [unowned view] (transform, velocity) in
    view.transform = transform
  })
  .disposed(by: disposeBag)
```

`transformGestures()` is a convenience extension which creates three gestures — a pan, a pinch and a rotation — attaches them to the view and returns an `Observable<TransformGestureRecognizers>`. The `TransformGestureRecognizers` struct simply holds the three recognizers.

The `asTransform()` operator turns the structure into an `Observable<(transform: CGAffineTransform, velocity: TransformVelocity)>`. The `TransformVelocity` struct holds the individual velocity for each of the gestures.

If you don't need the three gestures, you can disable one of them at configuration time, as the default configuration creates and attaches all three recognizers:

```
view.rx.transformGestures(configuration: { (recognizer, delegate) in
  recognizer.pinchGesture.isEnabled = false
})
```

Advanced usage

You'll sometimes need to use the observable for the same gesture at multiple places. Since subscribing to the observable creates and attaches the gesture recognizer, you only want to do this once.

This is a good opportunity to use the `share(replay:scope:)` operator, as shown here:

```
let panGesture = view.rx.panGesture()
  .share(replay: 1, scope: .whileConnected)

panGesture
  .when(.changed)
  .asTranslation()
  .subscribe(onNext: { [unowned view] translation, _ in
    view.transform = CGAffineTransform(translationX: translation.x,
      y: translation.y)
  })
  .disposed(by: stepBag)

panGesture
  .when(.ended)
  .subscribe(onNext: { _ in
    print("Done panning")
  })
  .disposed(by: stepBag)
```

Chapter 21: RxRealm

By Florent Pillet

A long time ago, in a parallel universe far away, developers who needed a database for their application had the choice between using the ubiquitous but tortuous Core Data, or creating custom wrappers for SQLite. Then Realm appeared, and all of a sudden using databases in applications became a breeze.

Database queries in Realm are "live": the contents of a `Results` collection update along with any database changes. Insert, modify or remove items and you'll immediately see the changes in the `Results` object. Additionally, fine-grained notifications can provide detailed information about changes in a `Results` object.

Same goes also for the `List` type, which allows you to build collections of objects, and even single objects you are working with will auto-update their contents should there be changes committed to the database meanwhile. All this makes Realm an ideal candidate for exposing these dynamic changes as observable sequences!

RxRealm, https://github.com/RxSwiftCommunity/RxRealm, is another project living under the RxSwiftCommunity organization. Its goal is to help you seamlessly integrate Realm into your reactive workflow.

Auto-updating results

A database query defines a collection of objects. At the most basic level, RxRealm wraps `Results` as an observable which fires once with initial contents, then again every time the collection changes:

```
let realm = try! Realm()
let result = realm.objects(MyObject.self)
```

```
Observable.collection(from: result)
  .subscribe(onNext: { items in
    print("Query returned \(items.count) items")
  })
  .disposed(by: disposeBag)
```

Every time you commit a change to the database that could affect `results`, the collection fires again.

Arrays

Getting an array instead of a Realm `Results` collection is easy:

```
let result = realm.objects(MyObject.self)
Observable.array(from: result)
  .subscribe(onNext: { array in
    print("Query returned \(array.count) items")
  })
  .disposed(by: disposeBag)
```

> **Note:** Since every object from the result has to be loaded from the database, there's both a memory and a time penalty to grab all objects as an array. Working with `collection(from:)` is usually what you'll need most often.

Asynchronous first item

Both `Observable.collection(from:)` and `Observable.array(from:)` emit the initial collection or array of items synchronously. At the time you subscribe to the observable (before the `subscribe(_:)` function returns), you receive the first element. This may interfere with your application, particularly when setting up user interfaces. A common source of bugs is to write `subscribe(_:)` while assuming that the code that follows has already been executed – but it hasn't for the first element.

Luckily, both functions actually take a second parameter which defaults to `true`. The actual signatures are `Observable.collection(from:synchronousStart:)` and `Observable.array(from:synchronousStart:)`.

If you want to let the first element be emitted asynchronously, pass `false` for the synchronousStart flag:

```
let result = realm.objects(MyObject.self)
Observable.array(from: result, synchronousStart: false)
  .subscribe(onNext: { array in
    print("Query returned \(array.count) items")
  })
  .disposed(by: disposeBag)
```

You will receive the initial contents when the initial Realm notification fires.

Changesets

RxRealm gives access to more elaborate observables. You can get changesets (the ones Realm notifies when results are updated) with `Observable.changeset(from:synchronousStart:)`. The observable sends the changeset along with the original collection of results:

```
let result = realm.objects(MyObject.self)
Observable.changeset(from: result)
  .subscribe(onNext: { (update) in
    if let changes = update.1 {
      // it's an update
      print("deleted: \(changes.deleted)")
      print("inserted: \(changes.inserted)")
      print("updated: \(changes.updated)")
    } else {
      // it's the initial data
      print(update.0)
    }
  }
  .disposed(by: disposeBag)
```

A variant of this API returns an observable of array and a Realm `ChangeSet`. For this, use `Observable.arrayWithChangeset(from:synchronousStart:)`.

Single objects

A final feature of RxRealm lets you observe a single object and get a new one every time it updates in the database. For example, if you store user settings in an object in the database, observe it at various places in your code to automatically update on settings change.

This is particularly handy for live updates being synced from other devices if you're using the Realm Mobile Platform:

```
let hideCompletedObs = Observable.from(object:
preferencesObject)
  .map { prefs -> Bool in prefs.hideCompletedTodos }
  .distinctUntilChanged()
let todosObs = realm.objects(Todo.self)
Observable.combineLatest(hideCompletedObs, todosObs) {
    hideCompleted, todos in
    if hideCompleted {
      return todos.filter { $0.completed == false }
    }
    return todos
  }
  .bind(to: tableView.rx.items) {
    (tableView: UITableView, index: Int, element: Todo) in
    // return cell here
  }
  .disposed(by: disposeBag)
```

In this scenario where your application displays a list of *todo* items, the list refreshes once initially, then again every time the "hide completed todos" flag changes in the user preferences.

In case you are interested in the changes to only certain properties of an object, you can use `Observable.propertyChanges(object:)` to subscribe to change events per property. In the *todo* app scenario from above, you might want to observe for changes on a given task's title, like so:

```
Observable.propertyChanges(object: task)
  .filter { $0.name == "taskTitle" }
  .subscribe(onNext: { change in
    print("property \(change.name) changed from: \
(String(describing: change.oldValue)) to: \(String(describing:
change.newValue))")
  })
  .disposed(by: bag)
```

Adding objects

RxRealm extends the `Realm` class with `add()` and `delete()` observers. You can use them to observe sequences of items to add or delete. Every time the sequence emits an object, it can be automatically added to or deleted from the database.

Consider the scenario where you need to query a remote server for new messages at regular intervals. When the API returns new messages, you want to see the messages added to the database (you're using RxRealm elsewhere in your application to automatically update the message list on database change):

```
Observable
    .timer(0, period: 60, scheduler: MainScheduler.instance)
    .flatMap { (_: Int) -> Observable<[Message]> in
      let messages =
realm.objects(Messages.self).sorted(byKeyPath: "dateReceived")
      if let lastMessage = messages.last {
        return MailAPI.newMessagesSince(lastMessage.dateReceived)
      }
      return MailAPI.newMessagesSince(Date.distantPast)
    }
    .subscribe(realm.rx.add())
    .disposed(by: disposeBag)
```

Simply ignore the value emitted by the timer, request all messages since the date of the last received message and pass the result on to RxRealm.

Be careful when you use `add()` on a Realm object. RxRealm retains the `Realm` database object for the duration of the subscription. If you don't want the subscription to retain the `Realm` object you can use one of the variations on the class itself: `Realm.rx.add()` or `Realm.rx.add(configuration:)` — the static method will fetch any existing `Realm` instance on the current thread and use it without retaining it.

Deleting objects

A similar endpoint lets you delete existing objects or collections of objects from the database:

```
let realm = try! Realm()
deleteSelectedMessagesButton.rx.tap
   .map { self.selectedMessages() }
   .bind(to: realm.rx.delete())
   .disposed(by: disposeBag)
```

Again, the `Realm` object is retained for the entire duration of the subscription.

Chapter 22: RxAlamofire

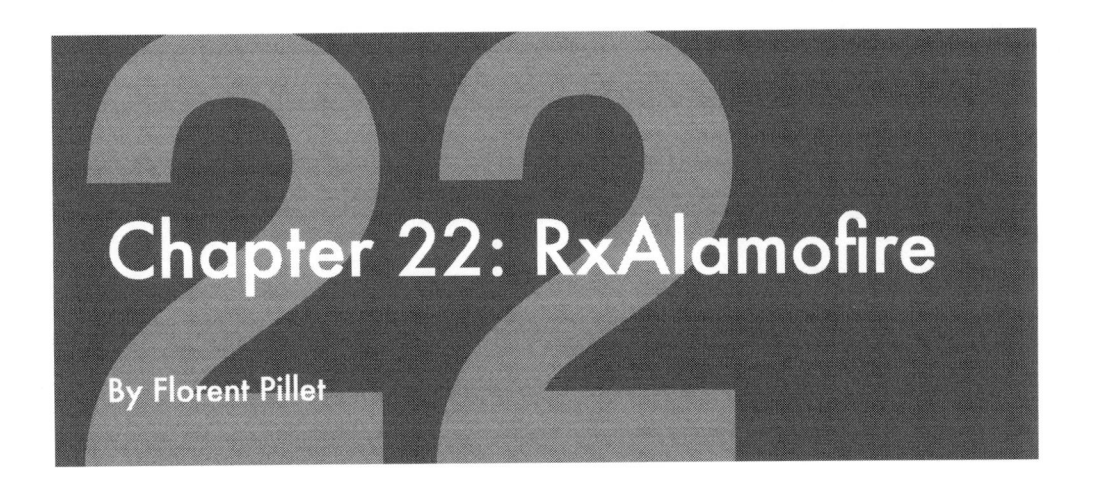

By Florent Pillet

One of the basic needs of modern mobile applications is the ability to query remote resources. You've seen several examples of this throughout this book, using the basic extensions to `NSURLSession` included with RxSwift.

Many developers like to use wrappers around OS-provided query mechanisms. The most popular undoubtedly is Alamofire https://github.com/Alamofire/Alamofire, a networking library with roots in Objective-C as it itself stems from AFNetworking https://github.com/AFNetworking/AFNetworking.

RxAlamofire https://github.com/RxSwiftCommunity/RxAlamofire is a project living under the RxSwiftCommunity organization. It adds an idiomatic Rx layer to Alamofire, making it straightforward to integrate into your observable workflow.

Most of the RxAlamofire API revolves around extending `SessionManager`.

Basic requests

It's straightforward to perform requests using the default `SessionManager` session. If you don't need to reuse a customized session, this can be your go-to request mechanism:

```
string(.get, stringURL)
    .subscribe(onNext: { print($0) })
    .disposed(by: disposeBag)
```

Most of the time you'll want to deal with and decode JSON, as simply as this:

```
json(.get, stringURL)
  .subscribe(onNext: { print($0) })
  .disposed(by: disposeBag)
```

The resulting observable emits the result as a decoded JSON object. Since the element type is `Any`, you'll need to further map for observable chaining, or cast it in the subscription.

You can also obtain raw `Data`:

```
data(.get, stringURL)
  .subscribe(onNext: { print($0) })
  .disposed(by: disposeBag)
```

RxAlamofire defines variants of these convenience functions prefixed with `request` (`requestString`, `requestJSON`, `requestData`), taking the same input parameters but returning an observable of a tuple of the `HTTPURLResponse` object along with the decoded body.

> **Note:** RxAlamofire requests are well-behaved observables. If you `dispose()` a subscription before the request has completed, the ongoing request is canceled. This is an important behavior of the framework, in particular when performing large uploads or downloads.

All of the above are convenience functions using the default `SessionManager`. Under the hood, they call the actual implementation defined as reactive extensions to `SessionManager`:

```
let session = SessionManager.default
session.rx.json(.get, stringURL)
  .subscribe(onNext: { print($0) })
  .disposed(by: disposeBag)
```

> **Note:** The `SessionManager` reactive extensions returning observables of tuple are prefixed with `response`, not with `request`. For example, you'll use `session.rx.responseJSON(.get, stringURL)` to obtain an `Observable<(HTTPURLResponse, Any)>`.

Request customization

The examples above didn't modify the default values for customized parameters, URL encoding and HTTP headers. But that's easy as well:

```
// get current weather in London
json(.get,
    "http://api.openweathermap.org/data/2.5/weather",
    parameters: ["q": "London", "APPID": "{APIKEY}"])
  .subscribe(onNext: { print($0) })
  .disposed(by: disposeBag)
```

The request URL will be `http://api.openweathermap.org/data/2.5/weather?q=London&APPID={APIKEY}`. You can also customize the request headers by adding a `headers` dictionary.

> **Note:** All the examples use strings as the request URL. All the APIs in RxAlamofire accept any object conforming to the `URLRequestConvertible` protocol, so you aren't limited to strings.

Response validation

The `request` and `session.rx.request` APIs let you perform further validation and manipulation by exposing the underlying `DataRequest`. You can then use AlamoFire extensions to perform validation, as well as RxAlamofire convenience extensions:

```
request(.get, stringURL)
  .flatMap { request in
    request
      .validate(statusCode: 200 ..< 300)
      .validate(contentType: ["text/json"])
      .rx.json()
  }
```

RxAlamofire also offers a `validateSuccessfulResponse()` extension performing the same status code validation as above.

Downloading files

You can download files to a destination determined by AlamoFire's `DownloadDestination` closure type:

```swift
let destination: DownloadRequest.DownloadFileDestination = { _, response in
  let docsURL =
FileManager.default.urls(for: .documentDirectory, in: .userDomainMask)[0]
  let filename = response.suggestedFilename ?? "image.png"
  let fileURL = docsURL.appendingPathComponent(filename)
  return (fileURL,
[.removePreviousFile, .createIntermediateDirectories])
}

download(URLRequest(url: someURL), to: destination)
  .subscribe(onCompleted: { print("Download complete") })
  .disposed(by: disposeBag)
```

Resuming a previously canceled download is also supported. Check out the `download(resumeData:to:)` API for more information.

> **Note:** the `request`, `download` and `upload` APIs all emit a single `AlamoFire.DataRequest`, `AlamoFire.DownloadRequest` or `AlamoFire.UploadRequest` at subscription time, then either complete or error.

Upload tasks

Uploading is equally easy. You can upload in-memory `Data`, stored files or even provide an `InputStream` as the data source:

```swift
upload(someData, to: URLRequest(url: someURL))
  .subscribe(onCompleted: { print("Upload complete") })
  .disposed(by: disposeBag)
```

The download and upload operators return observables of `AlamoFire.DownloadRequest` and `AlamoFire.UploadRequest` respectively. You can perform advanced processing by further handling of the emitted object.

Tracking progress

Track upload and download progress by extracting an `Observable<RxProgress>` from the `AlamoFire.Request` object emitted by request, download and upload APIs:

```swift
upload(localFileURL, to: URLRequest(url: remoteURL))
  .flatMap { request in
    request
      .validate()    // check acceptable status codes
      .rx.progress()
  }
  .subscribe (
    onNext: { progress in
      let percent = Int(100.0 * progress.completed)
      print("Upload progress: \(percent)%")
    },
    onCompleted: { print("Upload complete") })
  .disposed(by: disposeBag)
```

The `rx.progress` extension emits a `RxProgress` element at regular intervals on the main queue.

> **Note:** RxAlamofire exposes a rich subset of the even richer AlamoFire API. Make sure you explore the framework for more goodness!

Section VI: Putting it All Together

The "easy" part of the book is over. :] If you made it this far and are looking to learn even more in order to start creating production apps with RxSwift, this section is for you.

The two chapters in this section are going to help you learn how to build real-life applications with RxSwift.

The first chapter will cover the MVVM application architecture and show how a well designed ViewModel can power both the iOS and macOS versions of an app. You will look into building a flexible networking layer and touch on writing tests for your view models.

The second chapter, and the last one in this book, is going to build upon what you learned about the MVVM architecture and expand on it by adding services into the mix and scene-based navigation.

Once you finish working through this section, you will be one of the top RxSwift developers out there. There is, of course, more to know about Rx but at this point you will be able to figure out things further on your own.

Also, don't forget to give back to the community! It would not have been possible for us to put this book together without all the amazing Rx folks sharing their knowledge, code, and good vibes.

Chapter 23: MVVM with RxSwift

Chapter 24: Building a Complete RxSwift App

Chapter 23: MVVM with RxSwift

By Marin Todorov

RxSwift is such a big topic that this book hasn't covered application architecture in any detail yet. And this is mostly because RxSwift doesn't enforce any particular architecture upon your app. However, since RxSwift and MVVM play very nicely together, this chapter is dedicated to the discussion of that specific architecture pattern.

Introducing MVVM

MVVM stands for Model-View-ViewModel; it's a slightly different implementation of Apple's poster-child MVC (Model-View-Controller).

It's important to approach MVVM with an open mind. MVVM isn't a software architecture panacea; rather, consider MVVM to be a software pattern, which is a simple step toward good application architecture, especially if you start from an MVC mindset.

Some background on MVC

By now you've probably sensed a bit of tension between MVVM and MVC. What, precisely, is the nature of their relationship? They are very similar, and you could even say they are distant cousins. But they are still different enough that an explanation is warranted.

Most of the examples in this book (and other books about programming) use an MVC pattern for the code samples. MVC is a straightforward pattern for many simple apps and looks like this:

Each of your classes is assigned a category: the **controller** classes play a central role as they can update both the model and the view, while **views** only display data on screen and send events like gestures to the controller. Finally, the **models** read and write data to persist the app state.

MVC is a simple pattern that can serve you well for a while, but as your app grows you will notice that a *lot* of classes are neither a view, nor a model, and must therefore be controllers. A common trap to fall into is to start adding more and more code to a single controller class. Since you start with a view controller with iOS apps, the easiest thing to do is to stuff all your code into that view controller class. Hence the old joke that MVC stands for "Massive View Controller", because the controllers can grow to hundreds or even thousands of lines.

Overloading your classes is simply a bad practice, and *not* necessarily a shortcoming of the MVC pattern. Case in point: Many developers at Apple are fans of MVC, and they turn out amazingly well-built macOS and iOS software.

> **Note:** You can read more about MVC at the dedicated Apple documentation page: http://apple.co/2zKgwOR

MVVM to the rescue

MVVM *looks* a lot like MVC, but definitely *feels* better. People who like MVC usually love MVVM, as this newer pattern lets them easily solve a number of issues common to MVC.

The obvious departure from MVC is a new category named ViewModel:

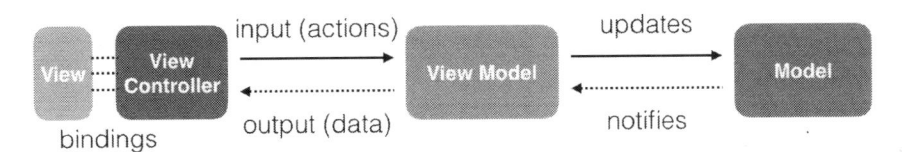

```
         input (actions)            updates
View─┬─View      ───────────►  View Model  ───────────►  Model
     │ Controller ◄───────────              ◄───────────
bindings    output (data)               notifies
```

ViewModel takes a central role in the architecture: It takes care of the business logic and talks to both the model and the view.

MVVM follows these simple rules:

- **Models** don't talk directly to other classes, although they can emit notifications about data changes.
- **View Models** talk to **Models** and expose data to the **View Controllers**.
- View Controllers only talk to **View Models** and **Views** as they handle view lifecycle and bind data to UI components.
- **Views** only notify view controllers about events (just as with MVC).

Wait, doesn't the View Model do exactly what the controller did in MVC? Yes... and no.

As mentioned earlier, a common issue is stuffing view controllers with code that doesn't control the view *per se*. MVVM tries to solve this problem by grouping the view controller together with the view, and assign its sole responsibility of controlling the view.

Another benefit of the MVVM architecture is the increased testability of the code. Separating the view lifecycle from the business logic makes testing both the view controller and the view model very straightforward.

Last but not least, the view model is completely separated from the presentation layer and, when necessary, can be re-used between platforms. You can just replace the view–view controller pair and migrate your app from iOS to macOS or even tvOS.

What goes where?

However, don't assume that *everything* else should go in your View Model class.

This would be the same madness as you sometimes end up with in MVC. It's up to you to sensibly divide and assign responsibilities across your code base. Thus, leave the View Model as the brain between your data and your screen, but make sure you split networking, navigation, cache, and similar responsibilities into other classes.

So how do you work with these extra classes, if they don't fall under any of the MVVM categories? MVVM doesn't enforce rules about these, but in this chapter you will work on a project that will introduce you to some possible solutions.

One good idea, which you'll cover in this chapter, is to inject all objects a View Model needs via its `init`, or possibly later in its lifecycle. This means you can pass long-living objects like stateful API classes, or persistence layer objects from view model to view model:

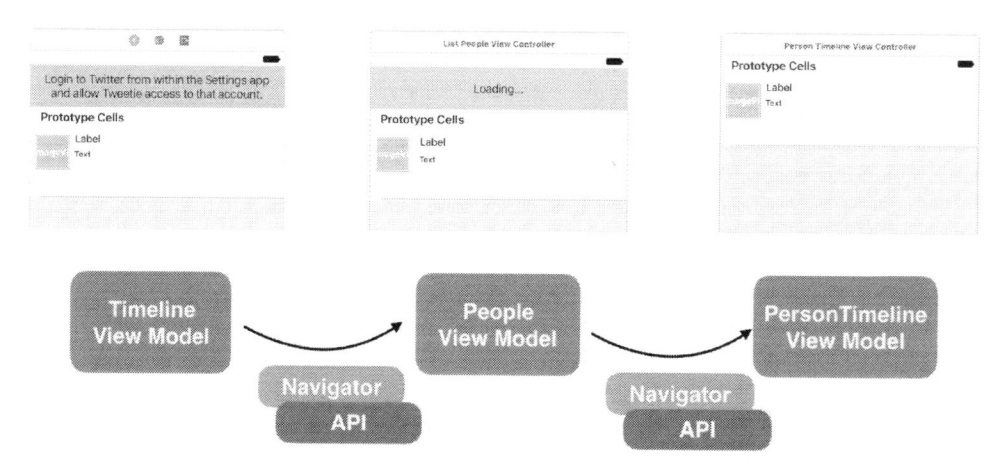

In the case of this chapter's project, **Tweetie**, you will pass things around in that fashion, such as the object taking care of in-app navigation (`Navigator`), the currently-logged in Twitter account (`TwitterAPI.AccountStatus`), and more.

But are smaller files the only benefit of MVVM? When used properly, the pattern allows for improvements over classic MVC:

- View controllers tend to be a lot simpler and really deserve their name because their only responsibility is to "control" the view. MVVM works especially well with RxSwift/RxCocoa because being able to **bind** observables to UI components is a key enabler for that pattern.

- The view model follows a clear *Input -> Output* pattern and are easy to test as they provide predefined input and testing for the expected output.

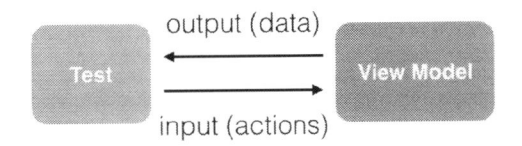

- Visually testing view controllers becomes much easier by creating mock view models and testing for the expected view controller state.

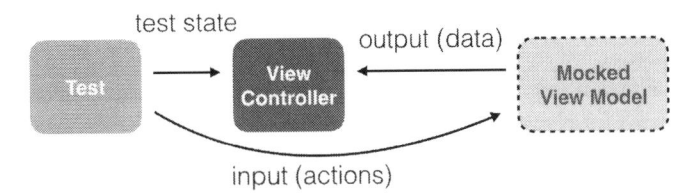

Last but not least, since MVVM is a great departure from MVC, it also serves as an enabler and an inspiration to explore more software architecture patterns.

Keen to try out MVVM? As you work through this chapter you'll see many of its benefits in action.

Getting started with Tweetie

In this chapter, you will work on a multi-platform project called Tweetie. It's a very simple Twitter-powered app, which uses a predefined user list to display tweets to the user. By default, the starter project uses a Twitter list featuring all authors and editors of this book. If you'd like, you can easily change the list to turn the project into a sports, writing, or cinema-oriented app.

The project has macOS and iOS targets and solves a lot of real-life programming tasks by using the MVVM pattern. There is a lot of code already included with the starter project; you'll just focus on the parts relevant to MVVM.

As you progress through this chapter, you'll witness how MVVM aids a clear distinction between the following:

- Code that has to do with UI and is therefore platform-specific, such as a view controller that uses UIKit for iOS, and a separate macOS-only view controller that uses Cocoa.

- Code that is reused *as-is*, since it doesn't depend on the specific platform's UI framework, such as all the code in the model and view model.

Time to dive in!

Project structure

Find the starter project for this chapter, install all CocoaPods, and open the project in Xcode. Take a quick peek into the project structure before working on any code.

In the project navigator, you will find a number of folders:

- **Common Classes**: Shared code between macOS and iOS. Includes an Rx Reachability class extension, and extensions on UITableView, NSTableView, and more.
- **Data Entities**: Data objects to use with the Realm Mobile Database in order to persist data on disk.
- **TwitterAPI**: A bare bones Twitter API implementation to make requests to Twitter's JSON API. TwitterAccount is the class that gets you an access token to use with the API, while TwitterAPI makes authorized requests to the web JSON endpoints.
- **View Models**: Where the three app view models reside. One is fully functional and you will work on completing the other two.
- **iOS Tweetie**: Contains the iOS version of Tweetie, including a storyboard and iOS view controllers.
- **Mac Tweetie**: Contains the macOS target with its storyboard, assets, and view controllers.
- **TweetieTests**: Where the app's tests and mock objects reside.

> **Note**: The tests won't pass until you've completed the chapter challenges, and you can use the test provided to make sure you complete the challenges correctly. Don't be surprised if things don't work right away!

Your task is to complete the app so users can see the tweets of all users in the list. You will start by completing the networking layer, then move on to writing a view model class, and in the end you will create the two view controllers (one for iOS and one for macOS) that use the finished view model to display data onscreen.

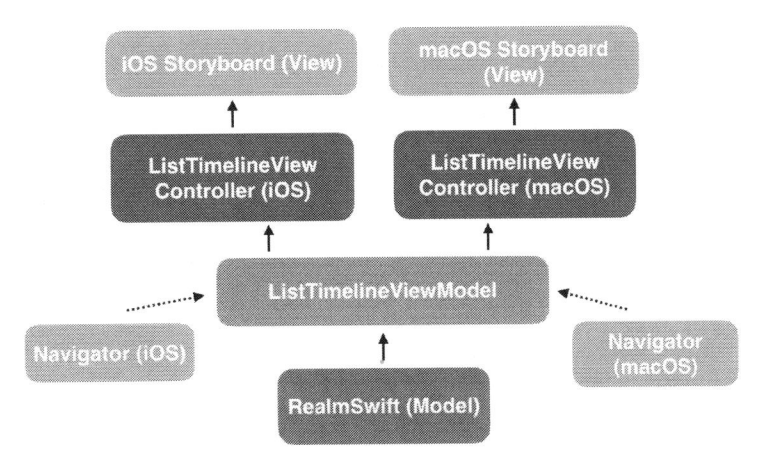

You'll get to work on a number of different classes and experience MVVM first hand.

Getting access to Twitter's API

To get this chapter's project up and running, you need to do a bit of initial setup. To fetch data from Twitter's API, you'll need to register for a free Twitter account and create an app on their platform.

If you don't have a Twitter account, you can register for free at https://twitter.com. If you're wondering who to follow, the twitter handles of this book's team are: @ashfurrow, @fpillet, @bontoJR, @icanzilb, @scotteg, and @crispytwit.

Next, you need to create an app and get your credentials to access the Twitter API. Visit https://apps.twitter.com/app/new and fill in the required details. Chose a **Name** and **Description** of your liking, then enter a **Website**; if you don't have your own page you can use "https://placeholder.com" for the time being.

You'll also need a placeholder URL for **Callback URL**; you can use the same value you entered for the website.

Make sure you agree with the developer agreement and click **Create your Twitter application** button. *Et voilà!* Your Twitter platform app is created!

Now select the **Permissions** tab, click the **Read only** radio button and then click **Update settings**. Your app will only read data, so there's no need for more permissions than that.

Finally, select the **Keys and Access Tokens** tab. Here you can see the credentials assigned to your app to access the Twitter API.

Open the Tweetie project in Xcode and make the following two changes:

1. Open **iOS Tweetie/AppDelegate.swift** and find the line `TwitterAccount.set(key:"placeholder", secret: "placeholder")`. Then replace the two placeholder values with your app's real key and secret.

2. Open **Mac Tweetie** and do exactly the same as above in the respective **AppDelegate.swift** file.

This will set up the iOS and the macOS projects with your credentials. You're now good to start working through this chapter!

Finishing up the network layer

The project already includes quite a lot of code. You've already been through a lot in this book, and we're not going to make you work through trivial tasks such as setting up your observables and view controllers. You'll start by completing the project networking.

The class `TimelineFetcher` in **TimelineFetcher.swift** is responsible to automatically refetch the latest tweets while the app is connected. The class is quite simple and uses an Rx timer to repeatedly invoke the subscription that fetches the JSON from the web.

`TimelineFetcher` has two convenience `init`s: one to fetch the tweets from a given Twitter list, and another to fetch a given user's tweets.

In this section, you'll add the code that makes a web request and maps the response to `Tweet` objects. You've already completed similar tasks in this book, so we've included most of that code in **Tweet.swift**.

> **Note:** People often ask where to add networking when working on an MVVM project, so we've structured this chapter to give you the chance to add networking yourself. There's nothing confusing about networking; it's a regular class you inject into your view models.

In **TimelineFetcher.swift**, scroll to the bottom of `init(account:jsonProvider:)` and find this line (it's just a placeholder to make the code run in the starter project):

```
timeline = Observable<[Tweet]>.empty()
```

Replace that line with the following:

```
timeline = reachableTimerWithAccount
    .withLatestFrom(feedCursor.asObservable(), resultSelector:
    { account, cursor in
        return (account: account, cursor: cursor)
    })
```

You take the timer observable `reachableTimerWithAccount` and combine it with `feedCursor`. `feedCursor` currently doesn't do anything, but you'll use this variable to store your current position in the Twitter timeline, indicating which tweets you've already fetched.

Xcode might display an error once you add this code, but ignore it for the moment. This will get resolved with the next code addition.

Now add the following to the chain:

```
.flatMapLatest(jsonProvider)
.map(Tweet.unboxMany)
.share(replay: 1, scope: .whileConnected)
```

You start by flatmapping the method parameter `jsonProvider`. `jsonProvider` is a closure that's injected into `init`. Each of the convenience inits is supposed to fetch different API endpoints, so injecting `jsonProvider` is a handy way to avoid using `if` statements or branching the logic in the main initializer `init(account:jsonProvider:)`.

`jsonProvider` returns an `Observable<[JSONObject]>`, so the next step is to map that to an `Observable<[Tweet]>`. You use the provided `Tweet.unboxMany` function, which attempts to convert the JSON objects into an array of tweets.

With these few lines of code, you're prepared to fetch the tweets. `timeline` is a public observable, so this is how your view models will access the list of latest tweets. The app's view models might save the tweets to disk or use them straight away to drive the app's UI, but that's entirely their own business. `TimelineFetcher` simply fetches tweets and exposes the results:

```
                                                    request
Observable<[Tweets]>     ┌──────────────┐         ╭╌╌╌╌╮    ┌ ─ ─ ─ ─ ─ ─ ┐
◄────────────────────────│TimelineFetcher│────────►      ────►  Twitter API
                         └──────────────┘◄────────╰╌╌╌╌╯    └ ─ ─ ─ ─ ─ ─ ┘
                                                    response
```

Since this subscription is called repeatedly, you also need to store the current position (or *cursor*) so that you don't fetch the same tweets over and over again. Just below the place you typed in the last piece of code, add:

```
timeline
  .scan(.none, accumulator: TimelineFetcher.currentCursor)
  .bind(to: feedCursor)
  .disposed(by: bag)
```

`feedCursor` is a property on `TimelineFetcher` of type `Variable<TimelineCursor>`. `TimelineCursor` is a custom struct that holds the oldest and latest tweet IDs you've fetched so far. In the above code, you use `scan` to track the IDs. Each time you grab a new batch of tweets, you update the value of `feedCursor`. If you are interested in the logic of updating the timeline cursor, have a look inside `TimelineFetcher.currentCursor()`.

> **Note:** We won't cover the cursor logic in detail, since it's specific to the Twitter API. You can read more about cursoring at http://bit.ly/2zLF7mx.

Next you need to create a view model. You'll use the completed `TimelineFetcher` class to grab the latest tweets from the API.

Adding a View Model

The project already includes a navigation class, data entities, and the Twitter account access class. Now that your network layer is complete, you can simply combine all of these to log the user into Twitter and fetch some tweets.

In this section, you won't concern yourself with controllers. Find the project folder **View Models** and open **ListTimelineViewModel.swift**. As the name suggests, this view model will fetch the tweets of a given user list.

It's a good practice (but certainly not the only way) to clearly define three sections in your view model code:

1. **Init**: In which you define one or more `inits` where you do all your dependency injection.

2. **Input**: Contains any public properties, such as plain variables or RxSwift subjects, which allow the view controller to provide input.
3. **Output**: Contains any public properties (usually observables), which provide the output of the view model. These are usually lists of objects to drive a table or collection view, or any other type of data a view controller would use to drive the app's UI.

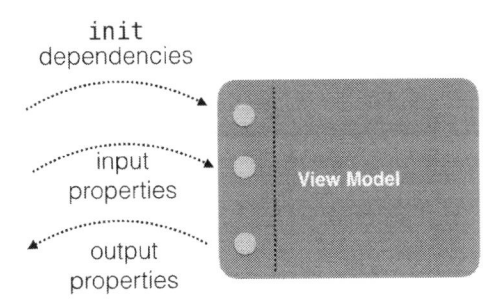

`ListTimelineViewModel` has a bit of code already in its `init` that initializes the `fetcher` property. `fetcher` is an instance of `TimelineFetcher` for fetching tweets.

Time to add more properties to the view model. First, add the following two properties, which are neither input nor output, but simply help you persist the injected dependencies:

```
let list: ListIdentifier
let account: Driver<TwitterAccount.AccountStatus>
```

Since those are constants, your only chance to initialize them is in `init(account:list:apiType)`. Insert the following **at the top** of the class initializer:

```
self.account = account
self.list = list
```

Now you can move on to adding the input properties. But what properties should those be, since you've already injected all the dependencies of this class? The injected dependencies and the parameters you provide to `init` allow you to provide input at initialization time. Other public properties will allow you to provide input to the view model at any time through its lifetime.

For example, consider an app that lets the user search a database. You would bind the search text field to an input property of the view model. As the search term changes, the view model will search the database and change its output accordingly, which in turn will be bound to a table view to show the results.

For the current view model, the only input you will have is a property that lets you pause and resume the timeline fetcher class. `TimelineFetcher` already features a `Variable<Bool>` to do just that, so you'll need a proxy property in the view model.

Insert the code below in the input section of `ListTimelineViewModel`, as marked with the handy comment `// MARK: - Input`:

```
var paused: Bool = false {
  didSet {
    fetcher.paused.value = paused
  }
}
```

This property is simply a proxy which sets the value of `paused` on the fetcher class.

Now you can move on to the view model's output. The view model will expose the fetched list of tweets and the logged-in status. The former will be a `Variable` of tweet objects, loaded from Realm; the latter a `Driver<Bool>` simply emitting `false` or `true` to indicate whether the user is currently logged into Twitter.

In the output section (marked by a comment), insert these two properties:

```
private(set) var tweets: Observable<(AnyRealmCollection<Tweet>, RealmChangeset?)>!
private(set) var loggedIn: Driver<Bool>!
```

`tweets` contains the list of the latest `Tweet` objects. Before any tweets are loaded, such as the point before the user has logged into their Twitter account, the default value will be `nil`. `loggedIn` is a `Driver`, which you will initialize later on.

Now you can subscribe to `TimelineFetcher`'s result and store the tweets into Realm. This is, of course, quite easy when using RxRealm. Append to `init(account:list:apiType:)`:

```
fetcher.timeline
  .subscribe(Realm.rx.add(update: true))
  .disposed(by: bag)
```

You subscribe to `fetcher.timeline`, which is of type `Observable<[Tweet]>`, and bind the result (an array of tweets) to `Realm.rx.add(update:)`. `Realm.rx.add` persists the incoming objects into the app's default Realm database.

The last piece of code takes care of the influx of data in your view model, so all that's left is to build the view model's output. Find the method named `bindOutput`, and insert:

```
guard let realm = try? Realm() else {
  return
}
```

```
tweets = Observable.changeset(from: realm.objects(Tweet.self))
```

As you learned in Chapter 21, "RxRealm", you can easily create an observable sequence with the help of Realm's `Results` class. In the code above, you create a result set out of all persisted tweets and subscribe for the changes of that collection. You expose the `tweets` observable to interested parties, which is usually your view controller.

Next you need to take care of the `loggedIn` output property. This one is easy to take care of — you simply need to subscribe to `account` and map its elements to either `true` or `false`. Append to `bindOutput`:

```
loggedIn = account
  .map { status in
    switch status {
    case .unavailable: return false
    case .authorized: return true
    }
  }
  .asDriver(onErrorJustReturn: false)
```

This is all the view model needs to do! You took care to inject all dependencies in the `init`, you added some properties to allow other classes to provide input, and finally you bound the view model's results to public properties that other classes can observe.

As you can see, the view model doesn't know anything about the view controllers, the views, or other classes that aren't injected via its initializer. Since the view model is so well isolated from the rest of the code, you can proceed to write its tests to make sure it works fine — even before you see any output on screen.

Adding a View Model test

In Xcode's project navigator, open the **TweetieTests** folder. Inside you will find a few things provided for you:

- **TestData.swift**: Features some test JSON, and test objects.
- **TwitterTestAPI.swift**: A Twitter API mock class that tracks which methods were called and records the API responses.
- **TestRealm.swift**: A test Realm configuration that ensures Realm uses a temporary in-memory database for the tests.

Open **ListTimelineViewModelTests.swift** to add some new tests. The class already has a utility method to create a fresh instance of `ListTimelineViewModel` and two tests:

1. `test_whenInitialized_storesInitParams()`, which tests if the view model persists its injected dependencies.

2. `test_whenInitialized_bindsTweets()`, which checks if the view model exposes the latest persisted tweets via its `tweets` property.

To complete the test case, you'll add one last test: the one to check if the `loggedIn` output property reflects the account authentication status. Add the following inside the class body:

```
func test_whenAccountAvailable_updatesAccountStatus() {
}
```

Since this is an asynchronous test you will use RxBlocking. You learned about that handy library in Chapter 16, "Testing with RxTest".

You will test the elements emitted by your view model's `loggedIn` property, and so you tell the observer to listen for `Bool` elements.

Now add the following:

```
let accountSubject =
PublishSubject<TwitterAccount.AccountStatus>()
let viewModel =
createViewModel(accountSubject.asDriver(onErrorJustReturn: .unavailable))
```

Next you create a `PublishSubject`, which you will use to emit test `AccountStatus` values. You pass the subject to `createViewModel()` and finally fetch a view model instance, all ready and set up for the test. Add:

```
let loggedIn = viewModel.loggedIn.asObservable()
```

Now that your subscription is in place, you can emit few test values. Add the following async block:

```
DispatchQueue.main.async {
  accountSubject.onNext(.authorized(AccessToken()))
  accountSubject.onNext(.unavailable)
  accountSubject.onCompleted()
}
```

Finally, subscribe to `loggedIn`, take 3 events and check if they are the ones you expect:

```
let emitted = try! loggedIn.take(3).toBlocking(timeout: 1).toArray()

XCTAssertEqual(emitted[0].element, true)
XCTAssertEqual(emitted[1].element, false)
XCTAssertTrue(emitted[2].isCompleted)
```

This code waits asynchronously for three events and then checks if the recorded events were the exact sequence of `.next(true)`, `.next(false)`, and `.completed`.

With that, the test case is complete. The highly isolated view model class lets you easily inject mock objects and simulate input. Read through the rest of the test suite class to see what else is being tested. If you figure out some new tests that would be useful, feel free to add them in!

> **Note:** Since the view models in the Tweetie project are so well-isolated from the rest of the app's infrastructure, you don't need to run the entire app to run a test. Peek into **iOS Tweetie/AppDelegate.swift** to see how the code avoids creating the app's navigation and view controllers during testing. Alternatively, you might disable the host app in testing altogether.

Now you have a fully functioning view model, which is also under test. It's time to make use of it!

Adding an iOS View Controller

In this section, you'll write the code to wire your view model's output to the views in `ListTimelineViewController` — the controller that will display the combined tweets of users in the preset list.

First, you'll work on the iOS version of Tweetie. In the project navigator, open the folder **iOS Tweetie/View Controllers/List Timeline**. Inside you will find the view controller and iOS-specific table cell view files.

Open **ListTimelineViewController.swift** and have a quick look. The `ListTimelineViewController` class features a view model property and a `Navigator` property. Both classes are injected through the `createWith(navigator:storyboard:viewModel)` static factory method.

You'll add two sets of setup code to the view controller. One will be some static assignments in `viewDidLoad()`, and the other will be bindings of the view model to the UI in `bindUI()`.

Add the code below to `viewDidLoad()`, **before** the call to `bindUI()`:

```
title = "@\(viewModel.list.username)/\(viewModel.list.slug)"
navigationItem.rightBarButtonItem =
UIBarButtonItem(barButtonSystemItem: .bookmarks, target: nil,
action: nil)
```

This will set the title to the list's name and create a new button on the right-hand side of the navigation item.

Next, on to binding the view model. Insert this into `bindUI()`:

```
navigationItem.rightBarButtonItem!.rx.tap
  .throttle(0.5, scheduler: MainScheduler.instance)
  .subscribe(onNext: { [weak self] _ in
    guard let this = self else { return }

this.navigator.show(segue: .listPeople(this.viewModel.account,
  this.viewModel.list), sender: this)
  })
  .disposed(by: bag)
```

You subscribe to taps on the right bar item and throttle them to prevent any double taps. Then you call the `show(segue:sender:)` method on the `navigator` property to show your intent to present the segue to the screen. The segue displays the list of people: members of the selected Twitter list.

`Navigator` takes care to either present the requested screen, or discard your intent if it decides to do so, as it might decide to ignore your intent to present the desired view controller based on other parameters.

> **Note:** Read through the `Navigator` class definition for more details about the class implementation. It contains the list of all possible navigable screens, and you can invoke these segues only by providing all required input parameters.

You also need to create another binding to display the latest tweets in the table view. Scroll to the top of the file and import the following library to easily bind RxRealm results to table and collection views:

```
import RxRealmDataSources
```

Then go back to `bindUI()` and append:

```
let dataSource =
RxTableViewRealmDataSource<Tweet>(cellIdentifier:
  "TweetCellView", cellType: TweetCellView.self) { cell, _,
tweet in
    cell.update(with: tweet)
}
```

`dataSource` is a table view data source, specifically suited to drive a table view from an observable sequence that emits Realm collection changes. In a single line, you configure the data source completely:

1. You set the model type as `Tweet`.
2. Then you set the cell identifier to use as `TweetCellView`.
3. Finally you provide a closure to configure each cell before it shows on screen.

You can now bind the data source to the view controller's table view. Add this code under the last block:

```
viewModel.tweets
  .bind(to: tableView.rx.realmChanges(dataSource))
  .disposed(by: bag)
```

Here you bind `viewModel.tweets` to `realmChanges` and provide the preconfigured data source. This is the bare minimum you need to drive the table view with animated changes.

The final binding for this view controller will show or hide the message on top depending on whether the user has logged in to Twitter or not. Append the following:

```
viewModel.loggedIn
  .drive(messageView.rx.isHidden)
  .disposed(by: bag)
```

This binding toggles `messageView.isHidden` based on the current `loggedIn` value.

This section showed you why bindings are a key enabler of the MVVM pattern. With your view controllers serving only as "glue" code, you can easily separate out concerns really easily. Your view model remains mostly ignorant about the current platform it runs on, as it doesn't import any UI framework as UIKit or Cocoa.

Run the app and observe all the bindings your shiny new view model drives:

As soon as the app completes the JSON request, the message at the top disappears. Then the fetched tweets "pour in" with a snappy animation. Finally, when you tap on the bar item on the right side, the app will take you to the users list view controller:

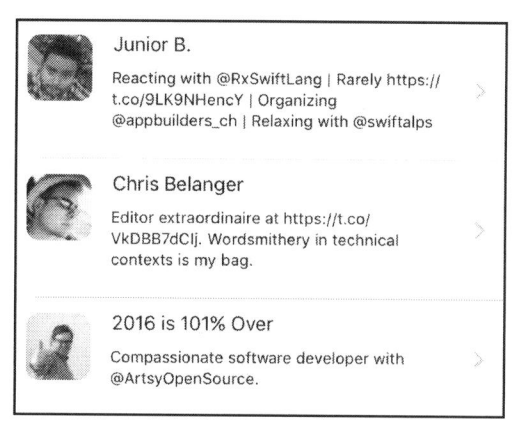

And that's that! In the next section, you will learn how easy it is to reuse your view model across platforms.

Adding a macOS View Controller

The view model doesn't know anything about the view or the view controller that uses it. It that sense, the view model could be platform independent when necessary. The same view model can easily provide the data to both iOS and macOS view controllers.

`ListTimelineViewModel` is precisely one such view model. Its only dependencies are RxSwift, RxCocoa, and the Realm database. Since those libraries are cross-platform themselves, the view model itself is cross-platform too.

You job is to switch to the macOS target of the Xcode project and build a view controller that mirrors the iOS one you built above.

From Xcode's scheme selector, choose **MacTweetie/My Mac** and run the project to see what the macOS starter project looks like.

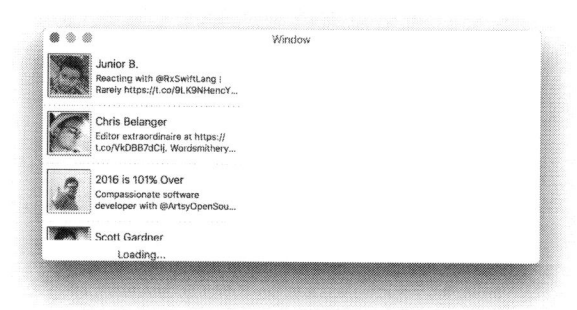

The app displays the list of all accounts included in the pre-defined Twitter list, but the right-hand side of the window remains empty. The blank view controller is the one that should be displaying the tweets timeline. When complete, it should look much like the tweet list you created for the iOS Tweetie app.

Open **Mac Tweetie/ViewControllers/List Timeline** and select **ListTimelineViewController.swift**. The file is named similarly to the iOS view controller file, but is located in the **Mac Tweetie** folder instead.

Start by displaying the name of the list at the top, just as you did in the iOS app. Add the following to `viewDidLoad()`:

```
NSApp.windows.first?.title = "@\(viewModel.list.username)/\
(viewModel.list.slug)"
```

Now you can move on to the bindings. If you skim through the code of the macOS view controller, you'll notice it uses the same view model and navigator classes as its iOS counterpart. That's great news, since you already know (and love) `ListTimelineViewModel`.

The view controller code is, in fact, almost identical to the iOS version! This code similarity is one of the many benefits of RxSwift. A lot of Rx code looks quite similar between languages as well. You will likely be amazed at the ease with which you can can read and understand Java written with RxJava, or JavaScript if it's written using RxJS.

Much like for the iOS view controller, scroll up the current file and import RxRealmDataSources:

```
import RxRealmDataSources
```

Now scroll down to `bindUI()`. To bind the view model's tweets to the table view, add:

```
let dataSource =
RxTableViewRealmDataSource<Tweet>(cellIdentifier:
"TweetCellView", cellType: TweetCellView.self) { cell, row,
tweet in
  cell.update(with: tweet)
}
```

Here you create a data source containing `Tweet` objects with a cell with identifier `TweetCellView` and configure each cell before it's reused by calling `update(with:)` on it. Now to create the table view binding. Add the code below:

```
let binder = tableView.rx.realmChanges(dataSource)
```

You create a binding between the table view rows and Realm changes by using the already initialized data source object.

Now you can simply bind the view model's `tweets` property to the configured binding. Add the following:

```
viewModel.tweets
   .bind(to: binder)
   .disposed(by: bag)
```

This binding should bring the table view to life. Run the app and observe :trollface: the tweets showing up in the right hand side of the window.

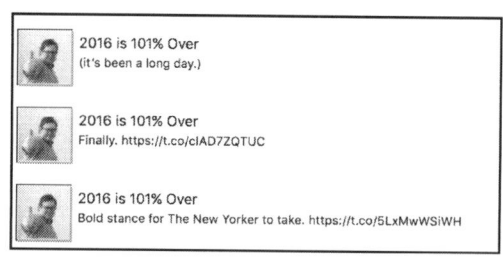

Is this the real life — or is this just fantasy? You didn't have to perform any networking, data transformation, or JSON validation?

Nope — you're working on the view controller and not on any other part of your app. The view model takes care of everything, so the only thing you needed to do was to bind the data to the UI.

You now have a basic understanding of how to split your code into a model, a view model, and a view with a view controller. MVVM certainly has benefits over MVC for anything beyond simple apps, but it's important to remember that MVVM isn't the only option out there.

MVVM is a particularly sweet pattern to use with RxSwift, since Rx makes creating bindings a straightforward task. This leads to cleaner code that is easier to read and test.

Other architecture patterns have different benefits, and there might be other libraries that suit those patterns better. But if you see MVVM + RxSwift as something you might want to learn, then definitely try out the challenges below!

Challenges

Challenge 1: Toggle "Loading..." in members list

On the screen displaying the users list, the *Loading...* label is always visible. It's useful to have the loading indicator there, but you really only want it to be visible while the app is fetching JSON from the server.

To complete this challenge, you will work on both the iOS and macOS apps.

First open **ListPeopleViewController.swift** in the iOS part of the project. In `bindUI()`, subscribe to `viewModel.people`, convert it to a `Driver` and map the elements to `true` and `false`. Emit `false` when `viewModel.people` is `nil`. Drive `messageView.rx.isHidden` with the resulting `Driver<Bool>`.

In the end you should see "Loading..." only when the app is fetching the JSON. Once it's completed, the label should disappear automatically.

Once you're happy with the result in the iOS app, move on to the macOS target. Since the view controller outlets have the same names, you can copy the code directly from the iOS view controller into the macOS app's **ListPeopleViewController.swift**.

Über challenge: Complete View Model and View Controller for the user's timeline

You've noticed that there is still a part missing in both the iOS and macOS app. If you select a user from the users list, you'll see a new, *empty* view controller appear.

As the über challenge in this chapter, you will finish the two apps in the project and display the personal Twitter timelines of selected users. If you want to try completing this challenge on your own follow the instructions below, otherwise the challenge folder for this chapter includes a solution, which you can read through.

In **PersonTimelineViewModel.swift**, you will find a property named `tweets`. Change this to a lazy variable and use the following code to initialize it.

```
return self.fetcher.timeline
  .asDriver(onErrorJustReturn: [])
  .scan([], accumulator: { lastList, newList in
    return newList + lastList
})
```

This code subscribes to the class' `TimelineFetcher` instance and gathers all emitted tweets in a list.

Then switch to the iOS **PersonTimelineViewController.swift**, scroll to `bindUI()` and add two subscriptions to `viewModel.tweets`.

- With the first subscription, drive the `rx.title` of the view controller. Display "None found" before you fetch the tweets along with the username of the user (from the `viewModel`) when the tweets show up.

- For the second subscription, get a data source object by using the provided `createTweetsDataSource()`, then map the tweets to a single `TweetSection` (consult the RxDataSources chapter if you need help), and drive the table.

For the macOS version of the app (in the corresponding **PersonTimelineViewController.swift**), use the provided `tweets` array property. Subscribe `viewModel.tweets`, update the `tweets` array and reload the table. You can optionally update the window title just as you did for the iOS app.

Now you should be able to open the user's list, select a user and see their personal tweet timeline appear in the app like so:

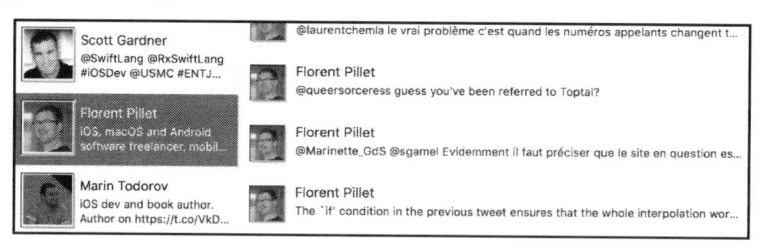

Chapter 24: Building a Complete RxSwift App

By Florent Pillet

Throughout this book, you've learned about the many facets of RxSwift. Reactive programming is a deep subject; its adoption often leads to architectures very different from the ones you've grown used to. The way you model events and data flow in RxSwift is crucial for proper behavior in your apps, as well as protecting against issues in future iterations of the product.

To conclude this book, you'll architect and code a small RxSwift application. The goal is not to use Rx "at all costs", but rather to make design decisions that lead to a clean architecture with stable, predictable and modular behavior. The application is simple by design, to clearly present ideas you can use to architect your own applications.

This chapter is as much about RxSwift as it is about the importance of a well-chosen architecture that suits your needs. RxSwift is a great tool that helps your application run like a well-tuned engine, but it doesn't spare you from thinking about and designing your application architecture.

Introducing QuickTodo

Serving as the modern equivalent of the "hello world" program, a "To-Do" application is an ideal candidate to expose the inner structure of an Rx application.

In the previous chapter, you learned about MVVM and how well it fits with reactive programming. You'll structure the QuickTodo application with MVVM and learn how you can isolate the data-processing parts of your code and make them fully independent.

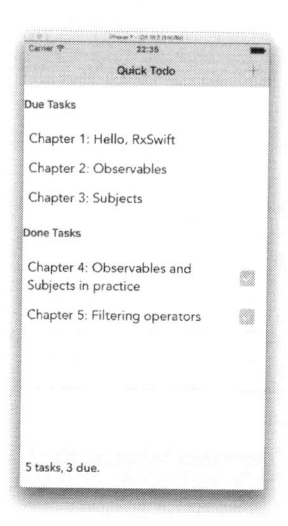

Architecting the application

One particularly important goal of your app is to achieve a clean separation between the user interface, the business logic of your application, and the services the app contains to help the business logic run. To that end, you really need a clean model where each component is clearly identified.

First, let's introduce some terminology for the architecture you are going to implement:

- **Scene**: Refers to a screen managed by a view controller. It can be a regular screen, or a modal dialog. It comprises a view controller and a view model.

- **View model**: Defines the business logic and data used by the view controller to present a particular scene.

- **Service**: A logical group of functionality provided to any scene in the application. For example, storage to a database can be abstracted to a service. Likewise, requests to a network API can be grouped in a network service.

- **Model**: The most basic data store in the application. View models and services both manipulate and exchange models.

You learned about ViewModel in the previous chapter, "MVVM with RxSwift". Services are a new concept and another good fit for reactive programming. Their purpose is to expose data and functionality using `Observable` and `Observer` as much as possible, so as to create a global model where components connect together as reactively as possible.

For your QuickTodo application, the requirements are relatively modest. You'll architect it correctly nonetheless, so you have a solid foundation for future growth. It's also an architecture you'll be able to reuse in other applications.

The basic items you need are:

- A `TaskItem` **model** that describes an individual task.
- A `TaskService` **service** that provides task creation, update, deletion, storage and search.
- A **storage medium**; you'll use a Realm database here and, of course, RxRealm.
- A series of **scenes** to list, create and search tasks. Each scene is split into a **view model** and a **view controller**.
- A **scene coordinator** object to manage scene navigation and presentation.

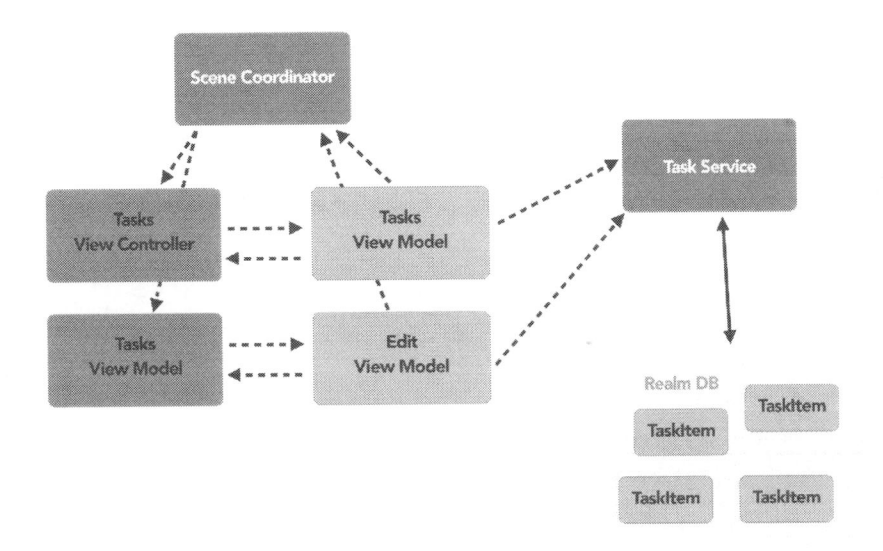

As you learned in the previous chapter, the view model exposes the business logic and the model data to the view controller. The rules you'll follow to create the ViewModel for each scene are simple:

- Expose data as `Observable` sequences. This guarantees automatic updates once connected to the user interface.
- Expose all ViewModel actions connectable to the UI using the `Action` pattern.
- Any model or data publicly accessible and not exposed as an observable sequence is immutable.
- Transitioning from scene to scene is part of the business logic. Each ViewModel initiates this transition and prepares the next scene's view model, but doesn't know anything about the view controller.

A solution to fully insulate ViewModels from the actual ViewController, including triggering transitions to other scenes, is laid out later in this chapter.

> **Note**: Data immutability guarantees total control over updates triggered by the UI. Strict observance of the rules above also guarantees the best testability of each part of the code.
>
> The previous chapter showed how to use a mutable property to update the underlying model with the help of `didSet`. This chapter will take the notion further by completely removing mutability and only exposing `Action`s.

Bindable view controllers

You'll start with the view controllers. At some point, you need to connect, or *bind*, the view controllers to their associated view model. One way to do this is have your controllers adopt a specific protocol: `BindableType`.

> **Note**: The starter project for this chapter includes quite some code. When you first open the project in Xcode it will not compile successfully, as you need to add few key types before you can build and run for the first time.

Open **BindableType.swift** and add the basic protocol:

```
protocol BindableType {
    associatedtype ViewModelType
```

```
    var viewModel: ViewModelType! { get set }
    func bindViewModel()
}
```

Each view controller conforming to the `BindableType` protocol will declare a `viewModel` variable and provide a `bindViewModel()` function to be called once the `viewModel` variable is assigned. This function will connect UI elements to observables and actions in the view model.

Binding at the right moment

There's one particular aspect of binding you need to be careful about. You want the `viewModel` variable to be assigned to your view controller as soon as possible, but `bindViewModel()` must be invoked only *after* the view has been loaded.

The reason is that your `bindViewModel()` function will typically connect UI elements that need to be present. Therefore, you'll use a small helper function to call it after instantiating each view controller. Add this to **BindableType.swift**:

```
extension BindableType where Self: UIViewController {
  mutating func bindViewModel(to model: Self.ViewModelType) {
    viewModel = model
    loadViewIfNeeded()
    bindViewModel()
  }
}
```

This way, by the time `viewDidLoad()` is called in your view controller, you're sure the `viewModel` variable has already been assigned. Since `viewDidLoad()` is the best time to set your view controller's title for a smooth push navigation title animation, and knowing you might require access to your view model to prepare the title, loading the view controller only when required is what works best for all cases.

Task model

Your task model is simple and derives from the Realm base object. A task is defined as having a title (the task contents), a creation date and a checked date. Dates are used to sort tasks in the tasks list. If you're not familiar with Realm, check out their documentation at https://realm.io/docs/swift/latest/.

Populate **TaskItem.swift** as follows:

```
class TaskItem: Object {
    @objc dynamic var uid: Int = 0
    @objc dynamic var title: String = ""

    @objc dynamic var added: Date = Date()
    @objc dynamic var checked: Date? = nil

    override class func primaryKey() -> String? {
        return "uid"
    }
}
```

There are two details you need to be aware of that are specific to objects coming from a Realm database:

- Objects can't cross threads. If you need an object in a different thread, either re-query or use a Realm `ThreadSafeReference`.

- Objects are auto-updating. If you make a change to the database, it immediately reflects in the properties of any live object queried from the database. This has its uses as you'll see further down.

- As a consequence, deleting an object *invalidates* all existing copies. If you access any property of a queried object that is deleted, you'll get an exception.

The second point above has side effects, which you'll study in greater detail later in this chapter when binding the task cell.

Tasks service

The tasks service is responsible for creating, updating and fetching task items from the store. As a responsible developer, you'll define your service public interface using a protocol then write the runtime implementation and a mock implementation for tests.

First, create the protocol. This is what you'll expose to the users of the service. Open **TaskServiceType.swift** and add the protocol definition:

```
protocol TaskServiceType {
  @discardableResult
  func createTask(title: String) -> Observable<TaskItem>

  @discardableResult
  func delete(task: TaskItem) -> Observable<Void>

  @discardableResult
```

```
  func update(task: TaskItem, title: String) ->
Observable<TaskItem>

  @discardableResult
  func toggle(task: TaskItem) -> Observable<TaskItem>

  func tasks() -> Observable<Results<TaskItem>>
}
```

This is a basic interface providing the fundamental services to create, delete, update and query tasks. Nothing fancy here. The most important detail is that the service exposes all data as observable sequences. Even the functions which create, delete, update and toggle tasks return an observable you can subscribe to.

The core idea is to convey any failures or successes of the operation through successful completion of the observables. In addition, you can use the returned observable as the return value in `Actions`. You'll see some examples of this later in the chapter.

For example, open **TaskService.swift** and you'll see `update(task:title:)` looks like this:

```
@discardableResult
func update(task: TaskItem, title: String) ->
Observable<TaskItem> {
  let result = withRealm("updating title") { realm ->
Observable<TaskItem> in
    try realm.write {
      task.title = title
    }
    return .just(task)
  }
  return result ?? .error(TaskServiceError.updateFailed(task))
}
```

`withRealm(_:action:)` is an internal wrapper to get the current Realm database and start an operation on it. In case an error is thrown, `withRealm(_:action:)` will always return `nil`. This is a good occasion to return an error observable to signal the error to the caller.

You won't go through the complete implementation of the tasks service, but in case you have a few extra minutes, you can read through the code in **TaskService.swift**.

Since the last thing you did was to add `TaskServiceType`, now open **TaskService.swift** and make it conform to that protocol:

```
struct TaskService: TaskServiceType {
```

You're done with the tasks service! Your view models will receive a `TaskServiceType` object, either real or mocked during the test, and will be able to perform their work.

Scenes

You learned above that in the chapter's architecture a scene is a logical presentation unit made of a "screen" managed by a view controller and a view model. Rules for scenes are:

- The view model handles the business logic. This extends to kicking off the transition to another "scene".
- View models know nothing about the actual view controller and views used to represent the scene.
- View controllers shouldn't initiate the transition to another scene; this is the domain of the business logic running in the view model.

With this in mind you can lay down a model where application scenes are listed as cases in a `Scene` enumeration, and each case has the scene view model as its associated data.

> **Note:** Thais is similar to what you did in the previous chapter in the `Navigator` class, but here navigation is even more flexible by using scenes

Open **Scene.swift**. You'll define the two scenes we need in our simple app, `tasks` and `editTask`. Add:

```
enum Scene {
    case tasks(TasksViewModel)
    case editTask(EditTaskViewModel)
}
```

At this stage, a view model can instantiate another view model and assign it to its scene, ready for transition. You also fulfill the basic contract for view models, which, as much as possible, shouldn't depend on UIKit at all.

An extension to the `Scene` enum that you'll add in a moment exposes a function which is the only place you'll instantiate a view controller for a scene. The function will know how to pull the view controller from its resources for each scene.

Open **Scene+ViewController.swift** and add this function:

```
extension Scene {
    func viewController() -> UIViewController {
```

```
        let storyboard = UIStoryboard(name: "Main", bundle: nil)
        switch self {
        case .tasks(let viewModel):
            let nc =
    storyboard.instantiateViewController(withIdentifier: "Tasks")
    as! UINavigationController
            var vc = nc.viewControllers.first as! TasksViewController
            vc.bindViewModel(to: viewModel)
            return nc

        case .editTask(let viewModel):
            let nc =
    storyboard.instantiateViewController(withIdentifier: "EditTask")
    as! UINavigationController
            var vc = nc.viewControllers.first as!
    EditTaskViewController
            vc.bindViewModel(to: viewModel)
            return nc
        }
    }
}
```

The code instantiates the appropriate view controller and immediately binds it to its view model, which is taken from the data associated to each enum case.

> **Note:** This function can become quite long when you have many scenes in your application. Don't hesitate to split it up into multiple sections for clarity and ease of maintenance. In a large application with multiple domains, you could even have a "master" enum for domains, and sub-enums with the scenes for each domain.

Finally a **scene coordinator** handles the transition between scenes. Each view model knows about the coordinator and can ask it to push a scene.

Coordinating scenes

One of the most puzzling questions when developing an architecture around MVVM is, "How does the application transition from scene to scene?". There are many answers to this question, as every architecture has a different take on it. Some do it from the view controller, because of the need to instantiate another view controller; while some do it using a *router*, which is a special object thats connects view models.

Transitioning to another scene

The author of this chapter favors a simple solution, which has proved to be efficient over the various applications he has developed:

1. A view model creates the view model for the next scene.
2. The first view model initiates the transition to the next scene by calling into the scene coordinator.
3. The scene coordinator uses an extension function to the `Scenes` enum to instantiate the view controller.
4. Next, the scene controller binds the controller to the next view model.
5. Finally, it presents the next scene view controller.

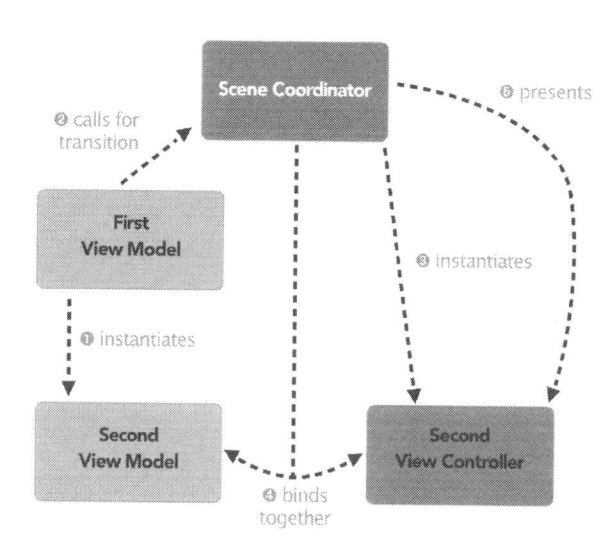

With this structure, you can completely insulate view models from the view controllers using them, and also insulate them from the details of *where* to find the next view controller to push. Later in this chapter, you'll see how to use the `Action` pattern to wrap steps 1 and 2 above and kick off a transition.

> **Note:** It's important that you always call the scene coordinator's `transition(to:type:)` and `pop()` functions to transition between scenes, as the coordinator needs to keep track of which view controller is frontmost, particularly when presenting scenes modally. Do not use automatic segues.

The scene coordinator

The scene coordinator is defined through a `SceneCoordinatorType` protocol. A concrete `SceneCoordinator` implementation is provided to run the application. You can also develop a test implementation that fakes transitions.

The `SceneCoordinatorType` protocol (already provided in the starter project), is simple yet efficient:

```
protocol SceneCoordinatorType {
  @discardableResult
  func transition(to scene: Scene, type: SceneTransitionType) ->
Completable

  @discardableResult
  func pop(animated: Bool) -> Completable
}
```

The two functions `transition(to:type:)` and `pop(animated:)` let you perform all the transitions you need: push, pop, modal, and dismiss.

The concrete implementation in **SceneCoordinator.swift** shows some interesting cases of intercepting delegate messages with RxSwift. Both transition calls were designed to return a `Completable` that completes once the transition is complete. You can subscribe to it to take further action, as it works like a completion callback.

To implement this, the code included in the project creates a UINavigationController *DelegateProxy*, an RxSwift proxy which can intercept messages while forwarding messages to the actual delegate:

```
_ = navigationController.rx.delegate
  .sentMessage(#selector(UINavigationControllerDelegate.navigati
onController(_:didShow:animated:)))
  .map { _ in }
  .bind(to: subject)
```

The trick, found at the bottom of the `transition(to:type:)` method, is to bind this subscription to a subject returned to the caller:

```
return subject.asObservable()
  .take(1)
  .ignoreElements()
```

The returned observable will take at most one emitted element to handle the navigation case, but doesn't forward it, and completes.

> **Note**: You may question the memory safety of this construct because of the unbounded subscription to the navigation delegate proxy. It's totally safe: the returned observable will take *at most* one element, then complete. When completing, it disposes of its subscriptions. If nothing subscribes to the returned observable, the subject is disposed from memory and its subscriptions terminate as well.

Passing data back

Passing data back from a scene to the previous one, such as when a scene is presented modally, is easy with RxSwift. A presenting view model instantiates the view model for the presented scene, so it can access it and can set up communication. For the best results, you can use one of these three techniques:

1. Expose an `Observable` in the second (presented) view model that the first (presenting) view model can subscribe to. When the second view model dismisses the presentation, it can emit one or more result elements on the observable.

2. Pass an `Observer` object, such as a `Variable` or a `Subject`, to the presented view model, which will use that object to emit result one or more elements.

3. Pass one or more `Actions` to the presented view model, to be executed with the appropriate result.

These techniques allow for excellent testability and help you avoid playing games with `weak` references between models. You'll see an example of this later in this chapter when adding the Edit Task view controller.

Kicking off the first scene

The final detail about using a coordinated scene model is the startup phase; you need to kick off the scene's presentation by introducing the first scene. This is a process you'll perform in your application delegate.

Open **AppDelegate.swift** and add the following code to `application(_:didFinishLaunchingWithOptions:)`:

```
let service = TaskService()
let sceneCoordinator = SceneCoordinator(window: window!)
```

The first step is to prepare all the services you need along with the coordinator. Then instantiate the first view model and instruct the coordinator to set it as the root.

```
let tasksViewModel = TasksViewModel(taskService: service,
  coordinator: sceneCoordinator)
let firstScene = Scene.tasks(tasksViewModel)
sceneCoordinator.transition(to: firstScene, type: .root)
```

That was easy! The cool thing with this technique is that you can use a different startup scene if needed; for example, a tutorial that runs the first time the user opens your application.

Now that you've completed the setup for your initial scene, you can take a look at your individual view controllers.

Binding the tasks list with RxDataSources

In Chapter 18, "RxCocoa Datasources", you learned about the `UITableView` and `UICollectionView` reactive extensions built in RxCocoa. In this chapter, you'll learn how to use **RxDataSources**, a framework available from the RxSwiftCommunity and originally developed by Krunoslav Zaher, the creator of RxSwift.

The reason this framework isn't part of RxCocoa is mainly that it is more complex and deeper than the simple extensions RxCocoa provides.

But why should you use RxDataSources over RxCocoa's built-in bindings? RxDataSource provides the following benefits:

- Support for sectioned table and collection views.
- Optimized reloads that only reload what changed, such as deletions, insertions, and updates, thanks to an efficient differentiation algorithm.
- Configurable animations for deletions, insertions and updates.
- Support for both section and item animations.

In your case, adopting RxDataSources will give you automatic animations without doing any work. The goal is to move checked items at the end of the tasks list into a "checked" section.

The downside of RxDataSources is that it is initially more difficult to understand than the basic RxCocoa bindings. Instead of passing an array of items to the table or collection view, you pass an array of *section models*. The section model defines both what goes in the section header (if any), and the data model of each item.

Section model

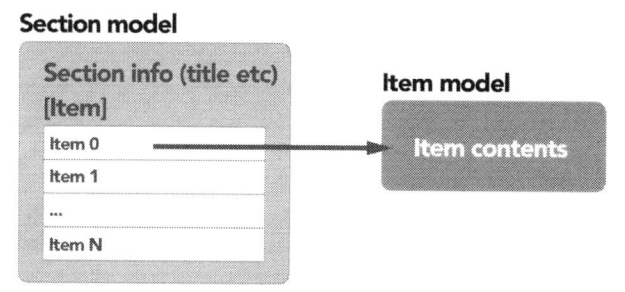

Section info (title etc)
[Item]
| Item 0 |
| Item 1 |
| ... |
| Item N |

Item model
Item contents

The simplest way to start using RxDataSources is to use the `SectionModel` or `AnimatableSectionModel` generic types as the type for your section. Since you want to animate items, you'll go for `AnimatableSectionModel`. You can use the generic class *as is* by simply specifying the types of the section information and the items array.

Open **TasksViewModel.swift** and add this to the top:

```
typealias TaskSection = AnimatableSectionModel<String, TaskItem>
```

This defines your section type as having a section model of type `String` (you just need a title) and section contents as an array of `TaskItem` elements.

The only constraint with RxDataSources is that each type used in a section must conform to the `IdentifiableType` and `Equatable` protocols. `IdentifiableType` declares a unique identifier (unique among objects of the same concrete type) so that RxDataSources uniquely identifies objects. `Equatable` lets it compare objects to detect changes between two copies of the same unique object.

Realm objects already conform to the `Equatable` protocol (see note below for a few gotchas). Now you simply need to declare `TaskItem` as conforming to `IdentifiableType`. Open **TaskItem.swift** and add the following extension:

```
extension TaskItem: IdentifiableType {
  var identity: Int {
    return self.isInvalidated ? 0 : uid
  }
}
```

This code checks for object invalidation by the Realm database. This happens when you delete a task; any live copy previously queried from the database becomes invalid.

> **Note:** Change detection is a little challenging in your case because Realm objects are a class type, not a value type. Any update to the database immediately reflects in the object properties, which makes comparison difficult for RxDataSources. In fact, Realm's implementation of the `Equatable` protocol is fast because it only

> checks whether two objects refer to the same stored object. See the "Task cell" section below for a solution to this specific issue.

Now you need to expose your tasks list as an observable. You'll be using your `TaskService`'s `tasks` observable which, thanks to RxRealm, automatically emits when a change occurs in the tasks list. Your goal is to split the tasks list like so:

- **Due** (unchecked) tasks first, sorted by last-added-first
- **Done** (checked) tasks, sorted by checked data (last checked first)

Add this to your `TasksViewModel` class:

```swift
var sectionedItems: Observable<[TaskSection]> {
  return self.taskService.tasks()
    .map { results in
      let dueTasks = results
        .filter("checked == nil")
        .sorted(byKeyPath: "added", ascending: false)

      let doneTasks = results
        .filter("checked != nil")
        .sorted(byKeyPath: "checked", ascending: false)

      return [
        TaskSection(model: "Due Tasks", items: dueTasks.toArray()),
        TaskSection(model: "Done Tasks", items: doneTasks.toArray())
      ]
    }
}
```

By returning an array with two `TaskSection` elements, you automatically create a list with two sections.

Now on to the `TasksViewController`. Some interesting action will happen here to bind the `sectionedItem` observable to the table view. The first step is to create a data source suitable for use with RxDataSources.

For table views, it can be one of:

- `RxTableViewSectionedReloadDataSource<SectionType>`
- `RxTableViewSectionedAnimatedDataSource<SectionType>`

The `Reload` type isn't very advanced. When the section observable it subscribes to emits a new list of sections, it simply reloads the table.

The `Animated` type is the one you want. Not only does it perform partial reloads, but it also animates each change. Add the following `dataSource` property to the `TasksViewController` class:

```
var dataSource:
RxTableViewSectionedAnimatedDataSource<TaskSection>!
```

The major difference with RxCocoa's built-in table view support is that you set up the datasource object to display each cell type, instead of doing it in the subscription.

Within the task view controller, add a function to create and "skin" the datasource:

```
fileprivate func configureDataSource() {
    dataSource =
RxTableViewSectionedAnimatedDataSource<TaskSection>(
        configureCell: {
            [weak self] dataSource, tableView, indexPath, item in
            let cell = tableView.dequeueReusableCell(withIdentifier:
"TaskItemCell", for: indexPath) as! TaskItemTableViewCell
            if let strongSelf = self {
                cell.configure(with: item, action:
strongSelf.viewModel.onToggle(task: item))
            }
            return cell
        },
        titleForHeaderInSection: { dataSource, index in
            dataSource.sectionModels[index].model
        })
}
```

As you learned in Chapter 18, "RxCocoa Data Sources", when binding an observable to a table or collection view, you provide a closure to produce and configure each cell as needed. RxDataSources works the same way, but the configuration is all performed in the "data source" object.

There's one detail about this configuration code that's key to this MVVM architecture. Notice how you passed an `Action` to the configuration function?

This is the way your design handles actions triggered from cells, that propagate back to the view model.

It's much like a closure, except the action is provided by the view model, and the view controller limits its role to connecting the cell with the action.

In the end, it works like this:

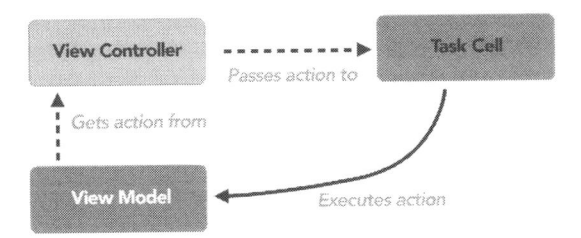

```
View Controller  - - - - - - >  Task Cell
       ▲          Passes action to
       ┆ Gets action from
       ┆
   View Model   <──── Executes action
```

The interesting part is that the cell itself, aside from assigning the action to its button (see below), doesn't have to know anything about the view model itself.

> **Note:** The `titleForHeaderInSection` closure returns a string title for section headers. This is the simplest case for creating section headers. If you want something more elaborate, you can configure it by setting `dataSource.supplementaryViewFactory` to return an appropriate `UICollectionReusableView` for the `UICollectionElementKindSectionHeader` kind.

Since `viewDidLoad()` is the place where the table view is placed in auto-height mode, that's a good place to complete the table configuration. The only requirement of RxDataSources is that the data source configuration **must** be done before you bind an observable.

In `viewDidLoad()` add:

```
configureDataSource()
```

Finally, bind the view model's `sectionedItems` observable to the table view via its data source in the `bindViewModel()` function:

```
viewModel.sectionedItems
    .bind(to: tableView.rx.items(dataSource: dataSource))
    .disposed(by: self.rx_disposeBag)
```

You're done with the first controller! You can use different animations for each change type in your `dataSource` object. Leave them at the default for now.

The cell used to display an item in the Tasks list is an interesting case. In addition to using the `Action` pattern to relay the "checkmark toggled" information back to the view model (see figure above), it has to deal with the fact that the underlying object, a Realm Object instance, may change during display.

Fortunately, RxSwift has a solution to this problem. Since objects stored in a Realm database use `dynamic` properties, they can be observed with KVO. With RxSwift you can use `object.rx.observe(class, propertyName)` to create an observable sequence from changes to the property!

Binding the Task cell

You'll apply this technique to `TaskTableViewCell`. Open the class file and add some meat to the `configure(with:action:)` method:

```
button.rx.action = action
```

You first bind the "toggle checkmark" action to the checkmark button. Check out Chapter 19, "Action", for more details on the `Action` pattern.

Now bind the title string and "checked" status image:

```
item.rx.observe(String.self, "title")
  .subscribe(onNext: { [weak self] title in
    self?.title.text = title
  })
  .disposed(by: disposeBag)

item.rx.observe(Date.self, "checked")
  .subscribe(onNext: { [weak self] date in
    let image = UIImage(named: date == nil ? "ItemNotChecked" : "ItemChecked")
    self?.button.setImage(image, for: .normal)
  })
  .disposed(by: disposeBag)
```

Here you individually observe both properties and update the cell contents accordingly. Since you immediately receive the initial value at subscription time, you can be confident that the cell is always up to date.

Finally, don't forget to dispose your subscriptions. Failing to do so would lead to some nasty surprises when the cell is reused by the table view! Add the following:

```
override func prepareForReuse() {
  button.rx.action = nil
  disposeBag = DisposeBag()
  super.prepareForReuse()
}
```

This is the correct way to clean things up and prepare for cell reuse. Always be very careful not to leave dangling subscriptions! In the case of a cell, since the cell itself is reused, it's essential that you take care of this.

Build and run the application. You should be able to see a default list of tasks. Check one off, and the nice animation you see is automatically generated by RxDataSources' difference engine!

Editing tasks

The next problem to tackle is the creation and modification of tasks. You want to present a modal view controller when creating or editing a task, and actions (such as update or delete) should propagate back to the tasks list view model. While not absolutely necessary in this case, as changes could be handled locally and the tasks list will update automatically, thanks to Realm, it is important that you learn patterns for passing information back in a sequence of scenes.

The main way to achieve this is to use the trusted `Action` pattern. Here's the plan:

- When preparing the edit scene, pass it one or more actions at initialization time.
- The edit scene performs its work and executes the appropriate action (update or cancel) on exit.
- The caller can pass different actions depending on its context, and the edit scene won't know the difference. Pass a "delete" action for canceling at creation time, or an empty action (or no action) for canceling an edit.

You'll find this pattern to be quite flexible when you apply it to your own applications. It is particularly useful when presenting modal scenes, but also to convey the result of one of more scenes for which you want a synthetic result set passed.

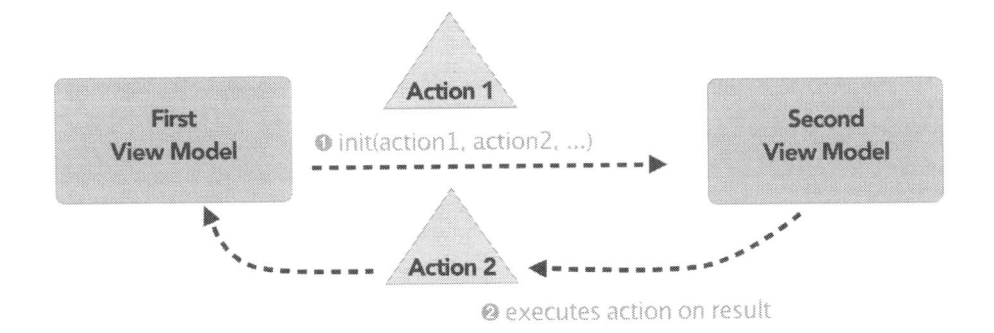

```
                    Action 1
    ┌─────────┐       ▲
    │  First  │  ❶ init(action1, action2, ...)
    │  View   │ - - - - - - - - - - - - - - ▶  ┌─────────┐
    │  Model  │                                 │ Second  │
    └─────────┘                                 │  View   │
         ▲                                      │  Model  │
         │                                      └─────────┘
         └ - - - - - - - - - - - - - - - - -
                    Action 2
              ❷ executes action on result
```

Time to put this into practice. Add the following function to `TasksViewModel`:

```swift
func onCreateTask() -> CocoaAction {
  return CocoaAction { _ in
    return self.taskService
      .createTask(title: "")
      .flatMap { task -> Observable<Void> in
        let editViewModel = EditTaskViewModel(task: task,
          coordinator: self.sceneCoordinator,
          updateAction: self.onUpdateTitle(task: task),
          cancelAction: self.onDelete(task: task))
        return self.sceneCoordinator
          .transition(to: Scene.editTask(editViewModel),
            type: .modal)
          .asObservable().map { _ in }
      }
  }
}
```

> **Note:** Since `self` is a `struct`, the action gets its own "copy" of the struct (optimized by Swift to being just a reference), and there is no circular reference - no risk of leaking memory! That's why you don't see `[weak self]` or `[unowned self]` here, which don't apply to value types.

This is the action you'll bind to the "+" button at top-right of the tasks list scene. Here's what it does:

- Creates a fresh, new task item.

- If creation is successful, instantiates a new `EditTaskViewModel`, passing it along with `updateAction`, which updates the title of the new task item, and a `cancelAction` which deletes the task item. Since it was just created, canceling should logically delete the task.

- Since `transition(to:type:)` returns a `Completable` and `CocoaAction` expects an `Observable<Void>` (this may change in the future), the last line in the `return` statement performs the required conversion to an Observable sequence of `Void`.

> **Note:** Since an `Action` returns an observable sequence, you integrate the whole create-edit process into a single sequence that completes once the Edit Task scene closes. Since an `Action` stays locked until the execution observable completes, it is not possible to inadvertently raise the editor twice at the same time. Cool!

Now bind the action to the "+" button on the `bindViewModel()` function of `TasksViewController`:

```
newTaskButton.rx.action = viewModel.onCreateTask()
```

Next, move to **EditTaskViewModel.swift** and populate the initializer. Add this code to `init(task:coordinator:updateAction:cancelAction:)`:

```
onUpdate.executionObservables
  .take(1)
  .subscribe(onNext: { _ in
    coordinator.pop()
  })
  .disposed(by: disposeBag)
```

> **Note:** To allow most of the code to compile, the `onUpdate` and `onCancel` properties were defined as forced-unwrapped optionals. You can remove the exclamation mark now.

What does the above do? Besides setting the `onUpdate` action to be the action passed to the initializer, it subscribes to the action's `executionObservables` sequence which emits a new observable when the action executes. Since the action will be bound to the **OK** button, you only see it executed once. When that happens, you `pop()` the current scene, and the scene coordinator will dismiss it.

For the **Cancel** button, you need to proceed differently. Remove the existing `onCancel = cancelAction` assignment; you'll do something a little more clever.

Since the action received by the initializer is optional, as the caller may not have anything to do on cancel, you need to generate a new `Action`. Therefore, this will be the occasion to `pop()` the scene:

```
onCancel = CocoaAction {
  if let cancelAction = cancelAction {
    cancelAction.execute(())
  }
  return coordinator.pop()
    .asObservable().map { _ in }
}
```

Finally, move to the `EditTaskViewController` (in **EditTaskViewController.swift**) class to finalize the UI binding. Add this to `bindViewModel()`:

```
cancelButton.rx.action = viewModel.onCancel
```

```
okButton.rx.tap
  .withLatestFrom(titleView.rx.text.orEmpty)
  .subscribe(viewModel.onUpdate.inputs)
  .disposed(by: self.rx.disposeBag)
```

All you have to do to handle the UI is pass the text view contents to the `onUpdate` action when the user taps the **OK** button. You're taking advantage of `Action`'s `inputs` observer which lets you pipe values directly for execution of the action.

Build and run the application. Create new items and update their titles to see everything in action.

The last thing to tackle is the addition of existing items. For this, you'll need a new `Action` that isn't temporary; remember that actions have to be referenced other than via a subscription, otherwise they'll be deallocated. As mentioned in Chapter 19, this is a frequent source of confusion.

Create a new lazy variable in `TasksViewModel`:

```
lazy var editAction: Action<TaskItem, Swift.Never> = { this in
  return Action { task in
    let editViewModel = EditTaskViewModel(
      task: task,
      coordinator: this.sceneCoordinator,
      updateAction: this.onUpdateTitle(task: task)
    )
    return this.sceneCoordinator
      .transition(to: Scene.editTask(editViewModel),
 type: .modal)
      .asObservable()
  }
}(self)
```

Did you notice the `Swift.Never` type for the returned sequence? Since `transition(to:type:)` returns a `Completable` sequence which, when turned to an observable sequence, translates to `Observable<Swift.Never>` (to indicate that no element is ever emitted), we also convey this information in the sequence type returned by the action.

> **Note**: Since `self` is a `struct` you can't create `weak` or `unowned` references. Instead, pass `self` to the closure or function that initialized the lazy variable.

Now, back in **TaskViewController.swift**, you can bind this action in
TaskViewController's bindViewModel(). Add:

```
tableView.rx.itemSelected
  .map { [unowned self] indexPath in
    try! self.dataSource.model(at: indexPath) as! TaskItem
  }
  .subscribe(viewModel.editAction.inputs)
  .disposed(by: self.rx.disposeBag)
```

s

You're using dataSource to obtain the model object matching the received IndexPath, then piping it into the action's inputs. Easy!

One final nitpicking point: you'll notice that after tapping a row to edit an item, if you press the **Cancel** button the row will stay selected. It's an easy fix with the do(onNext:) operator. Insert this code between the tableView.rx.itemSelected line and the map(_:) operator:

```
.do(onNext: { [unowned self] indexPath in
  self.tableView.deselectRow(at: indexPath, animated: false)
})
```

Build and run the application: you can now create and edit tasks! Hooray!

Challenges

Challenge 1: Support item deletion

You've probably noticed that it isn't possible to delete items. You'll need to make changes to both TaskViewModel and TaskViewController to add this functionality. For this challenge, start from the **final** project of this chapter. Once you complete the challenge, the users will be able to swipe on a task and delete it:

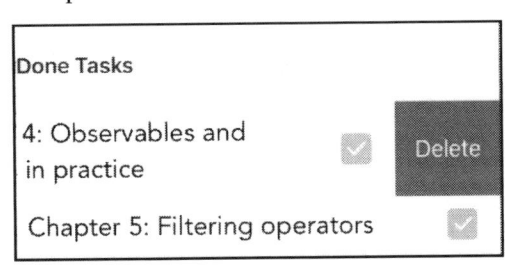

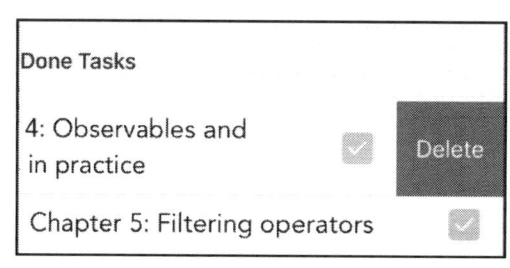

> Done Tasks
>
> 4: Observables and in practice ☑ Delete
>
> Chapter 5: Filtering operators ☑

The easiest way to get started is to put the controller in *edit mode* all the time. This will activate support for swiping right-to-left on cells so that you can reveal the **Delete** button. In `viewDidLoad`, you can turn that feature on this way:

```
setEditing(true, animated: false)
```

The second change will be in your `dataSource` object. You need to indicate that all the cells can be "edited". Dig through RxDataSources' `TableViewSectionedDataSource` class and I'm sure you'll find what you need to set. Hint: it's a closure, and you can simply return `true` in all cases.

Now you can get to the core of the challenge: handling the actual deletion. The solution to this challenge involves:

- Creating an `Action` in `TasksViewModel` such that, given a model item, will call the appropriate API in `TaskService`. Can you figure out its signature? If not, read on!

- In `TasksViewController`, bind this action to `tableView.rx.itemDeleted`. You'll have to figure out how to go from the `IndexPath` you receive to a `TaskItem`.

You won't reuse the existing `onDelete(task:)` function because it returns a `CocoaAction`, not an `Action<TaskItem,Void>`.

Challenge 2: Add live statistics

To make the UI more interesting, you want to display the number of *due* and *done* items in your list. A label is reserved for this purpose at the bottom of the `TasksViewController` view; it's connected to `statisticsLabel`. For this challenge, start from either your solution to the previous challenge, or from the chapter's final project.

Gathering live statistics involves the following:

- Adding a single new API to `TaskServiceType` (and its implementation in `TaskService`) to query both *due* and *done* items. Hint: use the `checked` date property in `TaskItem`; it's `nil` if the item is not checked. Every time a query returns a new result, that is, every time a change occurs in the database, produce an updated statistic. You'll need to run two permanent queries for that, filter one of them to exclude either checked or unchecked item, then use the `zip(_:_:resultSelector:)` RxSwift operator to produce the result.

- Exposing a new statistics observable in `TasksViewModel`. This is a piece of cake, since you did all the hard work in `TaskService`.

- Subscribing to this observable in `TasksViewController` and updating the label.

To make things easier, you can define a `TaskStatistics` tuple typealias in **TaskServiceType.swift**:

```
typealias TaskStatistics = (todo: Int, done: Int)
```

You shouldn't meet any particular difficulties in completing this challenge, aside from figuring out how to correctly filter Realm results. The interesting part is to see how you can structure new functionality and correctly spread it across the relevant components in your application.

Once you're done with this, reuse your statistics observable to update the application badge number dynamically. This is something you want to add to the application delegate in `application(_:didFinishLaunchingWithOptions:)`.

This concludes the final chapter of this book! We hope you loved it as much as we did. You now have a solid foundation of programming with RxSwift (and Rx as a whole) to build on as you continue your learning. Good luck!

Conclusion

> *"Why sometimes I've believed as many as six impossible things before breakfast."*
> — The White Queen, Through the Looking-Glass

We hope you're excited about all the new possibilities, previously seeming impossible, that developing with RxSwift has opened up for you!

Reactive applications are solid, easier to test, and very agile about their user experience. With data bindings, your apps' UI is always up to date and the highly composeable RxSwift operators allow you to craft complex app logic with a minimum of effort.

This book took you all the way from a complete Rx beginner, just learning about the pain points of asynchronous programming, all the way to being an RxSwift veteran. It's up to you now to couple your creativity with the all the knowledge you've gained from this book and create some impressive apps of your own!

If you have any questions or comments about the projects in this book, please stop by our forums at http://forums.raywenderlich.com.

Thank you again for purchasing this book. Your continued support is what makes the books, tutorials, videos and other things we do at raywenderlich.com possible. We truly appreciate it!

— Ash, Chris, Florent, Junior, Marin, Scott, and Vicki

The *RxSwift: Reactive Programming with Swift* team

Printed in Great Britain
by Amazon